The Multiracial
Experience

The Multiracial Experience

Racial Borders as the New Frontier

Maria P. P. Root
Editor

SAGE Publications
International Educational and Professional Publisher
Thousand Oaks   London   New Delhi

For information address:

SAGE Publications, Inc.
2455 Teller Road
Thousand Oaks, California 91320
E-mail: order@sagepub.com

SAGE Publications Ltd.
6 Bonhill Street
London EC2A 4PU
United Kingdom

SAGE Publications India Pvt. Ltd.
M-32 Market
Greater Kailash I
New Delhi 110 048 India

Printed in the United States of America

Library of Congress Cataloging-in-Publication Data

Main entry under title:

The multiracial experience: Racial borders as the new frontier/
   edited by Maria P. P. Root.
      p. cm.
   Includes bibliographical references (p.) and index.
   ISBN 0-8039-7058-7 (cloth: alk. paper).—ISBN 0-8039-7059-5
(pbk.: alk. paper)
   1. Racially mixed people—United States. 2. Ethnicity—United
States. 3. United States—Race relations. 4. Pluralism (Social
sciences)—United States. I. Root, Maria P. P.
E184.A1M89 1996
305.8′00973—dc20   95-34980

This book is printed on acid-free paper.

96 97 98 99 00 10 9 8 7 6 5 4 3 2 1

Sage Production Editor: Diane S. Foster
Sage Typesetter: Danielle Dillahunt

Contents

Part II: Identity

Part III: Blending and Flexibility

Part VI: The New Millenium

Glossary

The following terms appear frequently in this volume and in various oral and written discussions on racial mixing. The definitions provided here reflect the most common current usage.

Afroasian refers to people of African and Asian heritage.

Amerasian is the most inclusive term to refer to anyone racially mixed of Asian ancestry. It is also a transnational term referring to racially mixed Asians in other countries. Subsumed under this term are Afroasian, black Japanese, Eurasian, mestiza(o), and hapa (hapa haole). Amerasian originally referred to children of American and Asian national origin, usually fathered by white Americans. The term has been used broadly with children fathered by American servicemen in Asia.

Biracial refers to a person whose parents are of two different *socially* designated racial groups, for example, black mother, white father. In a less commonly used, but perfectly accurate meaning, biracial can also refer to someone who has parents of the same socially designated race, when one or both parents are biracial or there is racial mixing in the family history that is important to the individual. This use of biracial moves us away from requiring equal "fractions of blood" to recognize the prevalence of racial blending throughout American history. However, the social and psychological experience of the person who uses the term this way may be different from someone who is a "first-generation" biracial.

Eurasian refers to people of Asian and white European heritage.

Hapa haole or **hapa** is a term derived from the Hawaiian language. Although it was originally used to designate someone who was partially a stranger or outsider—Hawaiian mixed with other national and racial heritage—today it designates someone of Asian or Pacific Island origin mixed with European heritage. Some people are broadening its usage to be more similar to Amerasian.

Hypodescent refers to a social system that maintains the fiction of monoracial identification of individuals by assigning a racially mixed person to the racial group in their heritage that has the least social status.

Mélange, a French term for mixed, is a newer term used by many black/white individuals to indicate being of mixed racial heritage with no racial designation.

Mestiza(o) a Spanish-origin word, designates racial mixing of someone with Indian and Spanish ancestry. Not commonly used by young multiracial people, it now has a broader meaning, referring to people of Latino and European ancestry. Because of the shared Spanish ancestry, this term is also used by older Filipinos and Filipino Americans to refer to multigenerationally mixed or biracial Filipinos.

Miscegenation refers to race mixing in intimate dating and sexual relationships. Thus, antimiscegenation means against intermarriage or against race mixing. The last antimiscegenation laws were repealed in 1967 by a U.S. Supreme Court ruling in the case of *Lovings v. State of Virginia.*

Monoracial refers to people who claim a single racial heritage. It is also a system of racial classification that only recognizes one racial designation per person.

Mulatta(o), in its current usage, covers someone who is of varying fractions of African and European heritage. **Not all racially mixed persons view this as a positive designation.** Its original meaning has negative connotations; many believe the word is derived from the Spanish **mulato** for mule, the infertile hybrid between a donkey and a horse. The suffix suggests a diminutive status. Arabic origins have been suggested for this term.

Multiracial refers to people who are of two or more racial heritages. It is the most inclusive term to refer to people across all racial mixes. Thus it also includes biracial people.

Transracial indicates movement across racial boundaries and is sometimes synonymous with interracial. This term is most notably used in the context of adoption across racial lines.

The Multiracial Experience

Racial Borders as a Significant Frontier in Race Relations

MARIA P. P. ROOT

From the time I started elementary school to the time I started junior high, strangers, teachers, and friends' parents often let me know I was different by asking, "Where are you from?" I would name my street, my city, or a geographic marker near my house. But I knew these answers, although they sometimes stopped the inquiry, were not replying to the question they intended. Sometimes if the inquiry continued, I would give my birth country, the Philippines, a place I could no longer remember. For some strange reason, this of all answers seemed to satisfy them. Some would go further and knowingly ask, "Your dad in the military?" a question I dreaded and disliked. Then sometime in my teens, in the era of ethnic and racial pride movements, the question about my difference more frequently became "What are you?" By then I understood that the question was mostly about my physical ambiguity, asked by someone wondering "whose side I was on." I gave various fractions and explanations, trying to hurry my explanation away from this difference. Demographic changes require that the question must change again. It must move from an individual one to a

societal one. The larger question increasingly facing this nation
is, "Who are we?" &

The **biracial** baby boom that began in the 1960s practically guarantees
that anyone living in a large U.S. city knows someone who is racially
mixed—a niece or nephew, a confidant, a co-worker, a classmate, a
neighbor, a grocery store clerk, a friend of a friend. The contemporary
presence of racially mixed people is unmatched in our country's previous history. Interracial families and multiracial individuals are changing the face of America and the meaning and utility of race (from this
volume: Brown & Douglass, Chapter 20; Fernández, Chapter 2; Graham,
Chapter 3; King & DaCosta, Chapter 14; McRoy & Hall, Chapter 5;
Nakashima, Chapter 6). Ramirez (Chapter 4, this volume) observes that
these demographic changes will have impact on color-conscious remedies for social and political change.

 The U.S. Bureau of the Census (1992) forecasts that by the year 2050,
the representative face of America will no longer be white. Given the
history of U.S. race relations, the two most common reasons given for
this change are higher birthrates in communities of color and increasing
numbers of immigrants who are people of color. However, Alonso and
Waters (1993), Root (1992b, 1992d, 1995), Ramirez (Chapter 4, this
volume), and Waters (1994) are among those who believe that a third
factor will contribute to the complexion and momentum of this shift:
The self-identified multiracial population is increasing. *Time Magazine*
recognized this contribution in a special Fall 1993 issue. The cover portrayed Time's vision of the future face of America, a computer-generated
image of a young woman with Anglo-Saxon, Middle Eastern, African,
Asian, southern European, and Latino roots.

DEMOGRAPHIC TRENDS

Multiracial Births

 For the first time in history, the number of biracial babies is increasing
at a faster rate than the number of monoracial babies (U.S. Bureau of
the Census, 1992). The National Center for Health Statistics notes that
the number of monoracial babies has grown at a rate of 15% since the

early 1970s, whereas the number of multiracial babies has increased more than 260%. Although multiracial births represent a small portion of all babies born in the United States (3.4% in 1989, when race was recorded for both parents), this translates into over 100,000 births per year since at least 1989. More than a million first-generation biracial individuals have been born in this country since then. This figure will rapidly increase according to demographic projections, even if interracial marriage rates remain constant (Alonso & Waters, 1993).

Across racial groups, the trends are similar. The U.S. Census Bureau (1992) reported that while the number of monoracial black babies has grown 27% and the number of monoracial white babies 15%, the number of black/white biracial babies has grown almost 500%. According to the 1990 census, there were 39% *more* Japanese/white births than monoracial Japanese American births that year. In Native American communities, there are 40% *more* racially mixed babies than babies born to two parents who identify as American Indian. This trend was also present, although not as emphatically, for other Asian American and Pacific Islander American groups.

Interracial Marriage and Dating

The biracial baby boom followed the U.S. Supreme Court decision, on June 12, 1967, in *Loving v. State of Virginia,* to overturn the remaining state laws against interracial marriage (Spickard, 1989). Mildred Jeter, a black Native American woman, married Perry Loving, a white man, in the state of Virginia in 1958. They were subsequently sentenced to one year in prison by Judge Leon Bazile in 1959 for their interracial marriage.

Surveys of American attitudes toward interracial marriage over the last 25 years suggest that Mildred Jeter's and Perry Loving's children's and grandchildren's cohorts live in a social climate that is increasingly more accepting and more conducive to interracial relationships than was theirs. Since the pivotal 1967 U.S. Supreme Court decision in 1967, the Gallup Poll has surveyed black and white Americans about their attitudes toward interracial marriage five times—1968, 1972, 1978, 1983, and 1991. In telephone interviews, both groups have shown increased approval of interracial marriage: By 1991 more Americans approved (48%) than disapproved (42%) of interracial marriage (Gallup Poll, 1991). In 1968, 72% of Americans disapproved of interracial marriage.

This significant shift is driven primarily by a more favorable attitude among whites. Since the beginning of these polls, African Americans have had a significantly more favorable attitude toward intermarriage, compared to whites. Across racial groups, approval of intermarriage was associated with higher levels of education, living in large cities, higher incomes, living outside of the South, more liberal ideology, and being younger than 50.

U.S. Census Bureau figures confirm that attitude changes have translated into real demographic changes. The rate of interracial marriage has nearly doubled each decade since 1970. Interestingly, the media usually limits their reports of interracial marriages to those involving black/white couples, which account for 246,000 or .5% of married couples (U.S. Bureau of the Census, 1992). However, these couples represent only a fraction of interracial couples. Interracial marriage involving a black *or* white partner involves 2% of marriages or 1.2 million couples; these couples include African American/Asian American, American Indian/white, and African American/European American, and other possibilities. When we turn our attention to interracial marriage among people of color, excluding African Americans and Latinos, an estimated 1.5 million more couples are involved, representing an additional 3% of all marriages. However, the U.S. Census figures do not distinguish well between interethnic marriage (e.g., Chinese married to Japanese) and interracial marriage (e.g., Chinese American married to Native American) in these figures.

The interracial marriage rates for Latinos are more difficult to estimate, because this is essentially a multiracial group and the government-manufactured category of "Hispanic" is largely an ethnic identifier. However, the Census Bureau reports that 26% of people of Hispanic origin were married to someone other than a person of Latino heritage (Falcon, 1993). Falcon (1993) further breaks down the figures to show different rates of intermarriage for the different groups subsumed under the Hispanic label, for example, Cubans, Puerto Ricans, and Mexican Americans.

Many more individuals have dated interracially than married. By 1971, a Louis Harris poll sponsored by *Life Magazine* found that 45% of black and white respondents knew someone who had dated interracially. Based on responses by 77% of its participants, the pollsters theorized that young people of different races were basically going to do as they pleased, and elders were going to have less say. Almost 20 years later, the U.S. Census figures and two recent surveys confirm this 1971 forecast. In October 1989, a *Seventeen Magazine* survey found that 40% of the young—primarily white—women surveyed indicated they would date interracially, and 31% said they would be willing to marry interracially. In July 1989, Tenzer (1990) conducted a random survey of white women's beliefs and attitudes about interracial sexuality. He found that 65% of the women surveyed would date interracially, if there were no social taboo against it. And, as indicated by the Gallup Poll results (1991), the social taboos are loosening.

RACIAL CLASSIFICATION
AND GROWING PAINS

In 1977, the Federal Office of Management and Budget reflected this nation's social construction of race by establishing a policy to collect racial data by five *mutually exclusive* racial categories on federal and state forms (Sanjek, 1994). Consequently, the contemporary growth in the multiracial population is not easily gleaned from the racial classifications used in the U.S. Census.

Ironically, this country seems to be quickly outgrowing this five-race framework. In the 1990 decennial census (U.S. Bureau of the Census, 1992), the "other" racial category grew more than any other category—by 45% to 9.8 million people. This is larger than the monoracially identified Asian American population in the United States (7.2 million). McKenney and Cresce (1992) suggest two sources of this growth: a segment of the Latino population likely used the government-inspired designator Hispanic as a race, and a segment of the increasing multiracial population used "other" to indicate the monoracial framework did not work for them. Rodriguez (1992) noted that many Latinos responded to the race question using cultural frames of reference for defining race; race and culture are confounded, sometimes even with country of origin, in which a different system of race was employed. Thus, in the U.S. system of race, many Latinos were "other."

Added to these signs of growing pains, nearly a quarter million people "wrote in" a multiracial designator to the race question (U.S. Bureau of the Census, 1992). Waters (1994) examined the rules and procedures followed by the Census Bureau for classifying people who identified multiracially. Among the top 10 categories (217,565 people), four could not be retrofitted into the five-race framework (mixed, mulatto, biracial/interracial, or Creole). These people were converted to "others." The remaining six categories were black and white, white and black, Eurasian, Amerasian, white Japanese, and white Filipino. In these categories, most people were assigned a monoracial classification based on the first race they listed. In an exception to this rule, those identifying as Eurasian were classified as Asian rather than white.

U.S. history repeatedly demonstrates an ambivalence about recognizing multiracial people (Daniel, 1992a; Chapter 8, this volume). Regardless of additions or deletions of racial categories to the decennial census, a multiracial category has not existed for more than 60 years (Lee, 1993). Instead, classification has largely followed rules of hypodescent in a society that subscribes to monoraciality. In the 1700s, legislation was passed in several states to classify babies by mother's race (Tenzer, 1990). As a result, white slaveholders' multiracial babies were classified solely as black, increasing slave holdings.

These origins of hypodescent follow us into contemporary times. Waters (1994) pointed out that in 1978 the Federal Office of Management and Budget established a policy for classifying people of mixed racial origin. The policy directed individuals to classify themselves as people in their community would. In contrast to self-empowerment through self-designation, this instruction ensures that, if compliant, people will continue to apply the rules of hypodescent that ensure the continued "fit" of the mutually exclusive categories of the five-race framework (Daniel, Chapter 8, this volume; Zack, 1993). Of course, there is a problem if the respondent checks more than one box or assertively *or* accurately adds some category reflecting *multiracial* (C. C. I. Hall, 1992; in this volume: Brown & Douglass, Chapter 20; Fernández, Chapter 2; Field, Chapter 13; Graham, Chapter 3; King & DaCosta, Chapter 14; Root, Chapter 1; Standen, Chapter 15; Wardle, Chapter 23; Weisman, Chapter 10; Williams, Chapter 12).

The standing policy for classifying babies at birth also reflected hypodescent laws (Waters, 1994). Until a change in policy in 1989, biracial babies with a white parent were assigned the racial status of the nonwhite parent. Otherwise, multiracial babies of two parents of color, whether same or different race, were assigned the race of the father.

Waters (1994) noted that since 1989, new policy directs information keepers to designate *all* infants the same race as their mothers.

Further difficulties in racial classification of multiracial people stem from the situational and dynamic nature of race (Stephan, 1992; in this volume: Comas-Díaz, Chapter 11; Williams, Chapter 12). In a recent research study of how interracial couples classify their children, Alonso and Waters (1993) concluded that no uniform rule guided these decisions, though there appeared to be some parent gender-by-parent race interaction. Furthermore, parental determinations of their children's racial identity do not necessarily coincide with how their children identify themselves in later years.

The U.S. Office of Management and Budget, which oversees the U.S. Census categories, has started listening to leaders from multiracial community groups in this country, who want to open the discussion about racial classification and a multiracial category (in this volume: Fernández, Chapter 2; Graham, Chapter 3). Many researchers on multiracial identity have made the case for checking more than one box on categorical forms that historically forced a choice (e.g., Field, Chapter 13, this volume; C. C. I. Hall, 1980, 1992; Krieger, 1994). This is an alternative in a era of high-speed computers. A move toward this resolution would provide a way to obtain a more accurate understanding of the composition of this country. Alonso and Waters (1993) suggested that counting multiracial individuals in simulated population projections significantly affects the future composition of the United States.

THE BORDERLANDS

Although some are concerned that recognition of multiracial people will further exacerbate this country's problematic use of race, the contemporary context does not support this concern (in this volume: Hall, Chapter 24; Nakashima, Chapter 6). The current multiracial movement does not attempt to assert a superior position for individuals or families based upon race. It attempts to point out the archaic and destructive use of race; race has been constructed in the eye of the beholder of power. Root (1995) found evidence for this context change in the tendency for many multiracial people to identify as people of color or to insist on being essentially multiracial when forced to choose in a dichotomous framework. This choice does not represent the internalized default of hypodescent. It comes from learning to cope with oppressive experiences of objectification: being described as exotic, being stared at, being fantasized about as sexually special (Root, 1994b), or coping with the *What Are You?* question (Williams, Chapter 12, this volume). These experiences are not solely imposed by European-descended individuals; they are imposed from all sides in a manner that can choke the blended individual with a squeeze of oppression (Root, 1990; Zack, Chapter 9, this volume) in the form of "authenticity tests," forced choices, or unwarranted assumptions about one's identity. These experiences are also most consistent with bisexual and ambiguous gender status (in this volume: Allman, Chapter 17; Kich, Chapter 16; Streeter, Chapter 19).

Debate remains around whether or not the similar experiences of individuals of different mixes is enough to create a separate cultural group (Thornton, Chapter 7, this volume). Phenomenologically, evidence validates similarities in the experience of being mixed (Williams, 1992; in this volume: Brown & Douglass, Chapter 20; King & DaCosta, Chapter 14). Contemporary research and conceptualization on identity suggests parallels across different mixtures (e.g., Hall, 1980; Field, Chapter 13, this volume; Kerwin, 1991; Kerwin & Ponterotto, 1995; Kich, 1992; Murphy-Shigematsu, 1986; Poston, 1990; Thornton, 1983). Although this phenomenology may support the importance of recognizing multiraciality as a category, it does not support a separate cultural group by conventional definition.

Border Crossings

Unquestionably, the role of multiracial families and individuals in the forecasted demographic shift has structural implications for the meaning of race and race relations. Many people living in the borderlands of the 1970s' five-race framework recognize multiple types of "border crossings" that subvert this structure (Daniel, 1992b; Root, 1990; Weisman, Chapter 10, this volume). The active and habitual situational manipulation of race between foreground and background creates confusion. Confusion prevents the structure from subsequently reassembling itself the same ways; thus it creates the opportunity for deeper change.

There are different ways of experiencing, negotiating, and reconstructing the borders between races (Anzaldúa, 1987). The four ways described here have implications for thinking about the borders in similarly co-constructed dualities of masculine versus feminine and heterosexual versus homosexual identities.

One can bridge the border by having *both* feet in *both* groups, and in some cases even in other groups that are not originally associated with one's political existence as determined by others (Murphy-Shigematsu, 1986). This interpretation of border crossing is significantly different than that of straddling two worlds in a one-foot-in, one-foot-out metaphor that fractionalizes the multiracial person's existence. This new construction suggests the ability to hold, merge, and respect multiple perspectives simultaneously (Anzaldúa, 1987; C. C. I. Hall, 1992; Williams, 1992; in this volume: King & DaCosta, Chapter 14; Nakashima, Chapter 6; Standen, Chapter 15).

Another border crossing highlights the shifting of foreground and background as one crosses between and among social contexts defined by race and ethnicity (Miller, 1992; Root, 1990; Stephan, 1992; Zack, Chapter 9, this volume). The individual decodes their ambiguity to the perceiver or matches the demands of the social context (in this volume: Twine, Chapter 18; Williams, Chapter 12; Zack, Chapter 9). This experience is not to be mistaken for switching loyalties; it is the natural response to race as socially co-constructed by economics, by gender (Anzaldúa, 1987; Butler, 1993; Lerner, 1986; in this volume: Allman, Chapter 17; Streeter, Chapter 19), and by sexual orientation (in this volume: Allman, Chapter 17; Kich, Chapter 16). Thus one practices situational ethnicity and situational race (Stephan, 1992) as one might manipulate the extent to which any other aspect of identity—such as parent, worker, partner—is foreground or background in differing contexts (Thornton, Chapter 7, this volume).

In yet a third interpretation of the border, one decisively sits on the border (Anzaldúa, 1987; in this volume: Nakashima, Chapter 6; Weisman, Chapter 10), experiencing it as the central reference point. Anzaldúa (1987) referred to this border crossing as the experience of the "mestiza" consciousness. Such people insist on recognizing the essential character of human beings. They may insist upon viewing themselves with a multiracial label that cannot be deconstructed, like those who were moved from the multiracial category to the "other" category in the 1990 census because their self-designation could not be clearly defined in the five-race framework (Waters, 1994).

In the last border crossing, one creates a home in one "camp" for an extended period of time and makes forays into other camps from time to time. One might even move camp at some point in time. Again, loyalty is not the issue; rather, surrounding oneself by an environment that supports one's psychological, emotional, social, and political needs may guide this type of a crossing (in this volume: Nakashima, Chapter 6; Standen, Chapter 15; Streeter, Chapter 19). Thus people might change ways of identifying themselves over their lifetime (Root, 1990).

The border explorations I describe are now common among a critical mass of people of all racial backgrounds, but especially among multiracial people. The beginning of this structural change signals greater change to come (Hall, Chapter 24, this volume). As with any significant threat to a current social organizing structure, such as race, self-assigned border patrols insist on denying entrance (in this volume: Comas-Díaz, Chapter 11; Glass & Wallace, Chapter 21; King & DaCosta, Chapter 14; Root, Chapter 1; Zack, Chapter 9). Many multiracial people are not asking for permission but asserting the right to belong despite gate-keepers' discomfort (Daniel, 1992b; in this volume: Daniel, Chapter 8; King & DaCosta, Chapter 14; Root, Chapter 1; Streeter, Chapter 19; Wardle, Chapter 23). These border crossings are neither motivated by attempts to hide nor to denigrate some ethnic or racial heritage. Border crossing is part of the process of connecting to ourselves and to others in a way perhaps both more apparent and more accessible to multiracial people than to their monoracial counterparts. Regardless of whether one consciously participates in the "mixed race movement," border crossings serve to reopen a potentially different dialogue about race (in this volume: Glass & Wallace, Chapter 21; Nakashima, Chapter 6).

Border Language

Whereas a child of 5 learns to classify an object by two categories or features simultaneously, for example, a blue *and* green ball, most Americans are overwhelmed by—or resistant to—the possibility that someone is both black *and* white, African American and Asian American. The average American's limited ability to think about race results in a limited ability to converse about race. Our racial vocabulary provides border markers that are rigid reflections upon our history of race relations and racial classification (Lee, 1993). Without the experience of recognizing race in all its manifestations and shades, we can not shift its meaning, deconstruct it, or combine it.

The typical vocabulary and dialect for race hardly accommodates the biracial person. There are few positive or neutral words to refer to racially mixed persons on a daily basis. However, many negatively laden words exist for such people. For example, in 1990, I conducted a pilot survey on racial and ethnic self-designation with a junior college sample in Honolulu, Hawaii, a geographic location heralded for its racial blending. As part of the survey, I asked respondents to write down words that referred to someone who was racially mixed. I compiled a list of approximately 30 different words, the majority of which most racially mixed persons would consider derogatory. It was interesting how many of the labels captured the U.S. mythology about biracial people as confused or likely "race traitors." Many of the references were to animals, and most were labels used to refer to dogs; for example, mutt, mongrel, Heinz 57, and poi dog. This small window of vocabulary was useful because epithets and slang are metaphorical comments on a group's social location in a society; although Hawaii is a geographic location holding some of the most positive attitudes toward racial mixing, people living there had still been exposed to considerable negativity.

Self-designations are important vehicles for self-empowerment of oppressed people (Helms, 1990a). Labels are powerful comments on how one's existence is viewed. In this volume, many words and labels are used that will be new to many readers. (See the Glossary for definitions.) Some of the most frequently used words are monoracial, biracial, multiracial, transracial, hypodescent, and miscegenation. Among multiracial people, several terms have been coined to refer positively to themselves. People who have some Asian ancestry might refer to themselves, or be referred to by others, as Eurasian, Amerasian (Buck, 1930), black Japanese (Hall, 1980), Afroasian (Thornton, 1983), mestiza(o), or hapa (hapa haole). People with African ancestry use terms such as Afroasian, black Japanese (C. C. I. Hall, 1980, 1992), mulatta(o), LatiNegra(o) (Comas-Díaz, 1994b), or mélange. Whereas multiple terms that derive from phenotype exist in Latin cultures of origin (Comas-Díaz, 1994b; Daniel,

1992b; Rodriguez, 1994), fewer terms are available to refer to racially mixed people of Latino origin in this country. This is already an admittedly mixed population (Rodriguez, 1992). The term mestiza(o), which was infrequently used by younger generations of people of Latin heritage, has been positively reinterpreted by several different people (Anzaldúa, 1987; Ramirez, 1983). A new term, *LatiNegra* (Comas-Díaz, 1994b; Chapter 11, this volume) has been introduced to refer to people of African and Latina(o) heritage.

Language is important to the whole issue of race relations. Language may deconstruct the utility of the original concept. New terms, code switching between languages (C. C. I. Hall, 1980, 1992; Williams, 1992), and bilingualism are just a few indicators of increased cognitive flexibility. Flexibility is usually accompanied by increased complexity. We will need both to develop a language to negotiate the frontiers of the borderlands. Whereas some people suggest we need to make a radical change and eliminate the use of all racial language, I think the change can be accomplished by taking concepts people are familiar with and transforming them. The fact that race is a social construct, the meaning of which changes in location and over time suggests that it is still malleable. The multiracial dialogue inserts the confusion that may be necessary to accomplish flexibility and complexity for deeper structural change.

Although not all individuals or groups representing U.S. multiracial communities are unified in their solutions, almost all agree that opening the dialogue about a multiracial category for federal and state government racial classifications may be a way of dismantling racial construction as we know it (in this volume: Fernández, Chapter 2; Graham, Chapter 3). For the first time in U. S. history, the U.S. Bureau of the Census and its associated branches of government that use population data are seriously grappling with the issue of classifying multiracial people (Evinger, 1995). Hearings, focus group discussion, testimony, trial surveys, review of the emerging literature on multiraciality, and consultation have been among the methodologies used to determine what changes, if any, will be made to the census in the year 2000. Anderson and Fienberg (1995) observed: "The demands of future classifications must also meet two newer criteria—the needs of the civil rights enforcement machinery and an emerging claim of the 'right' of Americans to define their own identity" (p. 17). Many multiracial people are arguing that the lack of accurate identification of multiracial individuals may become a civil rights issue (in this volume: Fernández, Chapter 2; Graham, Chapter 3; Ramirez, Chapter 4).

In this country, three broad proposals exist: Some groups advocate a multiracial identifier on the race question of the census (in this volume, Fernández, Chapter 2; Graham, Chapter 3). Some health researchers advocate a second approach. In this era of high-speed computers, people should check all racial categories that apply, rather than limit themselves to one choice (Krieger, 1994). Such a choice allows the government to continue using the five-race framework while moving away from the concept of monoraciality. I suggest a third proposal. The race question confounds race and ethnicity, reinforces the fiction of racial purity, and continues to compile data that will be an increasingly inaccurate depiction of the U.S. population. Assuming that it might still be too radical to totally eliminate the question, what if it were reduced to determining whether or not the individual identifies as multiracial or monoracial? Could we not move on to the ethnicity and ancestry questions?

Lee (1993) articulated four sociological issues raised in interpretation of census data:

> 1) concern with race as defined by skin colour, in particular, the black or Negro population at the turn of the century and Asian and Pacific Islander populations as we approach the next century; 2) preoccupation with racial purity and the push to categorize individuals into "pure" racial categories and the problem of "mixed" and "other" races; 3) The transformation of many ethnic groups into a few pan-ethnic racial groups; and 4) the confusion of race and ethnicity. (p. 81)

These dialogues expose the irrationality by which the categories have been derived and enforced, exposing a distant and more recent history of racial classification.

Such conversations further destabilize the "us" versus "them" dynamics of racial conversations. Many multiracial people simultaneously represent both the "us" and "them" of white versus black, Korean versus African American, Asian versus white, Latino versus Asian. Therefore they bring a different sensitivity to the racial dialogue in an attempt to keep the best interest of their *communities* in mind. This experience represents the resolution of societal racial wars within the individual and allows for an integrated, prideful identity (Hall, Chapter 24, this volume). This pride is the result of inclusion and flexibility. Direct education and reinterpretation of the multiracial designation are important to this country now (Fernández, 1992b; in this volume: Brown & Douglass, Chapter 20; Fernández, Chapter 2; Glass & Wallace, Chapter 21; Graham, Chapter 3; Wardle, Chapter 23; Williams, Nakashima, Kich, & Daniel, Chapter 22).

The Issues

In reopening the dialogue around race from the multiracial perspective, several issues are tackled in this book. The book's organization reflects the concepts of human rights, identity formation, flexibility and blending of multiple statuses and identities, multicultural education, and the future of race relations in this country. The more prominent issues are explored and remain as questions for the dialogue on the border.

How might a multiracial concept dismantle our negative construction of race?

How can the contemporary construction of multiraciality be viewed as a positive statement on the changing meaning of race relations in this country?

How might lack of legal recognition of multiracial people in a monoracial framework deprive civil rights guarantees in some situations?

How can we better understand the construction of race by exploring its co-construction with gender and sexual identity?

How do we redefine the "borders" and the "centers" of reference with the changing demographics of this country?

How does the presence of multiracial people affect color-conscious political remedies for racism?

How do we incorporate multiracial concepts into multicultural education?

Can the multiracial movement deconstruct race to the point of making it clear how race has been used as a caste system in contemporary America?

How do multiracial grassroots organizations constitute a significant historical movement?

Are there enough significant similarities among multiracial people to constitute a separate cultural or ethnic group?

How do we redefine ethnicity when race is less central to the definition?

Are we further entrenching race into our social system if we achieve official recognition for multiracial people?

CONCLUSION

As W. E. B. Du Bois (1903/1975) forecasted at the turn of the last century, race and its borders have been prominent problematic issues during the 20th century, and this will continue to be true into the 21st century. Nevertheless, much progress has been made through legislative reform that attempts to undo the harm inflicted by the use of race in this country.

The 20th century can be noted for a significant amount of legislation that attempted to restore and guarantee human rights protection that was stripped away by the way race was constructed. For example, the third quarter of 20th-century history includes the dismantling of Jim Crow laws: desegregated schools were legally mandated with the 1954 decision in *Brown v. Board of Education*, public and private access to stores was assured, workplace affirmative action (though under reconsideration now) began in the 1970s, and integrated housing was spawned by the Fair Housing Act. The second reconstruction of civil rights resulted in the Civil Rights Act of 1964 and the Voting Rights Act of 1965. Discriminatory restrictive quotas for immigrants from "nonwhite" countries were replaced with the Immigration Act of 1965 (though, this too is being threatened). The repeal of antimiscegenation laws in 1967 with the *Loving v. Virginia* Supreme Court decision removed a major barrier to racial mixing, which is one official marker for the start of the biracial baby boom.

The fourth quarter of this century has concerned itself with the societal interpretations and adjustments to these attempts at deep structural change. The dialogue that multiracial people and their families have opened, while meeting with much resistance and wariness, may be part of moving to a deeper level of change to make the borders between race more permeable and eventually less discernable (in this volume: Brown & Douglass, Chapter 20; Fernández, Chapter 2; Graham, Chapter 3; Nakashima, Chapter 6; Ramirez, Chapter 4). The multiracial dialogue may help us dialogue more directly about the class structure of this country, which has been confounded with race and gender.

Many people are ready for more complex frameworks to understand and discuss race. The increasing presence of self-identified multiracial people opens the door for reconsidering the type of conversations we wish to have about race in this country. The multiracial perspective allows for different conversations about race than have typically occurred in forums around these issues, particularly as we redefine the borders and the center reference points. Many of us bring with us multiple perspectives, multiple loyalties, and an optimism that we can transcend race in our discussions of similarities and differences. Many people who identify monoracially have joined and initiated these conversations.

This volume continues and reopens conversations about race. More often, questions are raised rather than authoritative answers declared. Information is shared so that others can join in the work and awareness. It is our hope that our work and experience confirms not only an appreciation for the complex reality we have inherited in the way race has been defined and used to organize social relations in this country, but that the reader might feel some optimism that the multiracial experience and perspective can offer a strategy for positive change. Whereas Du Bois insightfully forecast that the problem of the 20th century would be the color line, my hope is that the boundaries among and between races will be the new frontier for changing the direction and structure of race relations as we begin the new millenium.

PART I

Human
Rights

I

A Bill of Rights for Racially Mixed People

MARIA P. P. ROOT

Countless number of times I have fragmented and fractional-ized myself in order to make the *other* more comfortable in deciphering my behavior, my words, my loyalties, my choice of friends, my appearance, my parents, and so on. And given my multiethnic history, it was hard to keep track of all the fractions, to make them add up to one whole. It took me over 30 years to realize that fragmenting myself seldom served a purpose other than to preserve the delusions this country has created around race.

Reciting the fractions to the *other* was the ultimate act of buying into the mechanics of racism in this country. Once I realized this, I could ask myself other questions. How exactly does a person be one fourth, one eighth, or one half something? To fragment myself and others, "she is one half Chinese and one half white," or "he is one quarter Native, one quarter

AUTHOR'S NOTE: This chapter is based upon a keynote address given by invitation of the University of California at Santa Barbara's student group, Variations, for the Second Annual California Statewide Multiracial Conference held at UC Santa Barbara, April 15, 1994. Carla Bradshaw's and Christine Hall's comments were helpful in the refinement of this manuscript.

African American, and one half Spanish" was to unquestioningly be deployed to operate the machinery that disenfranchised myself, my family, my friends, and others I was yet to
meet. ॐ

At some deep psychological level, the mechanics of oppression derive
from insecurities. When oppression is directed at whole groups of people,
the mechanics are similar regardless of the type of oppression. First, a
system of beliefs is constructed to preserve the self-interests of a group that
has economic and judicial power. These beliefs are then spread by word
of mouth. Second, data are collected, often by respected, intelligent
people, to establish the beliefs as factual so that those in power may
continue to think of themselves as moral and ethical. Together, the
beliefs and data are used to rationalize superiority of one group over
another. This rationalization justifies the fourth and last mechanism, social
distance; social distance makes it easier to depersonalize and dehuman-
ize the group that is viewed as inferior, so that there are few if any
opportunities to observe oneself in the *other*. Together, social distance,
rationalization, biased facts, and entrenched attitudes about race relegate multiracial individuals to object status, unconnected to humanity.
Subsequently, otherwise sensitive, intelligent people are relieved of the
moral obligation to resist or object to oppressive thought or action.

Most systematic oppression is based in paranoid delusions—a tightly
gathered system of beliefs and rationalizations and biased data gathering that create a fractured and illusionary reality that allows one to stave
off one's fears, even unconscious ones. Racism is the result of a delusion
about the meaning of differences in the service of coping with disproportionate fears of inferiority to or harm by the *other*. Racism is simultaneously ambivalent, arbitrary, and rigid. Thus, a phenotypically European person with an African American parent is seen as black, whereas
a person who looks phenotypically white with two parents of European
ancestry can be judged as white. Millions of people have been unwittingly drafted into collaboration with an insidious destruction of human life and spirit. Deep in our psyches, racism feeds on crumbs of
ignorance, insecurity, and fear.

Irrationality and economic incentive guide changes in the meaning
of race (Omi & Winant, 1986; Takaki, 1993), rather than a moral incentive
toward bettering the collective society. Therefore the boundaries and

labels defining the disenfranchised by race shift over time, as demonstrated by the history of the U.S. Census (Lee, 1993). The purpose of the classification system, which insists on clean lines between groups, always remains the same: to establish and maintain a social hierarchy in which the creators and enforcers of the system occupy a superior berth. Consequently, members of some group are always "deserving" of inferior status, until they are arbitrarily elevated to a higher status or a change in status provides economic advantage to those in power.

Although the mechanics of racism seem to start with those in power, the system is also maintained by the oppressed's internalization of the mechanics; for example, an insistence on singular ethnic or racial loyalties, colorism, and discrimination against multiracial people across all ethnic and racial groups in this country. Paradoxically, this internalization of the mechanics of oppression is a version of the hostage syndrome observed in prisoners of war. Prisoners take on characteristics of their captors and even defend their behaviors as their plight and ability to make sense out of an irrational reality are integrally linked with survival.

When race is constructed through the mechanics of racism, oppression chokes multiracial people from all sides (Root, 1990). This throttling and stifling takes many forms: forced to fit into just one category from school registration to U.S. Census surveys; affiliations forced with oppressive questions (e.g., "Which one are you?"); forced to "act right," "think right," and "do right" in order to belong; and forced to prove ethnic legitimacy in order to have an identity in an ethnically diverse society.

Chao (in press) thinks of racism as the "original sin" in America. Ironically, the descendants of the Europeans who came to the United States spawned the delusion around race (Spickard, 1992), replete with one-drop rules of hypodescent, classification of a biracial child's race by mother's race to increase slave holdings and absolve white slave-masters of paternal responsibility, anti-Asian legislation, displacement of Native Americans, and so on. Unquestionably, race is invidiously intertwined with most major U.S. institutions and social policies. For example, consider the power the U.S. Bureau of the Census has in reconstructing race every 10 years. It would also have considerable power to slowly deconstruct race.

Unfortunately, the oppressive squeeze created by the mechanics of racism has historically relegated multiracial people to deviant status or "mistakes," has minimized our contributions to society (despite the evidence), and/or has ignored our existence. Subsequently, the human rights of a growing segment of the U.S. population are compromised by the imaginary borders between social races.

The Bill of Rights proposed in this chapter was developed in the historical context of three interacting factors and the social forces that enable them:

1. a critical number of multiracial people of an age and in positions to give voice to concerns and injustices;
2. a biracial baby boom; and
3. a continued social movement to dismantle racism.

The affirmation of rights below reflects *resistance, revolution,* and ultimately *change* for the system that has weakened the social, moral, and spiritual fiber of this country. This chapter offers a set of affirmations or "rights" as reminders to break the spell of the delusion that creates race to the detriment of us all. (See Bill of Rights, p. 7.)

RESISTANCE

Resistance is a political act. It is also a nonviolent strategy for changing a status quo that perpetuates race wars and violates civil rights. To resist means that one does not accept the belief system, the data as they are presented, or the rationalizations used to perpetuate the status quo around race relations. In fact, the final test case that overturned all remaining state laws against interracial marriage in 1967 (*Loving v. Virginia*) came about because two individuals, Mildred Jetters and Perry Loving, resisted the laws prohibiting interracial marriage. Subsequently, the Supreme Court invoked an interpretation of the 14th Amendment to repeal these laws because they interfered with a basic civil liberty in this country, the pursuit of happiness.

Resistance also means refusing to fragment, marginalize, or disconnect ourselves from people and from ourselves. This is accomplished by refusal to uncritically apply to others the very concepts that have made some of us casualties of race wars. Four assertions listed following the Bill of Rights embody this resistance.

BILL OF RIGHTS FOR RACIALLY MIXED PEOPLE

I have the right
  not to justify my existence in this world
  not to keep the races separate within me
  not to be responsible for people's discomfort with my physical ambiguity
  not to justify my ethnic legitimacy

I have the right
  to identify myself differently than strangers expect me to identify
  to identify myself differently than how my parents identify me
  to identify myself differently than my brothers and sisters
  to identify myself differently in different situations

I have the right
  to create a vocabulary to communicate about being multiracial
  to change my identity over my lifetime—and more than once
  to have loyalties and identify with more than one group of people
  to freely choose whom I befriend and love

I Have the Right Not to Justify
My Existence in This World

Multiracial people blur the boundaries between races, the "us" and "them." They do not fit neatly into the observer's schema of reality. Questions such as "What are you?" "How did your parents meet?" and "Are your parents married?" indicate the stereotypes that make up the schema by which the *other* attempts to make meaning of the multiracial person's existence.

Many people still have a limited understanding of the racially mixed person's place in society. Images abound of slave masters raping black women, U.S. military men carrying on sexually illicit relationships with Asian women during wars along the Pacific rim, and rebels and curiosity seekers having casual affairs.

The multiracial person's existence challenges the rigidity of racial lines that are a prerequisite for maintaining the delusion that race is a scientific fact. The multiracial person may learn to cope with these questions by asking questioners why they want to know or how this information will be useful, or by simply refusing to answer.

I Have The Right Not to Keep
the Races Separate Within Me

The original racial system has been transformed and embedded into our country's political system by both the oppressors and the oppressed. A five-race framework adopted by the Federal Office of Management and Budget drives the categories of racial classification throughout the United States (Sanjek, 1994), leaving no room to acknowledge self-identified multiracial people.

Resistance means asking yourself the questions, Do I want to fit into a system that does not accommodate my reality? What would I be fitting into? What is the price? Will I have to be less than a whole person? Change often requires th e presentation of extremely different realities and strategies (Freire, 1994) in order to break free from rigid realities. Multiracial people have a place and a purpose at this point in history to cross the borders built and maintained by delusion by creating emotional/psychic earthquakes in the social system. Declaring multiple racial affiliations and/or ethnic identities may have this effect on other people.

The biracial baby boom, the debate over racial classification for upcoming decennial census taking, and contemporary research on biracial children clarify the question: What about the children? This question is based on the belief that race dictates differences in human needs and problem solving, that racial differences are irreconcilable. To prove otherwise, the biracial or multiracial person challenges the delusional biases upon which racism is maintained.

I Have the Right Not to Be Responsible
for People's Discomfort With My Physical Ambiguity

The physical ambiguity of many multiracial people, as well as mistaken identifications about their heritage, clearly challenges the notion of "pure race." The physical look of some racially mixed people is a catalyst for psychological change in how race is understood and employed. For example, many Eurasians are misidentified as Latino or Native Americans. Some words, such as *exotic,* referring to the physical appearance of multiracial people may be used as tools to reduce discomfort. Unfortunately, such terms declare social distance between people in the guise of something special or positive being offered (Bradshaw, 1992; Root, 1994a).

Jean Paul Sartre (trans. 1976) suggests that people define self in terms of the subjective experience of the *other*. In this case, multiracial people are the inkblot test for the *other's* prejudices and fears.

I Have The Right Not to Justify
My Ethnic Legitimacy

Tests of ethnic legitimacy are always power struggles, demonstrating the internalization of oppressive mechanisms. They employ social distance through the use of rationalized interpretation of behavior understood within an oppressive system of beliefs. These tests serve purposes of increasing divisiveness around ethnicity and delusions around race. These tests usually require that multiracial people exaggerate caricatures of ethnic and racial stereotypes. Those who initiate such struggles usually win, because they create the rules—or change the rules to suit themselves. Anyone who unquestioningly accepts these tests, begging for acceptance, remains a prisoner of the system (Freire, 1970). Belonging remains fragile.

The existence of multiracial individuals requires that the common definition of ethnicity be revised. Specifically, race must not be synonymous with it. We must also challenge the notion that multiracial people will be the harbingers of doom to ethnic solidarity or ethnic continuity. Research shows that ethnicity to some extent is dynamic over time and that multiracial people are variable to the degree to which they are ethnically identified (Mass, 1992; Stephan, 1992).

REVOLUTION

Everyone who enters into an interracial relationship or is born of racially different heritages is conscripted into a quiet revolution. People who voluntarily cross the border are often viewed in such strong terms as "race traitors," a sure sign that they have unwittingly created a emotional/psychic earthquake with emotional reverberations. They have refused to confirm the reality predicated on a belief in racial immutability and segregation at the most intimate level. Their resistance suggests that another reality exists. This suggests choice. Choice is frightening for some—often because it opens the door to the unknown in social relations and redefines self in relation to others.

The second set of four assertions further challenges the social construction of race in relationships. The individual has the right to resist this oppressive construction, as Paulo Freire (1970) observes:

> [The] marginal [person] has been expelled from and kept outside of the social system. . . . Therefore, the solution to their problem is not to become "beings inside of" but . . . [people] freeing themselves; for in reality, they are not marginal to the structure, but oppressed . . . [people] within it. (pp. 10-11)

I Have the Right to Identify Myself
Differently Than Strangers Expect Me to Identify

Asserting this right meets with tremendous social resistance in the form of comments such as, "You can't be . . ." or "You don't look . . ." Such declarations of self-identity challenge the classification schema of the reactor. The declaration also exposes the rules that this person follows. More and more people took this tack in responding to the 1990 U.S. Census question about race. Almost a quarter of a million people wrote in a multiracial identifier (Waters, 1994).

I Have the Right to Identify Myself
Differently Than My Parents Identify Me

Parents are not usually aware of the identity tasks their multiracial children face unless they, too, are multiracial. Parents often will racially identify a child in a way that they feel will make for the most welcome reception of their child socially—this means not challenging social convention but usually acquiescing to our country's rules around race, which enforce singular racial identities.

Sometimes race is avoided as a topic because parents do not know how to talk about it without pain. Sometimes they assume their ability to transcend racial barriers affords a certain protection for their offspring. Parents can support the identity process by inviting conversations about race so that the illogical rules can be exposed and children can be explicitly taught how to take care of themselves as potential targets of racism (Greene, 1990; Miller & Miller, 1990). Parents' invitations for conversations in which they attempt to understand how and why their multiracial children identify themselves the way they do promote self-esteem and foster respect and psychological intimacy. These conversations in any household support revolutionary change.

I Have the Right to Identify Myself
Differently Than My Brothers and My Sisters

Siblings can have different experiences and different goals and purposes that guide them and shape their experiences of themselves in the world. It is possible that gender influences how one comes to experience multiraciality, although this link is not yet clear.

I Have the Right to Identify Myself
Differently in Different Situations

Many biracial and multiracial people identify themselves differently in different situations, depending on what aspects of identity are salient. This "situational ethnicity" is often misinterpreted. In the novel, *The Crown of Columbus,* by Louise Erdrich and Michael Dorris (1991), one of the main characters, Vivian, a mixed-blood Native American woman, describes this process as watering whatever set of her ethnic roots needs it most. This changing of foreground and background does not usually represent confusion, but it may confuse someone who insists that race is an imperturbable fact and synonymous with ethnicity. The essence of who one is as a person remains the same. Changeability is a familiar process for most people, if they consider the roles by which they identify themselves in different situations: child, parent, lover, employee, student, friend, and so on.

Situational ethnicity is a natural strategy in response to the social demands of a situation for multiethnically and multiracially identified people. For example, participants in Stephan's (1992) research on people of Asian European heritage in Hawaii and people of Hispanic European mixed ethnic heritage in New Mexico usually gave more than one identity in replying to questions about how they experienced their own identity in five different contexts. Only 26% of people with mixed Japanese heritage, 11% of those with several different ethnic heritages in Hawaii, and 56% of people of mixed Hispanic heritage gave the same identification in each of the five situations posed. Funderburg's (1994) research on black and white biracial Americans reveals some similar process and exposes the formidable resistance and reluctance of outsiders to accept multiple ethnic identification.

CHANGE

The third set of assertions frees us further from the constrictions of racialized existences created by delusional beliefs and rationalizations. It directs change to build upon previous and current willingness to resist social convention and its implicit rules around race. It removes one of the most insidious barriers to collective power, social distance, and attempts to replace it with connection.

Connection is never accomplished through fear. Fear drives racism and other injustices. Connection is gained through the possession of respect, esteem, and love for oneself and others. Connection acknowledges that our social fates are intertwined and our present and future are dependent on how we interact with one another now. It is predicated on an appreciation for differences that is destructive to "racist unity" (C. K. Bradshaw, personal communication, January 1995). Connection, wholeness, and a sense of belonging decrease the likelihood that one can commit atrocities against another human being.

I Have the Right to Create a Vocabulary to Communicate About Being Multiracial

Society's vocabulary for race relations, the experience of being racialized, and the attempt to break free from concepts embedded in vocabulary requires some new terms. We must all take time and responsibility to reexamine vocabulary that has depicted racialized experience, the way Daniel (1992b) has done with his examination of the concept of "passing."

It is important to think about the meaning and origin of the terms that we use to refer to ourselves. New terms are necessarily being created by multiracial people as a step toward empowerment (Root, Introduction, this volume). Self-labeling is empowerment (Helms, 1990a). It is a proclamation of existence.

I Have the Right to Change My Identity
Over My Lifetime—and More Than Once

Identity is dynamic on the surface, whereas the core maintains some constancy. Identity is shaped by interpersonal, global, and spiritual experiences that are personally interpreted. This interpretation, however, is guided by cultural values. Thus it is possible to change one's identity over a lifetime as part of the process of clarifying or declaring who one is (Root, 1990). This is an extended conceptualization of situational ethnicity. The process of identity change may reflect a shift from a passive acceptance of the identity that society expects one to accept to a proactive exploration and declaration of who one believes oneself to be—and this may include identifying differently in different situations (Stephan, 1992). Ironically, these identities can even be the same, although the process is different (Root, 1990).

I Have the Right to Have Loyalties and
Identify With More Than One Group of People

You have the right to loyalties and identification with more than one group of people. In fact, this fosters connections and bridges, broadening one's worldview, rather than perpetuating "us" versus "them" schisms and antagonisms. The allegiance to a greater number and variety of people increases the individual's sense of connection. The sense of connection makes it less likely that people will hurt one another by ignorance or malice. We are all empowered by connection. *The more connected we feel, the less threatening differences feel.*

I Have the Right to Freely Choose
Whom I Befriend and Love

Who the racially mixed person chooses to befriend, and particularly love, does not necessarily declare his or her racial identity or ethnic loyalty. The social folklore that racially mixed people tend to "out-marry" is a statement of the rules of the social order including hypodescent, singular allegiances, and us versus them mentality. One has the right to judge people as individuals, to know that skin color, hair texture, or eye, nose, and mouth shapes are not what measures endurance during times of hardship in love and friendship. Connection, respect, and willingness to understand, compromise, and negotiate make relationships work.

I hope this Bill of Rights exposes how insidiously entwined the mechanics of oppression are in our everyday lives—systematic beliefs, biased data or interpretation of data, rationalization, and ultimately social distance. Oppression always fragments people, as energy and attention are diverted from the experience of wholeness. A society that creates race as a difference to contend with places inordinate importance on this difference in the most negative of ways. It obscures important facts about the essence of an individual. Subsequently, instead of being seen as a *dependent* variable, the result of conditions, race is now often manipulated in the daily news, daily conversations about the motives of individuals, and in research as an *independent* variable.

If we resist this fragmentation, if we revolutionize the way we think about identity and the self in relationship to the *other*, we begin to free ourselves from an oppressive structure. When we refuse to fragment ourselves or others, then we become capable of embracing the humanity in ourselves and in others. We become less fearful, less judgmental, and less subject to defining ourselves by other's opinions of us. Then we can approach differences with respect and wonderment rather than with fear. It is respect that gives us the courage for resistance, revolution, and change in tackling racial boundaries for changing race relations.

Government Classification of Multiracial/Multiethnic People

CARLOS A. FERNÁNDEZ

I cannot recall exactly when I first became aware of my identity as both an American and a Mexican. Perhaps it was as early as the age of 4, when we prepared to travel to Mexico for the Christmas holidays to visit my father's family in Mexico City. It was probably then that we took a trip to the Mexican Consulate in San Francisco to ensure that our travel papers were in order, at which time I learned that my parents had registered me at birth as a dual citizen of the United States and Mexico. Naturally, I asked a familiar question: Who or what am I? Am I half Mexican and half American? My parents' answer was emphatic: You are not half anything, but 100% both. The 200% solution worked at that young age, but the matter was not fully resolved.

By my early teens, the question arose again, this time in the "racial" terms that were so much a part of the movements of the 1960s and early 1970s, especially in the San Francisco Bay area. It was then that I learned of my father's mixed racial background and my mother's suspicion that even in her background, there might be some Native American ancestry. There

was no place for a "mixed" pride movement then, but the
question was never far from my mind. Funny how things
haven't changed. ⌖

Anyone whose "racial" or ethnic identification encompasses more than
one of the classifications currently employed by government, from local
school districts to federal agencies, is well-acquainted with the absurdity and insult of rules requiring a monoracial response on government
forms. Relatively few, however, are familiar with the unique American
historical-cultural origin of this peculiarity, its present-day incorporation into a federal regulation, and perhaps most important, the practical,
concrete consequences of its continuation.

We will review these issues, as well as recent efforts to obtain government recognition of the specific identity of multiracial, multiethnic
people and what such recognition might mean for society as a whole.

HYPODESCENT—AN AMERICAN TRADITION

It is certainly no revelation to most people in the United States that
someone who has any physical features typically associated with people of African ancestry will be regarded as "black." That they may have
light skin will not usually matter, if their features incorporate black African
elements. That they may actually also incorporate typically European or
Asian features in addition to the perceived African features also usually
does not matter. They may be regarded as "light-skinned" or "dark-
skinned," but it is usually taken for granted that they are black (Myrdal,
1944/1962). So accustomed are we to this reflexive classification that we
tend to forget how really odd it is. And yet if we take a moment or two
to analyze why we do this, a whole new dimension of understanding
about the larger race question itself is revealed to us, including, I would
argue, important and often overlooked clues to its resolution.

Origins

The American (U.S.) tradition of hypodescent, also colloquially known
as "the one-drop rule," has distant roots in the anti-Roman traditions of
northwestern Europe, principally among the Germanic populations

who were most resistant to the Roman Empire's invasions of their territories, a resistance that continued in the guise of the Protestant-Catholic conflicts across Europe (Dickens, 1966). These traditions were carried to English-Dutch North America, preconditioning the early European colonists against "papist" or "Roman" ways and attitudes. Among these was a deep mistrust for cosmopolitanism, associated as it was with despotic foreign imperial authority (Fernández, 1992a).

Reinforcing these predilections, most male colonists came to North America with their womenfolk, or else they found wives among their own segregated ethnic communities once they arrived in the English and Dutch colonies. Thus, at the beginning, there was relatively little chance that any significant numbers of people of a mixed descent would emerge, and hence no need to have any particular terminology for referring to them.

This virtual absence of multiethnic people extended as well to the offspring of the most taboo of interethnic liaisons, those between Europeans and non-Europeans, primarily Africans and Native Americans. In the earliest colonial period, such "multiracial" people existed, but they were so rare as to be viewed as aberrational. Only the most exceptional circumstance of the marriage of John Rolfe and the noblewoman Pocahontas was acceptable, and in that particular case, the securing of land titles was the overriding concern (Gossett, 1963). The only other exceptions existed outside the mainstream of society, in the frontier areas where solitary trappers or traders might take an indigenous mate. In these cases, the offspring stayed with the Indians and rarely became a part of colonial society.

With the passage of time, all types of interethnic liaisons increased among the various European nationalities and between Europeans and non-Europeans, as well. Gradually the number of individuals having diverse origins grew, and as these individuals began to be noticed, a terminology for referring to them was needed. Among the Europeans, it was ultimately the identity "American" that served this function of referring to multiethnic people and communities, overcoming the Anglo-exclusiveness of the more conservative elements in society by uniting people around the common cause of opposing British authority for all the reasons enumerated in the Declaration of Independence and more.[1]

The unifying term *American* worked among the European-descended citizenry as a surrogate for *multiethnic* or an equivalent term for two simple reasons. First, a significant portion (not necessarily a majority) of the "American" population was multiethnic and not just English, so sufficient numbers of people were more inclined to disdain overly Anglocentric attitudes. Second, even among largely English-descended families, England was not very popular, for the obvious reason of the recently concluded War of Independence, but also for reasons of religious difference that had accumulated over many generations and for reasons of class. England was still heavily burdened by its feudal past, whereas America had been populated by free farmers and indentured servants.

It must be pointed out, however, that although American was a term of identification that tended to suppress overt Anglocentrism and thus make a multiethnic identity seem unnecessary, strong countertrends persisted and even reasserted themselves, particularly when new immigrants began to arrive in significant numbers. Thus when the large-scale Irish and German immigrations began in the mid-19th century, so did various "theories" about Anglo superiority. In reaction to this, the immigrants found themselves forced to form fraternal societies based on their ethnic origins and to create their own forms of "affirmative action" through political patronage and various forms of self-help organizations, both legal and illegal (Handlin, 1957; Seller, 1977).

Initially, intermarriage between these new immigrants and the dominant Anglo majority was very limited, and thus the question of the identity of their offspring always defaulted to the term American without necessarily resolving the multiethnic implications of these liaisons. The absence of such a resolution is evidenced both by the rise of racist "No-Nothing" political movements, including the Ku Klux Klan, and by liberal progressive "melting pot" advocates such as John Dewey. Among the progressives, whose greatest influence was in public education, resolution was to be found in forcing conformity to Anglo American culture, whether accurate or mythological. The multicultural basis of American culture was thus once again subsumed, and the question of a multiethnic identity thereby suppressed. Nonetheless, the rate of intermarriage among European ethnic groups, including the later immigrants from southern and eastern Europe, gradually increased (Seller, 1977).

The history of intermarriage between European and non-European individuals took a much different course, for several important reasons.

First, as previously mentioned, there existed from the earliest period a cultural aversion to interethnic or interracial marriages among the Anglo and Dutch colonists, mediated in part by their religious beliefs and reinforced by the presence of marriage partners of their own ethnic communities. The prejudice thus engendered was only somewhat lessened with respect to intermarriage with non-Anglo Europeans, but it remains very powerful to this day with respect to marriages with non-Europeans. This prejudice sets the United States apart from Latin America, where the taboo against interracial marriages was greatly dampened by the policies and traditions of the Roman Catholic church, as well as by the secular cultures of the Iberians and, to some extent, the predominant Native American ethnic groups.[2]

Second, the two numerically significant non-European groups, the Native Americans and Africans, stood outside the body politic, internal nations without the rights of citizenship. This discouraged intermarriage, although it did not discourage liaisons outside marriage. As was mentioned before, the few products of interracial relationships under these conditions were almost invariably raised outside of the mainstream white society in the community of the nonwhite parent. Although their mixture was known, it was of little relevance to the institutions of American society, so classifying these mixed offspring was not important. To the extent that multiracial people were acknowledged, it was as a matter of informal discourse. But because the very idea of a multiracial person was so strange in Anglo American culture, terms of identity had to be borrowed, and they were, from that other part of America to the south, the countries of Spanish America, where history had taken another course and resulted in large numbers of multiracial people who were acknowledged both officially and informally. From Spanish, the term *mulato* (mule) was acquired to refer to people of mixed black and white ancestry. Many other terms such as *quadroon* and *octoroon* (from Spanish *cuaterón* and *octorón*, meaning one-fourth black and one-eighth black respectively) were similarly introduced.[3]

Third, the race theories of the 19th century (Gossett, 1963) posited natural boundaries between the European and non-European groups, placing a significance on these particular group differences, which were said not to exist or to exist to a much smaller extent within the different "races." These theories dovetailed nicely with Western political theories of international law and the natural rights of men. That is to say, "nations," or European ethnic groups, had rights under international law that were not recognized in the case of non-Europeans because they were not fully nations like the European (usually Western) ethnic groups, but races, mere groupings of people lacking the cultural complexities required of "real" nations. Therefore, the non-European races had no rights a white man was compelled to respect, whereas at least in theory, the peoples of Europe had "natural" rights over which they could fight, which they usually did with great abandon. In America, this same type of thinking meant that treaties with Native Americans were easily broken with little moral compunction, that Africans could be slaves (and later, be without civil rights), and that the sovereign territories of Mexico, the Philippines, Puerto Rico, and Hawaii could be flagrantly violated in contravention of international law (Lauren, 1988).

Taken together, the above-cited factors help explain the aversion to intermarriage and the resultant small proportion of the U.S. population that is perceived as multiracial.[4] However, given the fact that many, if not most, African Americans are actually multiracial, what accounts for the virtual absence of a term recognizing that fact?

It is sometimes pointed out, correctly, that government agencies in the United States did in fact employ multiracial terms historically. For instance, beginning in 1850, the U.S. census employed the term mulatto, and later, in the 1890 census, used the terms quadroon and octoroon. And in most of the states that discriminated racially in their laws— especially with respect to the ability to give testimony in a court of law, the freedom to live where one could afford, and the freedom to marry interracially—degrees of racial mixture were explicitly mentioned, often using the relevant popular terms such as mulatto, half-breed, and so forth.

What seems at first inconsistent with the contention that multiracial people have never been accorded recognition can be reconciled by how racial data were reported in the U.S. Census. Mulattoes were included as a type of black ("Negro" or "colored"), never as a type of white, although biologically they were as much white as they were black. And in all the racially discriminatory state laws, when mixture was mentioned, it was not to acknowledge some intermediate legal status, as in the caste systems of South Africa and colonial Latin America, but rather to deny multiracial people their rights as if they were not white at all.

Thus, in "recognizing" multiracial people, there has been a consistent denial of their independent identity.[5]

By way of comparison, why did this occur in Anglo America and not in Latin America? Besides the powerful and perhaps decisive effect of historically evolved cultural factors, part of the answer also lies in the way the anticolonial wars unfolded in the different parts of the hemisphere.

The wars of independence against England and Spain involved different populations. In Latin America, the bulk of the revolutionary armies were mestizos (Indian & white), *mulatos*, blacks, and Indians. The officers were typically termed *Creole*, or Spanish born in America, but in fact, most of them were mixed bloods habituated to concealing their origins to maintain their class standing in colonial society.

Unlike the United States, many of the countries of Latin America, including Mexico, abolished slavery in the process of establishing their independence. Among the leaders of these independence wars was a disproportion of multiracial individuals, many of whom had achieved prominence precisely because of the advantages they had enjoyed as the heirs of a Spanish landowner. In French Haiti, the revolutionary leaders were mulattoes who'd also been accorded an intermediate status. This phenomenon of the mixed-blood popular leader did not go unnoticed in the United States. In particular, the Haitian revolution was the cause of much agitation and fear in the United States (Ottley & Weatherby, 1967) and led to actions curtailing the rights of "free blacks," a virtual euphemism for mulattoes because they made up the largest proportion of the free black population. (Williamson, 1984)

The Texas "rebellion" against Mexico, which eventually led to the Mexican-American War, was also due in no small part to the abolition of slavery in Mexico in 1829, the product of Mexico's first two presidents, one a mestizo and the other a mixed blood of African, Indian, and Spanish ancestry who, to the Texans was, by all appearances, simply black.[6] Although the Texans were allowed a temporary exemption from abolition after they threatened rebellion, their apprehension about what lay ahead was too much to bear. That their fate might be in the hands of "a mongrel race" undoubtedly helped to push them over the edge (Price, 1967).

As the Civil War loomed, anxieties about the loyalties of mulattoes in the United States finally reached a crescendo. The mulattoes became increasingly aware of these feelings and began to react in precisely the way that had been feared; they allied themselves with the unmixed black population. As in Latin America, the mixed bloods came to represent a disproportion of the leadership of the ethnic African American community (Williamson, 1984).

As the federal troops left the South and Reconstruction ended, the notorious Jim Crow laws cropped up like weeds. Among these were antimiscegenation laws,[7] a key component of which was aimed directly at the mixed bloods. If interracial liaisons were prohibited, then the offspring of same were, in the eyes of the law, illegitimate. Henceforth, as in many states before the war, even in the North,[8] the offspring of what were termed interracial liaisons could not inherit property, an important basis for capital accumulation and thereby power.

As for the mulattoes who had emerged prior to Jim Crow, the segregation laws made no distinction between them and the masses of African Americans. With no choice legally available, self-aware mixed bloods accommodated themselves fully to the one-drop rule. Intermarriage with whites virtually ceased. The African American population, now including the mulattoes, became a new ethnic community, a "new people," as Williamson (1984) puts it. With this accommodation, resolution of the multiethnic, multiracial identity issue in America was once again deferred. Moreover, it became the source of much tension within the African American community itself (Russell, Wilson, & Hall, 1992).

In this same period of the 19th century there emerged various race theories that lent a "scientific" gloss to European—and specifically Anglo or "Nordic"—claims of superiority, including the idea that racial mixture resulted in debilitation and regression (Gossett, 1963). Thus the notion of racial "taint" suggested another reason to maintain segregation of multiracial people apart from the white community, in the interests of "racial purity." In this context, again, there was no special reason to distinguish people of mixed blood from their nonwhite parents.

Taken together—the early cultural abhorrence of intermarriage, the irrelevance of multiracial people to the mainstream society due to their numbers later on, followed by official recognition as equal members of an oppressed minority because of the perceived threat to slavery, supported last by the "abominable (and dangerous) mongrel" threat to the white race—all of these resulted in the rule that prevails to this day (although we are seeing signs of change), the rule of hypodescent, the one-drop rule.

Hypodescent and Other Minorities

The one-drop rule has had various applications historically with respect to other non-European ethnic groups in the United States, even as it came to be largely shaped by the dictates of the black-white racial dynamic (as in all matters racial). In a few states, discriminatory laws considered *any* nonwhite ancestry as proof of nonwhite status. Often such cases at law involved defining just what "nonwhite" meant. Once that was determined, the person was either white or nonwhite. Just as in the case of blacks, there was no intermediate status.[9]

In ordinary social practice, the rule of hypodescent continues to apply to anyone whose surname or appearance suggests a particular ethnicity, even when in fact they are multiethnic. The consequences of this can range from relatively innocuous, when the relevant ethnic groups are perceived as racially similar, to significant where one of the ethnic groups is an object of prejudice.

The need to classify people for civil rights purposes carried forward the traditional rule of hypodescent and applied it to other non-European groups deemed to be victims of racial prejudice. The one-drop rule is now an issue for all whose ancestry includes more than one of the groups designated as belonging to the "protected classes" of race and ethnicity for civil rights purposes.[10]

THE TRADITION TURNED UPSIDE DOWN

The advent of the Civil Rights Era of the 1950s and 1960s profoundly changed the situation of multiracial people in the United States. With leadership from the multiracial lawyer Thurgood Marshall and the progressive Chief Justice Earl Warren, the legal segregation of the African American community and all communities in the country was ended in education, housing, employment, and family life.

In 1967, the U.S. Supreme Court in *Loving v. Virginia* overturned the 16 remaining state laws against interracial marriages, thereby freeing individuals of all ethnic groups from the constraints of law on their choice of marriage partners. Not only could people marry across artificially maintained community boundaries, they and their families could now also live and travel where they pleased without fear of the law. An interracial family could now live in an integrated environment rather than being restricted to the community of the nonwhite partner. The children of these couples might go to school with children from a variety of ethnicities, including other multiracial children.

Meanwhile, the cultural isolation of ethnic communities was seriously challenged by the mass media, especially television and popular music. Rock and roll and Mickey Mouse reached into the far corners of the nation, desegregating the mass culture in an unprecedented way. The process continues unabated today on a global scale (Wattenberg, 1991).

The legal desegregation of American society proceeded on the basis of various court orders and civil rights laws that depended on continuing the classification of people by race. Logically, one could not mandate this or that action or program without reference to the types of people involved. Thus the very classifications that had previously been employed for purposes of denying civil rights now became useful in enforcing and monitoring these same civil rights (Glazer, 1983).

I say the very classifications, but this is not entirely true. In fact, the classifications employed in the implementation of the civil rights orders and laws were those provided by the U.S. Census Bureau. Consistent with the traditional hypodescent rule, the U.S. Census had, by the time of the Civil Rights Era, dropped the term mulatto.[11] No one (of whom I'm aware) stepped forward to challenge the simplified census racial scheme, probably because all were familiar with American culture and the hypodescent tradition and challenging it seemed a low priority in view of the larger civil rights questions.

Whatever first-generation multiracial people existed at the time were either fully acculturated in the African American community and had no doubt about their ethnic identity, or, if they were among the comparatively small but increasing number who were growing up and living in an integrated setting, they typically found themselves caught up in the charm and excitement of ethnic pride that spilled over from the civil rights movement. For many multiracial, multiethnic kids, their *political* identification with their minority parent's ethnic group became all-consuming, often with the acquiescence or even encouragement of their white parent.

However, the abstraction of a political identity is a very fragile thing in the light of reality. The reality in this case was that the legally enforced segregation of earlier times was no longer present to reinforce the old identity. The only force of any consequence in this regard was social pressure to identify according to familiar habits. But over time, and without the force of law, mere social pressure is supremely vulnerable to challenge and change.

That challenge and change began in the late 1970s and early 1980s when local groups of parents, multiracial adults, and others became concerned about the particular issues facing multiracial people in the generation literally born from the success of the civil rights movement. Among the most concrete and immediate of these concerns was precisely the official classification of multiracial, multiethnic people on government forms, particularly in the public schools. No longer were the habits of tradition enough to justify placing people in the position of denying the objective fact of their parentage. No longer was it seen as necessarily threatening to the advancement of civil rights to proclaim the right to assert one's actual ethnic identity.

In late 1988, representatives of local interracial groups formed the Association of MultiEthnic Americans (AMEA), the first nationwide group of its kind in the United States, to advance an awareness of the emerging population of multiracial, multiethnic people in this country (Brown & Douglass, Chapter 20, this volume). In June 1993, AMEA was at last able to present its testimony before the Census Subcommittee of the U.S. House of Representatives and to issue a challenge to the racist tradition of hypodescent, the last vestige of segregation in America, which is maintained by current federal regulation.

OMB DIRECTIVE 15

Following the enactment of the 1965 Civil Rights Act, the newly created Equal Employment Opportunity Commission required employers to report on the numbers of Negro, Oriental, American Indian, and Spanish American people they employed and produced Standard

Form 100 (EEO-1) for this purpose. Other agencies followed suit (Glazer, 1983).

By the 1970s, racial statistics gathered from agencies of government at all levels were becoming unwieldy, and standardization was deemed necessary. Mindful of this, the Office of Management and Budget (OMB) produced Statistical Policy Directive 15 (text is provided in Appendix 1). Directive 15 remains to this day the supreme authority for racial classifications in the United States, affecting all governmental agencies including the census, the public schools, social security, and so on. The directive also dictates classification policy to the private sector, through the EEOC and the Small Business Administration, as well as by way of example.

OMB Directive 15 sets forth five racial/ethnic categories: white, black, Asian/Pacific Islander, American Indian/Alaskan Native, and Hispanic. Also, the directive requires reporting in one category only for each individual counted ("check one only"). *Other* is not one of the reporting categories. Here we see the old rule of hypodescent enshrined in modern form.

Directive 15's stated purpose is to require government agencies at all levels to design their racial/ethnic query forms in such a way that the information provided can be reported in terms of one of the Directive 15 categories only. Thus people whose parentage encompasses more than one of the designated categories cannot be counted, except monoracially.

The Census

The census has always maintained its own format for asking about racial or ethnic information. However, even the Census Bureau is subject to the mandate of OMB Directive 15. This meant in 1990 that monoracial/ethnic responses were required in the race and Hispanic questions. Census policy requires that responses to "other race" be assigned to monoracial categories for OMB reporting purposes when these are written in. When multiple categories are stated, the Census Bureau reports the first race or ethnicity declared. Responses such as "multiracial" or "mixed" require a visit by a census taker to obtain a monoracial response (Nampeo McKinney, U.S. Bureau of the Census, personal communication, June 1992).

The Public Schools

Nowhere has the impact of OMB Directive 15 been more keenly felt by members of the multiracial/ethnic community than in the public schools. In fact, the classification dilemma faced by parents of multiracial children has led to the formation of many local interracial groups across the United States.[12]

Not only are all parents of multiracial children required to designate their children inaccurately and in a manner that effectively denies one of the parents, but some parents have encountered what is probably the most onerous and outrageous enforcement of the one-drop rule in any setting. As a matter of federal policy, school officials are empowered to visually inspect (the so-called "eyeball test") for purposes of racially classifying a student who chooses not to identify monoracially on school census forms ("No Place," 1989).

Apart from this appalling (and unconstitutional) practice, the requirement to give what can only be regarded as false information on a school census form challenges fundamental educational ethics, which one might suppose dictate the teaching of facts and truth. Pupils exposed to the one-drop rule as it appears on school forms are being taught, in effect, that government sometimes requires half-truths and pretense.

Public Health

The one-drop rule even reaches into the area of public health. Unbelievably, the National Center for Health Statistics (NCHS) maintains monoracial identifications in its records and statistics. This practice reached such absurd proportions that in 1989, the race of children of single mothers changed from race of the father to race of the mother. Apparently, it never occurred to the NCHS to record multiracial/ethnic children as multiracial or multiethnic. It is unbelievable that this sort of statistical method, based solely on the racist rule of hypodescent, is applied in a supposedly scientific setting. How this inappropriate and potentially dangerous practice might impact such vital concerns as screening for genetic diseases, assessing the needs of various populations, or organ-donor matching is a matter that deserves immediate attention (Polednak, 1989).

CHALLENGING HYPODESCENT

As I stated in my testimony to the Census Subcommittee, many of us who fit into more than one of the official racial or ethnic categories have come to realize that our very identity is a challenge to a deeply ingrained habit of American culture. More and more of us have come to understand that the mere effort to assert our right to identify ourselves accurately is perceived as a threat by those who believe they have a vested interest in maintaining the status quo in race relations. Some of us also understand that this means "our" issue is in fact an issue having broader significance for the whole society.

As I have argued elsewhere, the failure to accommodate what are regarded as interracial relations and people in the United States is at heart an unresolved American identity crisis, a dilemma that perpetuates ethnic and racial disunion and makes the resolution of the general race problem virtually impossible (Fernández, 1992a). The failure to recognize that some people transcend traditional communal boundaries based on race or ethnicity is equivalent to enshrining those very same boundaries and thereby preventing even the concept, let alone the reality, of national unity. It is not enough to proclaim "we are all Americans" if in fact we continue to separate ourselves, not just by labels, but in social practice.

A Beginning—Reforming OMB 15

During AMEA's testimony to Congress in 1993, and again in our testimony before the OMB in 1994, I presented an alternative to the current format of Directive 15, an alternative that incorporates essential reforms including government recognition of the existence of multiracial, multiethnic people.

AMEA proposed that OMB Statistical Directive 15 be changed by (a) adding a multiracial and/or multiethnic category and (b) providing a subsection for those choosing to identify as multiracial/ethnic to signify their racial/ethnic parentage in terms of the other listed categories (see Appendix 2). This proposal

  1. counts people accurately according to their actual identity;

2. provides statistical continuity by accounting for the racial/ethnic component(s) that may be relevant for various government studies and programs; and

3. avoids unnecessary and unwarranted government influence and interference in the very sensitive and private matter of personal identity, namely, forcing individuals to choose one parent over the other.

AMEA's argument is that OMB Directive 15 and all government practices that involve the gathering of racial/ethnic[13] statistics must dispense with the rule of hypodescent as a matter of civil rights under the U.S. Constitution. In fact, in my view, as things presently stand, it is likely that OMB Directive 15 will be challenged in the courts and will be reformed along the lines AMEA has proposed by court order rather than by implementation of Congress or the President. This is because (a) the multiracial community, such as it is, has neither the clout of money or votes to influence government directly and (b) there is significant opposition to dispensing with the one-drop rule in classifications from some in various ethnic minority organizations.

The most common concern we hear expressed is that counting multiracial/ethnic people might cause minority communities to lose benefits that are tied to numbers. However, many programs that benefit minority communities are actually gauged by the economic status of geographic areas rather than by direct counts of particular ethnic groups. Inner cities or redlined areas are targeted, not necessarily black or Latino communities.

With respect to programs that may be tied directly to the counting of particular ethnic groups, there is little logic. For what does it matter what the count is if the same multiracial people who might be included in the enumeration are also included as beneficiaries of the relevant program? What is "gained" by including multiracial people is also "taken back" when they take advantage of various programs. The net effect is at least zero.

The only civil rights programs of real consequence that depend on the counting of people under a racial or ethnic classification scheme are the Voting Rights Act and civil rights orders issued by the courts. Court orders affecting such things as integration obviously depend on the ability to gauge the numbers of various racial/ethnic groups. It is important, for example, to know whether a particular school is 90%

Latino while another is 90% white, or whether there is a 50-50 balance, or what the proportions of these groups may be in the local community where these schools are located. However, it may also be significant to know how many Latino or white students are actually multiethnic when an integration order is issued. What could be more indicative of real integration than the presence of students who manifest that integration in their parentage and in their identity? Are the courts overlooking an important factor simply because of the rule of hypodescent?

The Voting Rights Act is designed to address the dilution of the franchise of those ethnic groups who have been the demonstrated objects of prejudice in American history, such as African Americans and Mexican Americans. The act mandates the drawing of political district boundaries so that targeted groups may concentrate their votes and elect people who are more likely to represent their interests. In order to draw these boundaries, it is necessary to count people by ethnicity or race. In doing so, unknown numbers of people who are in fact multiethnic or multiracial are included in these counts because the enumerators—in this case, the U.S. Census—follow the one-drop rule as mandated by OMB Directive 15.

The fear we hear expressed is that implementation of the Voting Rights Act would become more and more difficult if multiracial people could identify themselves as such. The solution to this perceived dilemma lies in the original policy upon which the Act is based. To the extent that multiracial people have been the objects of prejudice as if they were fully monoracial, their interests in countering the effects of such prejudice are identical with the community of their minority parent. With this policy objective in mind, it makes sense to include them in the overall count for purposes of apportioning political districts.

One way to do this without denying multiracial, multiethnic people the right to accurately identify themselves on government forms is to dispense with the rule of hypodescent and permit people to indicate all classifications that apply to them instead of restricting them to check one only. The information thus gathered would thereby not exclude any ethnic group designation for purposes of applying (or not applying) a given civil rights program. The designation multiracial or multiethnic in this type of scheme would serve the dual purpose of providing a singular personal identity and creating a statistical device for indicating that a multiple answer was given by one and not several individuals.

The arguments of least legitimacy are those derived from an exclusively ethnocentric standpoint, that is, a separatist, racist philosophy that looks at the world only in terms of race war. Such an outlook regards interracial coupling as "sleeping with the enemy" and "genocidal." Multiracial people then become disturbing living reminders of interracial relationships. They can also be viewed as "agents of the enemy within" in that their loyalty to the "enemy" parent becomes disloyalty to the threatened group. The multiethnic person is also a bearer of "foreign" ways; they are "too white" or "too black," and so on. If they are included as "one of us," it is only after paying the admission price of denying the fact of their diverse heritage. Even then, multiracial people often feel compelled to prove their loyalty, typically resulting in the phenomenon of the "overcompensating multiracial," people who are "more pure" than their "pure" cousins. It is not unusual (although it is embarrassing and shameful) for such people to project their self-hatred onto other multiracial people who feel comfortable with and even proud of their multiracial identity.

Another form of this ethnocentric attitude emphasizes the importance of "unity." Somehow, unity of a given group is threatened by the assertion of a multiethnic or multiracial identity. Notice it is the assertion of the identity, not the fact of the identity, something that cannot be denied. But why is the open acknowledgment of a simple fact so threatening to unity? Primarily for the reasons that the openly racist ethnocentrist opposes multiracialism of any sort: unity against the enemy, unity to "preserve" the group, unity to advance ethnocentrism, and so on. The misapplication of the high-sounding term *unity* to deny multiracial people their identity (and not incidentally, one of their parents) is actually a low blow for a form of racism that any thoughtful multiracial person would be foolish to support, if for no other reason than self-preservation.

Unity in the interests of advancing civil rights is another matter. Certainly most multiracial people are in favor of this type of unity. But for this cause, there is no need to deny a multiethnic identity. People from all backgrounds can and do support civil rights. A multiracial person can even support the type of ethnocentrism that serves as a basis for organizing ethnic communities to defend their civil rights. The critical distinction here is between ethnocentrism (separatism or nationalism) as a goal versus ethnocentrism as a foundation or home from which one moves out into the world.

Finally, there is the argument that besides considerations of personal pride, multiracial people really have no issues of consequence that are comparable to the civil rights concerns of the recognized ethnic minority groups, such as African Americans, Latinos, Asians, and Native Americans. Therefore, these people say, why tinker with the existing racial classification scheme?

The first response to this sort of arrogant argument is that the current racial classification scheme is inaccurate on its face, and how issues are addressed is a secondary concern. That is, *policies should be based on facts, not facts based on policies.* Moreover our right to identify ourselves accurately is at least equal to the rights of people who may be classified monoracially.

Second, it is patently false that no issues particularly affect multiracial people. It ought to be quite clear to any socially literate person that a special bigotry is aimed at interracialism and interculturalism, and it is present in all ethnic communities, not just in the United States, but throughout the world in varying degrees. It is precisely the type of bigotry encountered among rabidly ethnocentric folks as previously described.

The Wedowee Incident

A concrete example of this "special" racism was front-page news early in 1994. At a high school assembly at the Randolph County High School in the eastern Alabama town of Wedowee, the principal reportedly told students that the school prom would be canceled if interracial couples attended. When questioned by student Revonda Bowen about how this would apply to her because her father is white and her mother is black, the principal reportedly said his rule was aimed at preventing "mistakes" like her.

Naturally, there was a furor, with many people calling for the principal's resignation, but also with many parents voicing support for the principal. On March 14, the seven-member Randolph County school board met and decided to suspend the principal with pay while the matter was investigated. Meanwhile, the Bowens filed a lawsuit in federal court charging that Revonda Bowen's civil rights had been violated under both the U.S. Constitution and Title VI of the 1964 Civil Rights Act (*Bowen v. Randolph County Board of Education*, 1994).

The Bowen case raised a fascinating question: Are multiracial/ethnic people protected by the civil rights laws? Although the answer to this question would seem to be yes, no court has ever made such a ruling, probably because, in most instances, the one-drop rule has made it unnecessary.

Where discrimination has occurred in those cases that have reached the highest courts, it has been the racial status of the victim as perceived by the bigoted perpetrator that matters. Following tradition, such people generally adhere to the one-drop rule. A person may in fact have one black parent and one white parent, but if he or she is the victim of discrimination, it is by being regarded as black, not multiracial.

The Wedowee case was obviously different in that the particular type of discrimination that occurred directly involved the biracial identity of Revonda Bowen. Her apparent abuse by the school principal wasn't because she was black, nor was it because she was white. It was *specifically* her multiracial status that offended the principal.

Unfortunately, the Bowens chose to settle their case without proceeding to trial, so the hoped-for ruling never occurred. But there is no doubt that some court will eventually have to make such a ruling, especially, and paradoxically, as people, bigots included, become increasingly conscious of multiracial people.

When and if a court finally rules that multiracial people are specifically protected by the civil rights laws, it will have a profound and potentially revolutionary consequence with regard to the whole matter of racial and ethnic classifications, both legally and socially. Multiracial/ethnic people would be recognized as a distinct class by an agency of government. The case could then be made that the multiracial community must be recognized by other agencies of government as well, such as the Office of Management and Budget, the Department of Education, the Department of Health and Human Services, the Census Bureau, and all the state and local government agencies across the country, in order to effectively and accurately address the particular concerns of our still-nascent community.

A more profound result than the long-overdue recognition by government of multiracial people would be the revolutionary impact of that recognition on our American culture. It would signal the demise of the one-drop rule and demonstrate the emergence of a new awareness about the realities of multiracialism. This transformation would not only impact the race issue generally but also our self-concept as a nation, by challenging obsolete notions of traditional communal boundaries. This would be an important development as we situate ourselves in the emerging global community.

CONCLUSION

The time for change with respect to accommodating a recognition of people who transcend traditional social boundaries, both officially as well as in ordinary social practice, is long overdue. The United States as a society cannot afford to further postpone the resolution of this issue. The very fabric of American society is held together by tenuous threads. Persistent racism slashes at the fabric, while our habit of hypodescent prevents us from making use of stronger binding material: the people in our society who are intimately connected with the diversity of ethnic groups that make up the country.

Although it is important to emphasize such sentiments as "we are all Americans" or "we are all citizens of the world," such pronouncements are insufficient and unsatisfactory, particularly as they are often convenient ways of denying the real separateness that people experience, irrespective of their formal citizenship. In recognizing multiethnic, multiracial people, we allow ourselves a clearer vision of what it means to say "I am an American" or "I am a human being." It allows us to affirm both our unity and our diversity, a sentiment that echoes in the motto *E Pluribus Unum*, believed by some to be the better interpretation of the melting pot thesis. It also paradoxically frees us from overconcentrating on our ethnic differences and instead affirming the other things we share in common, such as our democratic ideals and our desires for a better life for ourselves and our families.

Hypodescent belongs to another era. As we move into the 21st century, it must be left behind. There is nothing progressive about it for anyone or any group, and much that is backward. We need to let it go.

NOTES

1. In 1782, the Franco-American de Crevecoeur (quoted in Glazer & Moynihan, 1970), who nearly coined the term "melting pot," said:

I could point out to you a family whose grandfather was an Englishman, whose wife is Dutch, whose son married a French woman, and whose present four sons have now four wives of different nations. *He* is an American, who leaving behind him all his ancient prejudices and manners, receives new ones from the new mode of life he has embraced. . . . Here individuals of all nations are melted into a new race of men. (p. 288)

2. A collision of these differing attitudes is illustrated in Pitt's (1966) *The Decline of the Californios*. An African American barber who settled in Los Angeles in 1846 and married a *californía* was seen dancing with a white woman at a fiesta by a white American southerner, an occurrence that shocked him greatly.

3. Some of these other racial terms include sambo, derived from *zambo*, meaning mixed African and Native American; maroon, derived from *cimarrón*, a runaway slave; and mustee, derived from *mestizo*, literally mixed, but properly applied to someone of European and Native American ancestry. An illustrated catalog of these was produced in the 18th century for the King of Spain by the Irish cleric O'Crouley (A description of the Kingdom of New Spain in 1774, reprinted 1972 by John Howell Books, San Francisco). The illustrations are displayed in the Caracól Museum in Chapultepec Park in Mexico City.

4. In fact, it is more than a perception. People of mixed European and non-European ancestry are the largest portion of the population in most of the countries of Latin America, whereas even if all African Americans were counted as multiracial (which most are; see Williamson, 1984), they would still only constitute 12% of the U.S. population. Adding Latinos (Latin Americans in the United States, most of whom are also multiracial) brings the total up to about 20%, significant, but still much less than in Latin America.

5. Williamson (1984) cites as "exceptional" the societies of ante bellum New Orleans and Charleston. But these examples only further illustrate the point. In the first place, both cities were greatly influenced by the so-called "Latin model" of categorization; Charleston by way of Barbados (a British colony amid a sea of Latin culture), and New Orleans, by way of its history as first a Spanish and then a French colony. And even though there existed an informal acknowledgment of mulattoes, the distinction was insufficient to accord them any greater legal status than any unmixed black.

6. The first president of the Mexican Republic was Guadalupe Victoria (1824-1829). The second president was Vicente Guerrero (1829). Both men had served as generals during the War of Independence against Spain.

7. Of course, such laws had been enacted well before the Civil War in many states, including many in the North. The earliest of the antimiscegenation laws (1661) was instituted by the colony of Maryland, a reaction to the significant intermarriage (or simply, liaisons) between white indentured servants and blacks (Williamson, 1984).

8. See, for example, the case of *Bailey v. Fiske* (1852):

Abigail Jones [is], according to her testimony, but one-sixteenth part of Indian blood, and she must be considered a white woman. She was married to a mulatto, who could not be regarded as a white man. The marriage of white with colored persons was then forbidden by statute. Their children were therefore illegitimate, and they could not inherit from their father. (p. 77)

9. One case that is significant in illustrating this point, as well as demonstrating that race mattered more than class, occurred in a San Francisco courtroom in April 1857. Los Angeles landowner Manuel Dominguez, a signer of the California constitution of 1849 and a respected county supervisor, was prepared to testify as a witness when one of the lawyers raised the fact that Dominguez had Indian ancestry and therefore, under California law that barred Indians from testifying against whites, should be disqualified. The fact that Dominguez considered himself a mestizo made no difference. The judge agreed.

10. A "protected class" is a group of people sharing some common characteristic that is specially recognized as subject to the "strict scrutiny" test by the U.S. Supreme Court when evaluating governmental laws and actions with respect to the Equal Protection clause of the 14th Amendment of the U.S. Constitution. "Race" and "ethnicity" are two such classes, now regarded as virtually interchangeable. Under recent rulings of the high court, particular racial or ethnic designations are no longer relevant. As long as a law treats a group of people in racial or ethnic terms, even whites, it must be scrutinized using the highest standards ("compelling state interest") to determine if it can be justified constitutionally. See *Regents of the University of California v. Bakke* (1978) and *Richmond v. Croson* (1989).

11. Mulatto was no longer used starting in 1920, thus signifying the full enshrinement of the one-drop rule.

12. In fact, the AMEA affiliate, Interracial Intercultural Pride (I-Pride), won recognition of the first multiracial category in modern U.S. history (about 1980) for use in the Berkeley, California, public schools, a classification that remains in place to this day.

13. Under a Supreme Court ruling in 1987 (*Saint Francis College v. Al-Khazraji*), the terms "race" and "ethnic" are deemed legally equivalent.

The Real World

SUSAN R. GRAHAM

I attended the workshop, Race and Ethnicity: An Assessment of the Federal Standard for Race and Ethnicity Classification, which was organized by the Committee on National Statistics (CNSTAT) of the National Academy of Sciences February 17 to 18, 1994. I met with over 75 government agency representatives, demographers, academics, Census Bureau representatives, and educators. At center stage was what is referred to as the Office of Management and Budget (OMB) Statistical Policy Directive No. 15 on Race and Ethnic Standards for Federal Statistics and Administrative Reporting (text in Appendix 1). Simply put, Directive No. 15, which was adopted in 1977, defines and categorizes all people in the United States by race and ethnicity. Our mission at the workshop was to decide if Directive No. 15 warranted any changes or updates.

As executive director of PROJECT RACE (Reclassify All Children Equally), I was invited to present the case for multiracial children and adults to classify themselves as multiracial. The

AUTHOR'S NOTE: I am grateful to my children and my husband for their ever present support and encouragement. I also wish to express appreciation to the members of PROJECT RACE for their tireless work for our children and their confidence in me.

mood was clear: They would discredit my cause and dismiss me. I had few supporters and did not expect many open minds.

Waiting for lunch, I introduced myself to the woman next to me and told her I was at the workshop representing the multiracial community. "I'm glad I'm not you!" she said, and the people who overheard all laughed and nodded in agreement. We had just experienced 3 hours of listening to federal agency officials all state their reasons why multiracial people should *not* be allowed to have a category on forms requiring racial data. &

This chapter excerpts some of my rebuttal presentation at that meeting. It examines the real life examples I hear every day of children like my own son and daughter who are subjected to discrimination, civil rights injustices, and affronts to their self-esteem and personal dignity. The federal government reduces multiracial children and adults to "data cells;" therefore much of my argument addresses concerns about data needs. It is heartbreaking to me, as the mother of two multiracial children, to have to "play politics" with their futures, but that, in fact, is today's real world.

DATA NEEDS IN EDUCATION

Our educational system needs help in many ways: It is beset by violence, drug use, and marginal student performance. Parents blame teachers, teachers blame parents, and everyone blames government. However, everyone seems to agree on several things: Building character, developing high self-esteem, pride, and self-concept, are crucial to individual educational success.

Parents are instilling new pride in our multiracial children. We are sending them to school with the knowledge that they can be proud of all of their heritage. What happens then? In North Carolina, a teacher asked a multiracial teenager in front of the class, "You're so light, are you sure your mother knows who your father is?" In Georgia, a teacher said to a child, "You should go home and figure out what you are—you can't be both." In Maryland, a school secretary came into a kindergarten class and announced she was there to decide a child's race.

Schools are fighting back. The National PTA has endorsed a multiracial classification, which is very important to our success in the educational system. Progressive administrators are saying, "We don't care
what the federal government says, we will let our multiracial children
be multiracial. It's the right thing to do." Progressive schools are not
waiting for OMB Directive No. 15 to catch up with reality. Progressive
schools recognize that "valuing diversity" is more than just a fashion-
able phrase. Progressive schools want the multiracial classification, and
they want it now because of the following examples:

1. What happened in Wedowee, Alabama, is an example of overt
racial discrimination against a multiracial student, Revonda Bowen.
Hulond Humphries, principal at Randolph County High School, stated
in an open assembly that Revonda Bowen's parents had made a "mistake" (referring to her parents' marriage and her birth). Is Revonda
Bowen, a biracial student, entitled to be free from racial discrimination
as "guaranteed" by Title VI of the Civil Rights Act of 1964?

2. A fourth-grade student takes a national test with his peers. The
first question he is asked is his race. He is multiracial, and his race is not
listed on the test, although his peers see their races. He feels singled out
and becomes upset. His emotional state affects his test scores. Should a
multiracial child be subjected to lower performance and achievement
scores because OMB Directive No. 15 does not reflect his race?

3. Federal officials accused five Georgia school districts of unfairly
steering blacks into special education, remedial classes, and other low-
level programs. U.S. Secretary of Education Richard Riley expressed
concern about racially biased tracking in schools. Multiracial students
are also subjected to racial tracking biases. How can you accurately
know if there is racially biased tracking against multiracial students in
our country if you do not collect accurate racial data on them?

4. The National Research Council sent out a survey for recent
graduates of doctoral programs with instructions to "check only one
box" on the question of racial identity. Multiracial respondents were
not satisfied with the choices, because there was no multiracial category. The surveys were returned to those persons who chose more than
one box. One would assume a person who earned a doctorate degree

would know how to classify themselves racially. Why would the National Research Council collect inaccurate data?

DATA NEEDS IN HEALTH SERVICES

Does it matter medically if a person is classified as multiracial? I am not a medical doctor, but as the parent of multiracial children, I have concerns. In 1990, our 2-year-old daughter had an accident. My husband and I took her to Scottish Rite Children's Medical Center—one of the premier children's hospitals in the South. I was given a patient information form in the emergency room. It had a space for race that was only large enough to fill in an initial. If I put a "B" for biracial, they would, of course, interpret the B as black. If I filled in an M for multiracial, they would have no idea what it stood for. I chose to write "Biracial" in large letters across the page.

The triage nurse glanced at the form, then looked at my daughter, my son, my husband, and me and decided my daughter was black, based on her *perception* of our family. She asked if our daughter had ever been tested for sickle cell disease. Our 6-year-old son asked us if he could have it, too, and were he and his sister going to die.

I questioned several genetics specialists at Emory University and the University of Michigan Medical Center. Was this a concern? Should my children be tested? Was it ethical for hospital personnel to put fear into the mind of a 6-year-old child? The answers came back unanimously from the experts: no, no, and no. The possibility of one of my children having the disease was virtually the same as a child of two white parents. It was doubly unnecessary in this case, because I had genetic counseling and testing during my pregnancy with this child. Yet a white child coming into the same emergency room is not asked about sickle cell disease testing.

The Agency for Health Care Policy and Research reported its recommendation in the November 10, 1993, issue of the *Journal of the American Medical Association*: "Universal screening is the only way to ensure that all infants with Sickle Cell Disease will be identified early and thus have the opportunity to benefit from current knowledge regarding treatment of the disease" (vol. 270, no. 18, p. 2158). They went on to advise:

Screening programs that target specific high-risk racial or ethnic groups will not identify all infants with Sickle Cell Disease because it is not possible to determine reliably an individual's racial or ethnic background by physical appearance, surname, presumed racial heritage or self-report. (p. 2158)

On June 15, 1992, after meeting with representatives of PROJECT RACE, Scottish Rite Children's Medical Center added the category "Multiracial" to its listings of race codes and put administrative procedures in place to educate their staff about self-identification.

The Institute of Medicine has made several recommendations concerning regulation of health databases. One of its recommendations was that databases regularly analyze their information for accuracy. If multiracial people are not listed as multiracial, racial accuracy of data will never be achieved.

Other health questions frequently arise:

1. Black people are at greater risk of high blood pressure than the general population. Blacks get the disease one third more often than whites, they get it earlier in life, and they suffer it far more severely. Are multiracial people at high risk for some diseases? How can we know without accurate data?

2. The result of one study has shown the relative odds of low birthweight based on race of the married mothers and fathers, specifically of white and black non-Hispanic marriages in the United States from 1984 to 1988. The odds were the best for children of a white mother/white father; worse for those with a white mother/black father; even worse for those with a black mother/white father; and worst of all for children of black mothers/black fathers. This is critical health information, yet it does not include children of single mothers, nor does it take other racial combinations or socioeconomic factors into consideration. Should multiracial children be placed at high risk medically because OMB Directive No. 15 excludes them?

3. It is much more likely for people of the same racial or ethnic background to match as bone marrow donors, because human leukocyte antigens (HLA) follow racial background. The National Bone Marrow Registry, for example, is government funded and mandated,

and it therefore follows racial and ethnic guidelines as set forth in OMB Directive No. 15. No donor drives have been directed toward multiracial people, as they have with other racial and ethnic groups, therefore the donor pool for our children is inadequate. Kathleen Rand Reed, American Society of Minority Health and Transplant Professionals, said, "To search for donor matches, especially in bone marrow donation in populations as constructed by OMB Statistical Directive 15, is to lessen the efficacy in successfully locating a marrow match" (CNSTAT Workshop, February 17, 18, 1994). How many multiracial children will suffer or die as a result of inadequate medical classifications?

Parents of multiracial children are legitimately concerned about the medical treatment of their families. Politics must be put aside when the health of children is at stake.

DATA NEEDS IN EMPLOYMENT

The first case I heard of regarding employment problems was from an engineer who worked for a government contractor. He had requested a multiracial classification on his employment records. The employer refused, giving "government requirements" as the reason. The company solved its problem: They hired him as black and fired him as white. We can all understand that the company got its affirmative action number—erroneously. This is neither fair nor accurate.

The human resources director of one of the largest corporations in Georgia voiced a legitimate concern. Race is an item on the job application form. In 1992, 6% of job applicants refused to answer the race question. In 1993, 20% of job applicants refused to answer the race question. I asked the director why she thought such a high percentage refused to fill out race information. She told me the majority of people who refused indicated there was not an appropriate category for them.

The government anticipated this problem. The Equal Employment Opportunity Commission (EEOC) advises employers: "Eliciting information on the race/ethnic identity of an employee by direct inquiry is not encouraged." I submit that a secretary or interviewer in an employment office is *not* qualified to make this decision. The president of the corporation is not qualified to make this decision. No one is qualified to make this decision about another person.

Other examples of discrimination in employment:

1. A multiracial job applicant filled in "white" when made to choose one race classification. The personnel director, who knew her family, called and asked why she chose not to help the company fill its affirmative action requirements (by choosing the majority race instead of the minority race). Should discrimination occur because accurate data for multiracial employees do not exist?

2. More and more universities are actively recruiting faculty that can serve as role models for their student population, including: black, Asians, Hispanics, Native Americans, veterans, women, physically challenged people, gays, and lesbians. Multiracial students need multiracial role models, too. How will a university know if a prospective employee is multiracial if their data entries do not include the category and their hiring practices discriminate?

Let's be realistic. Multiracial children grow up to be multiracial adults, who join our workforce. We need to face this and remedy the situation now.

DATA NEEDS IN HOUSING

In 1993, a report by the Federal Financial Institutions Council (July, 1994) showed that black applicants for conventional home loans were rejected in 34% of cases, Hispanics in 25.2% of cases, whites 15.4% of the time, and Asians 14.5% of the time. How can we determine the rejection rate in housing for multiracial people and interracial families if banks, savings associations, credit unions, and mortgage companies are not required to gather racial data for this segment of the population?

LEGISLATIVE UPDATE

The states had to do what the federal government would not do. Ohio was the first state to mandate the multiracial classification on school forms in the state, effective July 31, 1992. Illinois was the second state. The state of Georgia passed the most progressive legislation for multiracial people in the country in February 1994. Sen. Ralph David Abernathy sponsored the legislation from my state. Senate passage was unanimous; House passage was overwhelming. (Senate Bill 149 has since been signed into law and became effective July 1, 1994).

This legislation mandates that all school forms, state agency forms, and employment forms and applications include the classification multiracial. It further mandates that no written document or computer software in the state of Georgia shall bear the designation of *other* as a racial or ethnic classification. In July 1995, Indiana and Michigan became the fourth and fifth states to enact legislation.

Ohio, Illinois, Georgia, Indiana, and Michigan. Five states, 10% of all states. Is that a significant percentage for demographers? I do not know. What I do know is that more states will follow. Texas and Maryland have also introduced legislation. What I do know is that in each state, legislators and interracial families are fed up with the lack of progress on the federal level for the rights of multiracial people.

THE CATCH-22 OF DIRECTIVE NO. 15

It remains critical to the success of a multiracial classification to pass legislation in as many states as possible. As the states respond to our community, they send a positive and strong message to Washington. But the federal government may not accept the multiracial numbers. The states must collapse the numbers back into the categories accepted by Directive No. 15: American Indian or Alaskan Native, Asian or Pacific Islander, black, Hispanic, or white. We are forced by the limitations of Directive No. 15 to use an allocation method that distributes the numbers by population of the collected group. It is hardly the perfect solution, but at least each group is fairly represented, and we accomplish the addition of the multiracial category until Directive No. 15 can be changed.

The PROJECT RACE proposal for a revised directive differs from that of some other organizations. We propose the addition of the classification multiracial to the five basic racial and ethnic categories without further breakdown. In other words, multiracial children would only check multiracial and not be forced to list the race and ethnicity of their mothers and fathers.

Our motives are threefold. First, to demand that multiracial children explain their heritage is unnecessary in most instances. Schools, employers, lenders, and others do not care about the breakdown. It is unnecessary for compliance purposes and only serves to satisfy curiosity. Second, if multiracial children are told they must further qualify themselves on forms, it says two things to them: You must do something your peers do not have to do; and we are not finished with your identification yet. Some government entities have actually argued that to list the races of the parents would require too much print on a form. Third, adopted people have told us that they may be uncomfortable with the mother's race/father's race format, because the races of their biological parents may be different from that of their adoptive parents.

However, it does remain necessary *in some instances* (i.e., medical data) to obtain a further breakdown of the multiracial category. Our proposed revision of OMB Directive No. 15 takes this into consideration by stipulating a variance, similar to the requirement for Indian tribes. Therefore, our proposed variance reads:

If a further breakdown of the multiracial category is necessary, a variance can be specifically requested from the Office of Federal Statistical Policy and Standard, but such a variance will be granted only if the agency can demonstrate a reasonable necessity for civil rights compliance reporting, general program administrative and grant reporting, or statistical reporting. If a variance is granted, the category format shall be:

Multiracial: It is necessary for federal compliance purposes to provide a breakdown of racial and/or ethnic origins for multiracial persons. Please specify the combination of your origins from the list below, which best describes your multiracial identification:
- American Indian or Alaskan Native
- Asian or Pacific Islander
- Black, not of Hispanic origin
- Hispanic
- White, not of Hispanic origin

Using the terminology of "multiracial identification," as opposed to mother's race/father's race, makes a subtle, but critical distinction. One of the main points we are articulating to the government is the absolute necessity of self-identification. For example, Directive No. 15 now states: "The category which most clearly reflects the individual's recognition in his community should be used for purposes of reporting on persons who are of mixed racial and/or ethnic origins." A change in this method of identification is crucial. "Eyeballing" by a teacher, employer, census enumerator, or anyone is subjective, highly inaccurate, and probably a violation of civil rights. No one should be allowed to "guess" a person's race based on the perceived color of their skin, on their surname, or on any other criteria.

We have replaced this antiquated method in Directive No. 15 with:

> Self-identification must be utilized for all persons. If self-identification is attempted and refused, the data shall default to one of the six categories, or be allocated to the six categories on a proportionate basis, as long as the method for category assignment is consistent for the reporting agency or group.

CURRENT STATISTICAL ISSUES

A concern that has been voiced to us, largely by demographers, is that of a loss of numbers to certain racial communities if a multiracial classification is implemented. I am personally offended at statements by these same people that entire groups of people are against the multiracial category.

Some have said, "blacks are against this." Senator Abernathy of Georgia, who championed our legislation, is a black leader. In fact, not one black legislator in Georgia voted against our bill. Incidentally, Georgia has the fourth-highest percentage of black legislators in the country. Majority Leader William Mallory of Ohio, the first state legislator to sponsor our legislation, is black. Many, many black educators, civil rights leaders, psychologists, educators, and others support the multiracial classification.

PROJECT RACE is not an organization made up only of partners in black/white marriages. We have Hispanic, Asian, and Native American members and advocates in all combinations. To trivialize their needs is unacceptable. But for the sake of argument, let's explore the perceived "loss of numbers" problem.

First, I would like to stress that the multiracial category enables multiracial people to have the choice of an accurate designation. It is an important option for any person with parents of different races. This does not mean that this choice is appropriate for everyone. Some multiracial people choose to identify with one race only. They have every right and every opportunity to do so in our society.

Now the census numbers. Example: I am white, my husband is black. My children are white by default on the census figures (whereby the children take the race of the mother). Minority groups have lost two numbers. Because in the majority of white/black interracial marriages, the mother is white, the federal government, by its "mother calculation" arbitrarily takes away minority numbers—exactly what we have been accused of doing.

Will millions of people "jump ship" from another classification into the multiracial classification? No. In the 1991-1992 school year, before a multiracial category was added to forms, 489 students in the Cincinnati Public Schools chose the classification of *other*. In the 1992-1993 school year, the first year of the multiracial category, 527 students chose multiracial. The category of *other* was eliminated beginning with the 1992-1993 school year. In the 1993-1994 school year, 629 students chose multiracial. Every racial and ethnic minority increased as well during those years. Did students in Cincinnati jump ship into the multiracial classification? No. We have similar results in the data from the Fulton County, Georgia schools.

Fear is irrational by its very nature. The fear of a loss of numbers is irrational. The fear that multiracial children will undermine the racial balance of this country is irrational and racist. The fear that a multiracial category will ruin affirmative action and entitlements for minorities is unproved and unfounded.

One last argument is that adding a multiracial category would be costly to states, government agencies, employers, and schools. This is simply ridiculous. All of our legislation, for example, includes phase-out provisions, although many school districts in Georgia voluntarily printed new forms and disposed of all existing forms. Businesses constantly change their forms. In fact, data cells are added all the time.

If the government never made any changes that affect forms, we could all stop worrying about tax changes and new health care plans. Virtually all computers and forms will need to change to accommodate the century update in 4 years to the year 2000, which will be much bigger and more costly than the change to accommodate the multiracial category.

CONCLUSION

Is it the job of government to make the demographic count "easy" or to make it meaningful and truly reflective of our society? We will not sit still for discrimination so that government numbers will not be disturbed. Omission of multiracial people is a form of discrimination. Our country has changed dramatically in the 16 years since the drafting of Directive No. 15.

In 1990, my child was considered white on the census, black at school, and multiracial at home, all at the same time. Obviously, something is very wrong. A child can be multiracial in a school in Ohio, Illinois, and Georgia, but not in Maryland, New York, or Colorado. I can legally demand that a hospital in Georgia classify my child as multiracial. I cannot cross the state line and make that request in Florida.

We all have a responsibility to ensure the best for all our children. Multiracial pride is no less valid than any other pride and no less valuable. You cannot say of my children, "They don't know who they are." But I can say, "You don't know who they are—you don't know where they belong." That is the problem we face today.

4

Multiracial Identity in
a Color-Conscious World

DEBORAH A. RAMIREZ

One day, while I was concentrating on an art project in grammar school, some older kids began to question me. "Where were you born?" Without thinking, I responded, "in America." They looked at each other in puzzlement. An older girl, continued, "But, what are you?" Impatient and exasperated, I repeated a version of my earlier response, "I'm an American." One girl persisted, "But what about your family?"

Much later, I understood the questions. In our white working-class suburb, my Latino features were different from those of my Irish and Italian classmates. These children weren't sure how to categorize me.

Later, at Harvard Law School, a small group of Mexican American students gathered to form its own group. They identified themselves as the Chicano Law Student Association. When I joined, my mother was furious. "You are *not* Mexican, you are half Spanish and half Mexican. My mother and my father are from Spain; only your father's family is from Mexico." Of course, I knew this, but my mixed ancestry didn't fit neatly within any existing framework, especially the one at Harvard;

the Chicano Law Student Association deliberately rejected the term "Hispanic" in order to distance themselves from the more prosperous white students of European ancestry.

I always felt as if I lived between worlds, in a confusing, ambivalent netherworld that defied categorization. I was not black; I was not white; I was not European; to many, I was not Latino. What was I? I felt the frustration, anger, and confusion of someone whose true identity remains unknown, ignored, or disparaged.

When I stumbled upon Maria Root's book on multiracial identity, I began to find the words to express my own identity and feelings. I no longer live "between worlds," I live in a multidimensional one. This essay is about that multidimensional world. ⚭

The passage of the Civil Rights Act of 1964 marked the culmination of the African American struggle for legal equality, ending nearly a century of legislative and judicial decision making that tolerated, and at times, even mandated, differential treatment of citizens on the sole basis of skin color. This monumental civil rights victory, however, could not be savored long. It became readily apparent that nondiscrimination under the law was not a panacea for centuries of oppression. As President Lyndon Johnson (quoted in Kull, 1992) explained in 1965,

> You do not take a person who, for years, has been hobbled by chains and liberate him, bring him up to the starting line of a race and then say, "you are free to compete with all the others," and still justly believe that you have been completely fair. (pp. 186-187)

Color-conscious legal remedies involved an effort to prevent the legacy of past discrimination, and an inevitable degree of continuing discrimination, from funneling African Americans into a permanent racial underclass. When courts and legislatures first created race-conscious remedies in the 1960s, the United States could be seen as a black and white society. Blacks constituted approximately 10% of the population, and whites nearly 90% (U.S. Bureau of the Census, 1964). Numerous other ethnic and religious groups suffered from past and present discrimination, but blacks were, for all practical purposes, the only racial minority group of significant size (U.S. Bureau of the Census, 1964). Asians or Pacific Islanders constituted a mere 0.5% of the population; Native Americans, Eskimos, and Aleutians 0.3%; and other races 0.1%. Although Latinos constituted an estimated 3.9% of the population, the U.S. Bureau of the Census lacked the methodology to identify Latinos and Hispanics as such, contributing to the perception of America as "black and white." This demographic reality led the Kerner Commission to conclude in its 1968 report on urban unrest: "Our nation is moving toward two societies, one black, one white—separate and unequal" (Report of the National Advisory Council on Civil Disorders, 1968).

Given the relatively small number of nonblack people of color, their inclusion in many color-conscious remedies was not problematic at the time. The parameters, funding levels, and eligibility for federal and state affirmative action initiatives—including business loans, college scholarships, school programs, housing subsidies, health funds, and most important, the Voting Rights Act of 1965—were determined by U.S. Census information detailing the number of people of color in the population. Consequently adding small numbers of nonblack minorities seemingly would have little impact on these color-conscious remedies, court orders, and legislative programs.

Since the 1960s, however, three important demographic trends have changed the face of America and its race relations: first, *the percentage of people of color has increased;* second, *the percentage of people of color who are not black has increased;* and third, *the number of people who consider themselves multiracial has increased.* These demographic changes affect existing color-conscious remedies in crucial ways. In fact, demographic shifts may be causing our race-conscious remedial system to implode. As the percentage of people of color in the population increases, so too will the "exclusionary" effects of affirmative action on nonminorities. Furthermore, because a growing percentage of the population of color is Latino, Asian, or Native American, rather than black, the potential for interracial conflict over the benefits and burdens of race-conscious measures is increased. Together the effects of nonminority exclusion and interracial conflict affect the political viability of race-conscious remedies as we know them.

In addition to demographic changes, the increasing phenomenon of multiracial identity confounds the simplistic notion of race underlying our color-conscious remedial system. Changed circumstances require a reexamination of our approach to the continuing problems of race, ethnicity, and discrimination. I believe two of the possible options for change—tinkering with existing, government-sponsored affirmative action or alternatively eliminating all racial preferences in favor of a color-blind approach—are both unacceptable. In their place, I offer a third alternative which I call *multicultural empowerment*. Multicultural empowerment acknowledges the importance of race yet penetrates beyond it to identify and incorporate the realities of political, economic, and social problems that cannot be solved through racial preferences. A new paradigm of multicultural empowerment will benefit all groups in the population, acknowledging that race matters without limiting identity to race alone. This chapter describes the three major demographic trends in greater detail. Subsequently, I reassess the wisdom of those remedies and discuss whether they should continue and, if so, what form they should take.

DEMOGRAPHIC CHANGES

The Percentage of People of Color
Has Increased From 10% to 25%

In 1960, 1 out of 10 Americans was a person of color; according to the 1990 U.S. Census, 1 out of 4 Americans view themselves as people of color (U.S. Bureau of the Census, 1992). Given the increase between 1960 and 1990, the percentage of people of color is likely to rise further in the next few decades. For example, between 1980 and 1990, the Asian American population grew at a staggering rate of 107.8% (U.S. Bureau of the Census, 1992). The Latino population increased by 53%, and the number of non-Latino African Americans by 13.2%. In sharp contrast, the number of whites increased by only 6%.

The increase in self-defined people of color may have important consequences for affirmative action programs and other race-specific measures employing racial classifications. Even when minorities constituted only 10% of the population, the exclusionary effect of race-conscious selection procedures provoked frequent criticism. Given a finite number of places or slots, any system that includes people on the basis of race necessarily excludes others on that same basis. As the proportion of people of color in the population increases, so too does this exclusionary effect. Whereas 10% of existing slots may have been set aside for people of color in the 1960s, similar programs in the 1990s will set aside closer to 25%. Indeed, in states such as New Mexico, where people of color currently make up more than 50% of the population, non-Latino whites are actually in the minority (Barringer, 1991). In California, where people of color now constitute roughly 43% of the population, non-Latino whites could well be a minority by the year 2000 if the recent past is prologue. Other states will likely follow. In Texas, the population of people of color has increased to 39%, in Florida, 27%, in New York, 31% (Barringer, 1991).

The already significant exclusionary effect will undoubtedly affect the political acceptance of color-conscious remedies. A question posed by Justice William Rehnquist during oral arguments for *Regents of the University of California v. Bakke* presaged this demographic trend and its implications for race-conscious measures. Justice Rehnquist asked: "What if the school raised the minority quota to *fifty* places in one hundred . . . would this be *invidious* discrimination, designed to harm white applicants?" Defense counsel Archibald Cox responded:

> I would say that as the number goes up, the danger of invidiousness, or the danger that this is being done not for social purposes but to favor one group as against another group, the risk, if you will, of a finding of an invidious purpose to discriminate against is greater. And therefore, I think it's a harder case. (Irons & Guitton, 1993, p. 309)

This discussion illustrates how the exclusionary effect looms over affirmative action programs as a benchmark for public palatability. The current debate in California over the Civil Rights Initiative, which would end affirmative action in state government and public universities, also demonstrates the intense backlash that this exclusionary effect can produce.

The Word "Minority" Is No Longer
a Synonym for African American

In 1960, blacks constituted 96% of the minority population. Today, the phenomenal growth in the Asian and Latino communities has altered the mix of people of color so that blacks now constitute about

50% of the population of people of color (U.S. Bureau of the Census, 1992). Indeed, projections indicate that early in the 21st century, Latinos will be the largest group of color in the United States (U.S. Bureau of the Census, 1993).

Over time, the concept of a single racial minority group has expanded from a black and white model to a multicultural one. This demographic trend is important because the affirmative action remedies created almost 30 years ago were conceived to protect and empower a single racial minority group. Today, that monolithic concept is a myth; instead, several distinct racial and ethnic groups make up the population of color. These groups are growing considerably in number and influence, each with its own diverse and separate cultures, languages, histories, religions, and politics.

As a result, affirmative action remedies originally designed to address the legacy of suffering and discrimination experienced by African Americans are increasingly benefiting *other* people of color. The exclusionary effect of these remedies grows at the same time their historic justification diminishes.

Reserving race-conscious remedies for blacks alone may alleviate these political and conceptual problems. But excluding other people of color, in turn, raises questions as to whether blacks are uniquely disadvantaged historically and, if so, whether this factor alone entitles them to exclusive remedies. If blacks are indeed uniquely disadvantaged, does the "lesser" history of discrimination against Latinos and Asians entitle them to a lesser remedy, or no remedy at all? In other words, do we treat Latinos and Asians as whites, as blacks, or as something in between? As the number of groups and subgroups included within the concept of people of color grows, so too does the risk of escalating conflict between and among those groups. For example, may an institution meet its affirmative action obligations simply by hiring Latinos, or must it instead hire a certain percentage of blacks, Native Americans, and Asians, as well?

Broad differences within racial and ethnic groups further complicate racial identities. The history of discrimination against Mexican Americans differs from that of Cuban Americans, although both groups are lumped together with Puerto Ricans, Dominicans, Central Americans, and others under the classification Hispanic. Although Haitians are considered black, their status as recent immigrants and the language barriers they face can separate and exclude them from more established segments of African American community. Filipinos, although classified as Asians, face a history of oppression at the hands of Spanish and American colonialists. Koreans still resent their country's historical oppression by Japan. Japanese and Chinese cultures and militaries have often clashed. Yet, in the eyes of the U.S. Census Bureau, as well as the courts and legislatures that implement race-conscious remedies, Filipinos, Koreans, Japanese, and Chinese are all classified under the single designation of Asian. An additional accounting problem arises with Latinos because the U.S. Census Bureau classifies these groups as an ethnicity, but many Latinos are also black or Asian. In other words, the census currently counts people on the basis of race, but ethnicity transcends race in the case of Latinos. As a result, black and Asian Latinos are counted twice as people of color. Although the census could avoid this problem by segmenting the nonblack, non-Asian Latino population into its own subgroup, treating that subgroup as the entire Latino category would substantially undercount the true Latino population.

Multiracial Minorities:
Erasing the Premise of a Single Racial Identity

The third important demographic trend to consider when reexamining race-conscious remedies is the increasing number of Americans who are not solely black, Asian, white, Latino, or Native American. Instead their heritage represents some combination of these racial categories, and they identify as multiracial. The emergence and increasing presence of multiracial Americans are transforming the face of America (Root, 1992d) and forcing lawmakers to reevaluate remedies and programs that rely on simplistic racial classifications (Graham, Chapter 3, this volume).

Although, at some level, all individuals are racially mixed, many do not know or acknowledge their full racial and ethnic backgrounds. Historically, our multiracial heritage has been concealed by an odd, racist American institution known as the "one-drop rule," which states that even a person with only one drop of black blood must be classified as black. Thus, although many estimate that 75% to 90% of the black population is, in fact, multiracial, these individuals are lumped into a monolithic black category (Wright, 1994). One scholar observes:

The so-called "one drop of blood" rule . . . maintains that a person is nonwhite if she has (at least) one drop of another race in her. This blatantly racist concept, originating in the ante bellum South, still exists today; Americans who are part-black are socially considered black and only black, by most Americans." (Lythcott-Haims, 1994, pp. 539-540)[1]

The one-drop rule was created to maximize the number of slaves. In contrast, the test used by the Bureau of Indian Affairs for identifying who is Native American, and thus eligible for certain government benefits, is more restrictive. In order to be classified as Native American, an individual must have an Indian "blood quantum" of at least one fourth. Other governments require enrollment within a federally recognized tribe, each of which sets its own membership qualifications. Some use blood quantums varying from one sixteenth to one half. Thus, unlike the historic, racist rule for African Americans, one drop will not necessarily classify an individual as Native American.

Although aimed at blacks, the one-drop rule incidentally fostered a pervasive American belief that all individuals belong to one racial group or another, but not both. As a result, partly out of ignorance, partly out of choice, and partly because of a racist American cultural tradition, most individuals do not choose to identify themselves in multiracial terms. Instead, most identify within a single racial group. This phenomenon perpetuates the myth that multiracial people do not exist.

Accordingly, federal and state data collection agencies, including the U.S. Census Bureau, compile racial and ethnic statistics on the premise that individuals identify within a single racial and ethnic group. This notion of monoracial identity is enforced by the decennial U.S. Census, which requires individuals to categorize themselves as a single race.

Self-identification enables the census to avoid determining whether a person of multiracial ancestry should be categorized as white, black, Asian, or *other*. If a woman's parents consider themselves white but she thinks of herself as Asian because her great-great-great-grandmother was Chinese, the Census Bureau will not challenge her if she checks Asian on the form. The Office of Management and Budget's 1980 Statistical Policy Directive No. 15 (text in Appendix 1) also relies on self-identification, advising people to designate the racial and ethnic group with which they most identify. However, by failing to provide categories for those who identify themselves as multiracial, the census ignores mixed-race individuals who may have been consciously raised in two or more distinctive cultural traditions. If these individuals choose to identify themselves in multiracial terms, attempts to impose a single racial classification upon them would relegate their multiracial identities to second-class status. Multiracial people view identity as multidimensional (Root, 1992d) and deserve acknowledgment and appreciation of all their heritages.

As one commentator observed,

> Forcing a Multiracial child to define herself only as black perpetuates the myth that Multiracial people do not exist. Since it is not acceptable to acknowledge one's Multiracial status, the Multiracial person suffers in silence. . . . Although society has told Multiracial people to choose, in actuality, society makes the choice for them. The rich diversity literally embodied by multiracial people remains hidden from view, hidden from discourse, hidden from recognition, and thus invisible. (Lythcott-Haims, 1994, p. 540)

The size of the multiracial population is difficult to estimate because of the lack of a multiracial census category. However, indirect data suggest tremendous growth (Root, 1992d). For example, one study of mixed marriages indicates that

> the number of children living in families where one parent is white and the other is black, Asian, or American Indian . . . has tripled from fewer than four hundred thousand in 1970 to one and a half million in 1990 and this doesn't count the children of single parents or children whose parents are divorced. (Wright, 1994, p. 49)

As the multiracial population grows, so too does the inadequacy of existing racial classification schemes. When more children are born to parents from different racial groups, two problems emerge. First, the existing racial classification scheme's reliance on self-identification creates opportunities for individuals to strategically streamline their identity in order to qualify for certain admissions programs or government benefits. For instance, consider admission standards that require Asians to score 90 on a test but admit blacks with an 84. An Asian-black applicant scoring 86 would be admitted only if he identifies himself as black rather than Asian. We could solve this problem by defining individuals' race and ethnicity for them, but this approach invites an inquiry we surely would like to avoid. Alternately, we could create identical racial remedies for all people of color. However, under this approach, are multiracial people of partial white ancestry to be deemed white or a people of color? Even if such determinations are possible, uniform remedies for all people of color threaten to dilute benefits historically intended for black Americans: Affirmative action programs may fill their ranks with Asians and Latinos, leaving blacks once again disenfranchised.

Second, if growth in the multiracial population prompts federal and state data-gathering agencies to create a multiracial category, individuals who currently identify themselves as black, Asian, or Native American may instead identify themselves as multiracial. Given the increasing number of multiracially identified individuals, a multiracial census category could generate a staggering statistical shift in population (Alonso & Waters, 1993; Root, 1992d). Maria P. P. Root notes that:

> Currently, it is estimated that 30-70% of African Americans by multigenerational history are multiracial; virtually all Latinos and Filipinos are multiracial, as are the majority of American Indians and Native Hawaiians. Even a significant proportion of white-identified people are of multiracial origins. The way in which the Census Bureau records data on race makes it very difficult to estimate the number of biracial people, let alone multiracial people, in the United States. Any estimates that have been made are conservative. (p. 9)

Creating a multiracial category would diminish the statistical strength of established minority groups. As the number of people claiming multiracial identity increases, membership in existing minority groups would necessarily decrease.

This statistical change would have enormous impact on matters immensely important to minority communities: electoral representation, the allocation of government benefits, affirmative action, and federal contracting rules. Certain districts created under the Voting Rights Act of 1965 to encourage minority representation might have to be redrawn as group numbers change. This statistical shift would also affect local school boards and civil rights agencies that use traditional minority categories. The federal government relies on monoracial categories to monitor a wide array of programs and entitlements, including: minority access to home mortgage loans under the Home Mortgage Disclosure Act, enforcement of the Equal Credit Opportunity Act, public school desegregation plans, minority business development programs, and enforcement of the Fair Housing Act. Creation of a multiracial category also has the potential to disrupt equal employment opportunity record keeping and affirmative action planning on the part of employers who are mandated to collect ethnic data under Title VII of the Civil Rights Act of 1964.

Clearly, the creation of a multiracial category for self-identification will have far-reaching effects on society and the administration of race-conscious remedies. Can the inevitable, interracial tensions heightened by these changes be reconciled?

WHERE DO WE GO FROM HERE?

Multicultural Empowerment

The changing demographics of our population are causing the current race-conscious remedial system to implode. Undoubtedly public and political support will erode as increasing numbers of people of color magnify the exclusionary effects of race-based programs on nonminority groups. Not only will friction increase between minority and nonminority constituencies, but conflicts will also arise between minority groups themselves until we learn to balance their conflicting claims. Finally, as multiracial individuals increase in number and demand recognition, our existing race-conscious framework must consider the viability of a multiracial category, as well as the consequences of allowing people to self-define race.

Race-conscious remedies must either adapt to changing demographics or perish. I see three possible approaches to reform:

1. Continue government-sponsored racial preferences and affirmative action programs, but create dispute-resolution mechanisms for interracial conflict and discern a method for acknowledging multiracial identity.
2. Embrace a color-blind tradition, flatly prohibiting any distinctions made on the basis of race or ethnicity.
3. Construct policies that confront problems stemming from race without relying upon racial classifications.

The first approach promotes equality of results; the second assures equality of process. I reject the results-oriented, traditional affirmative action paradigm, because I believe racial classifications are no longer appropriate for our multicultural and increasingly multiracial society. They exacerbate racial and ethnic balkanization, fail to acknowledge multiracial identity, and depend upon subjective data processing by bureaucrats. The existing classification system pits ethnic and racial groups against one another, destroying the potential for transracial alliances.

I also reject the second, process-oriented, color-blind paradigm because it disregards the reality of racial and ethnic discrimination. Like most Americans, I embrace the ideal that our legal system should not make distinctions on the basis of race, gender, or ethnicity. However, although race should not matter, it does. A scene in the movie *Philadelphia* illustrates this truism. When a judge articulates the color-blind model, explaining that in "my" courtroom, gender, race, ethnicity, and sexual orientation are completely irrelevant and any questioning about a witness's sexual orientation is, therefore, inappropriate, the lawyer to whom he speaks responds: "But with all due respect, Your Honor, we do not all live in this courtroom." By ignoring race, the color-blind approach fails to square with reality.

The third approach presents a new, more eclectic, paradigm. Premised on a principle of nondiscrimination, it rejects the second approach of color blindness, recognizing that race matters too much to be ignored. However, unlike the traditional affirmative action approach, which focuses exclusively on race, this new paradigm penetrates beyond race to identify the political, economic, and social problems at issue within specific government or institutional programs. Race may contribute to these problems, but race-conscious remedies alone pose insufficient solutions. Thus this third paradigm establishes a more complex notion of identity enabling individuals to define themselves by race *or* other factors that shape their sense of self. I call this new paradigm multicultural empowerment.

For example, interracial conflicts resulting from employment set-asides do not require race-based remedies. Recognizing the law's current hostility to voluntary employer affirmative action plans, Donald Munro (in press) advocates an alterative approach in the vein of multicultural empowerment:

> Self-interested employers and minorities should develop workable alternatives to racial preferences which could still achieve the positive goals of

affirmative action without running afoul of the many restraints on the practice. . . . One answer may be a shift away from race-based preferences altogether, and the adoption of affirmative action based on economic status and class history.

Munro's proposal has several benefits. First, a class-based system of preferences aids all poor people, regardless of race or ethnicity, facilitating consensus building on civil rights issues and creating solidarity among the disenfranchised. Second, his approach is a cost-effective replacement for existing racial preferences, which may be over- and underinclusive in terms of disadvantaged status. Third, if the alternative is eliminating affirmative action entirely, economic preferences represent a second-best remedial measure for minority groups, many of whose members will continue to qualify for benefits under the new scheme. Because Munro's approach eliminates race and ethnicity as proxies for need, it emphasizes the reality of each individual's identity in furtherance of the goals of multicultural empowerment.

It is my hope that future discussions about race in America focus on how we can empower people of color without using racial classifications. Munro's proposal provides one example. We need to have more discussions about other possibilities.

The Limits of Multicultural Empowerment

Despite its advantages, the multicultural empowerment paradigm does have its limits. I anticipate three major areas in which racial classifications may be unavoidable. The situation arises when institutions seek integration, proportional representation, or racially or ethnically balanced distribution of benefits. Although multicultural empowerment programs may encourage these goals, it cannot assure them; success may hinge on implementation of a traditional race-based affirmative action scheme. Second, if institutions attempt to solve overtly racial or ethnic problems, minority group membership may be an essential proxy for linguistic or cultural insight. Third, and most important, proven patterns of institutional bias may require racial and ethnic classifications to remedy past identified discrimination against particular groups.

Some would argue that these exceptions devour the rule. However, many examples represent a variety of race-infused situations that fall outside these three problematic categories. The multicultural empowerment paradigm may not work in every setting; however, policymakers should use racial classifications as a last, rather than first, resort. When implementable, multicultural empowerment provides enormous benefits.

NOTE

1. Several Supreme Court decisions explicitly and implicitly recognize the "one-drop rule." For example, *Loving v. Virginia* (1967) strikes down an antimiscegenation law defining as black anyone with an "ascertainable" amount of black blood, and *Plessy v. Ferguson* (1896) treats Plessy as "colored" despite his claim to be seven eighths white. More recently, the Court declined review of a Louisiana case in which plaintiffs failed to prove their parents were white under the state's racial classification statute provision: "a person having one-thirty second or less of negro blood shall not be described or designated as 'colored'" (*Doe v. LA Dept. of Health and Human Resources* [1986], dismissed for lack of a substantial federal question).

5

Transracial Adoptions
In Whose Best Interest?

RUTH G. McROY

CHRISTINE C. IIJIMA HALL

When I began researching interracial marriages and interracial identity, I realized how these issues generalized to many other groups who lived in two cultures. I saw the similarity between interracial marriages and gay/lesbian relationships in terms of possible lack of acceptance by families. I was also able to see the similarity between transracial adopted persons and racially mixed people. Children of transracial adoptions have parents of a different race; racially mixed children have parents of different races. These two groups most likely share some similar life experiences and identity processes. Thus I jumped at the opportunity to coauthor a chapter with Dr. Ruth McRoy, an expert on transracial adoptions. We blend our research, philosophies, and counseling experiences to discuss the pros and cons of transracial adoptions. &

Christine Hall

I have been interested in transracial adoption outcomes since the 1970s when, as an adoptions social worker, I placed children transracially. I often wondered about the outcomes of these placements, which I considered to be "experiments in interracial living." At the time, I was very optimistic that some 20 years later, race relations would have improved significantly and that racial differences between parents and children would no longer be an issue.

I believed that interracial marriages as well as transracial adoptions of black and white children would be commonplace. However, in 1995, race is still very much an issue in our society, and transracial adoptions continue to be very controversial. Over the years, I have had an opportunity to research transracial adoption outcomes, debate the significance of racial identity, testify in legal cases, and consult with adoption agencies that are challenged to defend their same-race or transracial adoption policies. I was delighted to have been asked to coauthor a chapter with Dr. Christine Hall, whose expertise is interracial identity and interracial children and families. Our collaboration has given us both greater insights into the complex dynamics of transracial adoptions policies and practices. &

Ruth G. McRoy

Transracial adoption, the placement of children for adoption across racial lines, has been the subject of much media attention as well as state and federal legislation in recent years. The definition seems to imply that Anglo American children, Native American children, African American children, Mexican American or perhaps Asian American children, might be placed with families who are of a different racial background than the children. However, in practice, the term *transracial adoption* typically refers to the one-way transfer of children of color into white families.

What is the rationale for this practice? Why do adoption agencies rarely if ever consider the placement of a Euro American infant with an African American family but often place African American infants with Euro American families. This chapter will provide an overview of this complex issue from a historical and policy perspective. Over the years, trends toward transracial adoptions have been reversed several times. Special attention will be given to the unique racial identity issues for

African American children who have been placed transracially. Case illustrations and implications for therapists are provided.

HISTORICAL BACKGROUND

The public child welfare system, designed in the 1930s primarily to provide temporary out-of-home care for dependent children, has always served a disproportionately high number of African American children. This disproportion continued to grow as private adoption agencies, established in the 1920s, were designed to find adoptive homes for white infants and babies for childless couples. Until the mid-1960s, adoptions were viewed as a "white middle class affair," as the majority of the clientele at private adoption agencies were white middle- and upper-income families (Morgenstern, 1971, p. 68). Adoption agencies, following the Child Welfare League of America's (CWLA) *Standards for Adoption Service* (1958), adhered to the placement philosophy that children with the same racial characteristics as their adoptive families could be integrated more easily (Benet, 1976; McRoy, 1989). In fact in many states, adoption across racial lines was prohibited. It was not until 1967 in Texas and 1972 in Louisiana that the last two state statutes denying adoption across racial lines were declared unconstitutional.

Several factors, however, led adoption agencies to begin to reconsider their adherence to "race matching" in adoptions. In the 1960s, private adoption agencies experienced a significant decline in the number of healthy white infants available for adoption, due to the widespread use of contraceptives, availability of abortions, and lessening of the stigma toward unwed parenthood. Some agencies closed their adoption programs completely, as the limited placements could not financially sustain them. Other agencies continued to experience a great demand from white families to adopt infants and established long waiting lists. Some agencies and families turned to intercountry adoptions as a source of infants. Still others introduced very stringent criteria for adoptive parenthood in order to decrease the number of eligible white families waiting to adopt. Some increased their efforts to encourage women of color to consider making an adoption plan in order to increase the number of infants available for adoption. With the concomitant focus on integration in the 1960s and the need for more infants to place with prospective white adoptive families, some agencies began to advocate for transracial placements. In 1971 about 2,500 black children were placed transracially (Simon, 1984).

In opposition to this practice, in 1972, the National Association of Black Social Workers (NABSW) issued a resolution that called for the cessation of transracial placements, asserting that "black children in white homes are cut off from the healthy development of themselves as black people"(NABSW, 1972, pp. 2-3). The position clearly influenced agency practice; between 1972 and 1975, the overall number of transracial placements significantly declined, and the number of in-racial adoptions of black children increased (McRoy & Zurcher, 1983).

The following year, the Child Welfare League of America revised its standards for adoption practice and acknowledged that in-racial placements are preferable because children placed in adoptive families with similar distinctive characteristics can become more easily integrated into the average family and community (CWLA, 1973). In 1978, Native Americans obtained passage of the Indian Child Welfare Act, which set federal standards for the removal of Indian children and requirements to seek Native American adoptive families for Native American children (Indian Child Welfare Act, 1978). In 1987, the Child Welfare League restated the 1973 position, emphasizing the right of children to be placed in a family that reflects the child's cultural identity and heritage, but such children should not unduly wait for a same-race placement when a transracial placement was possible (CWLA, 1987).

However, as the numbers of white infants and young children available for adoption has continued to decrease and the number of white families desirous of adopting has increased, agencies have gradually resumed transracial placements. In the mid 1960s, an estimated 31.7% of children born to unmarried women were placed for adoption (Cartoof & Klerman, 1982). It is now estimated that about 3% of white unmarried mothers place their babies for adoption (Bachrach, 1991). The National Council for Adoption estimated that about 25,000 infants under 2 years of age were placed for adoption in 1986 (Stolley, 1993). Yet the number of parents seeking to adopt infants continues to increase as infertility has increased. It is estimated that about 2.4 million couples have infertility problems and approximately 2 million white couples are seeking to adopt (Simon & Alstein, 1987). Most of these couples are seeking healthy white infants, but due to the declining supply, many will consider an infant or young child from another country, and some will consider a child of a different ethnic or racial background. However, the actual number of such adoptions is still very small; it is estimated that in 1987, white women adopting black children accounted for 1% of all adoptions (Stolley, 1993).

Another phenomenon influencing transracial adoptions is the growing number of children in foster care. In 1986, 273,000 children were in out-of-home care. Due significantly to the drug epidemic as well as the economic decline of the mid 1980s, however, by 1989, 360,000 children were in foster care. In 1991, that number was 429,000, and in 1992, the number had risen to 450,000. Many states estimate that about 15% to 20% of children in foster care need adoption planning, and as many as 85,000 children may need placement. Children of color are overrepresented in these statistics. In some states, such as New Jersey, Maryland, Louisiana, and Delaware, over half of the children needing placement are African American (Stehno, 1990).

As the number of African American children needing out-of-home placement exceeds the number of available African American foster families, these children are often placed in transracial foster care. Many children remain with these families, often separated from their siblings, with limited contact with their birth families or extended families for several years before they are either returned to their birth families or placed in adoption. In a growing number of court cases, white foster families are seeking to adopt black children whom they have fostered since infancy. In many of these instances, few if any attempts have been made toward seeking placements for these children with their extended family or making an in-racial foster placement before resorting to transracial foster care (McRoy, 1994, in press).

BARRIERS TO IN-RACIAL AND TRANSRACIAL PLACEMENTS

A number of factors account for the lack of minority foster and adoptive families to meet the growing needs of African American children. Most agencies have not responded to the changing racial demographics and needs of children and families (McKenzie, 1993). In both public and private agency programs, the majority of adoption workers and supervisors are white, and very little effort is being made to train in cultural competency or to recruit minority staff. The North American Council on Adoptable Children (Gelles & Kroll, 1993) has noted that agencies specializing in the placement of minority children, such as the Institute for Black Parenting in Los Angeles, are significantly more likely to make successful in-racial placements of African American children than nonminority (traditional) adoption agencies. The North American Council on Adoptable Children also reported that barriers to same-race placement include not only lack of minority staff, but agency fees, inflexible standards, and institutional/systematic racism (Gelles & Kroll, 1993).

Nevertheless, several states have called for the elimination of race as a barrier to white families adopting black children. Although most state statutes do not mention race in adoption decision making, three states, Texas, Wisconsin, and Pennsylvania, specifically stipulated that the state cannot prohibit or delay the placement of a child in foster care on the basis of the race of the child or family (Simon, Alstein, & Melli, 1994). Three other states, Arkansas, California, and Minnesota, have laws that require preference to be given to adoption within the same racial group. Moreover, they suggest an order for prioritizing placement decision making: blood relative, in-racial placement, transracial with a family that appreciates the child's racial heritage.

In 1994, the federal government became a major player in the debate about transracial adoptions. When Sen. Howard Metzenbaum of Ohio initially introduced the Multiethnic Ethnic Placement Act in a Floor Statement on July 15, 1993, he spoke of a white couple in Arizona seeking to adopt their 3-year-old black foster daughter, who had lived with them since the age of 3 months. He also spoke of a biracial couple in Minnesota who had been forced to give up their 4-year-old black foster son, whom they were trying to adopt. The senator stated that something must be done to help these and other children who were being denied the opportunity to be part of a stable and caring family, when a same-race family was not available. As passed in 1994, the legislation prohibits the denial of a placement solely on the basis of race but allows for consideration of the cultural, ethnic, or racial background of the child and the capacity of the prospective foster parents to meet the needs of a child of this background. The fact that this legislation is needed is indeed intriguing, as historically race has always been a major consideration in the placement of white children with white families.

Advocacy organizations composed primarily of families that have adopted transracially or through intercountry adoptions have taken positions suggesting that numerous family resources within the black, Hispanic, and Native American communities should be explored first before considering transracial adoptions. They encourage family reunification efforts, as well as the preservation of racial and cultural heritage through in-racial placements (Gelles & Kroll, 1993; see also Adoptive Families of America's (AFA) 1994 transracial adoptions position statement). In 1994, the NABSW called for family reunification, in-racial placements, and transracial placements only after documented efforts of unsuccessful attempts at in-racial placements (NABSW, 1994).

IN-RACIAL ADOPTIONS OF BLACK CHILDREN

Although we often hear the myth that African American families are not interested in adopting, the reality is that African American families adopt at a rate 4.5 times greater than European American or Hispanic families (Simon et al., 1994). In some places, in fact, African American families are on waiting lists for African American children, and some must compete with white families for an African American child. In some locations, white families have filed lawsuits alleging discrimination when an agency has given preference to a black family for a black child.

In 1994, the Child Welfare League of America suggested that the myth that African American and Latino families are not available to adopt has been perpetuated so that agencies can channel African American and Latino infants and preschoolers to infertile white couples who cannot adopt a white child. The league noted that such families are available not only for infants and preschoolers but for many school-age children. They recommend that if such families cannot be found for older children, then transracial adoptions should be considered with appropriate white families (Sullivan, 1994).

Although the actual numbers of African American children who have been transracially adopted is not available due to the lack of national reporting of adoption statistics, it is estimated that about 1,200 black children may be transracially placed each year. Because most of these children are infants and young children, the availability of transracial adoptions has not significantly affected the thousands of older black children needing permanent homes. Family reunification and in-racial foster and adoptive placements must be the goals for most of these children.

Nevertheless, thousands of black children have already been placed transracially, and it is to this group that we turn our attention now. Much of the controversy about transracial adoptions centers around the child's development of racial identity. The remaining sections of this chapter will address the racial/ethnic identity issues for transracially adopted black children.

Racial/Ethnic Identity in Transracial Adoptions

Racial/ethnic identity is but one component of self and personal identity. It refers to one's self-perception and sense of belonging to a particular group. It includes not only how one describes and defines oneself but also how one distinguishes oneself from members of other ethnic groups and the extent to which an individual has acquired behaviors specific to the particular racial group (McRoy, 1990). However, developmental theorists (Maslow, 1968; Erikson, 1963, 1968) believe that primary needs must be fulfilled before a person can move on to higher stages of development, such as identity. If initial stages are unfulfilled, identity development may be thwarted or problems may be evident in later life.

Maslow (1968) felt that one could not strive for self-actualization (total satisfaction with self and others) until basic pragmatic needs are met. These primary needs include physiological satisfaction of hunger, thirst, and tiredness. Secondary are safety needs, such as a stable, predictable environment free from anxiety and chaos. Once these primary and secondary needs are satisfied, the individual is free to seek the love and belongingness (identity) that stem from the affection from others.

Children who have been removed from their families of origin and moved between several foster homes may never have experienced a stable and predictable environment. Thus attachment, love, belongingness, and trust may be difficult to develop if the home environment changes frequently. In addition, many children may not have been able to grieve adequately the loss of previous caregivers.

Like Maslow, Erikson (1963, 1968) felt that a child should not want for food, shelter, and love. A child needs to trust unconditionally that mom and/or dad will always provide safety and provisions and that the parents will always be there when the child wakes from a nap. Without successful completion of this early developmental stage, Erikson believed that a child may not trust another human being or ever successfully move into and accomplish the other stages of development (including identity) that are crucial to normal psychological maturation.

In the case of transracial adoptions, it is clear that a white family can supply the food, shelter, stability, and love that will lead to building trust in a child of color. Whether a white family can supply a child with the tools for being an ethnic minority in the United States and for strong ethnic identity still remains in question. Miller and Miller (1990) found that African American and other minority children need to learn self-esteem, racial/ethnic awareness and pride, and survival/coping skills from their parents so they may function in the majority and minority cultures. The NABSW (1972, 1994) has also discussed coping mechanisms as a priority for healthy ethnic and mental health development. Although white families may be able to supply self-esteem, racial/ethnic awareness, and pride, it is unknown whether they can provide the coping and survival skills needed. Miller and Miller also suggest the need for "ethnically self-assertive role models" to complement the family support systems.

Because ethnic identity is a very complicated phenomenon, only some of the facets have been studied with populations of transracially adopted individuals. Specific researched areas are self-esteem, racial awareness, and racial classification choice.

Research on transracial adoptees has shown similar self-esteem patterns among black and mixed-race black children adopted by white families and black families and white nonadopted children (McRoy & Zurcher, 1983). It should be noted that McRoy and Zurcher (1983) refer to black and mixed-race black children adopted by white families as being transracially adopted. However, black and mixed-race children adopted by black families are referred to as being in-racially adopted. This distinction is made because historically and according to U.S. societal tradition, any person with "one drop of black blood" is considered to be black (Close, 1995). It should be cautioned that mixed-race black children in black families sometimes also encounter incidents of nonacceptance by black and other communities. This is well-documented in this volume.

In terms of racial awareness, McRoy and Zurcher (1983) reported that black and mixed-race black adolescents adopted by white families were more likely to refer to race when asked to describe themselves than were black children adopted by black families. Transracially adopted children may be more conscious of their racial group and adoptive status "since their physical dissimilarity to their family and peers is a constant reminder" (p. 129). Also, more discussions about adoption and race may occur in transracial situations because transracially adopted children may be asked about their adoptive status and racial difference in the family more often than in-racially adopted children.

In a study by McRoy, Zurcher, Lauderdale, and Anderson (1984), racial self-identification differences were noted between in-racially and transracially adopted adolescents. Of the 30 transracially adopted children in the study, 22 were racially mixed, and 5 of the 30 in-racially adopted children were racially mixed. However, when asked about their racial self-identification, none of the in-racially adopted children referred to themselves as "mixed." However,

> sixteen (53%) of the transracially adopted sample referred to themselves as being either "mixed," "part white," or "black/white"; nine (30%) referred to themselves as "black," three (10%) stated that their racial background was white, and one responded "Mexican." One adoptee indicated that race was unimportant and referred to his background as American. (McRoy et al., 1984, p. 36)

The mixed-race children in black families had been told that they would be socially defined as black, regardless of their actual black/white racial background; this was social reality. Seventeen (57%) of the 22 transracially adopted mixed race children were born to one black parent and one white parent. Five were actually black/Mexican, black/Latin American, black/Indian, and black/Korean. The varied multiracial backgrounds of these children may have led them to be more likely to self-identify as racially mixed. Also, their transracial adoptive parents were much more likely to emphasize their racially mixed background than were the in-racial adoptive parents.

McRoy et al. (1984) also assessed the 30 transracial parents on how they dealt with the issue of race and racial identity. They found three distinctive philosophies. The first was that of color blindness; the parents felt that everyone is the same and that color is not an issue. They had a strong white orientation and often deemphasized black racial identity and made no or minimal efforts to provide black role models for their black children. The second philosophy was one of acknowledging the adoptees' race and the need to provide black role models. In the third group the families acknowledged that their family was no longer white but interracial. Discussions on race were common. Black heritage was emphasized, and the family had black and white friends and role models.

These three differing philosophies brought about three distinct reactions in the transracially adopted youth. The color-blind families tended to produce children who deemphasized their black heritage and were reluctant to identify with any particular racial group. Many felt that human identity was more important than racial identity. The middle group produced children who referred to themselves as mixed or part white but saw no need to dismiss or deemphasize their black heritage. They generally had some contacts with other black children in their school environment but tended to live in white communities. The last group, with the multiracial orientation, produced adoptees who acknowledged a strong black identity (McRoy et al., 1984). Thus it appears that a color-blind family may not be able to prepare a child to develop defenses necessary for coping with racism. This should be taken into account in preadoption interviews. Denial or color blindness may not be an acceptable environment for producing a healthy ethnic identity. As stated earlier, parenting skills that include racial awareness and coping mechanisms to combat discrimination are essential for children of color.

We, the authors of this chapter, agree that same-race adoption is preferable, and all efforts should be made to overcome the barriers that have limited black families from adopting. If an in-racial placement cannot be made, we recommend consideration of families for transracial adoptions that can provide a loving, stable, and healthy environment for a child; that can fulfill the child's needs to feel positively about his or her racial group identity; and that can provide the coping mechanisms needed by people of color. Agencies should develop selection criteria based upon research findings on the types families that are most successful in preparing transracially adopted children for living in a race-conscious society.

A recent study (Kallgren & Caudill, 1993) evaluated seven agencies in four major metropolitan areas to ascertain if their transracial adoption programs were adequately preparing families for transracial placement. They found that agencies were not providing adequate literature on racial awareness, training sessions, or support systems and did not encourage families to live in integrated neighborhoods. Similarly, Vroegh (1992) reported the latest findings from a study of transracial adoptive families and noted that the majority were not making special efforts to promote race identity. The majority were living in all-white neighborhoods, and parents were advising children to ignore racial incidents. Agencies may not be heeding the advice of adoption advocacy groups and some researchers, who have called for the selection of transracial adoptive families that will be sensitive to and nurturing of the child's racial heritage and identity needs.

IMPLICATIONS FOR THERAPY

From our experience as therapists, working on ethnic identity issues is difficult and must be addressed at an individual level. Most problems confronted by individuals who encounter ethnic identity issues tend to emanate from society's need for rigid racial classifications. A person must fit into a single category of either African American/black, Hispanic/Latino/Mexican, Asian/Pacific Islander, Native American/American Indian, or white/Caucasian. The cultures connected with these categories are also seen as mutually exclusive. There is little tolerance or understanding of racially mixed identity or multicultural identity in the United States (Root, 1992b). Like the multiracial individual, the ethnic person raised in a white family may not fit solely into, or may not be totally accepted by, any of the traditional four cultures/races.

Transracially adopted persons may be confused about their ethnic/cultural classification. Black children adopted by a white families know they are African American but may not know how to interact (language, common experiences) with other black people comfortably.

This discomfort may lead to limited interaction with blacks while the need for identification still remains great.

An example of this situation is Sarah. She is a young, successful, educated, intelligent, and well-adjusted young woman (age 23) who is interracial (black and Korean) and was adopted by a white family at the age of 3. She has a wonderful sense of self but still regrets that she has not been accepted totally into the African American community. She does not talk or act the same way that many of her black peers do. However, she feels no superiority or inferiority to these peers; she just knows that they perceive her as "different." This fact denies her a complete belongingness in the black culture. She has some desire to learn how to "act black" but simultaneously rejects the need to do so. She knows she is black and is angered that she must prove this by acting in certain stereotypical manners. (She knows and has access to very few Asians so this issue has not surfaced as much.)

However, the foundations of love, stability, strength, and self-worth were instilled in her at a very early age by her adoptive family. Thus the predicted adjustment of Sarah is good. She does have an racial identity—racially mixed adopted by a white family. She is happy with this identity. It hurts her that her nonblack behaviors are interpreted as her trying to be white. If this becomes a greater problem in her life, she may learn to "act more black." This is similar to a study by Hall (1980) in which she interviewed racially mixed people who reported the need to learn "black demeanor." They learned how to talk in black English; understood more of the black experience by being around and living in black neighborhoods; and learned how to move, act, eat, and so on to fit in with and be accepted by the black community. Again, these racially mixed individuals never denied their black membership; however, they felt the need to acquire these behavioral traits to participate comfortably in the black community.

Sarah has numerous dynamics playing simultaneously. She is racially mixed, adopted by a white family, lives in a predominantly white city, but interacts with African Americans at school and social events. Her racially mixed background may have had as much to do with her peers' nonacceptance as her being raised by white parents. Research on racially mixed adults raised by their biological parents shows incomplete acceptance by the black community also (Hall, 1980). This is further exacerbated by the fact that Sarah did not learn "black" culture from her adoptive family. Although she may not have learned black culture, she has experienced discrimination like other people of color in the United States.

Concern about this lack of black culture/behavior is not a phenomenon that is exclusive to racially mixed or transracially adopted blacks. Upper-class African American families know they are black. Many fear that lack of exposure to other black children will be detrimental for their own children. Thus they expose their family to as many black families, media, culture, and role models as possible. The same strategy may be applicable for black children adopted by white families.

This is actually the case for Sam—a light-complexioned African American who was adopted by an upper-class white family at age 10. Sam's adoptive parents ensured the availability of black role models. In college, Sam met many more African American peers and role models. Sam's physical appearance is unmistakably black, and his demeanor is definitely black. He did not learn the demeanor from his adoptive parents; he learned it through his role models and the African American community. Sam's physical appearance and demeanor are not the lone traits that make him black. Sam has also shared the "black experience" of prejudice, anger, sadness, happiness, joy, love, rich culture, food, people, and so on. He experienced this throughout his 40 years. Sam is comfortable in his black world and comfortable in the multicultural world of his parents.

Sam's present identity and experience and Sarah's future reveal that racial identity is a developmental process. The strength and focus of the identity are influenced by experiences and maturity (Cross, 1978; Helms, 1990a). Age has been shown to be an important factor for ethnic identity choice in multiracial/multicultural individuals (Hall, 1980). Because society does not allow individuals to be in more than one racial/ethnic category, younger people tend to accept this limitation. As they mature, however, they begin to revolt against this confining definition and allow themselves a multiracial/ multicultural identity. Poston (1990) outlines the stages of multiracial identity as a developmental process. The same may be true for multicultural adoptees. As they mature, they feel more confident about themselves as individuals and therefore feel more confident about their ethnic identity. They classify themselves, like Sarah, as a racially mixed person adopted by a white family. They allow themselves a new "category." This has been shown true in research on racially mixed adults. Hall (1980) found that many of her black Japanese respondents saw themselves as a "new people or a new race." They developed a new ethnic group in which to belong. This new category did not deny the components of this group (black and Japanese); it is a new racial category that is a inclusive of all the components (Williams, 1992). Thus interracially adopted people may see themselves as black but expand that identity to being black people adopted by a white family—which becomes their new category of belongingness.

CONCLUSIONS

The declining availability of healthy white infants for adoption, the large supply of white families seeking to adopt infants and young children, the growing numbers of African American children in the foster care system, and the limited success of many agencies in overcoming the barriers to finding African American families are all factors that have led to the transracial adoption controversy. The media, judicial system, and state and federal legislative bodies have focused society's attention on this topic in recent years. Race matching has historically been an acceptable criterion for white children and families, and white families have rarely if ever had to compete with black families to raise white children. However, black families are having to compete with white families in order to raise black infants and children. The attention given to the controversy seems a bit ludicrous, as transracial adoptions currently represent only about 1% of all adoptions. Moreover, although touted as a possible solution to the need for adoptive families for the growing numbers of African American children in the foster care system, the majority of white families seeking to adopt desire healthy infants and young children, not the older black and mixed-race children in the system.

In the new millennium, attention must be placed on the reasons why such high numbers of African American children are removed from their families and placed in foster care. Recent news reports suggest that if the numbers of children in the system continue to increase, orphanages may be needed. Expanded economic opportunities, as well as family preservation services, may enable more birth families to parent their own children and reduce the risk of their entering the system and eventually needing another family.

Children that have been placed transracially must resolve feelings about their removal from their birth families and experiences in foster care, as well as feelings about being adopted and racial identity issues resulting from transracial placement. Families must be prepared to use mental health professionals as needed to help the child address issues of grief and loss as well as adoptive and racial identity. As some predict, we are becoming more racially polarized as a nation, these racial issues may become even more prominent over time. Therapists must be trained to assess problems that may stem from racial identity conflict and problems that stem from other sources. Much more research is needed to better assess the factors that influence the evolution of racial identity in mixed-race and transracially adopted people.

6

Voices From the Movement
Approaches to Multiraciality

CYNTHIA L. NAKASHIMA

Not long ago, I spotted the latest issue of *Newsweek* on the newsstand and felt my stomach tie into knots. The cover was intriguing—a photograph made of 20 smaller photos of faces that vary dramatically in skin tone and facial feature and which, presumably, belong to people who are "African American." Across the cover and the faces stood the question, "WHAT COLOR IS BLACK? Science, Politics, and Racial Identity." Oh-oh, I said to myself. What are they going to say about multiraciality *this* time?

It seems like I've been experiencing this a lot lately; and not just on days when Sally Jessy Raphaël or Oprah talk to interracial couples or multiracial people, but every time I see a magazine or newspaper article on the U.S. Census, or the "scientific" aspects of race, or the changing ethnic demographics of America. My first reaction is always to worry that, again, we will be portrayed either as the final hope for assimilation

AUTHOR'S NOTE: I want to thank Barbara Reid-Gomez for introducing me to the concept of the "elevation of hybridity" and its relationship to the multiracial identity.

(e.g., *Time* magazine's special issue, Fall 1993, on "The New Face of America") or as an evil force set out to destroy the gains made by people of color (Wright, 1994).

After this initial overreaction, I sometimes find that the topics of intermarriage and racially mixed people have been discussed fairly and with complexity, and that multiraciality was not used to bolster a particular political agenda. But sometimes I do not. The *Newsweek* issue, for example, places (strategically, I suspect) articles on the scientific and social meanings of race, the "one-drop rule," and biracialism alongside an article calling for "The End of Affirmative Action," featuring a large photo of an interracial couple asking to be judged by the quality of their work.

The dialogue on people of mixed race has recently been thrust into the arena of America's dominant cultural institutions and ideology. Beyond being a standard on television talk shows, issues of race mixture have now gained entry into the world of "legitimate" news and commentary such as *Time, The New Yorker,* and *Newsweek.*

This "mainstreaming" of multiraciality has developed alongside discussion of such critical and explosive racial/ethnic issues as affirmative action, multicultural education, welfare, immigration policy, and the "bell curve."

Concern over what role racially mixed people and the "multiracial movement" will play, and how they will be "played" in the larger race debates, has prompted me, along with many others, to think carefully about what it is that we are participating in. The following chapter grew out of my consideration of this issue, with the conclusion that our best hope and our biggest challenge lie in listening closely to all of the "voices" in the dialogue on multiraciality. ⟨⟩

In the past 10 years or so, the United States has seen the growth of what many are calling a mixed-race "movement." This refers to the emergence of community organizations, campus groups, magazines and newsletters, academic research and writing, university courses, creative expression, and political activism—all created and done by mixed-race individuals and members of interracial families, with the purpose of voicing their own experiences, opinions, issues, and interests.

Within the mixed-race movement, as in any social movement, there are differing perspectives on and approaches to the various issues. How both to conceptualize and to assert an identity as a multiracial person in America are tasks not easily agreed upon. And, as in any social movement, sometimes the differences cause tension. In examining the ideologies expressed in the dialogue on multiraciality, I have identified the following three approaches, or "voices" as dominating the discourse:

1. The struggle for inclusion and legitimacy in the "traditional" racial/ethnic communities
2. The shaping of a shared identity and common agenda among racially mixed people into a new multiracial community
3. The struggle to dismantle dominant racial ideology and group boundaries and to create connections across communities into a community of humanity

The purpose of this chapter is to discuss each of these approaches to and perspectives on multiraciality and to consider the ideological and practical issues and conflicts that have occurred or might occur between them. I will make the argument that each is legitimate, and in fact, central to the movement itself, and I will attempt to demonstrate how the three voices can be viewed as dimensions rather than divisions, both of the movement and of the experience of multiraciality. Finally, I will suggest that as dimensions, the three voices not only can peacefully coexist, but they can function to serve as a system of "checks and balances" in order to avoid what many consider to be potential dangers of the mixed-race movement (Daniel, 1992a; Njeri, 1991; Pagnozzi, 1991; Spencer, 1994; Thornton, 1992; Wright, 1994).

Before I begin to discuss the dominant voices of the mixed-race movement, I must mention that not everyone who expresses his or her experiences with multiraciality considers him- or herself to be part of the multiracial movement. But I believe that any discussion of the mixed-race experience that takes place today occurs within the context of the larger dialogue on multiraciality and both is affected by and affects this dialogue. Thus I am considering all of these individual expressions to be part of the dialogue on multiraciality, and, in this way, part of the mixed-race movement.

A PATTERN OF VOICES:
THREE APPROACHES WITHIN "THE MOVEMENT"

Certain themes and issues seem to be central to the experiences of multiraciality, across racial/ethnic mix, geographical location, and time period; for example, locating one's racial/ethnic identity in various contexts and at different life stages, being pressured to "choose" a monoracial identification by external forces, and questions and issues of group belongingness and loyalty (Anzaldúa, 1987; Chang, 1956; Far, 1909; Funderburg, 1994; C. C. I. Hall, 1992; Kich, 1992; Larsen, 1928/ 1986b; Root, 1994a; Tamagawa, 1932). Perhaps these can be considered parts of a "core" of the mixed-race experience, or perhaps simply a mixed-race version of the core of the human experience. But although there are important commonalities to being racially mixed in America, how individuals approach their multiraciality can vary dramatically—from person to person, and within a single person over time and place.

Within today's dialogue on mixed race, three dominant voices inform us on how to approach multiraciality. On the one hand, there is considerable overlap between the voices, to the point that many of us (myself included) subscribe to all three simultaneously. On the other hand, certain ideological incongruities exist, at least on the surface, that require sorting out. In order to begin this task, I want first to establish what the ideologies are.

The Struggle for Inclusion and Legitimacy in the Traditional Racial/Ethnic Communities

The struggle by mixed-race people for inclusion and legitimacy in the traditional racial/ethnic communities can take many different shapes; from people who want all of their racial/ethnic communities to accept mixed-race people as full members without erasing the differences of a multiracial experience, to people who want a specific racial/ethnic community to accept them as full members, without making issue of their multiracial background. Perhaps the most extreme form of the latter position would be to avoid the multiracial dialogue by "passing" as monoracial. But many people of mixed race, at least those whose parents are racially different from each other, are not willing or able to actively hide their heritage, and so they will very likely be forced to participate in the dialogue at some level—even if to say, "Well yes, my father is Irish, but I really identify as a Chicana" (Streeter, Chapter 19, this volume).

The struggle for inclusion and legitimacy in the traditional racial/ethnic communities can be expressed explicitly; this has occurred in many

Asian American communities, where mixed-race people have recently become active in demanding recognition and legitimacy (Fulbeck, 1994; Houston, 1991; King & DaCosta, Chapter 14, this volume). But more often the desire is expressed less explicitly, by exhibiting on the individual level one's ability to "fit in" to a community, thus "proving" that one's multiraciality does not preclude racial/ethnic authenticity.

One of the ways that racially mixed people might attempt to persuade others to believe in their authenticity is by the "badges" that they wear, such as clothing, hairstyle, speech patterns, mannerisms, name, and so on. Phil Tajitsu Nash, a man of Japanese/European American heritage, legally changed his middle name to his mother's Japanese maiden name when he was writing for Asian American newspapers (Lee, 1991-1992). Valur Edvardsson, who is Icelandic and African American, felt that he had to alter his speech and his behavior in order to prove his legitimacy among other African Americans (Funderburg, 1994). Norma Elena Soto (1994), a woman of Chinese, Mexican, Spanish, and French heritage, wondered which of her badges she might need on a given day in her poem, "Woman of Color":

> But, should someone
> see my white skin and
> question my credentials,
> how would I prove my qualifications?
> I could smile
> to slant my eyes,
> speak Spanish and disclose
> my Hispanic name . . .
> maybe pick up an accent
> and start bowing a lot. (pp. 5-6)

We also "prove" our racial/ethnic legitimacy through our associations with people—friends, lovers (Twine, Chapter 18, this volume), and even family members. Many of the multiracial people interviewed by Lise Funderburg (1994) discussed their awareness that their choice of friends, especially in their school years, made an enormous impact on how legitimate African Americans perceived them to be. Funderburg herself, who is European and African American, has discussed how people will automatically "dismiss" her because she looks "white" and is married to a European American man (Jefferson, 1994). Several years ago, when I won a scholarship from a Japanese American organization, I was happy and relieved when my Grandma Nakashima volunteered to accompany me to meet the sponsoring family at their home, because I knew that her presence would testify to my "Japaneseness."

Similarly, the desire for inclusion in a racial/ethnic community can be expressed by which badges and which associations we choose not to call attention to; so that a mixed-race male college student might hesitate to hug a white female friend in the company of an African American female friend (Courtney, 1995), or a mixed-race actress, trying out for an "Asian" role, might wear a wig to hide her very curly hair (McCunn, 1988). Some multiracial people are critical of this process of proving their authenticity, even as they participate in it. Kip Fulbeck (1994), a Chinese/European American artist, wrote in "anger and frustration" of how mixed-race Asian Americans "come in bright-eyed and hopeful to a place that could be home and find we have to change our names or adopt Asian ones to pass on paper" (p. 8).

Another way for mixed-race people to struggle for inclusion and legitimacy in the traditional racial/ethnic communities is by proving their knowledge of and attachment to the culture, history, and/or political interests of that group. Velina Hasu Houston (1991) has argued that Amerasians like herself, who have a parent who is directly from Asia, are "more richly grounded in Asian culture and custom" than many of the "pure-blooded" Asian Americans who define themselves as "real" Asians whereas mixed-race people are not (pp. 54-55). As Larene LaSonde, who is African American, Russian, Jewish, Scot-Irish and Cherokee, said, among other African Americans, "My politics had to be better than anybody else's, [and] my ethics had to be in place because I was never trusted. I had to be surer of my facts than anybody else" (quoted in Funderburg, 1994, page 334). The mixed-race writer Lisa Jones (1994b) recently took this method one step further in the African American magazine *Essence,* presenting her European American Jewish mother's knowledge and commitment to African American historical, cultural, and political issues.

The ways that mixed-race people struggle for inclusion and legitimacy vary, both by what kind of inclusion and legitimacy each individual wants from a community and by what each racial/ethnic communities requires of the individual (Root, 1994a, pp. 465-466). In many Asian American communities, physical appearance plays a very important role in the level of acceptance a mixed-race person experiences. Also, having an Asian surname, which suggests patrilineal Asian heredity, seems to be an advantage. In many Latino communities, where racial phenotype varies greatly, language is considered an important indicator of legitimacy. In the African American community, which also claims a wide range of physical types, a person's lifestyle and cultural behavior are given considerable weight. Each of these communities' criteria for belonging have arisen out of specific historical, cultural, and political contexts and continue to change as conditions change (King & DaCosta, Chapter 14, this volume).

I have purposefully avoided, until now, the situation of mixed-race people struggling for inclusion and legitimacy in the European American "community" because of the complexity of comparing the dominant society with nondominant racial/ethnic groups. The desire for inclusion and legitimacy in the dominant society is wrapped up in issues of power, access to resources, standards of beauty, and so on—something that monoracial people of color experience similarly to mixed-race people. There is probably an important distinction between the kind of legitimacy sought by a mixed-race person with European American family ties, compared to a person of color without those connections, but I have not explored this issue enough to consider it here.

In the case of mixed-race people who are struggling for legitimacy in a specific European American ethnic group, (e.g., the Italian American community), issues of belonging are more like those of the racial/ethnic groups that we have been looking at—for example, language, cultural behavior, name, and certainly physical appearance. Physical appearance is perhaps the most important badge of whiteness in contemporary society, although heredity (i.e., the one-drop rule) is still significant (Omi & Winant, 1986).

The Shaping of a Shared Identity and Common Agenda
Among Racially Mixed People Into a New Multiracial Community

The developing of a mixed-race community is what people generally envision when they talk about "the multiracial movement." The theory underlying this approach is that the experience of being racially/ethnically mixed has enough common themes to make people of mixed-race a meaningful reference group (Weisman, Chapter 10, this volume).

There are two "sites" where mixed racial/ethnic community building generally takes place:

1. Within a specific racial/ethnic community or communities (e.g., organizations that have been geared to specific racial/ethnic "mixtures," such
   as African/European American or Asian/non-Asian American, and their
   specific set of issues)
2. Across racial/ethnic communities with the goal of pan-multiracialism
   (e.g., organizations, such as the Association for Multiethnic Americans
   [AMEA], which unite around the more general issues of racially mixed
   people)

It could be argued that the first kind of mixed-race community building,
which takes place within a specific racial/ethnic community, is ideologically and strategically located somewhere between the first and
second voices because of the importance that it puts on the traditional
racial/ethnic communities.

One of the more obvious expressions of mixed-race community
building is, as I mentioned above, the many organizations that have
formed across the country for interracial families and racially mixed
individuals (Brown & Douglass, Chapter 20, this volume). Most of these
groups function primarily as social and support groups, publishing
newsletters that provide resources and information for mixed-race
families (e.g. lists of children's books with positive multiracial characters). But some of the multiracial organizations have been formed with
the goal of mobilizing around a common political need or issue, such as
racial classification or Amerasian immigration and resettlement (Brown &
Douglass, Chapter 20, this volume).

Another overt example of community building is the existence of
magazines—namely, *Interrace, New People,* and *Biracial Child*—that feature articles by and about interracial couples, mixed-race children,
families with transracially adopted children, and multiracial adults.
Interrace presents articles that speak to a mixed-race "community" on
issues such as "Best and Worst Cities for Interracial Couples, Families
and Multiracial People to Live," (Grosz, 1993) and "Popular Myths About
Interracial Couples" (Mills, 1992). The magazine regularly features celebrities who are either involved in an interracial relationship or who are
racially mixed themselves, in very much the same way that the traditional racial/ethnic communities feature their "own" celebrities.

A very recent phenomenon that reflects the growth of the idea of a multiracial community is the existence of books and films on the mixed-race experience, published and produced for a popular audience. There have been at least two anthologies of writings by people of mixed heritage in the past few years (Camper, 1994; Glancy & Truesdale, 1994). In each of these books, the introduction talks about the common themes, experiences, and yearnings of the writers, who, while culturally diverse, share a status as mixed. There has also been a deluge of nonfictional storytelling by people who are multiracial (Alexander, 1991; Haizlip, 1994; Jones, 1994a; Khanga, 1993; McAuliffe, 1994; Nunez, 1995; Scales-Trent, 1995; See, 1995; Williams, 1995). These personal histories, although perhaps not explicitly asserting a desire to build a mixed-race community, are certainly written and published in the context of the growing dialogue on multiraciality, and thus they reflect the idea that the mixed-race experience is both common enough and special enough to warrant published accounts.

Similarly, Funderburg's (1994) book, *Black, White, Other: Biracial Americans Talk About Race and Identity,* presents to the public the experiences and opinions of an impressive number of mixed-race people, all of whom are African/European American (although several mention additional race/ethnicities as well). She organized the book by topics but allowed her interviewees to speak for themselves, which highlights both the similarities and the differences within the mixed-race experience. Funderburg also acknowledged the mixed-race movement and asked the interviewees questions specifically on the issue of a multiracial community. The answers she received varied from

> For me, the same way black people have a sisterhood or a brotherhood, that's something that I felt toward this mixed guy who worked at the same restaurant I did—that we had this connection just because of who we were. (p. 319)

to

> I don't feel the compulsion to join (an organization), even though I like finding people with whom I share that background. (p. 341)

to

Start a little club? No, I don't think so. What do they do? Does everybody just sit around? (p. 321)

But regardless of the range of opinions and experiences within the book, its very existence expresses and contributes to some feeling of community between mixed-race people. Consider the quote by Mindy Thompson Fullilove, M.D., on the book jacket:

At last, the voices of my kind. Those of us who match each other but not our relatives, who live in a one-person demilitarized zone, who create a patchwork of self out of mismatched bits of group hate and individual love. At last to hear in these voices the first echo of my life. At last to be among, rather than between. This book is for us, and all who love us. Parents, friends, teachers, students—read and know us.

In academia, there has also been a recent explosion in interest on multiraciality (in this volume: Twine, Chapter 18; Williams et al., Chapter 22). Although scholarly research has historically treated people of mixed race as a population for the purpose of study, there tends to be a much greater level of sophistication in more recent research, extending the idea of a mixed-race population beyond the simple facts of heredity to encompass the common themes of the multiracial experience. This is reflected in Root's (1992b) edited volume, *Racially Mixed People in America,* and in Zack's (1995a) edited volume *American Mixed Race: The Culture of Microdiversity.* It is also the basis for many contemporary university courses on multiraciality (Williams et al., Chapter 22, this volume). For example, in a course on people of mixed race, literature that is normally looked at in the context of a traditional racial/ethnic group's literature might be viewed alongside other works by people of mixed race—such as, Nella Larsen's *Passing* (1929/1986a) and *Quicksand* (1928/1986b) with Leslie Marmon Silko's *Ceremony* (1977) and Diana Chang's *Frontiers of Love* (1956).

The Struggle to Dismantle Dominant Racial Ideology and Group Boundaries and to Create Connections Across Communities Into a Community of Humanity

The third approach to multiraciality is perhaps the most difficult to define because it comes in the greatest variety of forms. The central ideology is that binary thinking and the boundaries that it facilitates must be destroyed in order to destroy oppressions based on race/ethnicity, gender, sexuality, class, and so on (in this volume: Graham, Chapter 3; Wardle, Chapter 23). Mixed-race people, who do not completely "fit in" to any of the racial/ethnic groups but who frequently have ties to more than one, should use their neither/both positionality to resist and destroy the dominant racial/ethnic structure—to be, as Weisman (Chapter 10, this volume) calls it, "supraracial."

This ideology is clearly articulated in Zack's concept of *deracination*, which is aimed at mixed-race people but can hypothetically be adopted by anyone. Deracination refers to an "antirace" racial identity, similar to having no religious affiliation. As Zack (1992) put it,

> The concept of race is an oppressive cultural invention and convention, and I refuse to have anything to do with it. . . . Therefore I have no racial affiliation and will accept no racial designations. If more people joined me in refusing to play the unfair game of race, fewer injustices based on the concept of race would be perpetrated. (p. 9)

Although deracination might seem exotic, it is essentially the same as the philosophies on race that are expressed in certain religious theologies, such as that of the Baha'i; and in the frequent testimonies of mixed-race people whose parents told them to write in "human race" rather than to check any of the race/ethnicity boxes (Funderburg, 1994; Weisman, Chapter 10, this volume).

The other dimension to resisting racial ideology is the proactive building of connections and communication across racial/ethnic groups. Seeing mixed-race people as a "bridge" between cultures has been a common theme, both in recent discussions of people of mixed race (Kingston, 1989; Sperber, 1991) and in creative expression by people of mixed race. In an essay entitled, "Leaves from the Mental Portfolio of an Eurasian," published in 1909, writer Sui Sin Far discussed, among other things, her role as a "defender" of the Chinese in America. Her essay concluded, "I give my right hand to the Occidentals and my left to the Orientals, hoping that between them they will not utterly destroy the insignificant 'connecting link.' And that's all" (p. 132). European/Native American writers Louise Erdrich and Michael Dorris (1991) made a similar statement about what they refer to as "the lost tribe of mixed bloods": "As the hooks and eyes that connect one core to the other we have our roles to play. 'Caught between two worlds,' is the way we're often characterized, but I'd put it differently. We are the *catch*" (pp. 123-124). At Stanford University, a group largely composed of people of mixed race formed a group called Cross Cultures that "focuses on uniting students of different cultures in a comfortable, nonthreatening atmosphere" ("Stanford Group," 1994, p. 16).

Since the late 1960s, American society has toyed with the idea of people of mixed race as the "children of the future." In the past decade, multiculturalism, which places a high value on a society's diversity, has made the valuing of a mixed-race person's "microdiversity" (Zack, 1995a) all the more obvious (Weisman, Chapter 10, this volume). At the same time, the ideas of *multiple positionalities* and *transgressing boundaries*, which have come out of postmodern and deconstructionist dialogues on culture, have functioned to shift the emphasis away from the disadvantaged and "marginal" aspects of being neither/both to the advantaged and liminal aspects (Weisman, Chapter 10, this volume). Mixed-race people are viewed as a form of the "citizen of the world" model, along with others who are transnational, multilingual, multicultural, transgendered, and so on; they move back and forth across the various borders, existing above the limitations of having only one culture or language or government or gender. The titles of two recent conferences at the University of California, Berkeley—"Displacing Borders" and "Boundaries in Question"—give an idea of how multiracial people are being resituated by the contemporary intellectual community.

Gloria Anzaldúa (1987) developed the idea of the border crosser in her book, *Borderlands/La Frontera: The New Mestiza*. She described a "mestiza consciousness" that tolerates contradictions and ambiguities:

> That focal point or fulcrum, that juncture where the mestiza stands, is where phenomena tend to collide. It is where the possibility of uniting all that is separate occurs. This assembly is not one where severed or separated pieces merely come together. Nor is it a balancing of opposing powers. In attempting to work out a synthesis, the self has added a third element which is greater than the sum of its severed parts. That third element is a new consciousness—a mestiza consciousness. (pp. 79-80)

Anzaldúa's mestiza is anyone who defies categories—racial/ethnic, gender, sexual, or national. Similarly, Judy Scales-Trent wrote about her experiences as a "white black woman," and about how, although her mixed-race heritage makes her "different" from so many others, her difference has revealed the similarities between herself and so many others. Scales-Trent (1990) wondered

> why the system of dualism is so important: What is there about a contin-
> uum that is unsatisfying? frightening? . . . It is this system of rigid dualism
> that fosters so much anxiety when people don't fit into the categories
> neatly, when people "transgress boundaries." (p. 324)

Exposing the fallacy of race and group boundaries is something that multiracial people frequently engage in, perhaps especially those who have positive relationships with family members who are racially different from each other. At a panel discussion on the future of the African American community, one mixed-race panelist surprised the audience by shifting the discussion away from issues such as media images of African Americans and the development of black-owned businesses to a consideration of the experiences that we, as humans, share across race, ethnicity, gender, class, and sexuality—experiences such as birth, death, love, hate, fear, sex, illness, family. The panelist made the point that although the categories we "belong to" shape our lives in important ways, we also belong to the human experience, and what is essential about the human experience is also important.

DIFFERENT APPROACHES, DIFFERENT PERSPECTIVES: DISSENT IN THE MOVEMENT?

> Should [biracial people] unite to carve out a separate territory on the racial
> map? The very idea draws criticism from myriad corners: from Blacks . . .
> from Whites . . . and from biracial people who simply want to exist in one
> camp or the other without fanfare, or who have decided, because of their
> experience, that all ideas of race are fallacious. (Funderburg, 1994, pp.
> 321-322)

The mixed-race movement, as well as mixed-race individuals, is sometimes accused of sending out mixed messages about race and ethnicity. For example, do mixed-race people think that they are "like" people in the traditional racial/ethnic groups, or that they are different from them? Do they think that race is important, or that it is not important? These are questions that are asked of multiracial people not only by monoracial people, but by other multiracial people, and by themselves. I will now discuss some of the points of contention that can and do occur between the three dominant voices in the dialogue on multiraciality.

Many mixed-race people who assert a monoracial identity are suspicious of the motivations behind asserting a multiracial identity and worry about the potential damage that the movement might have on a specific racial/ethnic community (Funderburg, 1994; Jones, 1994a). Some feel threatened by the idea of a mixed-race identity and community, because an emphasis on what is common among mixed people might be interpreted as an emphasis on what is different between themselves and those who are "full-blooded." As one of Funderburg's (1994) interviewees said about the mixed-race movement:

> Somebody said "mixed" once, as in a race separate from Blacks and Whites. I was just like, "Excuse me? We have enough races as it is. . . . I have no desire to be put on a little pedestal . . . I don't need any more separation in my life. (pp. 320-321)

Also, mixed-race people who identify with one of their racial/ethnic communities to the exclusion of other communities have said that the mixed-race movement holds a bias toward identifying as multiracial and pathologizes those who do not identify this way (Chuan, 1993; Funderburg, 1994, p. 323; Jones, 1994a). Chuan referred to "interracial populism" and criticized *Interrace* magazine as "clearly not designed to encourage either dialogue or self-determination—on the contrary, it is trying to tell interracials what they can and can't be" (p. 93). Similarly, Jones (1994a) critiques those who she calls the "interracial/biracial nationalists," and asks "Is there now to be a biracial party line to tow and a biracial lifestyle to upkeep?" (p. 59).

On the other hand, people involved in the building of a sense of community among racially mixed people have criticized those who struggle for acceptance in a traditional group for being "beggars," for being disloyal to family members, and for being dishonest about their heredity. Jamoo (1993), a writer who has contributed regularly to *Inter-race*, posed the question of whether or not mixed-race celebrities who "pass" as monoracial should be publicly "outed" so that they can serve as role models for the multiracial community. He concluded that they should not be outed, but:

> It saddens me that the "closet" mixed-race people in Hollywood and elsewhere feel a need to pass as white to be accepted or that Pebbles has to pretend to be a black girl so she can sell more records. I guess they made their choices just as I made mine, the only difference is that I know I made the right one. (p. 83)

In this way, those who "deny" their multiraciality are held in suspicion very much as those who assert their multiraciality have always been.

Coming from the perspective that racial ideology is inherently oppressive and should be rejected in its entirety, the idea of mixed race is seen as a perpetuation and reification of something completely lacking in value. The use of *race* as a word and a concept is offensive in and of itself, and the desire for a multiracial community and identity is a dangerous step toward creating another racial and ethnic category, similar to the "Coloureds" of South Africa (Chuan, 1993; Spencer, 1994; Wright, 1994). In terms of postmodern thought, there is a concern with what is called the "elevation of hybridity"; in the context of race and ethnicity, that multiracials as a group are currently being culturally constructed and that they will not only join the other "groups" with their own set of boundaries and limitations, but that they might become the new ideal against which others will be degraded and oppressed. This concern was reflected in a keynote lecture given by a professor at a recent conference on cultural studies. The professor highlighted her point that scholarly fields such as women's and ethnic studies are problematic in their essentialism by disclosing that there has even been mention of creating a new field of multiracial studies.

If those who emphasize the destruction of racial categories find fault with the idea of a multiracial community, they also worry about those people of mixed race who struggle for inclusion in a traditional group. To them, this struggle is nothing more than an attempt to participate in a system that will inevitably oppress and degrade them. The only worthwhile struggle is against race itself—as Rainier Spencer (1994) said, both the attempt to create a mixed-race classification and the adherence to hypodescent function to validate the "racial fantasy" and the "racial fallacy" that imprisons this society.

The response to these claims, both by those who emphasize a monoracial identity and by those who employ a multiracial identity, is that although dismantling the racial schema is, indeed, a nice idea, racial ideology is a central feature of our society and that exalting the struggle to dismantle it is impractical, utopian, and, as one of Funderburg's (1994) interviewees stated it, "cheesey" (p. 328; see Weisman, Chapter 10, this volume). Association of Multiracial Americans (AMEA) has said, "It might be argued that racial and ethnic classifications should be done away with entirely. But such a view is utopian and also distorts the reality of continuing communal divisions based on race and ethnicity" (Spencer, 1994, p. 22). In addition, critics of the "citizen of the world" approach point out that there is considerable real value to the ties that people have to their communit(ies), so the danger of destroying group boundaries is that we will destroy what is inside these boundaries, too.

Finally, many multiracial people feel that the assertion that mixed-race people are models of multiculturalism or bridges between groups is an unrealistic and unfair expectation and that it threatens to erase the significance of race and racial oppression in this society. It also contributes to a resentment toward multiracial people and the mixed-race movement by drawing attention away from persisting inequality and focusing instead on the feel-good idea of a raceless or color-blind future.

Perhaps the most concrete expression of the ideological differences that exist between the three voices of multiraciality involves the struggle to reform racial classification (i.e., the U.S. Census). The various racial classification models that have been proposed and the debates surrounding these models are both symptomatic and symbolic of the ideological and strategic differences that we have considered (in this volume: Fernández, Chapter 2; Graham, Chapter 3; Ramirez, Chapter 4). Whether mixed-race people should continue to check "just one" racial category, should demand the right to identify multiracially, or should refuse to participate in racial classification at all is a debate that has come to dominate the mixed-race movement (Mills, 1993; Spencer, 1994; Wright, 1994).

COMMON GROUND:
POSSIBILITIES FOR AN INTEGRATED VOICE

Now that I have established the dominant three approaches to multiraciality and the ideological and practical conflicts that can and do grow out of differences between the approaches, I will argue that, as with the various races, there is nothing immutable that separates the voices from each other. In fact, each of the approaches is central to the experience of multiraciality, and many racially mixed people subscribe to all three simultaneously. Rather than viewing the three voices as ideological divisions in the mixed-race movement, they should be viewed as ideological dimensions of the movement.

The task, then, is to work on the construction of an integrated voice. This is not to say that diverse perspectives, on multiraciality or any other topic, is a thing to be overcome. Rather, the process of looking for a perspective that leaves room for diversity within is an exercise in *cognitive flexibility* (Kich, Chapter 16, this volume) and general tolerance. Also, in looking for a multiracial identity that allows for a variety of approaches, I believe that we might come across what lies at the heart of the multiracial movement.

The following is my attempt to construct a multiracial voice that integrates the three approaches discussed in this chapter: The ties that we have to our racial/ethnic communities matter to us, and we have the right to claim them and to have full access to them. But, we have other ties too, and the fact that we have multiple ties creates experiences that connect us to others who have multiple ties, contemporarily and historically, in the United States and abroad. This experience of having multiple ties simultaneously leads us to question group boundaries and to reject these boundaries as oppressive and false.

In viewing the voices as dimensions of a unified perspective, I want to consider the possibility that there is an element of process to the dimensions (Kich, 1992). *Perhaps people of mixed race shift their emphasis from one approach to another, in response to changes in their environment* (which can be related to age and development), and as they either find that certain of their needs have been met or have remained unmet by a specific approach. For example, a person who is biracial Japanese/European American might first explore his or her multiraciality in terms of his or her membership in the Japanese American community. Then, upon feeling secure in this identification, he or she may begin to recognize and explore the commonalities between people of all racial/ethnic mixtures. Through this exploration, he or she might learn that the concept of race is entirely dishonest and oppressive. At this point, he or she might begin to emphasize the task of "transgressing boundaries."

Although I believe that the processual movement through the voices would often occur in the order given in the example above—the emphasis first on the traditional communities, next on the multiracial community, and finally on a community of humanity—I can easily imagine the process operating in other orders. The process of movement through the dimensions is unlikely to be linear or with an ending point. But the dimensions are fluid to the extent that changing life circumstances can shift an individual's emphasis from one to another without signifying any core ideological change.

Implications of an Integrated Voice

Besides being an exercise in cognitive flexibility and tolerance, the integration of the three dominant voices in the dialogue on multiraciality has the potential to affect our work in multiple ways. Keeping in mind that each of the voices is valid and "normal" and that people of mixed race can identify with all three simultaneously can affect:

1. our research on and analysis of racially mixed people;
2. our agendas as activists in the multiracial movement; and
3. our understanding of ourselves and our needs as people of multiple communities and cultures.

A recognition of the centrality of all three voices might also serve as a system of checks and balances in order to avoid the potential "nightmares" (Wright, 1994) of the multiracial movement. By listening to the questions and the critiques that we pose to each other—Isn't the concept of mixed race an acceptance of the concept of race? Isn't a monoracial identification an internalization of the "one drop rule"? Do mixed race people have enough in common, experientially and culturally, to make "multiracial" a meaningful identity? Can a person of color survive in

America without a racial identity? What are the effects of multiracial identification on communities of color?—we can remain vigilant in steering the dialogue and the movement in the direction of destroying racial oppression.

In Chapter 10 of this volume, Weisman asks the question, "Is the identity "multiracial" a step in that direction, or a step toward the entrenchment of those racial categories that already exist? The answer that she gives is that it is both: Identification with other multiracial people can transcend and thus challenge traditional boundaries, but there is the danger of creating a whole new set of boundaries around what is multiracial and what is not.

In my opinion, we need to take "multiracial" in the direction of *supraracial,* without jeopardizing our communities of color and without giving up the connections that add value to our lives. Our best chance of achieving this is to enlist a variety of perspectives on what it is to be racially mixed in America. For many, being racially mixed means building connections between ourselves and our traditional communities. For many, it means building connections between people who are multiracial. For many, it means building connections with others on the basis of shared humanity. And for many, it means all of these things. Whether we are constructing a model of multiracial identity or a model of racial classification, we should recognize and reflect the diversity of voices that make up the multiracial movement.

PART II

Identity

7

⎔

Hidden Agendas, Identity Theories, and Multiracial People

MICHAEL C. THORNTON

My thinking on the present subject originates in struggling to create an identity out of two normally disparate ethnic heritages: black American and Japanese. Working with no role models made the process simultaneously problematic and enlightening. Tied up in these feelings was how I felt about the experience, how others interpreted it for me, fused with a need to fit in. Looking back on those years, I now know that I grappled with feeling out of place, an emotion partially related to adolescence but also to contradictory messages I received about my own heritage. I grew up on Army posts, where the overt ideology was that "we" and "they" were unrelated to race. The military prides itself as being in the forefront of racial tolerance. This contrasted with us Americans inside gates protected from the "natives," who were always people of color; and my father's encounter with racial prejudice in the ranks. Thus the message I received was that race was not a measure

AUTHOR'S NOTE: I wish to thank Maria Root for helpful comments on an earlier version of this chapter.

of who I was, but it was; the message said there was no implicit racial preference, when there was.

Even more ambiguous were the views about my multiple heritage. I saw a clear separation between all groups, with whiteness valued over "otherness," which included, in order, Japaneseness and blackness. I did not clearly fit anywhere. I adjusted to this order, with some variation. I could not be white, and being black was disconcerting—thus I highlighted my mother's heritage (or occasionally I would be Puerto Rican or even Polynesian because of my looks). The ultimate struggle for my own identity was to see through my "military training" and the popular ideology of racial preference, and then, on my own, to carve out a space as someone who contradicted ready-made models that did not allow for transcending explicit racial boundaries. With age and role models who, although not just like me, informed my experience nonetheless, I came to see that the world as it was given to me had no place for me in it. I had to create my own space, my own identity. It was indeed much more complex than researchers and other people's "common sense" allowed. The thinking in this chapter in one sense reflects where I am in my life today, informed by this personal and academic journey. ⌀

It is increasingly clear that racial ideology provides powerful and unseen frames to discussions of group relations. Reality is reduced to two conflicting and irreducible elements (Martinez, 1992). Unfathomably, phenomena with more than two racial groups are usually ignored. This dichotomous thinking is best seen in press coverage of the Los Angeles riots.

Some mass media viewed it as a black-white concern. *Time,* in an issue on the riots, devoted coverage to a poll about black and white feelings. Nonetheless, the press (otherwise known as the fourth estate) generally typified the Los Angeles conflict as a wellspring of black jealousy and hatred aimed at Asian Americans. Even when incorporating into this frame relations outside the black-white dichotomy, the media usually did so only in the opening paragraphs; coverage of black-Asian American relations, even as the magazines avowed the conflict was multiracial, quickly moved to a black-white frame:

Newsweek asserted that "the race crisis of the 1960s has been subsumed by the tensions and opportunities of the new melting pot: The terms 'black' and 'white' no longer depict the American social reality." Ironically, this sentence appears under a blocked subtitle of "Black and White."[1] (Thornton & Shah, 1995)

Although as a group the media described events in Los Angeles as reflecting society's growing diversity, individually the magazines rarely examined more than one relationship. In so doing, the fourth estate crystallized a complex situation into a dichotomous struggle, a tendency that was also found in coverage of Hispanic-black relations (Shah & Thornton, 1994). An inability—or aversion—to see beyond dualism obscures multiple truths, in this case, the Hispanic role in the struggle in Los Angeles. More Central American immigrants were arrested during the riots than any other group. Whatever the ostensible reason, omitting this alternate picture of riot participants is consistent with the racial ideology.

Perhaps the media are too easy a target. Science, one assumes, does a better job, moving beyond dualities into the complexities of life. Science is commonly seen as controlling for subjective aspects of discovery. But clearly even within science, ideologies disguise realities. This is perhaps no truer than for scholarship on multiracial people. In this chapter, I review paradigms applied to multiracial identity by focusing on implicit assumptions in these positions and what they imply about the objects of attention. What emerges are positions mirroring dualistic press coverage. I then use this discussion to argue that multiracial identity research is limited in two ways:

1. The debate over multiracials has been driven by political agendas revolving around two ideas: those who argue that we are a new and better people who provide the lie to the importance of racial differences; and those who point to this phenomenon as proof of the necessity for racial separation.

2. Because of these agendas, what kind of *people* we are remains a mystery. Who are we as men, mothers, lovers, and workers? Are we not other than walking racial identities, and thus a very limited kind of people?

After addressing these underlying agendas, I will suggest how we can begin to broaden our understanding of the rest of us.

RACIAL IDEOLOGY
AND ETHNIC IDENTITY

Traditionally, races are viewed as distinct; boundaries between them are meaningful to both experience and how life is ordered. Race is certainly a mechanism used to organize life. The historically based structural position of whites over blacks refers to a hierarchical arrangement in disbursing opportunities and resources. In this sense, races are deterministic and discrete. The problem arises when race is used as a proxy for experience and attitudes, a practice embedded in premises of social science literature and often used to measure behaviors and beliefs (Wilkinson, 1984).

Ethnic or group identity has two significant contributors: a thread of historical experience that each group member shares in and a sense of potency or strength inhering in the group. Neither is primarily or necessarily racial in nature. Because ethnicity is not biologically defined, it and race are not synonymous, nor do they measure the same things. Race, and its effects on behavior and attitudes, is usually measured by self-identification—usually a checked item from a finite number of racial/ethnic options. The assumption is that racial labels reflect a core identity rather than a role identity. A core identity is an essential self, strongly defended and stable. A role identity is a property of the self devised by each of us as we live out a set of socially prescribed positions, such as what our race means to us (Brittan, 1973, p. 165). I choose "black" from a list because I know that is what society calls me. This selection may reveal only that I can correctly choose the socially approved term. It may say nothing about my core identity.

Typically, social scientists analyze the force of race on attitudes and behavior as indicated in Figure 7.1. Its effects are explained by analyses diagrammed in Figure 7.2. Explaining the impact of race references experiential and environmental outcomes identified in Figure 7.2, although statistical models seldom provide a specific assessment of the former effect. The assessment is usually via the racial label. Thus, racial differences are given cultural explanations without obvious measures of experience or attitudes. In this way, biogenetic explanations continue to underlie analyses brought to discussions of race and race relations.

Nevertheless, it is clear that race only approximates an individual's social location and acts as a proxy measure of experiences that people

Figure 7.1: Conceptual Model

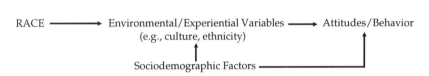

Figure 7.2: Explanatory Model

may encounter as a member of a group; it presumes that social expectations of group identity match personal experience. Based on racial stratification and the cultural aspects of ethnic group membership, there is no inherent association between race and ethnicity (Wilkinson & King, 1987).

If one's race provides indirect evidence of cultural heritage, or is synonymous with it, subgroup distinctions are semantic. Because Haitians and Jamaicans are termed black, (ethnic) variations between them are assumed to be minor. Not appreciating the differences results in treating race as a self-sufficient explanatory variable and overlooks how it is connected to other indicators—actual bonds to the group or experience with intolerance—that are closer to assessing racial life. Although the racial ideology treats them as uniform, races, and the experiences within them, are varied categories.

Thus, although race remains an important organizer of life—a measure of our worth and of where we fit into a hierarchy of societal preferences—it does not automatically determine with whom one feels bonds. Most people of a particular lineage feel a special affinity to that heritage. Nevertheless those bonds are not preordained, no matter what we believe.

This disorientation over the role of race in American life, and even in how we examine that life, provides background for discussing research on ethnic identity among so-called mixed-race persons. Most research fits them into a dualistic view of the world where membership can only lie with one group. Researchers so preoccupied with their ethnic/racial "mix" fail to explore their being mothers, sons, doctors, and plumbers or even the fact that they have feelings about life generally. Mixed-race people remain figments of and reflections of our imaginations, whether one worships or bemoans their presence. Hidden in all the rhetoric are code words, assumptions, and agendas seldom clearly stated but often explicit nonetheless. This results in researchers typically, and inaccurately, arguing that we are freed or imprisoned by our biologies.

Interracial Marriage

To examine the phenomenon of multiracial people, we must first briefly consider the broader context of multiracial families. (Maria P. P. Root provides a more detailed discussion in Chapter 1, this volume). In the United States, race is perhaps the most significant predictor of whom one will marry. Reflecting a number of issues, over three decades after attaining legal status nationally, interracial marriage is still resisted by most Americans. In 1992, for the first time since Gallup started asking the question, a slight majority of white Americans said they were against antimiscegenation laws. The wording of the question does not allow us to know their feelings about the unions.

The controversy interracial marriages create belies their numbers. Although they have risen steadily over time, interracial unions still constituted only 1.8% of all marriages in 1990, a tiny segment of the U.S. population. Furthermore, although it is popularly assumed that most of these unions involve blacks, only 2.2% of all black marriages are affected. Actually, white males and Asian American, Native, and Latino women are the prime candidates for interracial marriage. (For a more in-depth discussion of this topic, see Thornton & Wason, 1995).

Why interracial marriages remain controversial despite their small number is an issue not addressed here. Suffice it to say that these unions are a topic that links a number of factors at the heart of a stratified society. Examining these marriages provides insight into how race and gender function to connect kinship to political, social, and economic institutions (Pascoe, 1991).

MIXED ETHNIC IDENTITY

Clearly, interracial relationships draw so much concern because they encapsulate all our unresolved feelings about race. In a society that is racially stratified, where races are viewed as inherently separate, racial interaction has always been considered problematic (Spickard, 1992). Whereas these couples muddy the dualistic view of race, the products of their joining epitomize the inadequacies of this ideology. The presence of people of multiple heritage challenges basic assumptions of how racial life is organized.

In trying to understand where mixed racial offspring fit into society, questions revolve around the consequences of crossing distinct boundaries. "But what about the children? Won't they suffer because of how society views them? They won't fit anywhere, they are neither black nor white." Or "mixed children make the world a better place. They can see both sides." The first questions are concerned with what mixed racials symbolize in a troubled modern society, one in which distinct boundaries and roles are vanishing, as is predictability. The latter assertions view multiracial people as the hope of the future: able to freely flit across racial borders, and as a birthright to interact with assorted people and provide the seed for the destruction of race as a stratifying concept. But both views exaggerate. Both retain vestiges of the racial (racist) thinking that biology is key.

Offspring of interracial unions have always raised questions about how we define race. Historically it was simple. Mixed race referred to black-white offspring who were part of a two-tiered system: whites and blacks, with racially mixed people improved versions of blacks. A fitting identity was predicated on membership in one racial class. Given diverse racial features of present society, this dichotomy is all the more arbitrary. Recent changes in the racial composition of the United States have been the catalyst for emerging work that accents a history of race relations incorporating blacks, Native Americans, and others, accounts in which groups are so racially intertwined that separating them is all but impossible (Fernández, 1992b; Forbes, 1984, 1988).

Identity Paradigms

The social context presented above frames the current debate in the literature of the effects of multiple identity. A collaborator and I recently completed a review of the last 10 years of research on multiracial marriages and individuals (Thornton & Wason, 1995). The literature was dichotomous: Do multiracial people maintain stable, single-heritage identities or multiple-heritage identities? Those who found the former see multiple identities as untenable, whereas the latter see them as often superior to a single-heritage self-image. The newer work describes simultaneous membership and multiple fluid identities as common (Root, 1992a; Williams, 1992).

Three themes emerged from this review of the literature. The first was an approach to multiracials as problems. The second theme was what we called the equivalent approach, which described mixed and mainstream identities as comparable. Last, the variant approach envisioned mixed racial identity as a new phenomenon, presumably different than any before.

Problem Approach

Historically, in the most popular strategy to explore this issue, researchers viewed multiracial identity as inherently problematic. With few exceptions, these studies focus on black-white unions. Combining a majority and a minority image into one identity is problematic because of supposedly inherently contrasting attitudes and values found in the two groups. These groups, and therefore any person attempting to incorporate the two, are incompatible. This bimodal focus presumes that bonding with only one group is appropriate (i.e., mentally healthy). Thus these inquiries highlight risk factors (e.g., McKelvey, Mao, & Webb, 1992, 1993). Root (1992a) noted in this view that multiracial people are not a perfect fit anywhere; they are inherently "in between." Monoracial identification and social belonging cast multiracial people as deviant. Movement back and forth across color lines is viewed as a pejorative rather than a creative strategy (Daniel, 1992b; Nakashima, 1992). These studies rarely examine family context, usually choosing to generalize to the child from an examination of married couples (who are also at risk; see Thornton & Wason, 1995).

Much of the evidence for mixed race as problematic comes from clinical populations (e.g., Gibbs & Moskowitz-Sweet, 1991). An extreme example is a case study of one biracial child (Lyles, Yancey, Grace, & Carter, 1985). Assessed as facing novel demands, his parents were at risk and described as lacking the qualities necessary to assist him in the quest for a healthy identity. They were advised to feature positive aspects of their roots and, only when asked, to give him information on race. Finally, the authors exhorted the parents to be aware of their own prejudices and avoid interpreting the child's developmental struggles in racial terms.

Another study explored the problems encountered by an interracial family when dealing with the child welfare system (Folaron & Hess, 1993). Again, there was little to recommend these relationships. The article examined how the Indiana child welfare system failed to address the unique needs of mixed racial children placed in foster homes. The children endured bigoted extended families, including their own mothers, who often expressed mixed or negative feelings about them. Perhaps reflecting this prejudice, the children entered the welfare system youngest and were most likely to encounter disrupted reunifications and parents requesting placement. Compounding the hardships, service providers furnished no special services for them or their parents.

The problem approach underlies much of the social science research on ethnic identity. It is part of what Phinney (1990) described as a bipolar linear model, where identity lies along a continuum from strong minority group to strong mainstream ties. Strengthening one weakens the other. Therein lies the dichotomy: Strong group identity is negatively related to acculturation, for identity is tied to weakening one's ethnic identity. The internal struggle for mixed people lies in trying to maintain bonds to incompatible groups.

Equivalent Approach

The above approach envisions people, from birth, unable to cope with the mental stress of mixed racial status. Instead of seeing it as a problem, the equivalent paradigm characterizes mixed racial and monoracial identity formation as an assimilation process with similar outcomes, for multiracial people turn out little different from white peers;

racial background plays only a small role. Indeed, this work parallels that found in the more general discussion of Asian and Hispanic American identity, the primary concern being cultural aspects of assimilation and thus ultimately ethnicity (Porter & Washington, 1993). Unlike the problem approach, (American) cultural/ethnic patterns are the focus and not racial identity, which in part explains the similar patterns. These studies rely almost exclusively on samples from areas with large minority populations (the Southwest for Hispanics and Hawaii for Asian Americans) and exclude black-other combinations.

Grove (1991) found identities among college students of Asian white ancestry as similar to their Asian and white counterparts. The multiple-heritage individuals differed from Asian respondents in that they saw race as less important. Other studies on Asian white adults on the mainland and in Hawaii described comparable patterns. Although struggling to follow two cultural rules, with where they fit in racially, and in the nature of this struggle, they were found not to be a high-risk group (Ho & Johnson, 1990). Biracial (Asian white) males revealed higher socially desirable and lower intraception (rebellion and idealism) traits than monoracial males in Hawaii; biracial females were more extroverted than their monoracial counterparts. Increased risks of adjustment were not found (Johnson & Nagoshi, 1986).

Some authors described the important contexts of development among mixed racial people. Gibbs and Hines (1992) found 9 of 12 biracial children holding positive identities. Factors correlated with this phenomenon were being from an intact and upper-class family, experiencing integrated surroundings (school and neighborhood), leading a multicultural social life, and having warm family relations. Those with less positive identities were more likely from single-parent homes and lacked contact with the noncustodial parent's family and friends. Cauce et al. (1992) found biracials similar to control groups on aspects of family and peer relations (e.g., trust and alienation), life stress, psychological distress, behavior, and self-worth. They differed only in that they had less restrictive mothers.

One study suggested three stages of development among preadolescents (Jacobs, 1992). In the first stage, the children have an experience with color, yet do not learn the social importance of racial categorization. At the second stage, color constancy is developed, and children internalize biracial labels, which leads to racial ambivalence. At the third stage, ambivalence diminishes, and the children come to see group membership as determined by the parents and not by their skin color.

Ultimately the equivalent approach is interested in comparisons between majority and mixed individuals. It appears interested only in how mixed identities deviate from those of monoracial people. The problem approach assumes differences are inherently negative; the equivalent approach seems to allude to similarity as good.

Variant Approach

Much of the impetus for this viewpoint arises from work by people of multiple heritage (e.g., Mass, 1992; Root, 1992a; Valverde, 1992). The Stephans have been the most prolific in this perspective (Stephan, 1991, 1992; Stephan & Stephan, 1989) and are unique in their use of statistical models. They find biracial identification highly subjective, with variations even among those of similar biological heritage. Most identified with several groups without ill effects. Although the extent of exposure to cultures of origin helped explain its nature, it was not a necessary and sufficient condition for identification. People with little or extensive contact did not identify with cultures of origin. Among Japanese white individuals, contact with a Japanese religion was an important antecedent, whereas for Hispanic white blends, looks were associated with identification. The Stephans' work suggests that while it affects the individual, bicultural socialization generally leads to intergroup tolerance, language facility, enjoyment of minority group cultures, and better ties to single-heritage groups than the latter hold with one another.

Kich's (1992) description of three stages of identity development among Asian whites is another example of the variant approach. First, mixed racials feel discrepant from others. Second, they seek acceptance and to understand themselves; and finally they attempt to gain self-acceptance and assert their own biracial identity. Although the pattern of development overlaps with that of other adolescents, Kich describes a group ending with a distinct identity.

Kerwin, Ponterotto, Jackson, and Harris (1993) explored identity among school children and described them to be sensitive to both cultures and parents. Their parents were secure in their own identities and saw their children as multiracial. In a variation on this perspective focusing on black-white biracials, emerging work describes stages of development based on models developed for black adolescents. Poston (1990) used the identity model developed by Cross to describe stages of development among multiracial people. Stage 1, personal identity, is usually the first step in the identity process and found among the young who have not yet developed a group self-esteem. In Stage 2, individuals choose the group with whom they will identify. Here people are pushed to choose, and this choice is related to, among other things, status (ethnic background, home neighborhood) social support, and personal factors. The primary choices are between majority and minority. Multiple identity is rare because that demands more complex thinking than usually occurs at this stage.

Stage 3, enmeshment/denial, involves confusion and/or guilt about choosing a group to identify with, in part because of feelings of a lack of acceptance from other groups. This is also the stage, Poston argued, that is accented by the problematic approach. In Stage 4, individuals learn to appreciate having a multiple identity and attempt to learn more about themselves. Integration follows, Stage 5, where individuals become whole and cherishes all of their parts. Other work suggests that although the stages may resemble those of other adolescents, the final stage is unique (Kich, 1992; Johnson, 1992b).

This and the equivalent models of multiracial identity development follow a pattern described in Phinney's model of research highlighting a two-dimensional process. Although acculturation remains the theme, identity involves a process where both ethnic and mainstream bonds may be independent. One may have strong and/or weak ties with both groups (Phinney, 1990, pp. 501-502).

DISCUSSION

Although it is a popular debate topic, research on interracial relationships remains rare. Discussions have been dominated by a focus on black-white families as problematic and views of interracial families and individuals as marginal. This legacy continues, but new entrants to the debate bring a particularly notable focus on how multiracial status is mentally healthy. The implicit theme of all work in this area is, however, the question of whether races should intermingle. As such, interracial research is dominated by the history of race relations in this country and by political agendas.

The problem model, more than the other approaches, promotes the idea of sustaining clear boundaries between racial groups, for it views crossing racial boundaries as inevitably problematic. The quandary multiracials encounter is perceived as so severe because they attempt to bring together naturally antagonistic groups. Thus it is not surprising that upsetting the natural order will lead to chaos. Assimilation can never be the final outcome of the intermingling of races. Because of their racial mix, and society's reaction to it, multiracials cannot be mentally healthy.

The equivalent approach assumes that assimilation has occurred, because the interest is in how both sets of identities compare. The conclusion here is that no matter where multiracials start, they end up in the same place, with identities comparable to their monoracial peers. Focusing on patterns of personality common to our culture, these researchers characterize multiracial identity as acculturated to this society.

The variant and problem approaches describe differences between mixed and homogeneous populations. They further resemble each other in that they are cultural determinists: people are seemingly born with certain givens, having little choice in the matter. The variant approach evaluates the differences like cultural pluralists, however. In this view, individuals are likely to benefit from being able to draw from and exist in two contrasting worlds.

These paradigms are bonded by an either/or focus on differences or similarities. Ironically the point of reference in most models is implicitly mainstream America (cf. Cauce et al., 1992); after all, normality is usually predicated on majority patterns. The key for these paradigms is whether and how much multiracial identity differs from mainstream standards. The models part in their valuation of differences. However, focusing on differences and similarities tells us little about uniqueness.

This can be shown graphically. A and B are two ethnic identities arising from membership in two racial/ethnic groups; A is the majority and B is the minority group. Ethnic identity is for each mixed heritage individual a combination of A and/or B. The problem paradigm sees the mix as A or B. A true combination cannot occur for A and B are opposing poles. Furthermore, the appropriate identity is as a B; the lower-status ethnic heritage takes precedence. The equivalent approach, depicted by the model A + B, suggests combined identities come out as A or close enough so that they are indistinguishable from A (i.e., A + B = A'). This results in a single-heritage identity because the cultural artifacts of the majority culture seem to subsume other cultural influences such that the minority heritage disappears. The overtly different approach (the variant model) suggests that the identity is A and B, where each identity is juxtaposed. Instead of being combined or intermixed, mixed identity is two separate entities (minority and majority) lying side by side; the individual switches between them at appropriate moments. This enables them to interact in two different worlds by opening the door to two adjoining "rooms of information." The influence each has on the other is secondary. Instead of identifying with one group, the individual feels a bond with two. But incorporating both identities into one person does not seem to create a new sort of identity, merely two existing side by side. This is often the idea of biracial or bicultural.

What is missing are models of truly multiple identity: A × B and A × B × C, and so on, where there is an interaction among subidentities. Previous models of mixed ethnic identity ignore the effect of how combining two different identities may create something that is more than the sum of its parts. This is analogous to the current debate about the intersections of race, class, and gender in the lives of women of color (e.g., King, 1988). Are these social forces layered or interactive experiences? The growing consensus in this literature is that they are not simply layers, for these experiences are in reality so intermeshed that they cannot be pulled apart, as is implied by the layered view. The mixed-race literature rarely views identity as interactive. Blending two colors, for example yellow and blue, creates green, something completely different than revealed by either color separately.

Previous discussions ignore the "new colors" brought about by mixed identity. Focusing on comparison, I argue, has led us to a myopic view of mixed ethnic people. Missing is an understanding of mundane, normal, and indeed, unique aspects of their lives, such as the dynamics of family life and peer pressure, as well as how members of this group feel about topics other than race. To highlight potentially unique qualities among this group, this research tradition needs to examine very different sets of factors than has previous work.

PROPOSED RESEARCH DIRECTIONS
ON MULTIETHNIC IDENTITY

Ethnic Identity. Work in this area has assumed that multiple identity should result naturally from synthesizing several races in one person. The new work assumes that unless one identifies with a number of one's ethnic heritages, something is amiss—this mirrors the picture presented by the problem perspective. But this is an assertion with little empirical support. In work on black self-esteem, people who do not hold strong group identities may still have strong self-esteems (Porter & Washington, 1993).

Instead of assuming that race determines identity, we need to focus on the experiences and perceptions of multiracial bonds with other groups, discover if there is a multiple identity, and learn what about it makes it unique. These are the issues brought up in the literature on ethnicity. This is not to suggest that race is not integral to this understanding but merely that it explains only part of the phenomenon of multiracial identity.

Referencing work on ethnicity may be particularly useful for work on multiracials because along with assuming a unique identity, much of the work also seems to suggest that we are an ethnic group. What we know now could be explained by an overt identification with others we believe have a common experience. Is that connection parallel to bonds individuals hold with other ethnic groups? Or instead, is the association perhaps more akin to the bond between parents who have lost their children to disease, or to men who have played in the National Football League? If there is a truly multiracial or multiethnic identity, it has to be more than merely a common experience.

An ethnic/group identity is a complex interaction between personal and social definitions. Identity means to join with some people and depart from others, both within and without the group. Although society may try to impose identity in an absolute way, individuals often differ in how they define group boundaries and how strongly they identify with their own and other groups.

Phinney (1990) described several aspects of ethnic identity that offer a broader view of the kinds of issues the research on mixed racial people could tackle. Ethnic identity involves several components: awareness (understanding of one's own and other groups), self-identity (the label affixed to each group member), attitudes (feelings about one's own and other groups), and behaviors. To ascertain the nature of multiethnic identity, we need to distinguish our definition of a common ancestry, our shared history, the symbolic elements that make us a group. Do we have norms, values, even loyalties, all of which go to make us an ethnic group with a unique identity (See & Wilson, 1988). These unique factors need to be explicitly addressed in research and incorporated into a broader model of ethnicity. Race may be a less pivotal part of this process than previously attributed.

Phinney's review suggests other areas of possible focus. Group identity includes a sense of belonging that entails positive and negative attitudes toward both in- and out-groups. Although this makes intuitive sense, rarely in the empirical literature are feelings toward the group viewed as an admixture of positive and negative feelings or involving an affinity with some aspects of the group; nor are they coupled with attempts to dissociate from others (Jackson, McCullough, & Gurin, 1988; McAdoo, 1985). It seems natural that multiracial people would have mixed emotions about their status, especially if their ancestry lies with less socially desirable groups. This may result in being at once accepting of the overall status but troubled by aspects of it. Identity may in this way mirror experiences for all people of color raised in this country.

Content. Do we exist between groups? Is this our unique identity? Do our heritages exist side by side? If so, does this not parallel the idea of race and nation in the black context; and thus is not multiracial identity like other identities? It may be different but not unique. Perhaps the experience is actually little different from what other people of color go through, except that it is perceived to be very different.

If unique, our identity may be reflected in how and with whom we bond. Maybe we bond equally with the two parent groups (most others do not do this) or with some new kind of group we have created out of our own heads (the idea of imagined communities). Part of highlighting any potentially unique aspects to ethnic identity among mixed racial populations would be to examine their reference groups. Recent work in this direction has been fairly descriptive.

A paradigm developed by Boykin and Toms (1985) concerning areas of socialization might be useful in addressing this issue (Thornton, forthcoming). Boykin and Toms's idea of the triple quandary describes racial socialization among black children as involving an interplay between three major parental themes:

1. mainstream experience (i.e., influences of white, middle-class culture or so-called universals of family living);
2. minority experience (i.e., social, economic, and political forces that impinge on racial minorities, leading them to formulate a set of coping styles, social outlooks, and adaptive positions); and
3. cultural experience (i.e., styles, motifs, and patterns of behavior unique to blacks).

Parents may emphasize any one of these views over the others but probably incorporate them all in one form.

In using whites as the standard of racial/ethnic identity, with few exceptions, research on mixed racial identity has highlighted variations from the mainstream experience. The minority component is also to some degree stressed by the variant approach. But we cannot find unique factors without exploring who we are more directly. Such a focus would parallel the cultural experience described by Boykin and Toms (1985). If there are unique qualities to this identity, then we need to examine this in greater detail. A focus on whites implies assimilation and the internalization of beliefs in racial superiority (see, e.g., Cauce et al., 1992; Root, 1990). Thus the interest is in biculturalism rather than how within us there exists a multiculturalism. A comparative focus allows us to say how we are different but not why we are. Perhaps mixed identity is merely racial identity doubled—that is, monoracial people perhaps focus on one reference group; multiracials on at least two. This will remain unclear, however, unless we examine ourselves without reference to others, which is the cultural experience as identified in Boykin and Toms.

Group identity also entails ethnic involvement, the extent of contact with the cultural practices, language, religion, and political ideology, as well as the friends and neighborhoods. This is similar to the work done by the Stephans. Do multiethnic people possess unique types of bonding?

To answer these questions, we need to diversify the links studied. Clearly, this means first to include other nonwhite groups intersecting with each other. In part, the work focusing on whites points to cultural assimilation wherein racial complementarity is overlooked. How does this compare to groups within whom exist the bonds between two minority groups? This would also entail exploring the role of social class in the process. It seems most variant and equivalent paradigms use middle-class subjects. Perhaps grappling with these sorts of questions is limited to those who have the luxury to contemplate them and may be thus a class-based phenomenon.

Level of Analysis. Early-age experience is the focus for most of this work. Identity formation across the life span is rarely examined. How does it change with age? Does group identity differ after one leaves adolescence and enters adulthood and old age? Is what we discovered thus far primarily the normal transition through young adulthood compounded by adding race?

In examining only racial/ethnic identity, researchers ignore the broader person. Indeed, if portrayals of multiracials were applied to an individual, that person would be narrow and uninteresting, given a fixation on his or her race. What of other core and role identities we all have? What are our politics, our feelings about groups we are not part of? Are we good students? Who are our friends? Does our heritage make us into very different parents?

Put another way, in all the roles we play in our lives how important is our ethnicity? Where in our range of life roles do we place mixed identity? And does this change over the life course? Perhaps adolescents and young adults place it at the top of their list, but older multiracials may find it less an issue, devoting their time to parenthood, taking care of parents, and so on.

Researchers in other areas have begun exploring the relationship between group identity and personal identity. The latter is related to overall feelings about the self that transcend race but do not exclude it; the former highlights feelings toward the ethnic group. Although focusing on blacks, and ignored in research on Hispanics and Asian Americans, this work suggests that the two are distinct and often unrelated to each other (Porter & Washington, 1993). One can have a positive personal identity but weak ethnic ties. Is this the case among multiracials? Is this how we may be unique?

We give too little attention to the family's impact on identity. Outside the problem paradigm, few explore the family as a direct influence on the multiethnic identity. Most of our understanding of the family's influence is indirect, via scrutiny of intermarried unions. We don't know how their socialization patterns compare to those of other parents, nor how much their children's later development is predicated on family preparation. Knowing so little about the familial context is limiting, because identity is framed by environmental factors that include the family. The best way to examine any unique patterns in multiracial identity is to explore how multiracials are socialized. This may be the key to understanding the nature of this identity. In this context, we can better understand the influence of social class as well.

How do ethnic identity and other factors relate? What influences these relationships? Is proximity to the ethnic group important? Does contact with the in-group, political orientation, the racial balance of the community where the individual lives or grew up, or the level of commitment to and involvement in the in-group make a difference?

Finally, we must address cultural and structural forces that determine how multiracials view themselves and are viewed by others. Identity is a collective entity, not merely personal. Some work (e.g., Omi & Winant, 1986) shows the influence of larger social contexts on everyday experiences and interactions. However, day-to-day social activities also help shape the larger social context. How microlevel activities influence the macrolevel and vice versa is what has been called agency (Giddens, 1984, p. 9). Agency concerns events of which the person is a perpetrator; what happened would not have happened if that person had not intervened. How does grappling with this new kind of identity influence this society as it influences our attempt to come to a resolution of identity dilemmas?

CONCLUSION

Much of the ambiguity found in work on multiracial people can be attributed to the relatively recent move to make this population a serious area of study. Past efforts were desultory, researchers flitting in and out to make comments about the subject but rarely making it their expertise. We have witnessed growing pains in this new area of inquiry; in some sense, the field is in adolescence, perhaps ready to move into adulthood. This may be true in more ways than one. New researchers entering this field have had a very personal link to issues of multiple identity. I myself examined black Japanese Americans primarily because in so doing I could also explore and better understand my own development and identity. Through this work, I was able to clarify some of my own concerns. My interest in this area subsequent to my dissertation is a reflection of my becoming more removed from the heat of identity development and formation; I have entered a very different stage of my personal life, and this in turn has influenced my intellectual interests as well. I no longer fixate on my multiple heritage, for I now see it as one part, albeit a still important one, of my total self. In some sense when I did my study, I perceived my ethnic identity as almost all of who I was—or at least the most important part of who I was. It is no longer a pressing issue.

I am suggesting that part of the field has now moved beyond fixating on a single identity, needing to explore who we are in very narrow terms and even to justify our existence as a good thing. Having moved past an extended adolescence, and all the insecurities that entails, we are ready to look through the mist of our racial/ethnic identity to explore how it fits into the rest of who we are as human beings. Those who have the luxury of hindsight can now help the rest of us see the forest for the trees. One's (multi)ethnic or (multi)racial identity is important, but it is not everything. Our legacy should be to show the breadth and depth of what kind of people we are and can be.

NOTE

1. From *Newsweek*, May, 18, 1992, Newsweek , Inc. All rights reserved. Reprinted by permission.

Black and White Identity in the New Millennium

Unsevering the Ties That Bind

G. REGINALD DANIEL

One day in 1965, during my sophomore year in high school, two white female classmates approached me between classes at my locker and asked to borrow my history book. Right after they departed, the white guy whose locker was to my left said, "You know, we hang niggers for messing with white women." The black guy whose locker was on my left said, "Yeah, you might be a half-white nigga,' but you're still a nigga.'" Both laughed hysterically and went off down the hallway together, looking back at me and pointing their fingers mockingly. Within a few minutes, I got my composure and went on to class.

The rest of the day, however, I felt a sense of humiliation and could not get that scene out of my mind. When I went to sleep that night, I had a dream in which I was an octopus standing at the top of a very steep and lengthy stairway. One half of me

AUTHOR'S NOTE: I would like to acknowledge Nina Gordon, Adam Gottdank, and James U. Collins III for the feedback and moral support they provided in shaping revisions of this chapter.

was black and the other was white. I was wearing white tennis shoes on my black tentacles and black tennis shoes on my white tentacles. Just behind me was a large white statue of a blind-folded woman holding a scepter in one hand and a balance scale in the other. Right behind her was an a expansive white building with columns, which I knew to be the House of Justice.

Far below me at the bottom of the stairway there were millions of people pointing their fingers at me and laughing. I knew that they did not believe I could reach the bottom stair without tripping over my tentacles. As I descended the stairs my heart pounded. The tentacles went in all directions, inter-twining to the left, then to the right, sometimes forward, sometimes backward. I knew that I would fall at any minute. The crowd's laughter grew louder and louder as I approached the bottom of the stairway, and I felt I could go no further.

When I reached the last stair there was dead silence. Sud-denly all of the tentacles lunged forward and landed on the ground with absolute precision. I awoke somewhat startled and disoriented but absolutely clear about the dream's significance in terms of that day's events, and its even deeper meaning as to how I should live my life. ⚭

THE DIALECTICAL SETTING:
PLURALISM AND INTEGRATION

The rule of hypodescent (the "one-drop" rule) emerged in the late 17th and early 18th centuries as a means of increasing the number of slaves (Nash, 1982). It was buttressed, however, by the desire to main-tain white racial (phenotypical, ancestral) and cultural (beliefs, values, customs) "purity," as well as white privilege. By codifying the dichoto-mization and hierarchical valuation of "whiteness" and "blackness" origi-nating in European American and African American racial and cultural differences, this device has served as the basis for other legal and informal barriers to equality in most aspects of social life. This has included public facilities and other areas of the public (political, economic, educational) and private (residential, associational, interpersonal) spheres—particu-larly in the area of miscegenation (Davis, 1991). At the turn of the 20th century, these restrictions reached drastic proportions with the institutionalization of Jim Crow segregation. The one-drop rule, thus, has had fateful implications not only for intermarriages and blended offspring, but also for black and white relations generally speaking.

The dismantling of Jim Crow segregation—including the removal of the last legal prohibitions against intermarriage in 1967—and the implementation of civil rights legislation dissolved the formal barriers to equality. These changes have resulted in increased intermarriage and have led many couples to bring their black *and* white backgrounds to the identity of their offspring. The carriers of this new blended identity are primarily these "first-generation" individuals, but also include a smaller portion of "multigenerational" individuals. The latter have backgrounds that have been blended for several generations, and they are viewed by the general society as black but have resisted identifying solely with the African American community (Daniel, 1992a). In the 1990s, a growing number of these individuals are challenging the rule of hypodescent by "unsevering" ties with their European American background and European Americans; they seek to do this without diminishing their affinity with the experience of African Americans. They achieve this by affirming an integrative identity that has both the black and white communities as reference groups; or a pluralistic identity that blends aspects of the black and white communities but is neither. Most individuals display an identity that operates from many permutations on the integrative-pluralistic continuum (Daniel, 1992a, 1994). Considering that the possibility of affirming differences (pluralism) while nurturing commonalities (integration) appears ever more elusive in the schizoid racial/cultural maze of contemporary black and white relations, this identity, therefore, is an attractive and persuasive development.

EITHER BLACK OR WHITE:
SEVERING THE TIES

The Ties That Bind

European Americans, throughout Anglo America's history, have exploited racial and cultural differences between themselves and African Americans in order to maintain socioeconomic and political dominance. In the Old American South of the early 17th century, however, the number of blacks was comparatively small, and the distinction between white indenture and black slave was less precise than between bond and free (Tenzer, 1990). Consequently, a significant number of African-descent Americans were able to enjoy a measure of freedom in the public sphere, and in some cases, to become independent land-owners and employers of servants (Spickard, 1989). In the private sphere, phenotypical differences were somewhat accommodated— egalitarian pluralism (Marger, 1994)—and there were no laws prohibit-ing the commingling of ancestral lines—egalitarian integration (Daniel, 1992a)— despite strong social prejudice against miscegenation. This is indicated by the small, but not insignificant, number of blacks and whites of both sexes who intermarried or formed common-law unions of some duration and had legitimate offspring, alongside more wide-spread clandestine and fleeting liaisons that involved births outside of wedlock (Tenzer, 1990). Most of the latter, however, were between white masters and indentured, ór slave women of African descent, and in-volved extended concubinage and rape (Spickard, 1984; Tenzer, 1990). Furthermore, the coexistence of African and European centers of refer-ence that were of equal demographic significance, if not equal in popu-lation size, at times necessarily fostered an accommodation of differ-ences in beliefs, values, and customs—egalitarian pluralism. These same factors also served as the basis for a significant blending in perceptions of time, aesthetics, approaches to ecstatic religious experi-ence, an understanding of the Godhead, and ideas of the afterlife— egalitarian integration. Even the distinctive linguistic features of the Southern dialect are a creolization of West African and Old English speech patterns (Sobel, 1987). Egalitarian integration of beliefs, values, and customs through intermarriage or social intercourse, however, has often bordered on cultural grand larceny and certainly has not been transferred to equitable treatment in the educational, political, and socioeconomic arenas. Nevertheless, by the end of the colonial period, blacks and whites had forged a new Southern culture that in varying degrees was a blend of both (Nash, 1982; Sobel, 1987).

The Rule of Hypodescent

As African slavery became entrenched in society over the course of the 17th century, and the population of African descent expanded in order to meet these needs, slavery and African ancestry become inextricably intertwined in the Anglo American mind (Spickard, 1989). Subsequently, codes were promulgated to solidify the distinction between slave and free, which ultimately came to belie the distinction between black and white. Simultaneously, the Southern states, and some Northern states, began to enforce laws prohibiting sexual relations and intermarriages between whites and blacks (Dyer, 1976; Tenzer, 1990). Even in those states where interracial sexual relations and marriages were not prohibited by law, they continued to carry painful social consequences. These legal and informal restrictions, however, did not result in a marked decrease in miscegenation. The key change was a shift in public attitudes (Nash, 1982). Rape and extended concubinage, which conferred no legal status on the relationship and posed little threat to the slave system, continued to be tolerated as long as they involved white men and women of African descent (Tenzer, 1990). Marriage, on the other hand, which reflected an assumption that the two parties were social equals, could not be allowed (Spickard, 1989).

This change in attitudes had a profound effect on the offspring of black and white unions, whose legal status up to the time of the American Revolution had been ambiguous at best. With the expanding numbers of Free People of Color in the late 18th century and throughout the 19th century, Anglo Americans became more concerned with ensuring the precision of racial/cultural demarcations. The challenge that the blended individual implicitly presented to white socioeconomic and political domination, however, was feared more than the comingling of African and European beliefs, values, and customs or the blurring of phenotypical boundaries and ancestral lines themselves. Thus 18th-century lawmakers discovered that if legislation and public pronouncements against miscegenation were relatively unsuccessful at controlling the sexual impulses of the European American population, specifically males, there was little harm done so long as white domination was preserved by disowning the offspring of blended descent (Nash, 1982; Spickard, 1989).

Legal definitions varied from state to state. Informally, however, any African ancestry was used to classify a person as black, lest large numbers of blended individuals slip into the ranks of whites (Daniel, 1992b). Even those few individuals who "passed" into the white population necessarily were predominantly of European descent and carried very few, if any, "African genes" into the European American community. Consequently, only about 1% of the genes of European Americans are derived from African ancestors, although the total of European Americans with West African forbears would number in the millions (Davis, 1991). By winking at the exploitation of African-descent women by European American males, and defining all blended offspring as black, Anglo America found the rule of hypodescent to be the "ideal answer to its labor needs, its extracurricular and inadmissible sexual desires, its compulsion to maintain its [culture and ancestral lines] purebred, and the problem of maintaining, at least in theory, absolute dominance, superiority, and social control" (Nash, 1982, p. 285).

BOTH BLACK AND WHITE: UNSEVERING THE TIES

Breaking the One-Drop Rule

The rule of hypodescent, although designed to increase the number of slaves and divest offspring of European American slave masters and African American slave women from privilege associated with paternity (Nash, 1982; Tenzer, 1990), was reinforced by the desire to maintain not only white privilege, but also white racial and cultural purity. By dint of these facts, it served as the underpinning for a generalized system of both legalized and informal exclusion of blacks from contact with whites as equals by virtue of their racial and cultural difference— inegalitarian pluralism (Marger, 1994). These social dynamics, which culminated at the turn of the 20th century in Jim Crow segregation, encompassed both the public and private sectors of society, especially the area of intermarriage (Daniel 1992a).

The implementation of civil rights legislation over the last 30 years, however, has given blacks a comparatively greater opportunity to integrate with whites in both the public and private spheres. This, in turn, has led to increased intermarriage (Mitchell-Kernan & Tucker, 1990). About 98% of blacks and whites still marry within their respective communities (Lieberson & Waters, 1988), and out-marriage rates are highest among the middle and upper classes of both communities (Lieberson & Waters, 1988; Spickard, 1989). Urban centers on the West

Coast, such as Seattle, San Francisco, and Los Angeles, appear to have the highest rates of intermarriage (Monroe, 1992), but nationally there was a substantial increase from 65,000 black white interracial marriages in 1970 to 246,000 by 1992 (Funderburg, 1994).

The growing population born from these marriages since 1968 is estimated to range from 600,000 to several million (Funderburg, 1994; Gibbs, 1989; Gibbs & Hines, 1992), but these offspring had received limited attention from educators, researchers, sociologists, and mental health professionals prior to the 1980s (Wardle, Chapter 23, this volume). Previous research is outdated, contradictory, or based on small-scale case studies of children who were experiencing "problems" with personal identity and referred for psychological counseling (C. C. I. Hall, 1980, 1992). Most of these professionals stressed the importance for blended children to cope as African Americans, because society is going to view them as such. Consequently, they defined the children's mental health in terms of how successfully or unsuccessfully they achieved an African American identity (Wardle, 1987). Many intermarried couples, however, are integrating the plurality of their black and white backgrounds into the identity of their offspring and are using a variety of terms to describe them. These designations include rainbow, brown, melange, blended, mixed, mixed-race, biracial/bicultural, interracial/intercultural, and multiracial/multicultural (Wardle, 1987). The common denominator among these terms, however, is that they challenge formal policies and informal social attitudes that maintain the rule of hypodescent (Root, Chapter 1, this volume).

First-Generation and Multigenerational

Although most individual experiences of the past are unknown and unreported, there have been cases of notoriety, such as that of George and Josephine Schuyler, who in the 1940s encouraged their daughter, Philippa, to embrace both black and white heritages. Several groups that emerged between the 1890s and 1940s, also sought, with the support they provided intermarried couples, to help blended individuals affirm both their black and white backgrounds (Daniel, 1992a). More than 60 similar organizations have come into existence over the past decade (Brown & Douglass, Chapter 20, this volume). Composed primarily of black and white couples and their first-generation children, the membership in some cases includes other intermarried couples and their offspring. Most organizations also include a smaller number of multigenerational individuals who have backgrounds that have been blended for several generations and are viewed by the general society as black, but who have resisted identifying solely with the African American community (Daniel, 1992a).

The first-generation identity is derived from having one parent who is socially designated and self-identified as black and one who is socially designated and self-identified as white, regardless of whether these parents have multiple racial/cultural backgrounds in their genealogy. Consequently, first-generation blended individuals more frequently identify themselves as *biracial/bicultural*, irrespective of the multiplicity of actual backgrounds in their lineage. When asked to described themselves, they also respond, "I'm black and white," "I'm part white and part black," or "I'm mixed." Less frequent choices for self-description are multiracial/multicultural or interracial/intercultural (Daniel, 1994).

The multigenerational identity may encompass the experience of individuals who are socially designated as black but have two biracial parents; one parent who is biracial and one whose social designation and means of personal identification is African American; or a biracial parent and one whose social designation and means of personal identification is European American (or any other single racial/cultural reference group). More specifically, however, this identity applies to the experience of individuals who have parents, and/or several generations of ancestors, who have been designated socially as black although they have multiple racial/cultural backgrounds; these parents or ancestors may have resisted embracing single racial/cultural identities as African American (Daniel, 1994).

The identity of first-generation individuals is based on having *parents from more than one racial/cultural reference group* and generally involves the concrete and immediate experience of those backgrounds in the home and/or extended family. The experience of multigenerational individuals, however, may not have these specific backgrounds concretely delineated in the home and/or extended family (Zack, 1993). Consequently, their identity is primarily based on having *more than one parent racial/cultural reference group* in the more abstract genealogical past. Due to the fact that this generally includes many actual backgrounds (particularly Native American) along with African and European, as well as numerous ancestors, multigenerational individuals more commonly refer to themselves as *multi*racial/*multi*cultural (Daniel, 1994). Most first-generation and multigenerational individuals, however, use "mixed" as the most consistent alternate term to describe themselves (Daniel, 1994; Funderburg, 1994). Regardless of whether they are first-generation or multigenerational, all individuals who identify as blended must develop constructive strategies for resisting the rule of hypodescent (Root, Chapter 1, this volume). This mechanism challenges their comfort with both backgrounds and claim to membership in both communities. It also continually assigns them a socially defined identity that contradicts their personal identity (Root, 1990).

The contemporary first-generation experience, however, is frequently viewed as being a more justifiable basis for a blended identity. This is related in part to the removal of antimiscegenation laws in 1967 and the liberalization of the social ecology over the past three decades. More specifically, it appears to be related to the fact that this experience generally originates in the context of marriage and thus includes an element of choice. This confers equal de jure status on both parties and, by extension, equal legitimacy to both parent's identities. The one-drop rule, therefore, has been less consistently enforced, both de jure and de facto, in the case of their offspring (McRoy & Hall, Chapter 5, this volume).

This flexibility is not so readily extended to the identity of multigenerational individuals. Not only does that experience carry with it explicitly or implicitly the stigma of concubinage, rape, and illegitimacy, but also both parents and families of these individuals have been considered black by the larger society and to some extent have identified themselves with the black community. Furthermore, because most African-descent Americans have some European ancestry in their genealogy but identify themselves as black (Davis, 1991), multigenerational individuals are frequently at odds with the African American community and with first-generation individuals, as well. African Americans often accuse them of choosing to identify as blended in order to escape the societal stigma attached to blackness. Some first-generation individuals contend that their own biracial/bicultural experience is the legitimate starting point for a blended identity (Daniel, 1994). Restricting the parameters of the new blended identity to the experience of first-generation individuals born since the removal of the last antimiscegenation laws in 1967, however, seems myopic, despite valid differences between that experience and the experience of multigenerational individuals. This perspective ignores and invalidates the experience of earlier generations of first-generation individuals, as well as generations of their offspring, who have struggled, and continue to struggle, to liberate themselves from the ironclad shackles of hypodescent (Daniel, 1994).

Keeping the One-Drop Rule

The one-drop rule has become such an accepted part of the American fabric, however, that most individuals are unaware that this device is unique to Anglo America and specifically applied to African-descent Americans (Davis, 1991). The rule of hypodescent has been variously extended to other Americans whose blended lineage includes a "background of color," along with European ancestry. Generally speaking, however, these individuals are not invariably designated exclusively, or even partially, as members of that group of color, if the background is less than one fourth of their lineage. Furthermore, self-identification with that background is more a matter of choice (Davis, 1991). African ancestry, on the other hand, is passed on in perpetuity as a means of socially designating *all* future offspring as black, and thus it precludes any notion of choice in self-identification (Davis, 1991). Vast numbers of individuals— except perhaps African Americans—remain equally uninformed about the rule's oppressive origins and even more oblivious to the oppressive effects this mechanism has on blended individuals. Most Americans never question the rule's "illogic" (Spickard, 1992) and thus reinforce, if only unwittingly, the notion that blackness and whiteness are mutually exclusive, if not hierarchical, and objective categories of experience that have an independent existence of their own (Zack, 1993).

We cannot, however, ignore other attitudes and practices originating in less benign aspects of the one-drop rule, which not only continue to prevent its demise but also keep blacks and whites living largely in "separate, hostile, unequal" worlds (Hacker, 1992). The clearest indication of this schism is that African Americans, over the last half century, have challenged both the legal and informal inegalitarian pluralism barring them from integrating with whites as equals in the public and private spheres—including the area of intermarriage (Daniel, 1992a; Fuchs, 1990; Ringer, 1983). Generally speaking, however, they have not sought complete de facto integration in the private arena, especially as this relates to intermarriage (Davis, 1991). Considering the persistent Eurocentric bias in the larger society, blacks argue that intermarriage would not result in an egalitarian integration of African American and European American racial and cultural differences into a more inclusive commonality. Rather, it would lead to inegalitarian integration— assimilation—which would increase commonalities between blacks and whites by eliminating African American racial and cultural distinctiveness (Daniel & Collins, 1994; Yinger, 1981). What is envisioned instead is a mosaic of mutually respectful and differentiated, if not mutually exclusive, African American and European American racial/cultural pluralities—egalitarian pluralism. Both whites and blacks would have equal access to all aspects of the public sphere, with the option of integrating in the private sphere—egalitarian integration. In this case, the selective pattern would be voluntary, rather than mandated by whites; if and when blacks chose to integrate, they would do so as equals (Cruse, 1987; Daniel & Collins, 1994; Davis, 1991).

Increased integration, made possible by the dissolution of legalized inegalitarian pluralism, however, has allowed only a select few African-descent Americans to gain access to wealth, power, privilege, and prestige. Many of those structural gains also are very circumscribed and easily eroded (Winant, 1994). Furthermore, the privileged few tend to be disproportionately of more "visible" European ancestry and share similar sociocultural values, if not actual racial/cultural identification, with affluent whites by virtue of their socioeconomic status (Daniel, 1992a). The black masses, on the other hand, have been retained disproportionately in service and blue-collar jobs or pushed to the periphery of society the ranks of the underemployed and unemployed due to the continuing legacy of informal, yet no less deleterious, inegalitarian pluralism (Ringer & Lawless, 1989; Wilson, 1980, 1987).

Although most European Americans have repudiated notions of racial and cultural purity that supported the ideology of white supremacy, these trends do not indicate that the *hierarchical* relationship between blackness and whiteness that upholds white privilege has been dismantled. The achievement of comparatively greater integration by African-descent Americans indicates, rather, that the dichotomization of blackness and whiteness, originating in African American and European American racial and cultural differences has been attenuated. Although the rule of hypodescent remains the official law of the land, phenotype is thus gaining in importance over ancestry as an informal line of racial demarcation in the larger society; shared values, beliefs, and customs associated with class have increased in importance in determining social stratification (Daniel, 1992a). This type of integration, however, remains somewhat inegalitarian in that it furthers the illusion of power sharing without European Americans actually giving up structural domination and control (Allen, 1990; Cruse, 1987). Therefore, as European Americans become more willing to bend the one-drop rule, African Americans, understandably yet paradoxically, hold on to this device ever more tenaciously. They view it as a necessary, if originally oppressive, means not only of maintaining a distinct but equal African American racial and cultural plurality, but more important, of mobilizing blacks in the continuing struggle against white privilege (Davis, 1991).

Black No More or More Than Black?

The black community's resistance to relinquishing the rule of hypodescent, however, is more specifically related to its experience with strategies that have challenged it but that also compromised the mobilization of African-descent Americans in the struggle against white domination. Those tactics included integration through "passing," or the formation of pluralistic urban elites and rural enclaves, and they were motivated by the legal system of segregation, which sought to control the potential threat to white dominance posed by individuals of African descent (Daniel, 1992b). Consequently, these tactics were less a response to the forced denial of European ancestry and/or cultural orientation and more a reaction to being subordinated and being denied the privileges that these criteria have implied. Those strategies did resist the dichotomization of racial/cultural boundaries but operated respectively out of inegalitarian integrationist and inegalitarian pluralist dynamics by maintaining the hierarchical valuation attached to African American and European American racial and cultural differences. By so doing, these tactics were not only products of the Eurocentrism in the larger society but also responsible for a divisive and pernicious *colorism* among African-descent Americans. This phenomenon has often resulted in the preferential treatment of individuals who more closely approximate whites in terms of consciousness, behavior, and pheno-type within the black community as well as the larger society (Daniel, 1992a).

Like those other tactics, the new blended identity resists the dichoto-mization of racial and cultural boundaries. Yet, it is neither based on the desire to gain special privileges that would be precluded by identifying as black nor is it synonymous with the psychosocial pathology of colorism. This new identity, rather, resists both the dichotomization *and* hierarchical valuation of African American and European American cultural and racial differences (Daniel, 1992a). The new blended identity is not, however, indicative of someone who simply acknowledges, as do many blacks, the presence of African ancestry—in conjunction with other ancestries—in their background. This identity, therefore, differs from that of African Americans (who for the most part have multiple racial/cultural backgrounds but have a single racial/cultural identity as black) in that it replaces this one-dimensional identity with a more multidimensional configuration (Forbes, 1988). Nor is the new racially/culturally blended identity analogous to the multicultural identity model of Ramirez (1983). Ramirez's multicultural identity model is applicable to people—including individuals identified as African American and European American—who, irrespective of genealogy or ancestry, dis-play a general temperamental openness and sensitivity to racial and cultural differences, and thus have an affinity with the values, beliefs, and customs of more than one racial/cultural context or blend aspects of these contexts into a new personal synthesis, *due to exposure to multiple racial/cultural groups.*

This is not to say that there are no striking similarities between the objective behavior of individuals who display Ramirez's multicultural identity and those who exhibit the new racially/culturally blended identity. Nevertheless, the subjective motivation behind these two iden-tities differs considerably. The new blended identity is indicative of individuals who reference their sense of "we-ness" in both the black and white communities and feel a sense of kinship with both, directly in response to the *multiple racial/cultural backgrounds in their genealogy.* Exposure to these backgrounds enhances and unequivocally helps concretize this feeling of kinship. Simple awareness of those backgrounds, however, can catalyze this sentiment, and lack of contact does not preclude its presence (Daniel, 1994).

Playing the Middle by Embracing Both Ends

Due to the multidimensional nature of their identity, the new blended individuals are neither totally dependent on the cultural predispositions of any one racial group, nor are they completely free from the sociocultural conditioning of their racial backgrounds or contexts (Adler, 1974; Brown, 1990). The psychosocial configuration of their identity is premised instead on a style of self-consciousness that involves a continuous process of "incorporating here, discarding there, responding situationally" (Adler, 1974). Because the contemporary blended individuals maintain no rigid boundaries between themselves and the various contexts within which they operate, their identity has no fixed or predictable parameters. They are liminal individuals whose identity has multiple points of reference and, yet, has no circumference, due to the fact that it manifests itself *on* the boundary (Anzaldúa, 1987; Kich, Chapter 16, this volume). Their sense of being "betwixt and between," that is, their marginality, however, neither precludes an affinity with both blacks and whites nor translates into the social dislocation and personal alienation traditionally ascribed to blended individuals (Daniel, 1994; Kich, Chapter 16, this volume; Root, 1990).

Those traditional frameworks, which were formulated prior to the 1970s, argued that marginality itself is necessarily pathological and the source of lifelong personal conflict, characterized by divided loyalties, ambivalence, and hypersensitivity, due to the mutually exclusive natures of black and white backgrounds (Park, 1928; Stonequist, 1937). Admittedly, these theories emerged at a time when Anglo America was, in fact, significantly more hostile to forces supporting the affirmation of a blended identity. Specifically, however, they were acceptable to the prevailing ideology that focused on the "psychological dysfunctioning" of blended offspring, as a justification for discouraging miscegenation, rather than on the sociological forces that made psychological functioning problematic (Lempel, 1979). Park and Stonequist thus overshadowed other contemporary theorists who argued that marginality could potentially imbue individuals with a broader vision and wider range of sympathies, due to their ability to identify with more than one racial/ cultural reference group (Antonovsky, 1956; Goldberg, 1941; Green, 1947; Kerckhoff & McCormick, 1955).

The theories on "negative" marginality have been further refuted by theories formulated since the 1970s (Gist, 1967; Miller, 1992; Poston, 1990; Wright & Wright, 1972) and by data collected since the 1980s (Root, 1992d). Moreover, the concept of "positive" marginality has gained greater acceptance among health professionals and in the larger society as well. As a consequence, there is a growing consensus that blended individuals, in their odyssey to racial/cultural wholeness, may variously experience some of the ambiguities, strains, and conflicts that come "naturally" with marginality in a society that views black and white identities as mutually exclusive categories of experience. Yet those feelings can be significantly counterbalanced by a general sense of increased tolerance of differences and appreciation of commonalities, as an extension of their feelings of kinship with both blacks and whites (Daniel, 1994).

VARIOUS SHADES OF GRAY

Although the new blended individuals identify with both parent reference groups, there are differences in the affinity they feel toward their black and white backgrounds. Myriad variables determine this process. Data reveal, however, that the outcome is influenced less by the extent to which individuals display phenotypical traits commonly associated with their parent reference groups and more by the impact that society, peers, and family have had on their personal history (Bradshaw, 1992; Field, Chapter 13, this volume; Funderburg, 1994; C. C. I. Hall, 1980, 1992; Johnson, 1992a; Mitchell, 1990; Root, 1990, 1992d).

Information obtained between 1988 and 1995—through informal conversations with and observations of students attending the University of California campuses in Los Angeles, Santa Barbara, and Santa Cruz, as well as individuals participating in several California support groups—indicate that many blended individuals affirm an integrative identity that has both the black and white communities as reference groups; others embrace a pluralistic identity that blends aspects of both communities but is neither. Most individuals exhibit an identity that manifests itself in varying shades of gray on the integrative-pluralistic continuum (Daniel, 1994). As mentioned earlier, this spectrum can be broken down into three trends that are similar to Ramirez's multicultural identity model, yet differ in their subjective motivations: (a) synthesized identity, (b) functional identity/European American orientation, and (c) functional identity/African American orientation (Ramirez, 1983).

The Integrative Identity

Individuals displaying an integrative blended identity reference themselves simultaneously in the black and white communities. They are aware of being both similar to and different from their black and white reference groups, but they may, at certain times and in certain circumstances, lean toward either a European American or African American orientation. These individuals tend to be first-generation offspring, due to the likelihood of exposure to both backgrounds in the home and/or extended family (Daniel, 1994; Field, Chapter 13, this volume; Funderburg, 1994; Root, 1990; Tizard & Phoenix, 1993).

Synthesized Integrative Identity. These individuals identify with the black and white communities in fairly equal amounts. They feel comfortable in European American sociocultural settings but also are committed to issues concerning African Americans. This is demonstrated by their competent functioning and credibility in both communities and their ability to "shuttle" between both. More important, they exhibit a transcendent, or global, philosophy of life that accepts the commonalities among all humanity, while at the same time appreciating their differences (Daniel, 1994; Ramirez, 1983).

Functional Integrative Identity. These individuals variously identify with and function in both the black and white communities. Functional integrative/European American orientation individuals feel a greater acceptance from European Americans and are more comfortable in European American sociocultural settings. Functional integrative/African American orientation people feel more accepted by African Americans, are more comfortable in African American sociocultural settings, and are more committed to issues concerning the black community (Daniel, 1994; Ramirez, 1983).

The Pluralistic Identity

Individuals expressing a pluralistic identity blend aspects of both parent reference groups and move fluidly between both. Generally, however, they consider themselves to be neither black nor white but, rather, part of a new primary reference group composed of individuals sharing a blended identity, although they may variously have a European American or an African American orientation (Daniel, 1994; Field, Chapter 13, this volume; Funderburg, 1994; Root, 1990). A pluralistic identity, therefore, is more consistently embraced by multigenerational individuals, due to the fact that they frequently have not experienced both parent backgrounds in either the home or extended family. First-generation offspring, on the other hand, express an identity that operates variously out of both the pluralistic and integrative dynamics.

Synthesized Pluralistic Identity. These individuals reference themselves in both the black and white communities, as well as with other blended individuals, in roughly equal amounts. Although they feel comfortable in European American sociocultural settings, they also maintain a strong commitment to issues concerning blended individuals and African Americans. This is demonstrated by their competent functioning and credibility in the company of people from all three groups and by their ability to shuttle among all three. They display a transcendent, or global, philosophy of life that acknowledges the unity among all human beings yet appreciates their differences (Daniel, 1994; Ramirez, 1983).

Functional Pluralistic Identity. These individuals variously identify with blacks, whites, and other blended individuals. Functional pluralistic/ European American orientation individuals feel more comfortable in the company of other blended individuals and in European American sociocultural settings. They also feel more accepted by European Americans. Functional pluralistic/African American orientation individuals are more comfortable in the company of other blended individuals and in African American sociocultural settings. They also feel more acceptance from African Americans and have a greater commitment to issues concerning the black community (Daniel, 1994).

E PLURIBUS UNUM

These new identity models indicate that increasing numbers of individuals in the 1990s are resisting the rule of hypodescent by "unsevering" ties with their European American background and European Americans. They seek to do this, however, without severing their relationship with the experience of African Americans. Individuals affirm this new blended identity by operating from a *holocentric* point of view that recognizes the commonalities among blacks and whites (integration) but, at the same time, appreciates the differences (pluralism). Their identity not only affirms the complementary and simultaneous nature of pluralistic and integrative dynamics, but also challenges the inegalitarian modalities of both pluralism and integration that turn these differences into inequalities.

By so doing, the new blended identity recaptures elements that made black and white relations in early Anglo America appear to be comparatively more accommodating and reciprocal before the codification of the racial and cultural divide. More important, it points the way toward an egalitarian blending of pluralism and integration in which blacks and whites would be seen as relative, rather than absolute, extremes on a continuum of grays that is reflective of the essence, if not the specificity, of its varied racial and cultural components. In this system of integrative pluralism or pluralistic integration (Higham, 1975), differences thus become the basis upon which to forge a web of interdependent, yet flexibly integrated, racial and cultural pluralities that allow optimal autonomy for their individual constituents (Laszlo, 1987).

Correspondingly, European American identity would no longer be premised on the subordination of blacks (Helms, 1990a). African American identity, in turn, would be based on a pro-black, rather than anti-white, stance (Helms, 1990a). Both European Americans and African Americans would embrace their own whiteness and blackness, thus acknowledging the historical ramifications of these designations— without internalizing respectively any sense of "white guilt" and "black victimization" (Steele, 1990)—and taking collective responsibility for their future socioeconomic and political implications. Taken to its logical conclusion, this dynamic would lead blacks and whites beyond their separate and hostile worlds, by ensuring that wealth, power, privilege, and prestige are more equitably distributed among Anglo America's varied citizenry in the political, socioeconomic, and educational dimensions of society. More important, it would move the United States closer to realizing in the new millennium its image as the land of equal opportunity, an image it has touted during much of the 20th century.

9

On Being and Not-Being
Black and Jewish

NAOMI ZACK

I was born in Brooklyn in 1944. My mother was always a single parent, and she made a living as an artist. My father was African- and Native American. He was a gardener and had a large family whom I never met. I grew up vaguely "Jewish," mostly in Manhattan. I sometimes "looked Puerto Rican," which was evocative in its own way on the streets of New York City. People frequently asked me "what" I was and I did not have an adequate answer. My mother presented herself as the widow of a Jewish jeweler who had been killed fighting in World War II. Although her relationship with my father continued until I was 12, he was not identified to me as my father during my childhood, and I had little interaction with him.

I spent my early teens in Westchester County, where I learned from my peers that I did not look completely white. I found these experiences too shameful to discuss with my mother. When I was 16, I confronted her about my ancestry and she reluctantly divulged the "truth." I, in turn, disclosed this truth only to intimate friends, spouses, and my own children, over the next 30 years.

I have found my real racial identity through writing, during the past 5 years, and it may be the case that a lifetime of troubling experience and denial is the psychological motivation behind much of this work.

My present "position" on race is that it is an idea that now belongs in what Hegel called "the dustbin of history." The chapter below is an attempt to describe discomfort inherent in trying to "be" two conflicting "races," and I offer it as a specific example of the general failure of racial thinking as played out in one instance of mixed race. ⚘

The present impasse in black-Jewish relations will be overcome only when self-critical exchanges take place within and across black and Jewish communities not simply about their own group interest but also, and, more importantly, about what being black or Jewish means in ethical terms.

—Cornel West (1993, p. 109)

When Americans want to know what it means to be a black or a Jew, they often expect a definition of racial or ethnic identity from the standpoint of the person who has it. Because both blacks and Jews have traumatic group histories, the expected self-identification might be, "Being black means that at least one of my ancestors was kidnapped in Africa and brought to this country as a slave," or "Being a Jew means that fifty years ago some of my relatives were murdered in an attempt to exterminate all Jews" (Thomas, 1993). However, the question I want to address here pertains to the *being* part of racial and ethnic identity. Because these two groups are presently antagonistic, I will suggest that if one has both identities, given a choice, it is ethically better to not-be both black and Jewish. In that sense, not-being both identities presupposes that one cannot be either one alone. The resulting distance from one's own racial and ethnic identity opens a space to question the ethical assumptions and implications—which is to say the good faith—of any racial or ethnic identity.

BLACK AND JEWISH IDENTITY AND BEING

All racial identities are flimsy insofar as they rest on presumptions of underlying human biology: There are no general genes for race that can be used to predict the presence of specific racial traits; the specific physical traits that a culture may pick out as racial traits are not present in all members of any so-called race (Dubinin, 1965; Wheeler, 1995; Zack, 1993, 1994b, 1995a). American black identity is particularly problematic, given the absence of scientific support for the ordinary concept of race. There are no "drops of black blood" to support the system of racial designation in the United States, and the "one drop" that is sufficient for black designation reduces to the presence of one "black" ancestor.

But let us put this general problem of black race aside and go along with the social delusion that black people can be racially identified on the basis of some set of biological traits that every individual black person has. A person who has at least one black ancestor and a Jewish mother is considered racially black in the United States. But, on the basis of her Jewish mother, she is considered Jewish, because Jews define a Jew as someone who has a Jewish mother—having a Jewish mother is a sufficient condition for "natural" Jewish identity. Most contemporary American Jews and gentiles designate Jews as racially white. So is the person who is black and Jewish with a Jewish mother white? No, she is black, and in terms of official racial designation, her whiteness is obliterated. If Jewishness necessarily entails whiteness, then that means that her Jewishness is also obliterated. This could be a major problem for someone who is an observant Jew because practicing the Jewish religion imposes obligations that only Jews can fulfill. But this is not yet an internal problem, involving choice and conscience. It has to do with what others might superficially decide about someone, and in religious matters, among serious believers, it is best to be optimistic that if she wished to do so, a Jew who was also black would be "allowed" to participate in observances with other Jews who were not also black. After all, there are American blacks with no hereditary claims to Jewishness who appear to have successfully converted to the Jewish religion (Thomas, in press).

So let us now go back to the simple beginning and consider people who have a black ancestor and a Jewish mother. As far as they know, based on their family experience and history, they are thereby both black and Jewish, or Jewish and black, in terms of racial and/or ethnic identity. Assume that they are adults and can reflect on this identity and make choices about their relationship to it. That is, assume that there is always something about people in the privilege of their own thoughts and feelings that is other than any racial identity. Call that a conscious self. What does it mean for such a self to *be* that black and Jewish identity, or to *be* those black and Jewish identities?

Being something racially and ethnically confers membership in a population that is identified in the same way. (I am assuming that racial identity purports to be about biology and ethnic identity about culture.) This membership entitles one to participate in the population's particular styles of support, nurture, family, and politics. It gives one a claim to distinctive ways of talking, dressing, interacting, eating, and so on, and it gives other members of the population a presumed right to expect a degree of conformity or similarity in social dimensions of ethnicity (Appiah, 1990, 1992; Shrage, 1995). All of these shared ways of behaving add up to the social life of the race or ethnicity at any given time. Many are allowed to be matters of individual choice, to different degrees. For example, one can usually speak and dress differently from one's parents and still be a member in good standing. However, solidarity with other members of the race or ethnicity, including agreement on issues about which there is a broad consensus within the group, is often not negotiable. Members of races and ethnicities that share social lives within communities, especially if they generally perceive themselves to be at a disadvantage to other racial groups, as blacks and Jews do, expect a basic loyalty from all members. Although such loyalty is rarely a public, much less a scholarly, subject in itself, it is presupposed in interactions within the group and even more important, in interactions between the group and nonmembers. The implicit or explicit "group mind" message in the face of outside threat is this: If we belong to the same group, my enemies must be your enemies. If you are disloyal to us, you will still be identified as a black or a Jew, but you cannot really *be* a black or a Jew, because from the standpoint of our group hearts and souls, you will not exist.

The presumption of solidarity among the members of a disadvantaged or despised racial and ethnic group insulates individual members from outside oppression, aversion, and hatred, while they are within the group. But to be black or Jewish, in the best sense of this solidarity, confers security and protection only within the confines of the community to which one belongs. Given outside oppression and a shared history of slavery or genocide, the group life itself is never secure.

Against this insecurity, which is both practical and psychological for blacks and Jews, even the appearance of disloyalty becomes ethically important. People who appear to have strong reasons for being disloyal, even if they have done nothing disloyal as yet, cannot be fully trusted. They cannot be a full member of the group (Piper, 1992; Scales-Trent, 1995).

At this time in American history, there is no established, combined black and Jewish community for someone who has both black and Jewish identity. Therefore people who choose to be both black and Jewish can only do so through membership in each separate community. However, for the past 25 years in the United States, each community has become deeply distrustful of the other (Boyd, 1995). The black community is distrustful of all nonblacks, especially Jews, even though thoughtful exceptions are made in individual cases. The Jewish community is as separate from nonwhite communities as any other white community in the United States, both geographically and in terms of the economic, political, and professional interests that add up to social class. These interests of class unite Jews even if they are religiously unobservant; but unobservant Jews who are also black cannot assume to have the same solidarity extended to them by other Jews. Part of being Jewish in the United States in the 20th century allows for disclaiming one's Jewish-ness and "assimilating." Still, one has to be able to be a Jew "in good standing" for this non-Jewish Jewishness not to fracture one's being a Jew, and nonwhiteness added to nonobservance strains the presumption of Jewishness (Zack, 1992, 1994a).

Readers may think that the foregoing generalizations are too broad and pessimistic, and they may want to emphasize the exceptions. They may know black and Jewish people who are fully rooted in Jewish life or in black life and accepted without prejudice by their groups. But do they know anyone who is black and Jewish and fully accepted in either community with complete recognition and regard for the racial and ethnic identity that is not shared by the accepting community? Do they know any black and Jewish people who are fully accepted by black groups who recognize and value their Jewishness, and who are *also fully accepted by Jewish groups who recognize and value their blackness?* I am mildly skeptical about a positive answer to the first question and strongly skeptical about a positive answer to the second one at this time. The reasons lie in the nature of the antagonism between the two groups.

BLACK AND JEWISH
ANTAGONISM AND BEING

The antagonism between American blacks and Jews undermines the being of both groups. Attacks and counterattacks not only exploit each group's disadvantages as a minority but demonstrate a deliberate willingness to do so. As a result, intergroup trust has been seriously damaged. Here are some of the commonly acknowledged facts and issues around which this antagonism swirls.

From about the turn of the 20th century until the early 1970s, American Jews were generally important allies of American blacks (Hershel, 1992; King, 1992). Jews were personally sympathetic to the plight of American blacks; they supported their political efforts to gain civil rights and were philanthropically generous to programs for black education and social welfare. This Jewish liberalism culminated in the high percentage of Jewish freedom riders during the civil rights movement, as well as funding from Jewish organizations for social justice projects that benefitted blacks during the 1950s and 1960s (Berman, 1994; Carson, 1992).

The friendly alliance chilled and became twisted into strands that cannot now be unraveled without getting snagged by the racism on both sides. During the late 1960s, some black leaders began to advocate violent revolutionary action against all whites, including Jews. Afrocentric spokespersons, in identifying African Americans with nonwhite inhabitants of the Third World, began to denounce Israel's actions against the Palestinians as racist. The response was a decrease in organized Jewish interest in the problems of black Americans. Moderate to radical blacks in turn accused American Jews of racism and found narrow self-interest behind their previous assistance. Black extremist ideologues began to resurrect old European and Nazi myths and stereotypes of Jewish financial exploitation and international conspiracy. Meanwhile, throughout the 1970s and 1980s, American Jewish neoconservatives supported tougher anticrime policies and attacked affirmative action and social welfare programs with predominantly black client bases (Berman, 1994; West, 1993).

In the shadows of this antagonism lies the threat of violence against both blacks and Jews by neo-Nazi groups and the Ku Klux Klan, as well as diffuse and unpredictably combustible anti-Semitism and racism against blacks throughout the majority population of white Americans. The agents of this potential danger were previously acknowledged by both groups to be common enemies to blacks and Jews. The high media visibility of black-Jewish conflict constitutes, on the part of both groups, a covert and highly treacherous appeal to those still common enemies. Blacks know that the worst form of violent oppression and degradation that the black population has suffered in America was not dealt by Jews, but by white Christians. And Jews know that black anti-Semitism is only a widespread danger if it ignites the latent anti-Semitism among non-Jewish Americans.

So in fighting with each other in public, blacks and Jews are in effect addressing an audience that each side may hope is the real enemy of the other side alone but that is almost certainly the enemy of both sides. There is no way to inspire or ignite third-party punishment for the other side without also bringing it down on one's own side. To win is to lose.

A further dimension of the nastiness in black-Jewish antagonism is the opening of old wounds. When blacks accuse Jews of economic exploitation of the poor and international conspiracy to further their interests, Nazi propaganda reverberates. The Third Reich's attempt at genocide was the culmination of centuries of European anti-Semitism, which began with the "blood libel" of Crusaders who blamed Jews for the death of Christ. This religious anti-Semitism resulted in the expulsion of Jews from every major Western European nation by the early modern period; when and where they were permitted to remain, they were subject to pogroms in Eastern Europe, and their citizenship rights were severely curtailed throughout the Western world (West, 1993). An important part of Jewish being since World War II has been a sense of fulfillment about the existence of a homeland in Israel, for the first time in postbiblical history. But along with this satisfaction comes fear for the survival of Israel and fear lest the Holocaust be repeated. There is a deeply felt Jewish need to remember and reflect upon the Holocaust (Lang, 1990). Because Israel came into existence as a long overdue antidote to anti-Semitism and racism against Jews, Jews hear accusations of Israeli or Zionist racism as shocking insults.

American blacks have a history of oppression that includes kidnapping, slavery, murder, mutilation, rape, segregation, and systematic denial of opportunities to rectify the poverty and diminished status that are the legacy of that history. American blacks deeply feel that American whites generally dislike them and are not strongly committed to improving their disadvantages. For blacks, the worst harm of slavery is in the past. However, the awareness that a disproportionate number of blacks are in the criminal justice system and live in poverty makes Jewish neoconservatism sound racist insofar as it ignores the ongoing cultural disadvantages of blacks that are believed to cause incarceration and poverty. When Jewish neoconservatives attack affirmative action policies without proposals for alternative ways to correct for racial discrimination in American institutions, hopes for black betterment through public policy are undermined. This disappointment is made more bitter by the memory that earlier placement of black hopes in the public domain was based on advice from Jewish supporters, and the knowledge that recent economic gains within the black middle class have largely been due to increased black employment in the public sector (Boyd, 1993).

Finally, the matter of race itself, in the biologically false meaning of the term, adds an ultimately corrosive element to black-Jewish antagonism. During the European Jewish persecution, especially under the Third Reich, and throughout much of American history, Jews were considered to be a distinct race in comparison to Northern Europeans (Gordon, 1995, p. 2; Harrowitz & Hyams, 1995). French, Italian, Irish, Spanish, and Polish Americans were also considered to be distinct races in American social science until the 1920s and 1930s (Wacker, 1983). The nonwhite status of these other groups dissolved by the time of World War II, and the racial distinctivenes of Jews has considerably loosened since then. All of the European and also nonblack and non-Asian groups are now considered to be white within their own ethnic groups and in mainstream white American culture. In traditional as well as extremist black culture and in white supremacist culture, however, the requirements for white racial membership still restrict whiteness to Northern Europeans who phenotypically appear to belong to that group and who have no (traceable) nonwhite ancestors (Gwaltney, 1980, pp. 73-91, 206-219; Pleasant & Hardy, 1990, p. 43). This means that as a matter of seemingly factual belief, as well as convoluted racism—convoluted because it supports white racial purity, as defined by white supremacists (Ridgeway, 1990, pp. 13-17, 27)—many blacks do not consider Jews to be white. They think that Jews are passing and thereby exhibiting disloyalty to all other people who are officially designated nonwhite in a racist society (Pleasant & Hardy, 1990). From a Jewish standpoint, the experience of the Holocaust has made any mention of race in conjunction with Jewishness highly charged, to say the least.

From a black standpoint, the acceptance by some Jews of scholarly research that attempts to link low scores on intelligence tests with black racial membership reads as a particularly vicious form of racism (Gould, 1994). Jews are perceived to have disproportionately high representation in those occupations where high scores on intelligence tests are presumed to be an asset, and the periodic refusal of Jews to recognize what most blacks accept as the cultural bias of all IQ tests is read by blacks as yet another example of Jewish willingness to further their own group interests while refusing to concede their unfairness to blacks.

NOT BEING BOTH BLACK AND JEWISH

Because of what they have suffered, continue to suffer, and are afraid of suffering in the future, both blacks and Jews ought to know better than to engage in the kind of antagonism just described. That each group knows that members of the other group should know better only deepens the antagonism. For people who have both a black and a Jewish identity, the desirability of affiliation with both groups weakens in direct proportion to the amount of loyalty that is demanded as a condition of membership. On ethical grounds, people who think, feel, and have the ability to choose to be both black and Jewish hold back. They accept their dual racial and ethnic identity as a matter of social fact but cannot fully *be* it. Neither can they choose one side to the exclusion of the other because they will never be "black enough" to suit many blacks about their black membership, or sufficiently "real" Jews for Jews fully to accept them as a Jews. They could lie about the suppressed side and denounce it to the group of their affiliation, but that is unethical from the outset and psychologically unhealthy because they would then conceal and denounce something about themselves.

Holding back creates a space in which the good faith behind even the positive aspect of being something racially and ethically can be interrogated. Why should the presence of slave ancestors or persecuted ancestors serve as a foundation for present affiliation? Can one attach oneself to the past in such a way that the past automatically programs one for meaningful life in the present? Jean-Paul Sartre (1965) pointed out the absurdity of all such attempts in his analysis of the French anti-Semite, for example:

> The true Frenchman, rooted in his province, in his country, borne along by a tradition twenty centuries old, benefitting from ancestral wisdom, guided by tried custom, does not *need* intelligence. His virtue depends on the assimilation of the qualities which the work of a hundred generations has lent to the objects which surround him.
>   . . . [T]he anti-Semite flees responsibility as he flees his own consciousness, and choosing for his personality the permanence of rock, he chooses for his morality a scale of petrified values. (pp. 19-20, 23)

Sartre's philosophical point is that defining oneself in terms of one's ancestors is an evasion of responsibility based on the fantasy that one *is* one's ancestors. The descendant first chooses to act in accordance with values that he or she imagines were present in the past and then uses his or her own time and energy to do deeds and live a life in the present. The agent's present agency or ability to act is a reality that cannot be evaded without destroying the foundation of ethical action, which is responsibility. And the present ability to act is overlooked by the person who identifies with a character from the past. Personal responsibility begins in the present life of each individual.

However, the suffering of ancestors can cause present grief and anxiety, as it does for Jews who think about the Holocaust, or it can have a real legacy in present oppression, as does slavery for contemporary blacks. These painful inheritances seem to mitigate present responsibility because one did not choose the evils and suffering that befell one's ancestors and that seem to live on in one's own situation. But one can choose how to react to these tragic inheritances. Good faith requires that people who have to act in the present draw a line between the sphere of constraint that is a consequence of the past and the sphere of freedom that is where their own agency begins in the present; good faith requires that people recognize their own freedom, even if it is limited by social circumstances.

Suppose one picks out only the "positive" aspects of racial and ethnic black and Jewish identity, as a basis for affiliation. That would seem to be a rational option toward individual happiness and self-fulfillment. But is it right to accept the good without taking on the bad as well? Can people who have another racial identity be black or Jewish without having to deliberately "prove" each identity in ways that undermine their own sincerity, that is, *authenticity*? For example: If black Jews have to be deliberately "observant" in order to reassure other Jews that they are Jewish, isn't their piety made false? And if Jewish blacks have to "play down" a nonblack physical appearance in order to reassure other blacks that they are as black as anyone else, isn't their black appearance partly a costume that trivializes their black identity?

Let's return to the mode of holding back. When people who share their identity know or learn the identity of black Jews and extend invitations, does their private position of "holding back" mean they must always decline? It should not, if contact points for racial and ethnic identity are necessary for psychological well-being, which they seem to be in American life. The degree and nature of necessity would have to be an individual matter, to be determined by those who are holding back. Given their racial ambiguity, and the lack of an empirical foundation for all racial categories, they have a right to choose their racial affiliation, because it is in principle no different from any other form of group affiliation (Zack, 1995b). People who hold back from the antagonism between blacks and Jews will probably not be highly welcomed recruits or secure members of either group because it will be impossible to draw them into the bitter agendas. They may be accused of being antisocial, reserved, standoffish, hard to get, and so on. But there cannot easily be grounds for accusations of treachery. Their disloyalty will be out in the open simply because they "know better" and let it be known that they think others should know better, too. *That is the ethical part of holding back.*

Psychological well-being would also prevent mixed black and Jewish people from participating in intergroup antagonism. Because Americans habitually divide the human world into racial categories, racial difference is often more fascinating then racial similarity. As a result of this fascination, black and Jewish people may feel more "Jewish" among blacks than they do among Jews; and they may feel more "black" among Jews than among blacks. They therefore cannot be antagonistic to the other side without harming themselves, even though blacks may falsely imagine that black Jews are even more Jewish when with Jews than when with them, and Jews may make analogous false appraisals of their black being. Thus, although the existential limbo of not-being both black and Jewish, for someone who has both identities, may evoke emptiness and isolation at times and not be enthusiastically received by blacks or Jews, it does no harm to them or to the mixed person.

10

An "Other" Way of Life

The Empowerment of Alterity
in the Interracial Individual

JAN R. WEISMAN

The walls of my childhood home were covered with big sheets of cream-colored butcher paper, which were covered with my crayon drawings. One particular memory associated with my childhood artistic endeavors stands out—the memory of my mother continually telling me, "Don't color the faces."

My mother, a self-identified black woman, was trying to teach me not to view people as a color. With a child's reasoning, however, I took her literally. I drew page after page of people. All kinds of people, in all colors. Except for their faces. Their bodies were all shades of brown, tan, pink, and "flesh-tone," but, following my mother's directive, I left their faces the color of butcher paper.

Even as a child, I knew that people came in all different colors and other varied physical characteristics. I knew that these differences were popularly supposed to define "races." I knew what those races were, and that I didn't fit into any of them. One day, I learned the word *mulatto* at school. It was a revelation—a word that meant *me*! I eagerly shared this new knowledge with my mother that evening. "You're not a mulatto," she said, "You're a Negro." But that didn't seem quite right when she continually told me stories of my Jewish heritage, and when other Negroes stoned, spit on, and shot at me as they told me to "get out" of the all-Negro neighborhood where I had lived all my life. I knew that I wasn't white. I never had any desire to be white. I knew that whites would probably view me as a Negro. But trying to be a Negro among Negroes was a constant struggle.

I learned about South Africa, apartheid, and "Coloureds" in school. "Terrible system," I thought, "but at least they have a name for me." I knew very well what I was. What was the problem with other people, that they couldn't also accept the truth?

I joined the Peace Corps and went to Thailand, where the language had a word for me. *Loog kreung.* I could tell people that's what I was, and they would accept it. I didn't have to explain or argue. No one told me (as many Americans had) that there was "no such thing" as what I was. There were thousands of my people—Amerasians, born to Thai women and American soldiers—all over the country. I "adopted" one as a foster daughter through the Pearl S. Buck Foundation.

I moved to Berkeley, California, where I found many more of my people. I discovered that there was an actual class about my people taught at the University of California, Berkeley. Although not a student, I started attending meetings of the UC, Berkeley, interracial students' group, Miscellaneous (Multi-ethnic Interracial Students Coalition). I discovered that a local community organization of interracial people and families had been active for a decade. I joined that organization—Interracial, Intercultural Pride (I-Pride), and served on its board of directors. I came out as a mixed-race woman, defining myself and my community in my own terms. It is to others who have similarly declared themselves to be "other than 'other' " that this chapter is dedicated. &

WHAT'S IN A NAME?

Helms (1990a) noted that the American Civil Rights Movement opened the opportunity for racial minority groups to declare the names by which they wished to be known. No longer accepting the appellations Colored or Negro, Americans previously so identified proclaimed themselves black. Other groups also announced autonyms that differed from the terms previously applied to them by outsiders—for example, Oriental became Asian; American Indian became Native American. Surrounding these new labels were feelings of group pride, solidarity, and empowerment. As Wetherell and Potter (1992) noted, the discourse of race does not simply reflect racial ideology; rather, the very construction—or deconstruction—of race can be affected and effected through the use of language. Whether on an individual or a group level, speaking one's name is an act of self-validation; choosing that name even more so.

Many Americans of mixed racial descent are currently engaged in this process of self-validation. In refusing to accept the labels traditionally applied to them, many of these individuals are also refusing to accept marginality as a defining feature of their life experiences. In naming themselves, they are defining a place where they belong— where they are at the center rather than on the periphery. They still recognize that they are *other*, but their *other*ness is claimed rather than assigned, positive rather than negative.

In anthropology and other social sciences, the condition of being *other* is known as *alterity* (see Martin, 1990, and Taussig, 1993, for discussions of models of alterity in other contexts). In this chapter, I will draw on various constructions and theories of alterity in order to contrast the positive alterity available to interracial individuals with earlier ideas of alterity as marginalizing, negative, and/or psychopathological. This construct of interracial identity will be placed within a framework of "positive alterities" of various types. Finally, I will examine the possible impact of identities constructed around positive alterities on the development of non-race-based identities in the United States.

THE BIRTH AND
ENUMERATION OF *OTHERS*

Births to parents of differing races currently represent approximately 3% of all births in the United States (Barringer, 1989), and the incidence of mixed-race babies has increased at 26 times the rate of any other group (Smolowe, 1993). However, as has been noted by Nakashima (1992), Davis (1991), and others, people of mixed-race descent officially do not exist in the United States. According to census and other official forms that follow the 1977 Statistical Directive 15, issued by the U.S. Office of Management and Budget (OMB), the races of the United States are black; white; American Indian, Eskimo, or Aleut; and Asian or Pacific Islander, with "Hispanic origin" added as a second-layer ethnic category (text in Appendix 1).

A significant number of Americans, however, do not find themselves reflected in these official racial categories and are working for the legitimization of alternative identities. Since 1970, the number of people indicating a racial/ethnic identification of *other* on the U.S. decennial census form has increased more than five-fold (Rajs, 1991, p. 8; U.S. Bureau of the Census, 1970, Table 190; 1990, Table 3). Fernández (1992a) noted that *other* is the fastest-growing response to the racial/ethnic identification question among Californians, and he expressed the opinion that many of these respondents are people of mixed racial background, frustrated by the traditional "check one box only" directive.

Research has demonstrated that a large number of multiracial individuals in the United States do in fact feel constricted by the American practice of limiting legitimate racial identification to one—and only one—box. Hall (1980) noted that, when presented with an open-ended query rather than the usual boxes, Americans of mixed black Japanese ancestry chose an identification that reflected both of their heritages. These results have been duplicated in later studies of interracial Americans (e.g., Kich, 1982; Mar, 1988; Thornton, 1983; Wilson, 1985).

THE MARGINS AND
THE PATH TO THE CENTER

Many racially mixed individuals are now declaring themselves *other* than one of society's traditional boxes, even where that option is still not officially available to them. They check more than one box, refuse to choose, and declare "write-in identities." Recent scholarship, much of it by individuals of mixed racial heritage or otherwise belonging to an interracial family, has also helped to legitimate the option of choosing an *other* identity. Daniel (1988) stated that

today's comparatively more fluid intergroup relations and more icono-
clastic attitudes toward racial identity, fruits of the civil rights movement,
seem themselves to be reflective of even more fundamental epistemologi-
cal shifts that are seeking to move our society away from the "either/or"
paradigm of binary thinking, which clearly delineates things into mutually exclusive categories, to one that incorporates concepts of "partly,"
"mostly," or "both/and." (p. 333)

According to the "marginal man" theory first posited by Park (1928)
and further developed by Stonequist (1937), racially mixed individuals
experience marginalization as the result of being prevented from making their racial reference group their membership group. Racially mixed
people were typically seen as rejecting one parent group while remaining unsuccessful in their attempts to secure acceptance into the other
parent group. It was assumed, of course, that the group rejected would
be the one less valued by society, whereas the group whose acceptance
was craved by the marginal individual would be the one more valued
—often white. In a line of reasoning that has become ingrained in the
American mind-set, it was held that until mixed-race people gave up
the quest for whiteness and accepted the racial status imposed by a
racist society, they were doomed to a tragic life of *other*ness.

Although the adoption (with the emphasis on conscious choice rather
than ascription) of society's racial identification is still seen as a viable
path toward the resolution of *other* status (Root, 1990), racially mixed
people who consciously adopts an *other* identity actually become *other
than other.* They are no longer *other* by virtue of partially or not belonging, but by virtue of *completely* belonging to a group that is different
from all, yet overlaps with many other existing groups. (For a more
in-depth discussion of models of overlapping identities, see Mennell,
1995). No longer is the racially mixed person's existence relegated to the
margins (and even associated with other species, as can be found in the
title of a chapter in Seligman (1939): "Fruit Flies, Rabbits, Dogs, Sala-
manders, and Hybrid Groups of Men in Many Parts of the World").
Rather, their identity is positioned squarely within a framework of
positive alterity.

Stuart and Abt (1973, p. 165), writing about interracial marriage and
multiracial individuals, hold that identity maintenance is not possible
in the absence of a reference group. A self-proclaimed position of alterity
provides many racially mixed individuals with such a reference group
in which to ground their identity. Many researchers have noted that the

adoption of a "mixed race" reference group is indicative of the healthy internalization of a mixed-race identity (see, for example, Kich, 1982). Many mixed individuals, in claiming a mixed identity (in any of its semantic variations, e.g., mixed, multiracial, mulatto, Eurasian, etc.), express a feeling of solidarity with other mixed people—of whatever mixture as defined in whatever local environment—all over the world, thus establishing a reference group and community that transcends traditional boundaries. Other mixed individuals choose other identities based on nonracial factors, such as occupation, avocation, or resistance to labeling.

In noting some of the issues surrounding objection to the creation of a multiracial census category, Thornton (1992) called into question whether multiracial Americans in fact constitute, or *can* constitute, a "community." Noting the potential diversity of such a putative community, Thornton stated:

> There is little evidence indicating other than some superficial basis for commonality between groups of different racial mixture . . . [W]hat seems to bind multiracial people is not race or culture, but living with an ambiguous status, an experience similar to that of all people of color. Facing a different set of dilemmas does not make one an ethnic or racial group. . . . While there is experiential rationale for identifying a unique experience, that alone is not reason enough, and does not provide a consistent basis, to describe multiracials as one sort of people. (pp. 324-325)

Searle (1994), in her review of Anzaldúa (1987), likewise questioned Anzaldúa's positing of "Chicano Spanish" as a basis for her "outside the boxes" ethnic identity, asking, "Is this a legitimate 'culture' and 'language'?" Thus the question is raised, is the existence of a community a necessary precursor for the existence of an identity? Or, to phrase the question another way, in seeking a reference group in which one will be recognized, how important is it that one's reference group be recognized by society as a legitimate community?

THE NEW CENTER

I hold that recognition of one's reference group by society in general is not as important as recognition of that group by those who seek to belong to it. Primordial identities—identities based on elements considered to be "in the blood" and/or unchangeable, such as race, ethnicity, or one's place of birth—were long considered by social scientists to be the only viable identity choices. Many Americans, especially outside of academic circles, would still hold to such assumptions. However, I maintain that it is possible to hold a viable identity that is not only *not* primordially based but is not based on any previously recognized community. I further maintain that the continued adherence to such an identity by a steady or increasing number of individuals can in fact lead to the societal recognition of such new forms of identification.

Several theorists suggest that not only is this possible, but it in fact occurs. Leonard (1992) noted that, in the early 1900s, Americans of mixed Punjabi-Mexican descent identified with neither of the foreign communities in which their parents originated, but with a community invented for themselves in rural northern California. Appadurai (1993) noted that a "search for nonterritorial principles of solidarity"—that is, identities not based upon a geographically locatable community—is taking place in the world today (p. 417). And Kotkin and Van Agt (1991) posit a model of transnational identity centered on capitalist economic endeavor, in which one's identity is based not on any primordial criteria, but on "mastery of the cultural, technological, and scientific imperatives of [the] times." (p. 46)

In seeking an *other* reference group, many interracial individuals are seeking to resist, challenge, and/or transcend society's notions of the legitimacy of personal identity and community. The fact that the group they have chosen is neither recognized by society nor geographically locatable therefore does not matter to them. In fact, such lack of recognition by those not in the group may serve to heighten the sense of positive alterity that interracial individuals experience by such identification. They have created and named the group, and they can locate it (and their place within it) when others cannot. Having access to a community to which others fail to see the entrance can be an exciting and liberating experience for interracial people, who for so long have been excluded from more traditional groups, or tried to keep one foot inside the door of a group to which they could not fully belong.

Gupta and Ferguson (1992) noted a trend away from viewing hybridity, and the position of being betwixt-and-between that arises therefrom, as marginal and negative. They held that such a position, not confined to society's usual definitions, actually represents "a more adequate conceptualization of the 'normal' locale of the postmodern subject" (p. 18). One result of these changes in attitude has been that being "mixed" is—in stark contrast with earlier, disparaging portrayals—now often exalted as being the embodiment of the multiculturalist or postmodern ideal. Motoyoshi (1990) wrote that, "Mixed-race persons serve not only as models, but as prototypes. They are quite possibly our first glimpse of a new race" (pp. 88-89). This sentiment is mirrored in the popular press. Njeri (1991) predicted that the emergence of the mixed-race community may be the most important social phenomenon at the turn of the century.

Some popular media have already proclaimed the arrival on the scene of this new group of people. Many Americans saw and read a special Fall 1993 issue of *Time* magazine, which featured on its cover a computer-generated image of a multiracial woman with the headline "The New Face of America." A letter from the managing editor explained that the hypothetical woman's background included Anglo-Saxon, Middle Eastern, African, Asian, Southern European, and Hispanic ethnicities. The letter likened the woman to a modern-day Eve and proclaimed that several magazine staff members became infatuated with the image the moment it appeared on their computer screen. (Such exoticization and romanticization of mixedness is not limited to the present day but has been taking place at least since the heyday of European colonialism and American frontierism. For discussions of the exoticization of interracial individuals in literature, see Bentley, 1993; Berzon, 1978; Herzog, 1983; Scheick, 1979; Warmbold, 1992.)

THE CENTER AND
THE PATH TO THE MARGINS

The legitimation of multiracial identity as expressed in both the scholarly and the popular press has also lead to challenges to traditional racial identification among non-mixed-race people. In 1991, a group of Caucasian Americans in San Jose, California, organized for the recognition of their own multiethnic heritages. In a letter to the editor that appeared the August 1992 issue of the *I-Pride Newsletter*, a representative of the group—the European American Studies Group—expressed solidarity with I-Pride's efforts to change traditional racial and ethnic descriptors:

> With regard to the U.S. census reform, please be advised that we will support
> any innovations you may propose if you will support our campaign to allow
> for us European Americans to express our richly textured cultural and
> ethnic diversity more easily.... Our members are fully multicultural and we
> are tired of being colorized ("white"), tribalized ("anglo"), and racialized
> ("caucasian") in wholly inappropriate ways. (Warner, 1992, p. 2)

This show of support by the European American Study Group is not welcomed by all mixed-race individuals, however. Some react strongly to what they perceive as the appropriation of mixed identity by individuals recognized by society as monoracial. Perhaps because mixed-race individuals are only now beginning to realize the liberation of identifying as *other* than the prescribed boxes, many are anxious to guard their newly embraced identities. In doing so, they may apply the same hurtful and exclusionary tactics that have been used to keep racially mixed people at the margins.

At an October 1992 conference sponsored by the organization Multi-Racial Americans of Southern California (MASC), a debate arose among participants in one session regarding exactly who "qualified" as mixed. Continuing after the session concluded, the debate focused on a Caucasian-appearing participant who, in session, had argued for her right to claim a multiracial identity based on black ancestry some generations back. Some also noted the fact that the session leader himself was not first-generation mixed and had not been "raised mixed," but had decided in adulthood to claim this identity.

Contributing to the debate, still other session participants—representatives of various colleges and universities—stated that their institutions had noted an increase in the number of students claiming multiracial identities, creating difficulties in determining to what extent such claims were genuine versus spurious attempts to gain affirmative action benefits. It was noted that the University of Arizona, for example, faced a particular problem with heretofore Caucasian applicants claiming Native American identification on the basis of a recently discovered ancestor. The university has had to devise a "test" (including an interview to judge the applicant's or student's degree of tribal knowledge) to determine the validity of such claims.

An example from my own experience will serve to further illustrate the difficulties in defining the varieties of perceived "mixedness" and one's right to claim such an identity. Due to bureaucratic mix-ups, I was surveyed a total of seven times for the 1990 U.S. Census—twice by mail, twice by a door-to-door enumerator, and thrice by a telephone enumerator. Asked for racial/ethnic identification, my response was always "Other." Asked for elucidation, I responded each time, "mixed." Responses from enumerators ranged from "mixed what?" to silent perplexity to "Is that part of the Asian/Pacific Islander group?" My response was even met with an enthusiastic, "I'm mixed, too—German and Irish!"

NEW POSITIONS, NEW PATHS

What, if anything, does this apparent trend—among both monoracial and multiracial peoples—toward identifying outside the traditionally prescribed racial categories imply as far as the development of a model of non-race-based identity in the United States? Is the identity multiracial a step in that direction, or a step toward the entrenchment of those racial categories that already exist?

Many parents of multiracial children do in fact endeavor to impart to their children the ideal of a non-race-based identity. Although discouraged by many scholars of multiracial identity development who stress that, given the salience of race and the realities of racism in American society, multiracial children need a racial (e.g., biracial) label, many parents teach their multiracial children that race doesn't matter, that everyone is the same under the skin, and that they are not a race but are "just human beings." For such parents, secure in their adult identities and ideals, memories of childhood and adolescent identity struggles and the need to belong are often faint and blurred. These parents consciously work at encouraging their children to consider themselves citizens of the world, not bound by the artificial group boundaries of any society. Their children often cannot appreciate the ideals they are trying to impart until they are adults themselves. Nevertheless, multiracial individuals who have been raised with these ideals (and some who have not, but have come into them on their own) often do come to identify with communities beyond the traditional racial group or even the nation-state.

Some have posited that the increased numbers and sources of immigration into the United States—combined with the current emphasis on multiculturalism versus assimilation—will have more of an impact on American thinking about race and levels of identity than has any earlier discourse on this topic. The United States now includes a number of residents and citizens who, because of the particular ethnic and racial dynamics of the place in which they were raised, are uncomfortable with the identities imposed on them by the American system. This fact is sometimes raised in support of the hypothesis that notions of group affiliation and identification in the United States are changing, or in support of the suggestion that such notions *must* change. Others, however, noting the entrenchment of current American racial attitudes, are skeptical of the possibility of change. Davis (1991), in discussing American acceptance of the principles of hypodescent and the "one-drop rule," particularly as applied to individuals of African American ancestry, stated that

> none of the world's known alternatives to the American definition of who is black now seems at all likely to be given serious consideration in the United States. . . . It seems unlikely that the one-drop rule will be modified in the foreseeable future. (pp. 184-186)

(As noted elsewhere herein, however, the rule was in fact already being challenged at the time of his writing and is showing signs of changing.)

It may be surmised, then, that multiracial identity is seen not as transcending race-based identification, but as accepting of the concept of race and the need to be "raced." There are those, however, who endeavor to transcend the very notion of race in their self-labeling. What impact does a rejection of even multiracial identity have on the level of salience of racial identity, or the ideal of non-race-based identification, in American society?

Gupta and Ferguson (1992, p. 18) have noted that both the subjective experience and the objective perception of being mixed tend to call into question societal and nationalist notions of purity, homogeneity, and integration. However, if one is looking to multiracial people as the harbingers of some coming utopia of non-race-based identification, one is likely to be disappointed. If for no other reason than the small number of such individuals, their impact on the status quo is likely to be limited. Although a multiracial identity choice might (indeed, has already begun to) achieve legitimacy, complete devaluation of the concept of race is not likely to take place in the absence of promotion by the country's majority group. The aforementioned European American Studies Group is not yet well-known outside of its local area; in any event, its official agenda of promoting the option to identify with the various countries of origin of one's ancestors rather than with any reified racial designation still legitimates rather than challenges the idea of identification through recognized communities.

The challenges posed to the traditional American way of racial identification by those of multiracial heritage, and the alternative, "unboxed" identities that have increasingly been adopted by those who do not find themselves represented under the traditional racial categories, may cause some of those who had previously not examined society's beliefs and practices regarding race to begin to question some of their assumptions regarding the reification and delimitation of race and races. However, the effect has not yet been such as would undermine the basic American tendency toward racialization. In some ways, the alternative identities called for by multiracial advocates reinforce the racial status quo by demanding a legitimate place within the model. An analogy may be seen in Appadurai (1993), who stated that "Even as the legitimacy of nation-states in their own territorial contexts is increasingly under threat, the *idea* of the nation flourishes" (author's emphasis) (p. 424).

Appadurai (1993) further cautioned that, given the constant flow of people to, from, and around their original homelands in today's world, the United States must address the issue of how "to construct a society *around* diasporic diversity" (p. 425), keeping in mind that members of such diasporas might choose to place their transnational identification foremost, while retaining the option of dual citizenship. This admonition could also be applied on the level of racial identification as it concerns multiracial people—after all, if not for diasporas and other migrations, multiracial people would likely not exist in such numbers as they do today.

And in the same way that Appadurai (1993) said "no existing conception of Americanness can contain this large variety of transnations" (p. 424), it could also be said that no existing conception of race is able to encompass the new discourse being opened by Americans of more than one racial heritage. Many are confused or threatened by the choices of identity being made by those of multiracial background, as well as the demands for the legitimization of such choices. An understanding of the fact that loyalty to one parent group does not necessarily preclude similar loyalty to the other, even when, as might happen, one's primary loyalty is to a third group, would help alleviate the unease currently faced by many of those who were brought up in an easy acceptance of the idea of (mono-) nation-based and (mono-) race-based identities.

THE END OF THE PATH

As one matures and one's horizons widen, it becomes evident that there are many more systems of human classification than exist in our own society. A person considered "black" in the United States might, upon trying to claim that identity in Africa or Latin America, be advised that he or she is actually something other than black. In Asia, an American-recognized black person with no Asian ancestry might find no socially acceptable "box" applicable to him. Rather, after going through all the choices presented, he or she might find himself having to check some generic *other* category. A white person who in his or her own society does not claim a hyphenated (e.g., tied to ancestral origins in a different place) identity might, in parts of Europe or other locations, find that he or she is not allowed to be simply white but must be something other than that.

The social nature of the race concept ensures that we all will be *other* somewhere, if only we travel far enough. Racially mixed Americans may legitimately insist that, at least in our own society, our existence be recognized to the same extent as other groups. We may chafe that they are able to see themselves named whereas our name never appears and we are relegated to a catch-all category for other such unrecognized souls. However, we must keep in mind that those whose names appear in our records may be anonymous in some other place, that we are not the only peoples unrecognized by our own society, that even peoples officially recognized do not always recognize themselves according to official designations, and that *other*ness is not necessarily a negative condition. By refusing to be *other*-ized and instead declaring ourselves *other than other*, we claim our rights and privileges as members of a community of our own definition.

PART III

Blending
and Flexibility

LatiNegra
Mental Health Issues
of African Latinas[1]

LILLIAN COMAS-DÍAZ

"Soon you will find out why we call you *moyeta*," Mami told me in preparation for our trip to Mayaguez to visit my father's family. After years of living in Chicago, interrupted by numerous moves between the continent and the island, my family decided to reside permanently in Puerto Rico. The trip from Yabucoa to Mayaguez (two towns on opposite sides of the island) seemed to symbolize my parents' struggle about their differences. Living in Yabucoa, my maternal extended family was a support system that embraced me during my conflict with belonging. Abuela, Abuelo, Titi Paulina, Elba, Alberto, Didi, Birla, Naydy, were all magical names in my childhood. There were no names associated with my paternal extended family, except for *negrita*, *prieta*, *grifa*, *jabá*, and *moyeta*—words filled with ambivalence and contradiction.

AUTHOR'S NOTE: The author would like to thank Rhea Almeida for her insightful editorial suggestions; Janice Petrovich, Angela Ginorio, Sandra Laureano, and Mercedes del Valle Rana for their contributions; and María Providencia Scott for her inspirational influence.

167

The profound physical differences between my brother and I could be best described by his winning the Carnation Baby Award in Chicago, an award given to the baby who epitomizes health and (white) beauty. My brother won this award at a time when political correctness was present only in *espiritistas* seances. Although my "you don't look like my sibling" brother used to tease me by calling me *moyeta,* I secretly liked the *mal nombre* (bad name). I learned that *moyeta* meant being black and ugly, but it also meant "we love you anyway."

Our odyssey to Mayaguez was punctuated by the fact that as an only child of divorced parents, Papi had never been close to his family. In fact, we only saw his mother sporadically because she was busy in New York earning a living as a successful "Spanish psychic." His father, *el inteligente* (the intelligent one) was a respected professor; he had remarried and was eager to meet us. When we arrived at Grandpa's house, my 6-year-old brother ran out of the car yelling: "Abuelo, abuelito, where are you?" Running closely behind I followed. When Abuelo emerged, my brother screamed "Watusi!" and hid behind me. In front of me stood a 6 foot 2 inch black man with white kinky hair, who looked like an African warrior king. His penetrating stare was filled with tears.

During our trip back to Yabucoa, Papi complained of not feeling well and blamed the fish he ate at Abuelo's house for his illness. "Fili, why are you the only one sick if we all ate that fish?" asked Mami. My brother kept asking: "How can I be so white if Abuelo is so black?" As for me, I secretly smiled, realizing that *moyeta* meant belonging to and bridging between two disparate sets of families. &

YOU DON'T LOOK LATINA!

This assertion is a continual reminder to the LatiNegra that a significant portion of her culture and ethnicity is forcefully denied. The LatiNegra is the African Latina who is perceived beyond any doubt as black by both the North American and the Latino communities. The LatiNegra is the daughter of African American (Caribbean, North, Central, and South American) and Latino parents. Although there are some differences between the African North American LatiNegra and the African Caribbean LatiNegra, the racial exclusions faced by both LatiNegras embrace many commonalities. For instance, the denial of LatiNegras' Latinness is equally emphasized by all communities. Consequently, the LatiNegra constitutes a classic example of racial exclusion, marginality, and disconnection. Frequently, her combination of race, ethnicity, and gender result in her being a minority within a minority.

This chapter addresses racial and life cycle exclusions of LatiNegras and their impact on the mental health of these women. Due to the heterogeneity among these populations, I will concentrate on LatiNegras with a Caribbean background. I emphasize themes prevalent among multiracial women, such as acceptance and belonging, sexuality, and identity (Root, 1994a), which have also been identified as prevalent among LatiNegras (del Valle, personal communication, 1993). Family and collective dynamics surrounding LatiNegras' unique experiences often include intense ambivalence, racial projection, conflict in ethnoracial loyalty, shame, racial and gender stereotyping, and guilt. Vignettes will be used to illustrate particular points. Clinical data have been altered to protect confidentiality.

HISTORICAL AND SOCIOPOLITICAL CONTEXT

The Latino/Hispanic population embraces a rich tapestry of races and ethnicities, including but not limited to Native Americans, Africans, Spaniards, and other Europeans. The presence of the African heritage varies among the diverse Latin American countries. For instance, Brazil, Columbia, Cuba, the Dominican Republic, Ecuador, Panama, Puerto Rico, and Venezuela have significant black African populations, whereas countries such as Uruguay, Chile, and particularly, Argentina have virtually no blacks due to racial genocide. Black individuals from West Africa were sold as slaves in the Spanish Caribbean to work in sugar cane plantations. Consequently, the population with African ancestry is highly visible in the Caribbean, particularly in Cuba, Puerto Rico, and the Dominican Republic. Moreover, Cuban, Dominican, and Puerto Rican LatiNegras often share historical, cultural, and geopolitical commonalities.

Racial Glossary

In discussing the issues affecting the LatiNegra, I need to define my terms. I use the term *LatiNegra* as opposed to African Latina, in order to avoid the partial or total negation of the Latinness in African Latinas by the Latino community. Within the Spanish linguistic usage, the first word—Latina—is the primary denomination, whereas the second word—Negra—is the secondary denomination or adjective. African Latinos have objected to the Spanish use of the terms Africano Latino or Negro Latino because this semantic usage reflects the racism of denying the Latinness of African Latinos (Zenón Cruz, 1975). The term LatiNegra attempts to recognize both ethnicity and race, while resisting the society's systematic negation of African Latinas' Latinness. This systematic negation is the product of racism. In a culture that values interconnectedness, the external forces of racism are so powerful that they result in oppressing and separating Latinos through color lines. Consequently, the term LatiNegra is an empowering affirmation of both the Latino and African components of the African Latina's multiethno-racial identity.

Racial differences among Caribbean Latinos are expressed according to gradations of color and features. For example, *mulata* is the equivalent of female mulatto; *jabá* is the light-skinned woman who has features that indicate black ancestry—equivalent to the African American *yellow*; *grifa* is the female with white features who has frizzled or kinky hair; *trigueña* is the female who is olive skinned; *morena* is darker than the trigueña, *india* has Indian characteristics, and *negra* or *prieta* is the black female (Comas-Díaz, 1989; Jorge, 1979; Longres, 1974).

Relationships between individuals with different racial appellations are mediated by historical, political, social, and economic factors. During slavery, lighter skinned blacks (presumably the progeny of white plantation owners) were preferred over darker skinned slaves as house servants. Although this preferred treatment did not shelter them from slavery or abuse, the difference in treatment affected the relationships between lighter and darker slaves, creating jealousies and resentments (Greene, 1992). As a result of this legacy of North American preferential treatment based on skin color, many black and white people developed skin color preferences, feelings, resentments, and distortions about such preferences (Greene, 1992). This legacy is also present in the Caribbean.

Racismo: Latino-Style Racism

Many Caribbean Latinos describe their racial background as a rainbow, acknowledging their mixed Indian, Spaniard, and African heritage. Contrary to the North American dictum that one drop of African blood makes you black, one drop of white blood makes you at least not black in the Latin Caribbean (Longres, 1974). The historical recognition of the rainbow racial composition of the Spanish Caribbean was partly the outcome of the Catholic religion. Although the church officially discouraged intermarriage, its condemnation of sexual cohabitation as living in sin facilitated the legalization of interracial unions. Also, common-law marriages have a history of more frequent legal recognition in the Latino society than in North American society. Therefore, the offspring of such unions were often recognized by the society.

The Spanish Caribbean history of relative miscegenation allows people to recognize their African ancestry. For instance, Puerto Ricans who look white cannot deny their African heritage. The saying, *Y tu abuela dùnde está?* (And where is your grandmother?), illustrates that Puerto Ricans have a female ancestor (i.e., grandmother, great-grandmother) who was black African, and thus they cannot deny their own blackness regardless of phenotype or how nonblack they appear to be. The emphasis on the femaleness of the black ancestor derives from the collective memory of dark females being sexually enslaved and raped by conquistadores or other white Europeans. This emphasis acknowledges the intersecting influence of misogyny and slavery. However, racism among Latinos is very much alive, regardless of the visibility of the African Caribbean abuelas.

Racismo or Latino-style racism permeates all spheres of the society from education, politics, religion, arts, and business to social, personal, family, sexual, and interpersonal relationships (Zenón Cruz, 1975). Racismo is a classic example of internalized racism. For example, many Caribbean Latinos have difficulty accepting their own blackness and often accuse each other of being black and or having African ancestry (racial projection). The reply, *el que not tiene dinga tiene mandinga* (the individual who does not have dinga has mandinga) asserts that Latinos who don't have dinga (Indian heritage) have mandinga (African heritage) (Zenón Cruz, 1975). Many times this reply is used to combat racist remarks, racial projection, and covert racismo.

Internalized racism is pervasive in the Latin Caribbean media. The media often portray the idealized image of Caribbean Latinos as being nonblack. The Puerto Rican movie, *Lo que le pasó a Santiago* (What happened to Santiago), nominated for the 1990 foreign movie Oscar, did not have black, *jabao,* or *grifo* actors. This behavior can be interpreted as an attempt at "passing," or Latino Caribbeans' effort to appear as nonblacks. Passing involves a racial denial and active attempts to be perceived (by self and others) as white, or at least, nonblack. Greene (1992) has argued that among African Americans, passing has been used historically as an adaptive survival mechanism, enabling its users to avoid imminent harm or to obtain goods, services, or jobs that would otherwise be denied because of discrimination. However, she also warned that when passing is accompanied by the belief that being black is a sign of inferiority, it represents an expression of internalized racism. Similarly, the darkest actor in *Lo que le pasó a Santiago*—a dark Indian-looking trigueño—played the role of a criminal. This casting sublimi-nally designates criminals as being nonwhite individuals.

Compared to North American racism, racismo is a different con-struct. Racismo is a dynamic, fluid, and contextual concept that is often associated with social class. Regardless of color, the higher the person's social class, the whiter the person is perceived to be, and thus less subjected to racismo, therefore, people can change their color when they change their socioeconomic class. Thus racismo is highly contextual-ized, but it is not as institutionalized as North American racism. Due to the specific historicopolitical context and the relativity of color and racial attributions, many Latinos pride themselves in being nonracist. This assertion is at best a distortion or denial, and at worst a racist act. Zenón Cruz (1975) asserted that a mechanism of covert racismo among Caribbean Latinos is racial projection. He argued that when asked directly about racismo, many Latinos may not identify themselves as racist, although they identify their neighbors, friends, and even rela-tives as being racist, thus attributing to others their own racismo.

Racismo tends to operate differently from racism. It appears to be relatively covert compared to racism because the Latino Caribbean society is historically more racially integrated than the North American one. The covert nature of racismo among Caribbean Latinos acquires complex connotations, due to both its societal and individual dimensions. An example of an individual dimension is racial perception. Both racial perception and identification comprise subjective and highly complex processes. Racial perception of others is also related to perceptions of one's own race. As an illustration, Ginorio (1971) empirically examined racial perception in Puerto Rico, finding that individuals' perceptions were closely associated to their own racial identification. In other words, a trigueña may be racially perceived differently by two individuals according to their particular self identification. The same trigueña may be perceived as being darker by a darker observer and lighter by a lighter observer. Del Valle (1989) replicated Ginorio's study in the United States, obtaining similar findings.

Although different, racismo is as painful, dysfunctional, and destructive as its North American counterpart. The combination of racism, sexism, and classism contributes to the covert nature of racismo, and this covert nature further involves the rejection of LatiNegras. It has been shown that there is a sociocultural glass ceiling for the LatiNegros in general, and for the LatiNegra in particular (Ramos Rosado, 1986). Although Latinos may not object to socializing with LatiNegros, they profoundly object to their offsprings' decision to marry LatiNegros. Particularly, having a LatiNegra daughter-in-law, as opposed to a Lati-Negro son-in-law, is often perceived as marking the decline of the family's status and class. As an illustration, it is usually more acceptable for a female to marry down by marrying a LatiNegro, than for a male to marry down by marrying a LatiNegra. Due to their gender, Lati-Negros often have more options for marriage—LatiNegras, Latinas, and white or African American females. If the LatiNegro marries a nonblack female, such a liaison is less threatening than a LatiNegra marrying a nonblack man.

Marrying a LatiNegra is contrary to the Latino dictum of *adelantar o mejorar la raza* (literally, to improve the race)—going through a whitening process by marrying someone light-skinned or white (Jorge, 1979). Therefore, LatiNegras are not perceived as desirable potential spouses because they do not improve the race; instead, they damage the race (Zenón Cruz, 1975). This process is compounded by the fear of *requintar* (from the word fifth), or the inheritance of African traits not manifested in the parents or grandparents but present in a fifth generation (great-grandparent) ancestor. Thus nonblack Latinos fear that their African ancestry has greater probability of *requintar* in their children, grandchildren, or great-grandchildren if they marry LatiNegros or nonwhite Latinos. The fear of requintar may acquire obsessive proportions in that individuals engage in excruciating racial denial and projection. These dynamics are perpetuated in an elitist, racist, sexist, and patriarchal system.

The primary role of the mother in the socialization process among Latinos also contributes to the rejection of LatiNegras as potential wives. LatiNegras are considered more threatening to the family racial character (even to the national racial character) than LatiNegro fathers. Latina mothers are expected to be physically and emotionally present in the lives of their offspring, whereas such expectations do not necessarily apply to fathers, who occasionally are allowed to be emotionally and physically distant. Consequently, LatiNegro fathers are less visible than LatiNegra mothers, whereas the presence of the LatiNegra mother is harder to hide in the family racial closet. A visible LatiNegra mother is a clear sign of her children's mixed racial ancestry, reducing their opportunities to *adelantar la raza,* and thus limiting their attractiveness as potential spouses.

Marrying a LatiNegra may also tap into internalized racism and misogyny, due to the racial and gender connotations attributed to LatiNegras. These processes are facilitated by the special racial and gender projection that LatiNegras may engender in a patriarchal and covertly racist society. I expand more on these issues in the section on racial and gender dynamics.

The realities of LatiNegras are compounded by the interaction of gender, race, class, and sexual orientation. LatiNegras' circumstances are very different from those of other Latinas. The unique realities of the Caribbean LatiNegra are beginning to be acknowledged. For example, the Puerto Rican Office of Women's Issues sponsored a 1992 conference on the black Puerto Rican woman (de Guzman, personal communication, 1993). Another example of this recognition is the formation of LatiNegra organizations, such as the *Unión de Mujeres Puertorriqueñas Negras* (Union of black Puerto Rican Women) (Petrovich, personal communication, 1993). Unfortunately, the issues of the LatiNegra in the United States have received minimal attention (Jorge, 1979).

COLLECTIVE CONTEXTS:
FAMILY AND COMMUNITY

Latinos in the United States are identified as both ethnic and racial minorities. Many Latinos' racial experiences in the United States surpass the individual and family level and need to be viewed as a collective experience, where all are forced to confront and question their racial identity. The individual and institutionalized racism prevalent in the United States encourages a racial division among Caribbean Latinos. Most of them are multiracial individuals, and while living in the continental United States, they frequently internalize North American racism. Mainstream society, with its polarized racial identification, often forces Latinos with African heritage into defining themselves as either black or white.

LatiNegras' needs for acceptance and belonging to their families and communities are plagued by conflict. Traditionally, the family acts as a buffer between children and their outside world. However, Latino families do not buffer LatiNegras against racism or racismo. Bearing different gradations of color, family members may be unable to cope with the North American racism. One or both of the LatiNegra's parents may not be considered African Latinos and cannot teach her the coping mechanisms to deal with racial prejudice and discrimination as a black woman. They are unable to racially socialize their LatiNegra daughter. Racial socialization involves warning black girls about the racial dangers and disappointments without overwhelming or overprotecting them (Greene, 1990). Although the LatiNegra's parents may be able to effectively teach her how to cope with ethnic discrimination and prejudice as a Latina, they cannot empower her by teaching her emotional defenses and coping skills as a black female. Racial and gender socialization is further complicated by the great differences between the non-LatiNegra mother's racial experiences and those of her LatiNegra daughter.

The LatiNegra who is a lesbian is even more severely affected relative to her needs for acceptance and belonging. Besides the mainstream society's racism, sexism, and heterosexism, many lesbians of color face the additional stress of coping with the gay and lesbian community's racism, plus the heterosexism, sexism, and internalized racism of their own ethnic community (Greene, 1993; Kanuha, 1990). This situation creates profound conflicts in the lesbian LatiNegra's loyalties, as well as paradoxes within her identity and sense of belonging. For instance, Kanuha (1990) argued that for many lesbians of color, the contradiction in feeling safe yet afraid as lesbians in their ethnic communities is evidence of the pervasiveness of both racism and sexism. She recognized a critical tie between homophobia and sexism, in which many people of color identify lesbianism as a white phenomenon, thus blaming the existence of lesbians of color on white feminism. The outcome of this process is that the lesbian LatiNegra is further excluded from all the communities to which she attempts to belong.

The Latino family's lack of racial socialization and racial coping skills affects the LatiNegra differently than the LatiNegro because, culturally, females tend to derive self-esteem from receiving approval from significant others. In the general culture, women have been socialized to assume primary responsibility for family relationships (Walters, Carter, Papp, & Silverstein, 1988). Traditional Latino gender roles stipulate that females subordinate their individual needs to those of the group. Many Latinas have an extended, collective, and contextual definition of themselves. The extended self is validated only by its functioning in relationship and in harmony with the group (Nobles, 1980). The extended self-definition posits that women perceive themselves as being individuals within a collective and nonlinear context and, therefore, their relationships to others and need for individual and collective survival are central to their well-being and sense of continuity (Comas-Díaz, 1994a). Although the concept of well-being and the sense of group continuity may appear to enforce traditional gender roles within the family, the extended self promotes a combined instrumental (rational) and expressive (emotional) concept of womanhood prevalent among many women of color (Comas-Díaz, 1994a).

The family is the major source of socializing cultural values, mores, beliefs, and behaviors. Within this context, the LatiNegra's own family can be a source of both approval and rejection in the form of racismo. The family's racial rejection complicates the process of self-acceptance for the LatiNegra. For instance, Franklin and Boyd-Franklin (1985) argued that racial socialization was enhanced in the context of love and support for the child, but it was negatively affected when it occurred in the context of parental contempt and rejection, as in the case of many LatiNegras. Consequently, the LatiNegra's self-esteem suffers. The family dynamics often target the LatiNegra for racial exclusion due to the intersection of race and gender. The LatiNegra's individual characteristics are viewed through the lens of female blackness and often acquire negative connotations. For example, a colicky baby may be identified as *esa prieta majadera* (that bothersome black female baby) whereas a nonblack colicky baby may engender concern or be identified as a *majadera*, without any allusion to her color. From infancy, the LatiNegra learns to associate her blackness with negative attributes. Moreover, during childhood, adolescence, and adulthood, she frequently hears parents and family members making racist-sexist remarks toward other LatiNegras.

Internalized racism, colonization, and oppression are often present among many Latinos, particularly among those with visible African ancestry. The dynamics of internalized sexism and racism are frequently channeled at the expense of the LatiNegra. This process becomes heightened when the family has recently immigrated and copes with learning a new culture, language, and racial dynamics. Many Latinos face the racial cultural shock that results from being perceived in a racially dichotomous manner (black or white), being racially discriminated against, subjected to an overt individual and institutionalized racism, and being considered genetically inferior due to their race.

The racial cultural shock may persist even for generations after the family's translocation. In other words, LatiNegras whose families have been in the United States for several years may still be ill-equipped to deal with racism. Among Latinos with African ancestry in the United States, feelings about self and others are related to color differences between the LatiNegra and others. Many nonwhite Latinos, such as trigueños, jabáos, mulatos, and grifos, experience racial identity diffusion in that within the Latino context they may be considered nonblack, but in the North American context they are perceived as nonwhite. Consequently, the LatiNegra represents a painful mirror that nonwhite Latinos with internalized racism may want to break. She is the reflection of their blackness, and due to her powerlessness resulting from racism, sexism, and classism, the LatiNegra is racially excluded. She searches for self-definition at a great risk to herself. Many of these feelings and dynamics often generate destructive relationships between LatiNegras and their siblings, parents, relatives (Thomas, 1967), and friends (Rivera, 1982).

Many Latino families do not have appropriate socialization skills within an overt racist environment. For example, Greene (1990) argued that women who have been confronted early on in life with direct and open racial discrimination, who have had it accurately labeled for what it is, and who received family support in developing strategies for overcoming and enduring it may be better prepared to manage racial discrimination later in life. She added that women who were forced to address racial discrimination with little or no support, or who confronted it in more subtle and indirect forms, may be less prepared to address it and may be at greater risk for internalizing its destructive aspects. The LatiNegra is obviously at a disadvantage due to her lack of family support in coping with racial discrimination as a black woman. Frequently, the LatiNegra's lack of family support results in a negative self-internalization. The pervasiveness of racism and the varied efforts and methods blacks use to minimize its damaging effects on themselves can be accurately perceived as a major source of stress (Greene, 1990). Many nonblack Latinos do not experience this type of racial stress and thus cannot minimize its negative effects on their LatiNegra daughters.

Latino groups and communities are collectively incompetent to deal with the type of racial discrimination confronted by LatiNegras. As previously indicated, Latinos with African ancestry may find it difficult to accept their own blackness due to their internalized racism and colonialism. Those Latinos with visible African heritage often harbor negative attributions of being black, which are then externalized and projected onto the LatiNegra. In a poignant article describing the experience of being a Puerto Rican LatiNegra, Jorge (1979) asserted that her multiple minority status engendered shame and feelings of inferiority, which were reinforced by the Latino culture and dominant society at large. Unlike an African American female, the LatiNegra cannot expect nor does she receive the protection of her family against racism. Moreover, the LatiNegra's mother did not prepare her to become a black woman by communicating the racial and sexual dangers, stereotypes, and realities that confront black females, nor how to interpret them, or to cope with them.

Blackness often produces intense ambivalence among Latinos. The personal and collective African heritage makes blackness a part of the self that is both loved and hated. The loving black abuela is a source of both nurturance and shame. The African queen may be sexually exciting as a lover, but she is rejected as a potential wife. The ambivalence is further concretized in the usage of language, where the same racially derogatory terms, such as *negra* and *prieta*, are also expressions of affection (Zenón Cruz, 1975). This linguistic usage is similar to the use of the word *nigger* among some African Americans as a term of familiarity and endearment. Mixed-race Latinos also struggle with their own blackness at an intrapsychic level. Their reaction to the LatiNegra frequently involves a confrontation of their own blackness. Such confrontation encompasses intense conflict, shame, and guilt, resulting in the rejection of the LatiNegra. Consider the following vignette.

Antonio, a nonblack Puerto Rican male, was married to Ann, a white Anglo Saxon Protestant (WASP) woman. Antonio began an affair with Celia, a LatiNegra of Cuban background. As the relationship unfolded, sexual difficulties began to emerge. On one occasion, Celia experienced sadness (due to the illicit status of their liaison) and began to cry during lovemaking. Antonio trivialized the incident by responding that blacks cry when they are having sex. This type of defensive reaction is frequently found among individuals with diffused racial identity.

As a racially mixed man, Antonio's marriage to Ann may be interpreted as an internalization of the white middle-class female beauty ideal. However, having an affair with Celia may indicate ambivalence and a search for a more integrated racial identity. This search, notwithstanding Antonio's insensitive behavior toward Celia, appears to be a reflection of the combination of sexism and racism through the projection of racial and sexual dynamics. As indicated earlier, the projection of racismo and of blackness is a racial defense mechanism among many Latinos.

Racial and Sexual Dynamics

LatiNegras are exposed to the mainstream's racism and sexism, in addition to racismo and sexismo from the Latino community. They are stripped of their humanness, denied their individuality, and devalued.

Individual and institutional racism complicate Latinegras' experiences. They are frequently rejected by both the mainstream white and the Latino societies due to their blackness. Such double rejection often leads to the development of solidarity with African Americans. The African American and the LatiNegro community both share the common denominator of being black in an openly racist society. For most African Americans, racism is an active expectation requiring adaptation to ongoing levels of stress connected to survival and inextricably bound up in physical characteristics that are always visible (Greene, 1990). The commonality in the LatiNegra's experiences with African Americans facilitates identification with this group.

Many LatiNegros in the United States adapt and tend to assimilate to the mainstream society as African Americans. In some cases, they may change their accent, adopting a nonstandard black English (del Valle, personal communication, 1993; Seda-Bonilla, 1970). When color supersedes ethnicity and culture as the source of identity for Latinos with African ancestry, they often assimilate into the racial antagonisms of the United States (Longres, 1974). The result is that lighter Latinos may marry white Americans, Latinos, or other nonblack individuals, whereas darker Latinos will marry African Americans or other blacks. Consequently, marital liaisons between LatiNegras and African Americans can be common.

The LatiNegra who marries an African American man often gives birth to non-Latinos. The ultimate outcome of this process is the total assimilation of LatiNegros to the African American group without identifying—socially, emotionally, and politically—with the Latino community (Jorge, 1979). The total assimilation into the African American community is aided by the conflict in racial loyalties that many LatiNegros experience when they become members of the African American diaspora. This conflict is illustrated in anecdotal and autobiographical materials. For instance, in discussing his experiences growing up as a Hispanic in Spanish Harlem, Edward Rivera (1982) told the story of his LatiNegro Puerto Rican friend, Panna, whose African American friends prevented him from interacting with his nonblack Puerto Rican friends on black turf. Such conflict often leads to the LatiNegros' immersion into the African American group at the exclusion of their Latino identification.

SEXUALITY

The intersection of gender and multiraciality involves confronting the oppressive mythology associated with being a mixed-race woman (Root, 1994a). As black females, LatiNegras often conjure up ideas of exoticism, evil, dark power, sensuality, and strong sexuality. There is no other area that engenders more fantasies than the strong sexuality attributed to the LatiNegra. Within the racist and sexist North American society, there is a level of sexual fantasy regarding the possession of and dominance over the sexuality and sexual behavior of women who are unfamiliar to the male (Root, 1992b). The mixed-race woman is considered the stereotypic unusual sexual being (Nakashima, 1992).

The LatiNegra exemplifies the unusual sexual being within the Latino culture. Many Latinos project diverse sexual fantasies onto the LatiNegra. These fantasies mediate LatiNegras' real and assumed sexuality. For example, having sex with a LatiNegra can be considered aphrodisiacal (*afrodisíaco* in Spanish). Moreover, there is the perception that the LatiNegra has no control over her sexuality, and thus, can engender the same effect in her sexual partner; or on the contrary, she has an inhibitory effect.

Another fantasy is that the LatiNegra's strong sexuality is transmitted by osmosis. Within the Caribbean Latino community, having a LatiNegra lover can be a testament to the man's sexual prowess. For example, a nonblack Puerto Rican man told his Dominican LatiNegra lover: "I like being with you because when men see us together they know that I . . . [perform cunnilingus with] you."

Many of these sexual fantasies can transcend the traditional gender roles. For instance, having a LatiNegra lover can heighten fantasies of power and powerlessness, with its dimensions of dominance and submission enacted in the sexual act. These dynamics can also transcend sexual orientation. Although embodied in a specific sociopolitical context, the effect of race within lesbian relationships can also be subjected to externalization of internalized oppression. Consider the following vignette.

A lesbian couple decided to move in together after 6 months of dating. Their sexual behavior involved sadomasochistic activities with Áurea, the white Cuban woman, as the active partner. Soon after their move, Áurea began to physically attack Luisa, her LatiNegra Puerto Rican lover. The situation escalated to the point that Luisa gave Áurea an ultimatum. As a result, they entered couples counseling. During the initial session, Áurea said: *I will never hit a white lover.* In other words, she was responding to the racial collective unconscious that blacks have been slaves and thus deserve to be physically abused. The racist hierarchical attributions of blacks being inferior to whites were evident within this dynamic. Moreover, Áurea had internalized the cultural dichotomous attributions of females as being either all good or all bad (Virgin Mary/Eve; Madonna/whore) (Almquist, 1989; Comas-Díaz, 1987). Within this context, the LatiNegra epitomizes the stereotypical bad woman. Further exploration revealed that Áurea had dissociated from her own African ancestry by displacing onto Luisa her internalized racial oppression. Thus, by oppressing Luisa, Áurea was rejecting parts of herself. This dynamic reflects an image whereby identification with the aggressor occurs in a racist, patriarchal, sexist, and heterosexist society.

As the previous vignette suggests, the sexual arena can become the soul's mirror. Many Latinos with mixed racial ancestry often deal with racial ambivalence within themselves. Thus being sexually involved with a LatiNegra can produce a confrontation with such ambivalence. As an illustration, Juan, a racially mixed Cuban male, began a relationship with María, a Cuban LatiNegra. Juan experienced sexual impotence and terminated the relationship with a cry of "I cannot screw my father!" Regardless of gender and sexual orientation, Juan had identified María with his own LatiNegro father. Consequently, racial identity had transcended gender identity. Juan was plagued by guilt due to immigrating from Cuba and leaving his LatiNegro father behind.

Closely related to the LatiNegra's sexuality is the issue of dark or occult power, which is attributed to many LatiNegros. For example, Zenón Cruz (1975) argued that people in the Caribbean trust a black folk healer more than a white one and are more afraid of black witches than they are of white ones. Consequently, one of the ways for LatiNegros to obtain respect is through the practice of *espiritismo* (spiritualism), *curanderismo*, and/or *santería*. Females tend to predominate in the area of spiritual healing among Latino communities (Espín, 1984; Mays & Comas-Díaz, 1988). Historically, women in most cultures have resorted to healing and magic as a means of empowerment (Bourguignon,

1979). Similarly, many Latinas, particularly the LatiNegra, gain power through their roles as folk healers such as curanderas, espiritistas, and santeras (Comas-Díaz, 1988; Espín, 1984; Koss-Chioino, 1992). The Catholic church's hierarchical definition of God as a white male, in addition to the prohibition against women becoming priests, seems to provide an impetus for the proliferation of female healers among many Latinos. The influence of female folk healers can be so pervasive that Boyd-Franklin and García Preto (1994a) advised family therapists to consider the Latino family's involvement with curanderas, santeras, and espiritistas.

In summary, there is a defensiveness among LatiNegras stemming from the oppressive racial and sexual dynamics. Sexually, the LatiNegra is not allowed to be an individual. The paradoxes that surround her life—unattractiveness but strong sexuality; oppression but dark power—all have an effect on the LatiNegra's sense of identity.

IDENTITY

The question of racial ancestry becomes a threat to the LatiNegra's identity. She is forced to come to grips with the reality of her racial identity. She is often denied the ability to define herself, which is essential to empowerment (Collins, 1990; Helms, 1990a). As a mixed-race woman, she is also denied the opportunity to claim membership in and identify with more than one racial or ethnic group (C. C. I. Hall, 1992; Root, 1990). The LatiNegra differs from other mixed-race women in that she does not engender curiosity regarding her racial identity. There are no ambiguous features—she is perceived as being black. However, like other biracial women, the LatiNegra needs to accept both sides of her racial heritage and has the right to declare how she wishes to identify herself racially—even if this identity is discrepant with how she looks.

The LatiNegra's racial exclusion and her lack of acceptance and belonging to the Latino community is doubly painful. She often experiences a fragmented identity. Multiracial identity can jeopardize the LatiNegra's sense of belonging to a group. For example, Root (1994a) argued that a major difference between African Americans and multiracially identified African Americans (such as LatiNegras) was not necessarily their racial heritage, but that the latter group identifies as multicultural and feels a kinship with more than one group. However, such identification may also be related to a desire to pass as nonblack by not identifying with the group of lowest racial and social standing (African Americans). For instance, Almeida (personal communication, April 1993) asserted that some dark-skinned Asian Indians would prefer to be mistaken for Latinos than blacks. Nonetheless, it is vital for the LatiNegra to be able to identify with multiple groups, particularly with the Latino and the African.

Attribution of the *other* is a dynamic highly relevant to the Lati-Negra's identity. *Other*ness refers to the process whereby an individual's attribution of people of different ethnocultural background helps the person to define his or her own concept of self. For instance, women in the general population have been described as men's *other* in that they are defined in reference to men and not men in reference to women (de Beauvoir, 1953). Moreover, Kovel (1984) asserts that Europeans' fantasies about Africans and Native Americans helped the former to define themselves. Similarly, Jenkins (1985) has argued that for white Americans, people of color may be a cultural representation of the polar opposite. The notion of *other* creates a dichotomous thinking and objectification, where difference is defined in oppositional terms. The dynamics of color and racial projection create a dramatic polarity, the projection of the not-me (Collins, 1990). The *other* gains meaning only in relationship to the counterpart (Fanon, 1967).

Women of color have been identified as the *other's other* in terms of being the man of color's *other* and the white woman's *other* (Comas-Díaz, 1991). Collins (1990) believes that maintaining images of African American women as the *other* provides ideological justification for race, gender, and class oppression. This justification can be generalized to include LatiNegras, in that they are doubly marginalized and racially excluded within their own group, as well as being outsiders in the population as a whole. As the target of sexual-racial projection, the LatiNegra is the paragon of *other*ness. She is not self-defined; instead, she is defined by others. Consequently, she often copes with severe identity conflicts. If she only identifies as a Latina, she denies her blackness. If she only identifies as a black, she denies her Latinness. Denial of one aspect of her identity implies denial of the self and heritage, plus sacrifice of personal integrity (Mizio, 1983).

LatiNegras' identification with a single group involves an ethnoracial denial as well as a psychocultural denial. Although the denial of ethnoracial identity may be a racial coping mechanism, it also leaves the denier vulnerable to loneliness, personal isolation, and political powerlessness, devoid of the opportunity to correct and transcend distorted ethnoracial perceptions of the group and of herself (Greene, 1992). The ethnoracial denial fosters a psychocultural denial of the self. By identifying exclusively with one group, the LatiNegra renounces herself by replacing a multiracial identity with a single racial one. Consequently, one of the LatiNegra's fundamental tasks is to preserve herself by affirming and integrating her multiethnic and racial identity. Many times, her fragmented identity surfaces during mental health treatment and needs to be addressed in that arena.

The LatiNegra spends an inordinate amount of energy in her ongoing struggle with the mainstream group's and Latinos' racial, gender and ethnic prejudices. Like other mixed-race women, LatiNegras do not necessarily identify racially with their physical appearance or with the way they look (black). They are caught between three diverse (and sometimes, antagonistic) worlds—black, Latino, and white—and racially excluded from all. Their marginality binds them in a conflict of racial loyalties without a satisfactory resolution of their racial identity.

Physical Appearance

Physical appearance is a central component of female identity in a patriarchal and sexist society. As indicated previously, among many Latin Caribbean societies, race is related to class and thus it can more flexible and fluid. For example, a LatiNegra from a higher socioeconomic class (although this is highly infrequent due to the Caribbean historical connection between blackness and low socioeconomic class) is not socially perceived as being black; instead she may be perceived as morena or trigueña. Social class, the dictum of adelantar la raza, still governs the LatiNegra's physical appearance and her suitability for marriage. The constructs of colonization and internalized colonization add to the objectification of the LatiNegra, who often represents the antithesis of the white male colonizer.

The issue of physical appearance is a pervasive theme among mixed-race women (Root, 1994a). The LatiNegra's physical appearance is often a target of racism and covert racismo. Regardless of color, males and females in the United States are immersed in and intoxicated by white female beauty standards. Due to pervasive media influence, many African American females, African Caribbean females, and LatiNegras grow up with a fantasy of aspiring to be white (as girls they are forced to identify with Snow White or Barbie, and as young and adult women, with white fashion models or those nonwhite models who have Caucasian features). These dynamics can result in hopelessness about their physical appearance and self-hatred due to their blackness.

In the Latin Caribbean, the covert nature of racismo is also illustrated in female beauty standards. Blackness (dark color, black features, kinky hair, and body shape) tends to have implications for attractiveness only and not necessarily for racial inferiority. Although the LatiNegra is not considered intellectually inferior, she is definitively considered unattractive. The LatiNegra's physical appearance is the antithesis of physical desirability and attractiveness among many Caribbean Latinos. According to Longres (1974), to be *rubia* (blond or fair) and or with light eyes is aesthetically prized. He added that straight hair is considered an indication of beauty, whereas *pelo malo* (literally bad hair, refers to kinky hair) is generally considered the ugliest and most condemning feature a person may have. As an illustration, the racial categorizations of grifa and jabá attribute blackness primarily based on the texture of the hair (kinky).

The denial and rejection of the LatiNegra's female blackness have serious implications for her self-esteem. Nonwhite Latinas such as trigueñas, grifas, morenas, and indias may externalize their internalized racism by attempting to whiten themselves through torturing their hair and scalp by chemically straightening their bad kinky hair, by using bleaching creams, and by generally trying to look less black. Although these attempts carry high physical and emotional costs, these nonwhite Latinas appear to have more degrees of freedom in terms of their racial identity than LatiNegras who cannot modify their blackness. However, many LatiNegras resort to an arsenal of weapons to attempt to whiten themselves, often resulting in pain, frustration, and hopelessness. Some LatiNegras may engage in torturing and life-threatening activities; for example, an 11-year-old girl was taken unconscious to the hospital emergency room after using a clothes pin to close her wide nose in order to make it narrow and thus to look less black.

The LatiNegra is resented and rejected due to her blackness, which is often defined as kinky hair, thick lips, wide hips, and dark color. Blackness evokes expressions of ridicule, rejection, and hostility. Female blackness, with its compounded racism and sexism, is often a target for negative remarks, even from significant others. Jorge (1979) provides several of these painful examples. For instance, the demand *Cierra esa bemba!* (Close your mouth!) commands the LatiNegra to avoid leaving her lower lip (generally thicker lip) hanging. (The word *bemba* is a pejorative term referring to a thick-lipped mouth.) As a child, the LatiNegra often suffers insults to her self-esteem from a loved caregiver. For example, while her hair is being combed by a mother or maternal figure, the expressions *Maldito sea este pelo!* (Damn this hair!) or *Dios mío, este pelo!* (Dear God, this hair!) engender feelings of inadequacy, unattractiveness (Jorge, 1979), and self-hatred.

MENTAL HEALTH ISSUES

Self-Esteem

The LatiNegra's socioculturally imposed identity conflict affects her self-esteem. Being multiracial in itself poses no inherent type of stress that would result in psychological maladjustment; however, the distress related to being multicultural is likely to be a response to an environment that has internalized racist beliefs (Root, 1994a). This type of distress stems from oppression and is frequently metamorphosed into low self-esteem.

The LatiNegra's self-esteem problem is exacerbated by the identification of multiracial individuals as the racial and or ethnic group with lower perceived status by the higher status group. Although both African Americans and Latinos have a low social status within the North American society, the history of racism and white supremacy tends to assign even a lower status to those individuals who look black (Root, 1994a). Due to her socially imposed low self-esteem and inferior social standing, the LatiNegra experiences powerlessness and learned helplessness.

The politics and dynamics of race, gender, and class add to the singularity and uniqueness of the LatiNegra, threatening her identity and sense of continuity, thus further eroding her self-esteem. The stressful and traumatic circumstances surrounding the lives of LatiNegras are compounded by the racism and sexism from both the Latino and mainstream communities. Being considered at least three minorities in one—black, Latina, and female—is a tremendous psychological burden that needs to be understood (Jorge, 1979) and addressed, particularly in the therapeutic process. Consequently, LatiNegras' membership in multiple minority groups often endangers their identity, decreasing their self-esteem.

Trauma

LatiNegras experience a multiple trauma. They confront trauma at a historicopolitical, transgenerational, psychosocial, and personal levels. LatiNegras' history of societal and political trauma includes slavery, oppression, and subjugation as black females. The historicopolitical context of their racial and gender exclusions constitute ancestral traumatic events that are embedded in LatiNegras' collective unconscious. Moreover, this historical trauma is the precursor of contemporary racial and sexual discrimination in the midst of hostile environments. The cumulative dose of discrimination may become so toxic that the processes of denial or suppression are similar to those in posttraumatic stress disorder (PTSD), where emotional flooding and disorganized behavior can be triggered by subtle clues, reminders, or even mini-instances of what has been suppressed (Hamilton, 1989). Similarly, Vasquez (1994) argues that Latinas' chronic exposure to racism can lead to powerlessness, learned helplessness, depression, anxiety, and PTSD. This traumatic situation is exacerbated for LatiNegras, who confront multiple societal and psychosocial barriers due to their assigned inferior status dictated by gender, race, ethnicity, and class.

LatiNegras are further exposed to what Root (1992c) called *insidious trauma,* or the cumulative effect of racism, sexism, dislocation, and other types of oppression. She argued that insidious trauma is frequently associated with the low social status attributed to individuals who are devalued because they are different from those in power due to an intrinsic identity characteristic such as gender, race, or sexual orientation. As members of multiple powerless minority groups, LatiNegras often become a target for racial, gender, and class victimization. As indicated previously, LatiNegras are oppressed and victimized through racial and sexual exclusions by the dominant group as well as by their own communities.

LatiNegras are also exposed to transgenerational trauma. Given their families' powerlessness and absence of racial and gender socialization, this trauma and victimization cycle perpetuates itself from one generation of LatiNegras to the next. The lack of societal and psychocultural reparation for the LatiNegra within the Latino community reinforces the transgenerational trauma. The LatiNegra's transgenerational trauma has a psychosocial component. The trauma inflicted by their own communities and families creates a psychosocial victimization. Due to internalized racism, the rejection by the LatiNegra's own group results in disempowerment and fosters her internalization of negative views of herself. Thus the LatiNegra is unable to racially socialize her daughter as a black female and to convey to her a positive sense of self.

Many LatiNegras experience added trauma at a personal level. They confront several traumata in their lives, which leave indelible effects on their functioning and self-esteem. Traumata refer to little traumas or events that when coupled with general life stresses and reduced environmental and psychological resources can bring the LatiNegra to the traumatic stress flashpoint (Puig, 1991). The message that LatiNegras are inferior due to their combination of gender, race, ethnicity, and class further adds to their victimization. This type of victimization acquires a sense of progression. Powerlessness breeds more powerlessness. Unfortunately, many LatiNegras are caught in a cycle of oppression, discrimination, trauma, and victimization and are often subjected to revictimization.

RECONSTRUCTION OF THE LATINEGRA

I have introduced the issues surrounding the LatiNegra, who constitutes a classic example of racial exclusion, marginality, and disconnection. She is caught between three diverse worlds—black, Latino, and white—and racially excluded from all. Her marginality binds her in a conflict of ethnoracial loyalties without a satisfactory resolution of her identity. The paradoxes that surround her life—unattractiveness but strong sexuality; oppression but dark power—all have an effect on the LatiNegra's sense of identity. Consequently, the LatiNegra often suffers from identity conflicts and needs to integrate her fragmented identity within her cultural and familial contexts in order to combat guilt, shame, and feelings of inferiority engendered by her combined racial-ethnic and gender status. The denial of one aspect of her identity implies denial of the self, her mixed-race heritage, and her cultural continuity.

LatiNegras' unique experiences are often framed in a collective context of intense ambivalence, racial projection, resentment, and racial and gender stereotyping. One of the LatiNegra's fundamental tasks is to preserve herself by integrating and affirming her dual racial and gender identity. The reconstruction of the LatiNegra involves healing the trauma and her wounded sense of self through the reclaiming and celebration of her prismatic racial, ethnic, and gender identity. Feminist family therapy approaches that incorporate collective elements are best equipped to deal with the unique circumstances of LatiNegras.

NOTE

1. This chapter is excerpted with permission from: Haworth Press, Inc., Binghamton, NY, 1994. LatiNegra: Mental health issues of African Latinas, *Journal of Feminist Family Therapy*, 5(341), 35-74.

Race as Process

Reassessing the "What Are You?" Encounters of Biracial Individuals

TERESA KAY WILLIAMS

To prepare for an ethnographic study on the identity construction and presentation of gay Latino homeboys in the spring of 1994, I began frequenting popular gay Latino dance clubs and other informal gay Latino hangouts.[1] As I stood observing and taking notes of the social interactions in one dance club setting, a Latino man approached me and began speaking to me in Spanish. I politely replied, "No hablo Español." Without missing a beat, he made a swift linguistic transition from Spanish to English and asked, "Are you white?" as his gaze locked onto

AUTHOR'S NOTE: Many people and organizations must be acknowledged for their contributions to the ideas that informed this chapter.

My family: the Williams family in West Virginia and the Suzuki family in Japan; my parents, Nobue Suzuki Williams and Tracy James Elwood Williams; my brother and best friend, Tracy Jay; the girls, Pinky, Brandy, and Pebbles.

My teachers and mentors: Sucheng Chan, Walter Allen, David Lopez, Melvin Oliver, Don Nakanishi, Haunani-Kay Trask, David Stannard, Judith Babbitt, and Franklin Odo.

191

my face. When I hesitantly responded, "I'm part-white," he redirected, "Which parent is Mexican?" Although my misidentification as Latina is so common that I have come to expect it, I pondered why this Latino man explicitly asked me if I were white? If "race" is so obvious, could he not tell? What was it about the combination of my inability to speak Spanish, my phenotype, and whatever other social cues I projected that prompted his series of questions? My phenotype screams, Latina, yet this man had to make sense of my lack of Spanish language proficiency. By soliciting whether or not I was white, this man may have felt it would explain my racial-behavioral mismatch. The fact that he had to ask implies that if indeed I were so obviously white, as my freckled güera skin might suggest, I did not completely fit the presupposed phenotype of a white person. After I explained that my mother is Japanese and my father is Irish/Welsh American, this man uttered in discontent, "Japanese? No, you're lying. If you don't want to dance, just say so." (Williams, 1994-1995). An accumulation of these incidents of racial misidentification has motivated me to further question fixed, statistical conceptualizations of race in the social sciences and to explore its "lived" complexities. ⚭

Racial ideology provides individuals with a unified system by which to understand and experience society (S. Hall, 1992; Prager, 1982). Woven into the core of American national consciousness is the insistence that

---

My friends and allies: Luis Xicay-Santos; Lobo Palombo; Velina Houston; Maria Root; Christine Hall; Cynthia Nakashima; Becky King; Steve Ropp; George Kich; Stephen Murphy; Michael Thornton; Sabrena Taylor; Brian Fung; April Elkjer; Lee Corbett; DeDe Howard; Que Dang; Erica Schmitt; Esther Trejo; Wei-Ming Dariotis; Erin O'Brien; Christine Armstrong; Joe Guziel; Shawn Griffin; Kip Fulbeck; Naomi Zack; Paul Spickard; Russell Leong; Glenn Omatsu; Curtiss Rooks; Eric Wat; Diane Fujino; Mari Sunaida; Amy Hill; Kevin Yoshida; Edith Chen; Kathy Shamey; Kenyon Chan; Nancy Brown; Ari Rosner; Dave Lemmel; Myra Mayesh; Marjie Lee; May Chan; Elias Garcia; Gene LaPietra; David Cervantes; Martin Mirano; Lil' Mario of Escandalo; "Naomi" Williams; Lazaro Concepcion; Eddie Asturias; Arturo Martinez; Eric Garcia; the employees and customers of Circus and Arena who shower me with *cariño* each week; and the faculty and staff at UCLA's Asian American Studies Center and UC Santa Barbara's Asian American Studies Department.

"the races" are monoracially constructed, distinctly pure, and fundamentally different. That is to say, America operates on a belief system—real or not—that is thoroughly, rigidly, and necessarily based on the essential differences of racial groups (Farley & Allen, 1989). No other social reality than that of racially mixed people questions the one-dimensional racial structure upon which America has founded and built its national identity.

In highly racialized U.S. society, one's assignment into a sociopolitically defined single racial group is necessary in order to be a socially recognized, functional member of the society. Individuals are coded and recoded into various membership groups—one of the most powerful identifications being that of race. Although definitions of race are continually being contested and transformed, race itself remains a critical organizing category that the society has socialized its members to notice immediately (Omi & Winant, 1986). Thus race gives a person membership into an ongoing social world and provides one with a social location from which to measure one's likeness to or difference from others. Without being able to code, categorize, and attach racial meanings to these "obvious" visual classifications, one often finds oneself in a state of discomfort and momentary crisis (Omi & Winant, 1986, p. 62). Within a social landscape where race plays an important role in one's livelihood, the socially ambiguous white/nonwhite biracial person has often been portrayed as confused, lost, and homeless (Bradshaw, 1992; Nakashima, 1992; Williams, 1993). These so-called poor, mixed-up biracial children are whom one is supposed to think of, a racist society cloaked in compassion warns, before one selfishly involves oneself with a romantic partner of another race. However, the growing social scientific research on multiracial identity indicates that biracial individuals often employ innovative coping strategies to make sense of their social ecology and to transform their social ambiguity into complex identities (Alipuria, 1990; Hall, 1980; Kich, 1982; Lemmel, 1992; Murphy-Shigematsu, 1986; Root,

The following organizations: MASC, AMEA, Amerasian League, UCSB Variations, UCSC Students of Mixed Heritage, Hapa Issues Forum, Black Gay and Lesbian Leadership Forum, Asian Pacific Aids Intervention Team, Gay Men of Color Consortium, GLAAD-L.A.'s People of Color Committee, Minority Aids Project, and Bienestar.

Finally, much thanks to all of my students from Santa Monica College, California State University at Northridge, UCLA, and UCSB and to the 20 biracial interviewees for sharing and illuminating.

1992b; Rosner, 1993; Thornton, 1983; Weisman, Chapter 10, this volume; T. K. Williams, 1991).

This chapter examines the identity formation of racially mixed non-white and white individuals of African/European and Asian/European ancestries; their "racial ambiguity" motivates these biracial people to negotiate racial and cultural membership and taken-for-granted racial meanings in creative, innovative, subversive, and transgressive ways in their day-to-day interpersonal encounters. This suggests that the social-psychological processing strategies of biracials may differ fundamentally from their monoracial counterparts. In examining the personal and public identities of nonwhite/white biracials, who represent the mixture between racial subordinates and superordinates, these biracials' situationality and locality become one of the most important sociopolitical signifiers of racial production, presentation, and contestation in American society's racial and social organization.

This pilot study has been conducted in two stages, using interviews and a short survey to glean the qualitative experiences of the participants. In doing so, this chapter attempts to rethink *What Are You?* encounters, which imply social displacement and racial ambiguity, as well as the social significance of such encounters to biracial individuals' identity construction. Thus far, 20 exhaustive, ethnographic interviews have been conducted with 10 African/European American biracials and 10 Asian/European American biracials. Because of the lack of official statistics on biracials and the relatively unorganized nature of biracials as a sociopolitical group, this study has relied almost exclusively on snowball sampling as opposed to any elaborate scientific data collection methods (e.g., random sampling). Through my personal and professional contacts, I have called for white/nonwhite biracials as research participants. The findings of this study are subject to revision and modification as new information is revealed and new light shed. As the rich stories and narratives of the biracial individuals in this study disclose, the socioeconomic class, area of residence, parents' gender and marital status, interviewees' gender and sexual orientation all vary tremendously. These differences and variations often play key roles in influencing how people articulate, understand, present, and identify with their biraciality.

The social positionality of nonwhite/white biracials is an important sociopolitical site within American society's racial landscape. How power is attained, how membership is assigned, and how resources are allocated between and among monoracially identified groups are directly related to the social placement and displacement of nonwhite/white biracial populations. Thus, this chapter addresses:

1. The structural issues of how newly formed and transformed social identities are conceptualized, sustained, and elaborated; and

2. The social-psychological issues of how individuals participate in the making of their social identities through their daily interactions. *What Are You?* encounters of biracial individuals illustrate how intricately connected structural and social-psychological forces contribute to the formation of a biracial identity and throw into question taken-for-granted racial assumptions.

BLACKS AND WHITES:
THE OPPOSITIONALIZING OF RACE

The pervading belief that blacks and whites are different sociologically and biologically is nowhere more prevalent than in the notion of miscegenation or "race-mixing." Hernton (1965/1988, pp. xii-xiii) has described how interracial black-white sexual relations have fundamentally shaped the American psyche. American society has long treated relations between African Americans and European Americans as hypersexualized, operating under the ideological assumption that black-white miscegenation is a result of pornography and pathology (Hernton, 1965/1988, p. xiii).

As racist ideology began to permeate the American psyche and organize a social structure, blacks and whites became informed on how they were to perceive and subsequently treat each other. Despite their separate social locations, both black and white people came to agree on the "negative" effects of interracial sexual unions. Despite the erection of rigid social boundaries between black and white and the construction of an elaborate ideology to enforce and maintain this separation, upon contact, blacks and whites almost immediately began crossing the color barrier. Black-white miscegenation dates back to the early colonial period; it became widespread and took place within the socioeconomic context of southern American slavery under thoroughly unequal and brutally coercive circumstances. Russell et al. (1992) explain that miscegenation, or race mixing, became widespread as Europeans, Africans, and Native Americans mixed their seed and substance to produce a kaleidoscope of skin tones and features. But these primary race groupings differed sharply in their civil liberties and political freedoms. Subtle variations in appearance took on enormous consequence in meaning, especially among Negroes. Against a backdrop of love and rape, politics and war, and ultimately, power and privilege, attitudes about skin color evolved in America. (pp. 9-10)

Due to the white patriarchal structure that tightly governed southern life, in most cases, white men fathered mulatto children by slave women. However, it was not so uncommon for white mistresses to bear mulatto children as well. Black and white indentured servants (and slaves) crossed racial/sexual barriers. Although few and far between, interracial marriages also took place. In colonial America, miscegenation in the forms of rape, lust, love, cohabitation, and marriage all took place within and across class divisions.

Race mixing between whites and blacks within and across class lines both in the North and the South pointed to the direct contradiction of maintaining this division when the boundaries were being blurred at an alarming rate (Bennett, 1982, p. 304). The emergence of the mulatto population testified to that. By 1860, 13% to 20% of the African American population had European ancestry (Genovese, 1974, p. 414). Williamson (1984) has pointed out that at the turn of the century, the notion that mulattoes were fathered by northern Yankee and scalawag intruders was popularized. Along with this idea was an implicit southern hope: if the unwanted northerners would leave, so too would the mulattoes (Williamson, 1984, p. 136).

Race mixing between blacks and whites and mulattoes and whites, respectively, lessened when slavery was briefly interrupted by the Civil War and Reconstruction although soon replaced by legalized segregation. As the distinction between blacks and whites was once again restored, mulattoes and blacks increasingly engaged in "internal miscegenation" and "forced endogamy" (Daniel, 1992b; Williamson, 1984). By the 1920s, the African American community became a predominantly mixed-race group; yet around the same time, the census dropped the mulatto category altogether. Through generations of miscegenation between blacks and whites, and internal miscegenation between mulattoes and blacks, light-skinned versus dark-skinned colorism (which emulated white racism) evolved within the African American community. Thus the multiplicity of black-white multiracials was suppressed through the social, legal implementation of "one-drop" hypodescent policies (Davis, 1991).

ASIANS AND WHITES:
THE "ALMOST WHITE" MIXING

The incorporation experiences of Asians into American society since the 1830s were also highly racialized, with the intersection of race and sexuality informing social relations (Almaguer, 1994, pp. 160-162). Like other nonwhites, the Chinese were perceived as threatening to the purity of the white race. Ronald Takaki (1989) has explained,

> White workers referred to the Chinese as "nagures," and a magazine cartoon depicted the Chinese as a bloodsucking vampire with slanted eyes, a pigtail, dark skin, and thick lips. Like blacks, the Chinese were described as heathen, morally inferior, savage, childlike, and lustful. Chinese women were condemned as a "depraved class," and their depravity was associated with their physical appearance, which seemed to show "but a slight removal from the African race." Chinese men were seen as sensuous creatures, especially interested in white women. (p. 101)

The first antimiscegenation laws, passed in the 1660s, barred relationships with African Americans, but California's antimiscegenation laws were aimed at preventing Asians and European Americans from marrying. In 1878 at the California constitutional convention, an alarmed John F. Miller (quoted in Takaki, 1989), proclaimed,

> Were the Chinese to amalgamate at all with our people, it would be the lowest, most vile, and degraded of our race, and the result of that amalgamation would be a hybrid of the most despicable, a mongrel of the most detestable that has ever afflicted the earth. (p. 101)

In 1880, California passed a law prohibiting the legal marriage of any person of European descent with a "Negro, mulatto, or Mongolian" (Almaguer, 1994, p. 161).

In Sacramento, California, in 1913, the year the Alien Land Law was passed preventing Japanese immigrants from owning land, at the height of the anti-Japanese movement, a white minister by the name of Ralph Newman (quoted in Spickard, 1989) said,

> Near my home is an eighty-acre tract of as fine land as there is in California. On that tract lives a Japanese. With that Japanese lives a white woman. In that woman's arms is a baby. What is that baby? It isn't white. It isn't Japanese. It is a germ of the mightiest problem that ever faced this state; a problem that will make the black problem in the South look white. (p. 25)

This statement by the California minister revealed that feelings against black-white relations (sexual or otherwise) have been so strong and so deep that even when other forms of miscegenation (e.g., Asian and white) have been denounced in the United States, it has always been measured against the standard of black-white relations.

From 1898 when the United States obtained the Philippines from Spain after the Spanish-American War until this island nation's independence in 1934, Filipinos entered the United States as nationals, unlike their Chinese and Japanese brothers who, upon arrival, had been designated, "aliens ineligible for citizenship." Filipinos initially came as government-sponsored students called *pensionados*. However, many began occupying economic niches that required manual labor. Like the Chinese and Japanese before them, they too were thrust into a hyperracialized reality. Takaki (1989) noted,

> Beneath these sexual anxieties lay a fear of Filipino men as a threat to white racial purity. Relationships between Filipino men and white women represented "a hybridizing at the bottom, often under the most wretched circumstances, of the lower racial stocks." This "race mingling" would create a "new type of mulatto," an American Mestizo. (p. 329)

In 1930, Judge Rohrback (quoted in Takaki, 1989), notorious for his anti-Filipino public stance, had referred to Filipinos as "little brown men about ten years removed from a bolo and breechcloth. . . . [Filipino men] were sensuous creatures, 'strutting like peacocks and endeavoring to attract the eyes of young American and Mexican girls' " (p. 327). Furthermore, the judge warned that if this "present state of affairs" continued, there would be "40,000 half-breeds in California within the next ten years" (p. 329). After their arrival and settlement in the United States, Filipino *pinoys* courted, dated, and even married European American women, slipping through the legal loophole of California's antimiscegenation law. That is to say, Filipinos were not considered Asiatic or Mongolian; they were Malay. In 1934, the California legislature amended the law and inserted Malay, along with "negroes, mulattos, Indians, and Mongolians," as racial groups ineligible to marry members of the white race.

Race in America is fundamentally based on a black-white binary system, yet a hierarchy of racial classification has been constructed, with each socially designated, politically defined group being measured against this dual racial structure of white at the top, black at the bottom. Asians and other groups of color have also experienced their share of racialization, as well as systematic exclusion based on their racialized reality. Much like the "one-drop rule" that has socially engineered an African American racial group and allocated power, privilege, and prestige to only those who are legally defined as belonging to the white racial group, during World War II one eighth or more of Japanese ancestry was the criteria for forcibly removing Japanese Americans from their homes and placing them into internment camps.

THE INTERVIEWS

The Racialization of Biracial Experience

Meanings of race are formed and transformed, according to Omi and Winant (1986), through "the process by which social, economic, and political forces determine the content and importance of racial categories, and by which they are in turn shaped by racial meanings" (pp. 61-62). "Racialization," they explain, refers to "the extension of racial meaning to a previously racially unclassified relationship, social practice, or group" (p. 64). A series of personal encounters inform individuals as to their racial status in American society. By the time one has become an adult, one's racial membership within a hierarchically structured, racialized society has been concretized. From birth to adulthood, race as a taken-for-granted organizing tool of social reality transfigures into something obvious, natural, and common sensical (Omi & Winant, 1986; Thornton, 1992).

Many biracial interviewees in this pilot study have explained how they learned about their racialized self through social interaction. They identified specific interactional incidents as having foisted race onto them and alerted them to their racialized existence. One 25-year-old biracial African American/European American woman explained,

> Growing up, you don't think about race much. I mean it's always there, but you're busy trying to grow up and do kid things. It's only when the accumulation of those "racial moments" keep happening—some are subtle, some are more blatant in-your-face—then, you begin to say "hey, I'm different." I think most black people or racial minorities know what I'm saying. Like, my parents were these real "love sees no color" types who just thought if they'd love me enough, I wouldn't face much trouble; after all, I am very light. I don't know if my parents consciously thought that since I'm light, I'll be OK. I guess they were saying since I'm light or close to white, I won't have to worry about what my race is. Well, they were wrong. Kids are cruel. These kids' parents are cruel. Love isn't enough, sometimes . . . when you're getting pulled and pushed by blacks *and* whites.

A 23-year-old African American/European American man also discussed how he came to know "the dilemma of race" through "incidents" in his life that he later pieced together as an adult with a racial awareness. He stated,

> I never thought of my race as a dilemma until when I was 5 or so. This white kid on my block called me a nigger out of the blue. Just out of the blue! For some strange reason, I knew this was a bad word and that it had something to do with the fact that my mom was different [mother is African American], but I didn't really comprehend the full picture. These are the kinds of incidents when you look back, it gets you so damn angry you wanna go start a riot or something, like you've been betrayed by a society that has lied to you all these years. See, you gotta develop an awareness about these things. Once I lifted my blinders and realized that we got a lot of racial cleaning to do, then I was able to make sense of all the racist remarks and fights and all. As a child, you don't know what hit you. Kids are mean, yeah, but they also act out the racism they learn.

An Asian/European American biracial woman whose racialized experiences were more subtle also recounted how lived experiences taught her she was racially separate from her peers. Although this Eurasian woman first asserted that she had been "accepted by all groups" and has not been "discriminated against" by anyone, she then recalled,

> Just once, when I was about 8 years old, I think. I went over to my friend's birthday party. Her cousins were visiting from Minnesota. Her male cousin who was about 13 said "Ooh, you're Chinese. You're Chinese. You eat stink-food." Without missing a beat, my friend says to him (her cousin), "You dummy, she's Japanese." Thinking back now, it's so strange. Maybe, my friend's mother told them my dad was Japanese, but it just seemed so out of nowhere that this kid said this. And my friend actually knew I was half-Japanese, and I never ever said anything verbally to her. I guess just by knowing my dad, she already labeled me. I was really hurt. I thought I was just like them, but when this boy pointed out my Asian side, especially in this negative way and my friend stated my race as Japanese, it really told me that my difference was always apparent to them.

Another Asian/European American woman explained how her racial self-image was blatantly challenged in one particular encounter with a European American person.

> I always thought I looked white, I guess because my Korean (American) friends said I looked really white. They joked about my blondish-brown hair and green eyes. Then one day this white person called me a flat-faced slant-eye. This was a blow to the image I had developed of myself from my mom and my (Korean) peers always telling me how much of a Caucasian I was. I always thought of myself as a white person who was part-Korean. Most of my friends are all Korean. Most Koreans assume I'm white so they don't ask me "What are you?" I used to think Caucasians thought I was one of them too, but now I'm not sure. Sometimes Spanish (Latino) people just start speaking to me in Spanish, so I guess they think I'm Spanish. Right now, I'm going through this self-evaluation period in my life where I'm questioning my race. I feel like I'm going to have to choose one over the other, but no matter which one I choose, I'll never fit in because while people will accept me like my Korean friends do, they'll think I'm of a different race.

In contrast, a 20-year-old Asian/European American biracial male stated that Asian Americans pointed out his racial difference. He said,

> Whites always saw me as white. They never said nothing about racial stuff so I assume I was accepted as one of them. It was the Asians that always

told me how I wasn't Asian. I hated going to [Asian] church functions because these kids would call me names. I asked my mom one day to leave my dad home so I wouldn't be seen as too white. I think what they said to me really affected my self-esteem. When I now walk into a room full of Asians, I wonder what they're thinking, like "Why is this white dude here" or something. I feel a little insecure around Asians. I feel like a kid back in church again when I'm around them. Those feelings come back from when I was a kid, all over again.

A series of these critical moments contribute to the racialization of the identities of biracial individuals and the identification of their difference from their monoracially-identified parent groups. These experiences thus serve as puzzle pieces to the external component of biracial individuals' racialized identities, which are often, but not exclusively, separate from both white and nonwhite monoracially identified individuals. Psychologist Carla Bradshaw (1992) has noted that the ambiguous external racial coding or variegated phenotypical appearances of the racially mixed significantly contribute to their ambiguous, displaced social position. People's own understanding of their identity is filtered through cumulative racial experiences. The process by which people come to understand their racialized selves is inextricably linked to their group's social location in the society and the social ecology of the environment in which they are raised (Cross, 1991; Miller, 1992; Root, 1992b). It often means seeing themselves through the lens of others, usually the superordinate racial group but also monoracially identified minority groups, as well, or what W. E. B. Du Bois (1903/ 1975) called, "the veil."

Identity formation is complex, interactive, and ever-evolving, yet racial designations have been created and employed to simplify, sort, and rank individuals into fixed, exclusive categories. Placing racial designations is like trying to frame a moving picture. Yet, as well-socialized members of a racialized society, biracial individuals are also—at times—rigorous defenders of racialization and its employment in their everyday lives. The aforementioned "racial moments" that were thrust upon the interviewees illustrate how taken-for-granted assumptions about race and racial labeling sometimes come into conflict with how one understands oneself as a member of a group or how one wears his or her racial uniform (Takaki, 1989), resulting in racial dissonance (Kich, 1982).

The Sociological Significance
of *What Are You?* Encounters

The sets of assumptions and the layers of social meanings attached to specific racial groups become the social gauge for how one is to understand, respond to, and interact with people as representatives of these groups. Omi and Winant (1986) referred to these series of preconceived racial notions upon which we base our understanding of the social world as "a compass for navigating race relations" (p. 62). When the racial compass fails, the *What Are You?* question is prompted. This question is often posed innocently and unintentionally. Psychologist Carla Bradshaw (1992) has noted that "it reveals an awareness of unfamiliarity due to variances in physical features" (p. 77). Thus the social-psychological underpinnings of this question assumes the foreignness and nonbelonging of phenotypically ambiguous individuals.

In addition to physical appearance, Omi and Winant (1986) have said that when people are racially designated as card-carrying, uniform-wearing members of a specific racial group, they are expected to look and act a certain way—to be in accordance with their racial formula, to follow the racial script. Comments such as "You don't look Chicano," "You don't talk black," or "You don't act Asian" reveal racial expectations. Moreover, the question *What Are You?* that is so often asked of racially mixed people unveils the racial, social disorientation of the person asking the question as much as it potentially dislocates the person being asked. The racially mixed person may feel doubly *other*ed by such constant interrogation (Bradshaw, 1992), because the person who asks this question conveys his or her organization of society. The interrogator seems to be saying,

> In my construction of the world, your look, your speech, your behavior, your mannerisms, your name, and your overall presence do not have a place. You defy my limited understanding and social application of race. I have no label to fit you, to pigeon-hole you, and therefore to make assumptions about you. I need to know what you are so I can ease this discomfort I feel for being unable to peg you.

And thus, the *What Are You?* question represents what Nash called "biracial people's mucking up the system" (quoted in J. Williams, 1990,

p. 3) and what Omi and Winant (1986) referred to as "a momentary crisis of racial meaning" (p. 62) by the asker of the *What Are You?* question.

Both sociologist Michael Thornton (1992) and journalist Lisa Jones (1994a) have asked what biracial/multiracial people have in common. Does being biracial in and of itself, or possessing multiple racial loyalties, warrant separate political recognition (e.g., a distinct census category)? Thornton and Jones argue that perhaps the only commonality biracials have with one another is their sense of difference from the American mainstream. Many biracials and their allies who are attempting to make a claim for political recognition are searching for something, anything, to bind all biracials and multiracials together. Social and racial ambiguity, fluid identities amid rigid racial boundaries, and a groundedness in duality and multiplicity have been noted as defining biraciality and binding the biracial experience (Root, 1992b). The *What Are You?* encounters thus become concrete, identifiable experiences that bind a great number of biracial people together and fortify their sense of biraciality. The *What Are You?* question so commonly asked of biracial individuals is a poignant and striking theme that runs through all of the 20 interviewees' stories in this preliminary study.

A 24-year-old African American/European American biracial man discussed what Omi and Winant referred to as a crisis in racial meaning for the observer of phenotypically ambiguous individuals. He explained,

"What are you?" Boy, that's a question I try to dodge every day of my life. Maybe, even several times a day. I don't mind getting asked, but I don't like to answer it. I try to feel out the person, you know, their motives and stuff. I think [I get asked] cuz I look pretty mixed, like I could be anything. I also think it has to do with my name [an Anglicized surname], my so-called standard-sounding English with a dab of X-generation, hip-hop talk. Yet, I look sort of white, but not really. Not enough to be black, not enough to be white. I'm not easily identifiable. I really think that what I represent turns other people's worlds upside down. Some [people] get really angry at me for not giving them the answer they want to hear, insisting that I belong to this group or that group. It's their problem, not mine. It took me a while to understand that, but now that I know, I have the power to determine—at least for that moment—who I am and how they are going to respond to me. I turn it back on them now. I've decided I'll never let others make me feel crappy about myself when they are the ones who are asking a highly personal question about the very essence of who I am.

Learning to negotiate her dual racial affinities and to cope with her racial ambiguity have given this 21-year-old biracial African American/European American woman the experiential tools to expand her racial boundaries beyond her parent groups. She reflected,

Not looking black has been both a source of pain and a source of pride. I'm not trying to be conceited or racist against my own. I got rejected a lot, but I also got a lot of attention. It's a paradox. Because I don't even look like a light-skinned sister, I pass for Italian, Latina, white, and someone the other day said I looked like I was one of those Asian and white mixes, hapa, right? Well, when white kids find out that my dad is black, then I am suddenly treated differently, needless to say I went from being one of them to being a nigger (excuse my language). Then, black people totally distrust me, you know? If I claim I'm black, I have to prove myself and some blacks even laugh at me, like I'm a white girl trying to be black. But, if I don't wear a shirt that says, "I'm black and proud" all the time, then I'm a sell-out, Oreo, wanna-be trying to pass cuz I'm ashamed of being black. . . . Maybe, because I have the luxury of passing, I actually freely claim my blackness, but then move in other racial circles too. I've learned to be true to my multicultural self. I don't let what others say get to me. I just tell people to judge me on my actions. I support all causes for freedom, including many black causes because they are my causes, about my people. But because other groups can claim me based on my looks, I also feel a closeness to them. That's why I support Chicano studies and biracial peoples' things and all. They're my causes too. It's weird, I don't think someone who belongs to one race and who looks and feels loyal to only one race can understand.

A biracial African American/European American man in his mid-20s, who identifies monoracially as an African American, drew upon his biraciality when having to struggle with being gay as well. This respondent has connected the *other*ness of his white ancestry with the *other*ness of being gay. He explained,

My mother died when I was really little. I hardly remember her. Just that she had pretty, soft hands. She was white. My mother's family really didn't accept us completely. I grew up around black people. I'm black. I mean, in a way, I wished I could've known my mother and all but I'm really glad that I have a strong black identity. It's hard enough being black, I don't need to be mixed on top of that. I didn't like being light because I'd get asked *What Are You?* so much, so I might've overcompensated a bit, but now it's not an issue. . . . When I was first coming to terms with being gay, it was so hard. Being light, other people asked me, What Are You? but being gay, I asked myself, "What the hell am I?" Being gay and being light are considered sissy characteristics for a black man. Trying to put on a straight act when you're really attracted to other guys was harder than trying to be black when you know deep down inside you were given birth to by a white woman, even though in some ways they are similar. In some ways that white part of me and the gay part of me worked to console each other. I had two secrets. Both were painful. But they were also my source of strength. These two secrets became challenges to myself to learn to love all of me. Believe me, I'm glad I went through what I went through, but I never wanna go through that again or have anyone else go through that. Today, I consider myself to be a black, gay man who's light-skinned so when I'm asked, "What Are You?," I say "I'm black and gay."

Although this respondent anchors his racial identity within a monoracial frame of reference due to his upbringing, environment, socialization, and absence of one parent, he possesses a consciously articulated multiple identity as a light-skinned, African American, gay man.

A 28-year-old Asian/European American biracial man said that he locates his identity in relationship to his parents and explained the layers of conscious identity struggle these encounters facilitate for him. He reflected,

Yeah, people ask me all the time, *What Are You?* Some of my friends get really sick of it. But I can't help it if people ask. I don't know what it is about my looks that provokes this question. It's kinda flattering. Except the other day, this person, I think he was white, he said, "Are you a Euroasian?" I never heard that term so I busted out laughing. He got really upset, like he was offended or something. So, I asked him back, "Are you a Euroasian?" and he said, "I'm obviously an American-bred white boy." Well, he wasn't that obvious. He could've been Latino or something. His hair was darker than mine and his speech was very nonwhite. I replied by saying that my dad is Filipino and my mom is Swedish and German. I feel like I don't have my own racial identity. I have a racial identity through my parents. For me, being mixed is really a positive thing. Some people— usually of color—say I'm being treated like an exotic object, but I don't see it that way. I get a lot of attention, and it feeds my ego. I think I struggled more as a gay man. Being gay, it's hard on your self-esteem. Now that I'm out and feeling good about myself, my mixed identity also adds to my positive self-image.

Erving Goffman (1959) argued that the "presentation of the self" results from a dramaturgical interactive process between the social actor and his or her audience in which roles are played, impressions are fostered, and encounters are staged. A 25-year-old biracial Asian/European American man told how his racial manipulation and presentation can work for or against him in a highly racialized society.

> Yeah, I get asked *What Are You?* a lot . . . I think society sees me and my friends as men of color. It can be good and it can be bad. I also see myself as a man of color. That's the great part. I have a sense of belonging. It gives me a kind of masculinity that both Asians and whites don't have. But the downside is like the other day, I was speeding on the freeway and the LAPD stopped me. I get stopped by the cops all the time. That's when I have to stress that I'm Japanese or white or both. When I got pulled over that other day, the cop asked me for my ID. My name isn't Spanish. . . . It's a common black or white last name so it's kind of ambiguous. He was such an asshole. He asked me if I was a gang member or if I had drugs in my truck. The cop starts calling into his headquarters, "One Mexican, 25-year-old, male. . . . " As he was doing this, I was getting pissed, but I knew that I had to shift my speech patterns to standard English and to reveal my true race because it's stereotyped more favorably than Mexicans. I know that sucks, but I was arrested before because that cop thought I was black, so my survival was on the line. After the cop was done, I said, "Excuse me sir," real politely, "I'm not Mexican. My father is white and my mother is Japanese." From that moment on, the cop changed. I don't know if he was embarrassed because he misidentified me or because as a Japanese/white man, could he not see me as a drug dealer or gang member. My speech can also be considered nonethnic, which contrasts to my Latino-looking appearance so that's one edge I have. I really have to manipulate myself and project different selves in order to survive in a society that treats brown and black males like shit.

Because of this Asian/European American biracial man's lived experiences as a man of color, he has developed a sociological understanding of the social location of the various racial groups to which he belongs and to which he is mistakenly assigned. In addition, he is acutely aware of how race, gender, class, and culture (e.g., use of standard English) get played out in his life. This understanding allows him to "manipulate" his outward race and "project different selves" during social interaction (Goffman, 1959); it permits him in-group membership among his racially and culturally mixed friends of color. Yet, this interviewee can also powerfully subvert the racial system when he is being challenged and having "race done to him" by authorities whose presupposed racial ranking could have serious life-threatening consequences for him. This biracial individual has learned to "do race" with twists and turns, stepping in and out of the racial molds prescribed to him by the larger society that projects race onto him.[2] At times, he may engage in a calculated effort to do race, whereas at other times, his racial actions and projections may be far more subconscious.

The *What Are You?* question has been posed and perceived largely as possessing negative implications by the asker of the question and negative consequences for the respondent (Bradshaw, 1992), indicating marginality, alienation, and exoticization of biracial people. However, most respondents in this pilot study, who have long thought about and processed their *What Are You?* encounters had complex interpretations about what this question implied about their parents, about their parent groups, about themselves, and about the society at large. Many interviewees expressed that these encounters gave them a social-psychological platform to articulate and proclaim their identities during the interaction, to rethink their identities and to empower themselves long after the encounters had taken place, regardless of the interrogators' motives or their uses of biracial individuals' responses to the *What Are You?* question (i.e., the asker rejects the biracial person's self-identity, monoracially recodes the biracial person according to social customs, accepts the biracial person's proclamation, reorients himself or herself to a definitive identity amid the biracial person's racial ambiguity, and so on).

Although what others think of them, how others perceive them, and subsequently how others treat them racially certainly inform their self-understanding, the biracial interviewees' explanations of their *What Are You?* encounters reveal that they are not mere receivers of social messages or conformists to prescriptive racial categories. They are also active participants in shaping their identities and creating social reality. Not only do biracial individuals "get race done unto them," but they also do race as well (Lemmel, 1994, personal communication). Biracial individuals often create new meanings of race during social interaction, sometimes forcing those with whom they interact to rethink their assumptions and shift their understanding. Biracial individuals must constantly negotiate and renegotiate their in-group membership as their contestations of racial meanings alter, solidify, or expand racial boundaries. At times, their racial identity choices rigorously defend the rigidity of racial boundaries as stated by the biracial black/white respondent who today identifies as a light-skinned black, gay man. At other times, their racial identity choices undermine and subvert racial dichotomization through fluidly moving about the various boundaries without shifting the core of their biracial identity, (e.g., the black/white woman who feels a personal affinity to Chicano, biracial, and African American causes, all as her "own"; the Asian/European American man whose larger identity is that of a man of color). The salience of race in the lives of biracial individuals waxes and wanes while its significance continues to underpin their social and political identities. Thus, What Are You? encounters illustrate that race is indeed a process of social interaction, being created and re-created, defined and redefined as biracials encounter others in the backdrop of a highly racialized society.

CONCLUSION

From the early racialized periods of American history until quite recently, the social legitimacy of racially mixed people remained uncontested. With the coming of age of racially mixed people, popular literature now regularly features stories about biracial people, biracial scholars conduct social scientific research by and about themselves, biracial students organize educational conferences and publish journals on biracial identity and the mass media highlights high-profile biracial individuals who often nonchalantly discuss or casually refer to their multiple racial identities in public forums. Although biracial people are still portrayed within the sociohistorical context of single-race definitions and the limitations of an institutionally and ideologically racist social structure, old racial paradigms are being challenged as the discourse on race evolves and incorporates multiple racial agencies. The ever-growing presence of biracial individuals exposes the contradictions of the stated national ideology of racial purity and separation.

The study of multiple social identities illustrates the important intersection between micro and macro social relationships (Omi & Winant, 1986; Root, 1992b). The social location and dislocation of biracial populations within any given social group or institutional context reveal how racial group boundaries are constructed, sustained, and transgressed via formal and informal membership rules; they tell how groups acquire and maintain status, power, and resources within the larger system of race relations; and they inform the society's organizing rationale for racial stratification. The social positionality of racially mixed populations—be they Asian/European American (Kich, 1982; Mass, 1992; Murphy-Shige-matsu, 1986; Nakashima, 1988; T. K. Williams, 1991), Asian/ African American (Hall, 1980; Thornton, 1983; T. K. Williams, 1991), mestizo Latinos (Graham, 1990; Menchú, 1984; Xicay-Santos, 1993), mixed-blood Native Americans (Wilson, 1992), or black/white (Gibbs, 1992; Lemmel, 1992; Miller, 1992; Rosner, 1993) serves as an important so-ciopolitical site for racial contestation both interpersonally and struc-turally. The examination of multiple social identities such as biraciality not only offers new ways of understanding the concept of race or revolu-tionary ways of processing self, but moreover, it provides sociological insight into how ideological vestiges still inform our ever-shifting social landscape, bridging the present with the past and connecting the micro with the macro.

NOTES

1. In the summer of 1992, my former student and good friend, Kevin Yoshida—a bilingual Spanish/English speaking, biracial Japanese American/Euro American man, took me to Arena and Circus discos in Hollywood and Robby's in Pomona. Inspired by the people I met and came to know and love at Circus and Arena, I began conducting an ethnographic study. Many members in these particular gay, Latino settings are in fact first-generation biracials. Some of them, like Kevin, are not even part-Latino, yet have been accorded Latino membership as they "do race" and "have race done" to them in the field site.

2. Sociologists in the field of ethnomethodology, such as Harold Garfinkle (1967), Candace West and Don H. Zimmerman (1991) and ethnographer Barrie Thorne (1994) have examined how one "does gender." The socially constructed nature of race or doing race has striking parallels with gender or doing gender.

13

Piecing Together the Puzzle

Self-Concept and Group Identity in Biracial Black/White Youth

LYNDA D. FIELD

The idea for my research originated in a conversation with my then clinical supervisor Christine Chao, while I was a predoctoral graduate student in clinical psychology. Chris is Euroasian, her husband is African American, and they had just had their first child. She and I had often talked about race and ethnicity, because at the time I was exploring my own developmental issues of ethnic identity. We shared in common a strong identification as women of color but also the awareness that our mixed heritage brought up a variety of issues that might or might not be unique to our multiheritage status. My graduate training was focused on children and adolescents and while watching Chris' infant daughter, we speculated about her identity development. Chris suggested that I develop this topic into my dissertation. I recall vividly the excitement that the idea instilled.

An initial trip to the library in 1989 encouraged my interests; at the time the published literature in psychology on biracial individuals was extremely sparse. In reading the few articles that were published in academic journals, I was concerned by the overrepresentation of case studies, particularly because they portrayed biracial children and adolescents as having poor self-esteem and as being maladjusted. Yet, I knew that although some of my peers of mixed racial and ethnic heritage had gone through periods when identity conflicts were dominant, all were well-adjusted individuals. I saw a need for a systematic study of self-concept and adjustment in biracial adolescents. I chose to study those of black and white heritage, because this group in particular had been most pathologized in both academic literature and in the public press. At the time I was also enamored with William Cross's theory of racial identity development and Janet Helms and Thomas Parham's revisions of this theory. I had been analyzing my own development within that framework; thus this conceptual model heavily influenced my thinking while writing my dissertation. ⚏

In increasing numbers, couples are crossing racial and ethnic barriers and forming interracial unions. Thus a significant number of children being born today are biracial. Opponents of interracial marriages have argued that children of these unions will face numerous obstacles and become maladjusted (see reviews by Gordon, 1964; Henriques, 1974; Spickard, 1989). Much of the concern has centered around the development of self-concept and racial identity in biracial adolescents and young adults.

In our race-conscious society, biracial children are confronted with questions regarding their racial heritage early in their development. Historically there has been the concern that biracial children were at risk for failing to develop a positive racial identity and consequently a positive sense of themselves. This thinking was based in part on the idea that the hierarchical nature of race relations interferes with the biracial child's ability to identify with one or both parents, and one or both of their racial/cultural heritages. There has also been concern that rejection by one or both racial groups leaves biracial children at risk for developing a marginal identity, poor self-concept, and behavioral maladjustment (Benson, 1981; Gibbs, 1987).

Although the well-being of biracial individuals has been of some interest to scholars and clinicians for many years, there have been few empirical investigations. Some support for the view that biracial individuals are at greater risk for negative self-concepts has come from clinical case studies (Gibbs, 1987; Lyles et al., 1985; Sommers, 1964; Teicher, 1968). However, these studies are inherently biased because they relied solely on a clinical sample. The data were gathered from individuals who were having difficulties and sought help, not from a general sample of biracial individuals. Several recent studies of non-clinical samples of biracial adults have provided a more optimistic view of biracial individuals (Hall, 1980; Kich, 1982; Murphy-Shigematsu, 1988; Nakashima, 1988; Poussaint, 1984). These studies suggest that being biracial enhances one's self-concept through the development of a multicultural identity. However, the studies contain methodological problems that prevent us from being able to generalize from their findings. These problems range from sample ascertainment bias, to the overreliance on semistructured interviews and the failure to use standardized instruments and comparison groups. Root (1992a) has argued that although scientific methodology views the absence of a comparison group as a methodological flaw, it may actually be a strength. She has expressed concern that when comparison groups are employed, they often define what is normative behavior.

Two recent studies of black-white biracial adolescents have used psychometrically sound measures of self-worth and adolescent adjustment (Cauce et al., 1992; Gibbs & Hines, 1992) with nonclinical samples. Cauce and associates compared 22 biracial adolescents to their minority peers and found no significant differences between the two groups. However, these adolescents did not initially identify as biracial but instead identified as either black or Asian, depending on their minority heritage. Their dual racial heritage was only discovered during interviews. This excluded the population of biracial adolescents who identified as white, biracial, or had not developed a solid orientation. Gibbs and Hines's study of 12 biracial adolescents found that the majority showed good self-esteem and did not report significant behavioral problems. However, 3 of the 12 (25%) did show evidence of poor adjustment. These biracial adolescents had more negative self-esteem and greater ambivalence over labeling themselves as black. The methodology employed did not allow for a causal explanation for these findings.

RACIAL IDENTITY THEORY

Racial identity theorists such as William Cross and Janet Helms have written about the importance of understanding the relationship between racial identity and self-concept. Cross (1991) has theorized that one's self-concept is made up of two multidetermined factors: *personal identity* (PI) and *reference group orientation* (RGO). PI is believed to be made up of various facets of the self, excluding factors related to racial/ethnic group membership. In contrast, RGO is typically defined as a pattern of behavior, interests, and values that is associated with a particular racial group (Helms, 1990b). Since the development of racial identity theories in the 1970s, there has been an ongoing debate regarding the relationship between self-concept and RGO (Cross, 1991). The majority of these theories have hypothesized a strong relationship between the two constructs. It has been argued that adoption of a RGO that requires denial or distortions of self and/or racial heritage places the individual at risk for developing a negative self-concept and poor adjustment (Helms, 1990b). Helms has argued that the adoption of a white RGO by an individual of black racial heritage is associated with a negative self-concept. Would this apply to biracial adolescents of black and white heritage? A study was designed in part to address this question.

DESCRIPTION OF THE STUDY

In 1991 I was a graduate student at the University of Denver in Denver, Colorado, and conducted this research for my doctoral dissertation. The study was a systematic investigation of the relationship between biraciality, RGO, and self-concept in a sample of adolescents who have one black parent and one white parent. The population of interest had a low base rate in the general population; therefore it was necessary to try several strategies to recruit subjects. Most adolescents were obtained through word of mouth, or "snowball" sampling, a methodology frequently used in studies of multiracial individuals (Hall, 1980; Kich, 1982). Many contacts in minority communities were used to spread the information that a study was being conducted, and biracial teens were being paid $5 for spending 45 minutes to complete several questionnaires. Applicants were asked to provide the names of other biracial teens they thought might be interested in participating, and this almost always produced one or more subjects. The same procedure was used to recruit African American and Caucasian subjects.

Data were collected from 31 biracial adolescents. Two natural comparison groups were used, one containing 31 African American and a second containing 31 Caucasian adolescents. The three groups were closely matched on age, gender, demographic location (e.g. racial composition of neighborhood), and socioeconomic status (SES, defined as the Hollingshead & Redlich 2-factor theory). Despite efforts to match, an analysis of variance (ANOVA) revealed significant racial group differences in SES when SES is computed solely based on father's education and occupational status. Fathers of African American adolescents had significantly less education and lower occupational status, $F(2, 82) = 3.57; p < .05$, than fathers of biracial or Caucasian adolescents. The ages ranged from 13 to 18, with a mean of 16.5 years of age. Although attempts were made to recruit equal numbers of males and females, each group contained 19 girls and 13 boys. The adolescents all lived in the metropolitan Denver area. However, they came from a cross-section of neighborhoods, including predominately white suburbs, racially integrated middle-class urban areas and predominately black suburbs and urban areas. Efforts were made to match the location of black subjects to biracial adolescents. Biracial youths came from families with the highest divorce rate (50%) compared to those of the black (35.5%) and white (25.8%) youths. However, this difference was not statistically significant.

All subjects were offered the option of coming to the researcher's office at the university or having the researcher come to their home. Most participants were seen at home. All adolescents completed four questionnaires. With the exclusion of a demographic questionnaire, all measures possess good psychometric properties. The Self-Perception Profile for Adolescents (Harter, 1986) was used to measure global self-worth, as well as the separate self-concept domains of perceived social acceptance, physical attractiveness, and romantic appeal. The Youth Self-Report (Achenbach & Edelbrock, 1987) was used as a measure of behavioral adjustment, and a Reference Group Orientation Scale was developed (Field, 1992) based on the Dual Acculturation Scale (Guzman, 1986). In order to obtain a separate measure of behavioral functioning, parents of the adolescents completed the Child Behavior Checklist (Achenbach & Edelbrock, 1983). A demographic questionnaire was designed for the purposes of this study. In addition, biracial teens were asked to complete an optional semistructured interview. These interviews varied widely, depending on the teens' ability to discuss and share their experiences. Some teens quickly answered the questions and were done in a few minutes while others went on for 1 or 2 hours.

RESULTS

A series of Multiple Analyses of Variance (MANOVAs) were used to assess the relationship between race, self-concept, RGO, and behavioral adjustment.

Self-Concept

There were no significant differences between the racial groups in either their global self-worth or the specific domains of self-concept (i.e., perceptions of social acceptance, physical attractiveness, or romantic appeal), F (2, 90) = .64, p = ns. When only global self-concept was assessed, biracial adolescents reported neither more negative nor positive perceptions of themselves than did their minority and majority peers. However, this picture changed when RGO was added to the equation.

Reference Group Orientation

The questionnaire employed to measure RGO focuses on the adolescent's participation and enjoyment of the culture of both the black and the white community (e.g., friendships, dating partners, music, and clothing styles, etc.). It was not a measure of the psychological construct of racial identity (e.g., seeing oneself as a member of a particular racial group). Thus all adolescents could potentially hold a bicultural RGO. However, it was hypothesized that monoracial adolescents were more likely than biracial peers to hold a monoracial group orientation. A chi-square analysis confirmed predictions that RGO is highly related to a teen's racial group membership; $\chi^2(4, N = 93) = 48.37, p < .00001$. The pattern of race and RGO association is presented in Table 13.1.

Table 13.1 Reference Group Orientation (RGO) by Racial Group

	White RGO n (Percentage)	Black RGO n (Percentage)	Bicultural RGO n (Percentage)
Race			
White	24 (77)	1 (3)	6 (19)
Black	1 (3)	20 (64)	10 (32)
Biracial	5 (16)	14 (45)	12 (39)

In this table, it is evident that biracial teens had the most diverse pattern of RGO. Biracial youths were not significantly more bicultural in their orientation (39%) than their black peers (33%), but both groups were more bicultural in their orientation than their white peers (19%).

RGO and Self-Concept

The measure of RGO employed allows for four orientations: bicultural, black, white, or marginal. Based on Helms's (1990b) conceptualization of the relationship between RGO and self-concept with individuals of black racial heritage, it was hypothesized that biracial and black adolescents who held a RGO that caused them to feel uncomfortable with all groups (e.g., a marginal orientation) or one that devalued their black racial heritage (e.g. a white orientation) would also show significantly more negative global self-worth and specific domains of self-concept. Two MANOVAs employing planned comparisons were used to investigate this hypothesize. The first used only the data for the biracial adolescents and the second combined the data for biracial and black adolescents. RGO was the independent variable, whereas global self-worth and the specific domains of peer social acceptance, romantic appeal, and physical appearance were the dependent variables. No significant differences were found between black and bicultural orientation; however, comparisons between a black and white orientation were significant (Table 13.2).

Table 13.2 Self-Concept Domains by Reference Group Orientation
(RGO) for Biracial Adolescents

Self-Concept Domain	n	Mean	SD
Global Self-Worth			
RGO			
Bicultural	11	3.1	.72
Black	14	3.3	.56
White	5	2.4	.72
Social Acceptance			
RGO			
Bicultural	11	3.4	.52
Black	14	3.4	.54
White	5	2.8	.54
Physical Appearance			
RGO			
Bicultural	11	2.9	.62
Black	14	3.4	.48
White	5	2.6	.60
Romantic Appeal			
RGO			
Bicultural	11	2.9	.62
Black	14	3.4	.48
White	5	2.6	.60

Planned Comparisons (RGO)
Black × bicultural multivariate test of significance: $F(1, 27) = 1.6$, $p < 0$ ns
Black × white multivariate test of significance: $F(1, 27) = 2.19$, $p < .10$
Global self-worth: Univariate $F(1, 27) = 8.39$, $p < .01$
Social acceptance: Univariate $F(1, 27) = 3.98$, $p < .06$
Physical appearance: Univariate $F(1, 27) = 4.44$, $p < .05$
Romantic appeal: Univariate $F(1, 27) = 7.29$, $p < .01$

In summary, biracial teens who had a RGO that reflected comfort with their black racial group—a black ($n = 14$) or bicultural ($n = 11$) orientation—demonstrated more positive self-concepts than did biracial teens who chose a white ($n = 5$) RGO.

Behavioral Adjustment

Behavioral adjustment was assessed from both the adolescents' perspective, employing the Youth Self-Report, and from their parents' perspective, employing the Child Behavior Checklist. A series of MANOVAs

Table 13.3 Parental Report of Behavioral Adjustment by Race

YSR-Behavior Problems	n	Mean	SD
Internalizing			
*Biracial	32	52.9	8.1
White	31	50.8	10.8
Black	31	51.3	9.1
Externalizing			
Biracial	32	56.5	7.7
White	31	51.6	10.1
Black	31	52.1	7.6
Total Behavioral Problems			
Biracial	32	54.6	7.8
White	31	50.7	10.4
Black	31	51.4	8.7
Group effects (Race)			
Multivariate test of significance: $F(2, 91) = 1.16, p < .17$			
Internalizing (Univariate): $F(2, 91) = .23, p < .65$			
Externalizing (Univariate): $F(2, 91) = 3.08, p < .05$			
ANOVA total behavior problems $F(2, 91) = .72, p < .18$			

*There were originally 32 subjects, but one was subsequently dropped.

were conducted. Although there were no significant racial group differences in adjustment based on parents' reports, a difference was found for the adolescents' self-reported behavior. A MANOVA was conducted in which race was the independent variable and the Youth Self-Report "T" scores for externalizing and internalizing, as well as the total behavior problems reported, were the dependent variables. Although the multivariate F was not significant, there were significant racial group differences in the amount of externalizing behavior reported, Univariate $F(2, 91) = 3.08, p < .05$ (see Table 13.3).

Although the results indicate that biracial adolescents reported more externalizing behavior than did their black or white peers, and this was statistically significant, it is not clear that this finding represents a meaningful difference. The 4- to 5-point difference in scores simply indicates that they reported perhaps one additional problem such as lying, fighting, and so on. However, it is notable that a similar trend was found by Cauce and her colleagues in their 1992 study (personal communication, 1992). This finding was not explained by RGO; there were no significant differences in behavioral adjustment based on RGO.

Subjective Pieces of Identity

Racial/ethnic identity is a complex construct that many theorists and researchers struggle to operationalize. Current measures of reference group orientation tend to give us a more behavioral measure of the extent to which individuals participate in various cultures. In fact, in revising the current measure, the author relied on a focus group of African American teenagers who responded to two questions, leading to very behavioral descriptions: What do black teens do that is different from white teens? If you had a black friend and thought they were "acting white," what would they be doing?

Whereas outward behavior is an expression of more subjective identity states, there is also a separate component of associated feelings and thoughts. An attempt was made to gain information about these thoughts and feelings in a separate questionnaire. It obtained demographic information and asked the youths to write down which ethnic/racial label they applied to themselves. The instrument also included questions regarding their comfort level with their racial heritage, which race they most identified with, which group they felt and thought like, which background they would choose to be, and which racial group they most resembled. In addition, a series of six questions attempted to assess their comfort among black and white peers of the same social class and age in three different settings; informal gatherings, at school, and at a place of employment.

The biracial adolescents responses were examined within each of the three RGOs. In general, all reported feeling *very comfortable* to *comfortable* with their racial heritage. Black-oriented biracial adolescents (n = 14) were most likely to chose a black identity label (n = 9), with the remainder choosing biracial. These youths tended to feel most comfortable among black peers, and most felt they looked black, although two indicated that they looked white. However, they reported identifying most with being biracial and felt most like a biracial person. If they could be of any racial background, these youths were almost equally divided between choosing to be black (n = 8) and choosing to be biracial (n = 6).

The biracial youths who held a white RGO (n = 5) all reported feeling somewhat more comfortable in white groups than in black groups, with the exception of the classroom setting, where it did not matter. All indicated that *biracial* was the racial/ethnic label that they used for themselves. None of these youths reported identifying with black people, and instead chose white or mixed race even though more than half would choose to be black if they could have any heritage ($n = 3$), and they felt black or biracial. All but one indicated that their physical appearance was most similar to black people. The other adolescent chose Hispanic.

The biculturally oriented group ($n = 12$) gave the most varied and difficult-to-interpret responses. When asked to write down the ethnic/racial label they used for themselves, half wrote black and half wrote biracial. Only two felt they most identified with other biracial peers, the rest were divided evenly between identifying most with black and white peers. Similarly, they were divided in how they felt inside (e.g., black, white, biracial, *other*) and what race they most looked like. The biracial adolescents who had a bicultural orientation reported feeling equally comfortable in black and white informal gatherings and in the classroom, but were somewhat less comfortable in predominantly white employment settings.

If anything can be concluded from these results, it is that the relationship between various components of racial/ethnic identity is extremely complex. For example, biracial adolescents may apply a monoracial racial/ethnic label to themselves (e.g., black), yet be very bicultural in their lifestyle, while feeling more identified with other biracial adolescents, and desiring to be black.

Comparing the current results to findings reported a decade earlier by Hall (1980) provides some interesting contrasts. Hall's 1980 study of 30 black Japanese adults (mean age 24 years) employed similar methodology. She defined ethnic identity as the label a participant chose from a checklist. She then examined numerous factors in relationship to the identity choice (e.g., knowledge of each culture, friendships, demographic variables, etc). Hall found that a majority, 18 respondents, chose a black identity label, while 7 chose a biracial identity label. She found that choosing a black identity label was associated with a predominance of black neighbors and friends, knowing more about black culture, and feeling less accepted by Japanese Americans. Being a younger biracial individual increased the likelihood of identifying as black. In contrast in the present study, although the biracial adolescents were slightly more likely to hold a black RGO ($n = 14$) than a bicultural one ($n = 12$), summing across RGOs, the biracial black-white adolescents were more likely to use a biracial identity label (n = 21) than a black label (n = 11). Furthermore there was no clear relationship between the use of an ethnic identity label and the extent to which the adolescents interacted within each cultural group, as measured by the components of RGO (e.g., friendships, romantic relationships, music, language, clothing styles, etc.) or age; the average age for each RGO group was 16 years, with the white-oriented youths edging closer to 17 (16.8).

One possible explanation for this pattern of findings is a generation/cohort effect. At the time these adolescents were developing, the late 1980s, there was more widespread discussion in the national media regarding biracial children and a growing realization that monoracial labels did not adequately capture their heritage. Compared to the adults in Hall's study, the adolescents in the present study are more likely to have been encouraged to identify themselves as having mixed racial heritage. They therefore are more likely to make this choice when asked to choose an identity label, but it may not reflect their complex feelings about their identity or their cultural orientation. The failure to find a pattern between the various components of racial identity may also reflect a developmental process in which the adults in Hall's study had progressed further.

DISCUSSION

The results of this study indicated that biracial adolescents had self-concepts that were just as positive as their monoracial peers. The overall finding that biracial adolescents had positive self-concepts is extremely important in light of the historical pathologizing of biracial children in the popular media. Although most biracial adolescents were doing well, biracial adolescents who adopted a white RGO might have greater difficulty developing a positive self-concept than biracial or black peers who adopt either a black or bicultural orientation.

How can we understand the results of this study in the context of ongoing research and theorizing about the relationship of RGO to self-concept? Helms (1990b) has argued that simply holding a white RGO may not negatively affect a black person's self-concept; rather it is the active rejection of the black culture and its reflection of internalized racism that lead to negative consequences for the self. In the present study, interviews with the adolescents supported this theorizing. Although some of the biculturally oriented biracial adolescents appeared to participate more in the white community than in the black, none expressed negative feelings toward being of black heritage or toward the black community. In contrast, the white-oriented youths tended to immerse themselves in the white community and expressed negative feelings about their black heritage.

The impact of a white RGO in this study must be interpreted with caution, because the key findings are based on a small number of subjects ($n = 5$, 16% of the sample). However, when this investigator combined the qualitative interviews with the questionnaire data, the resulting profiles were compelling. The case of Mary provides a strong example.

Mary was an attractive 17-year-old female who grew up with her white mother and white stepfather but had regular contact with her black father. In many areas, Mary appeared well-adjusted: she was an A student at a competitive school, had many friends, and was an excellent athlete. Mary's mother saw Mary as well-adjusted, according to her ratings on the Child Behavior Checklist. But privately, Mary's mother mentioned to the interviewer her concern that Mary may be too hard on herself. On the RGO scale, Mary's scores indicated that she holds a white RGO, and in the interview, she articulated her discomfort in the black community.

I have never wished I was all black but I have wished I was all white, because like all my friends are all white, and there are all these stereotypes about blacks, and if I'm in a group of all whites sometimes I feel, like I wonder if they will all like me or anything, you know what I mean. Like all the guys I date are white . . . black guys are like aggressive, . . . they just want to get a girl and think that they are everything. They go down the halls yelling and like they are just more aggressive.

I feel more comfortable in all white than in all black settings, even though its sorta weird, because me physically, I am black. I look black, but inside me I am white. I act it. I think it. It's like in an all-black setting I feel like I look OK but I feel I am acting different. Whereas in an all-white setting they might look at me but like I act the same way [they do].

During the interview Mary expressed unhappiness with her identifiably black physical appearance. This unhappiness was vividly reflected in Mary's scores on the Self-Perception Profile for Adolescents, where she scored two standard deviations below the mean on the scales of physical appearance and global self-worth. One possible explanation for the negative association between a white orientation and Mary's poorer global self-worth and adjustment is that in using a white reference group, Mary employed a standard of beauty that dramatically deviates from her own attractive black physical features. Recent research in the area of self-concept (Harter, 1990) has found that one's assessment of one's physical attractiveness is highly correlated with one's global self-worth, and this relationship is especially strong in young women.

Mary's negative feelings were beginning to be translated into poorer behavioral adjustment—her score on the Youth Self-Report depression subscale was approaching clinical significance. Mary is an example of a biracial youth who holds a white RGO. For her, this orientation was associated with negative self-perceptions of physical attractiveness, poor global self-worth, and a higher rate of behavioral maladjustment. However, it is important to make clear that associations do not necessarily substantiate causation.

PIECING TOGETHER THE PUZZLE

Although the results of the study can be interpreted within Helms's (1990a) model of racial identity development, this theory is based on "Nigrescence" models of black identity development. One key question is how appropriate a single-race identity model is for biracial individuals of white and nonwhite heritage. Biracial identity theorists (Hall, 1980; Kich, 1992; Poston, 1990; Root, 1992a) are currently in the process of developing new ways of understanding racial identity development in biracial individuals. Poston (1990) has based his model of biracial identity in part on the work of Cross (1987). Poston (1990) articulated stages of development similar to Nigrescence models but he linked his stages more closely to age. The first stage, *Personal Identity*, occurs in early childhood, when there is little awareness of race/ethnicity and one's RGO has not developed. Stage 2, the *Choice of Group Categorization*, occurs when one is forced to choose an identity. In outlining the factors that influence group choice, Poston incorporated three factors from Hall's (1980) research and theorizing: status factors, social support, and personal factors. *Enmeshment/Denial* follows, which is a stage characterized by negative emotional reactions to having chosen a single identity that does not recognize one's dual cultural heritage. In the fourth stage, *Appreciation*, individuals begin to appreciate their multiple identity and broaden their RGO. However, they still tend to identify with one group, which continues from the Choice stage. In the final stage, *Integration*, individuals tend to recognize and value all of their ethnic identities. Poston noted that the Enmeshment/Denial phase is the most difficult time of adjustment and is most commonly seen in children and adolescents, whereas most adults achieve a healthy integration.

Poston's model, particularly the concept of a stage of appreciation, can help us to understand the complexity of findings regarding the various components of racial/ethnic identity in the present sample of biracial adolescents. However, the model does not offer an explanation for the finding that similar biracial adolescents who adopted a black or bicultural RGO had positive self-concepts whereas those who adopted a white RGO had significantly poorer self-concepts. It is important to note that this is not simply a function of age; the mean age across the three orientations was the same, 16 years with little variability. The finding of a relationship between white orientation and poor self-concept points to the importance of an orientation toward people of color for the development of a positive self-concept in biracial adolescents. Communities of color have much to offer biracial people. These communities have learned to cope with common experiences of racism and can help teach coping skills (Greene, 1990). In addition, they offer youths standards of beauty, emotional expressiveness, interpersonal distance, degree of extraversion, and comfort with physical intimacy that is often quite different from the white norm. These are standards by which the individual might find affirmation.

LIMITATIONS OF THE STUDY
AND FUTURE RESEARCH DIRECTIONS

The present study is one of the few systematic studies of self-concept in biracial adolescents. The results add valuable information to the unexplored area of the relationship between RGO and self-concept in biracial adolescents. However, like all studies, it has several limitations.

Although the sample of 31 biracial adolescents is one of the largest studied, it is still a small number from which to generalize research findings. A key finding, the impact of a white RGO on self-concept, is based on only five subjects (16%). Future research will need to employ large samples of biracial teens in order to explore this phenomenon more thoroughly. This study was conducted in a metropolitan area where racial groups were not rigidly segregated. Helms (1989) has proposed that racial identity is influenced by the racial climate of a particular geographic region. Studies of biracial adolescents in other parts of the country may find different patterns of results. For example, in areas of greater segregation, the rates of bicultural orientation may decrease in the black and the biracial populations (Root, 1990). In addition, if there is greater tension between the racial groups, the biracial adolescents may have internal struggles mirroring and reflecting the struggles of society as they attempt to develop a healthy identity.

This study offers a jumping-off point for other researchers who are interested in better understanding the intricate relationship between various aspects of racial/ethnic identity, identity development, and self-concept.

14

Changing Face, Changing Race

The Remaking of Race in the Japanese American and African American Communities

REBECCA CHIYOKO KING

KIMBERLY McCLAIN DaCOSTA

Growing up in Chicago, I can't remember a time when I did not know that I was part Japanese American. My mother taught us about internment; we played with our "Japanese" dolls; and we ate our hot dogs and bologna cooked in *shoyu* (soy sauce). Although our hot dogs, like our home, were not "normal," to my sister Debbie and me, they were.

When I first came to California to attend graduate school and began teaching in the Asian American Studies department, this notion of myself as Japanese American was seriously challenged for the first time. Many of my students wanted to know my qualifications to teach Asian American studies. "You don't look Japanese so how would you know about racism?" they would say. Clearly I was not Japanese American enough.

From Chicago to California, the social context changed and with it my acceptance as a member of the Japanese American

227

community. Other *hapas* (a Hawaiian term that has come to refer to mixed-race Asian Americans) in California invited me to attend a Hapa Issues Forum meeting, and I did, but with reservations. What I found was that this once individual and anecdotal experience was made collective within the Hapa Issues Forum organization. No longer was being hapa an individual challenge, but one that was shared collectively—multiraciality was and is moving from being an individual isolated experience to one that is increasingly collectively organized, not only with Japanese American hapas, but also in coalition with multiracial people of many different heritages. This chapter was born out of one such group, the Multiracial Alternatives Project, which sparked an intellectual dialogue about the mixed race-experience in comparative perspective. ⚐

Rebecca Chiyoko King

When I was in high school, my older sister, Ellen, was very active in the black campus community at Brown University. In her senior year, she was elected president of the Organization of United African Peoples, the black student union. I remember celebrating the news with Ellen and my mother in the kitchen one afternoon. Mom congratulated Ellen with a big hug and kiss and offered this (with a wry smile), "Just don't tell anyone you're only one quarter black." At this we all burst into laughter—laughter that expressed as much relief as it did humor. Mom had spoken the "secret," pointing out an irony that we had all been thinking but did not immediately articulate—that a woman who was of only partial African descent could be a leader in the community. But why was this ironic? We were all aware of a long history of mulatto leadership and participation in the African American community. But we were also aware that in our times, being multiracial in the African American political community was a reality to be tolerated and not something to be celebrated or even talked about, except in the limited context of slavery and rape. We understood that to articulate an identity as multiracial left us vulnerable to accusations of divided allegiances and threatened our belonging in a community that we regarded as our psychological home. We also knew that although people may be tolerant of a *bi*racial leader, being only one-fourth black might be less tolerable.

Perhaps even more ironic for my sister and I was that our mother's comment forced us to acknowledge for the first time that although we identified ourselves as black, or if pushed further, biracial, our heritage was more complex than that. Yet we did not have a frame of reference for articulating multiraciality with that level of specificity.

As an adult, I still call the black community my "home," but if I am to participate in the community, it must be a place where I can bring my mother into that community's conversation, where I can voice my experience in its totality. I have become interested in the ways other mixed-race African Americans are attempting to do likewise. &

Kimberly McClain DaCosta

According to Omi and Winant (1986), racial formation is, "the process by which social, economic, and political forces determine the content and importance of racial categories, and by which they are in turn shaped by racial meanings" (p. 68). This chapter analyzes the mixed-race experience in comparative perspective by extending Omi and Winant's theory of racial formation and applying it to case studies of the participation of mixed-race people, both individually and collectively, in the African American and Japanese American communities.

FOUR FACES OF RACE

Most people realize that race is socially constructed, which means that although they know that race is not "real" in a biological sense, they cannot just refuse to use race as an analytical category, cannot simply individually change what they want race to mean, nor can they ignore that race has very real consequences.

But what exactly does it mean to say that race is a "socially constructed" concept? There seem to be four levels at which race is socially constructed; we call these the four "faces" of racial formation. For the first face of race, we borrow from the sociology of gender. Like gender, race is something that one "does" (West & Zimmerman, 1991). It is something that you actively practice in your everyday life. But "doing race" happens on two distinct levels, within individuals and between individuals. George Herbert Mead (1934) did not theorize explicitly about race, but his theory of the *self* as the "ability to take oneself as an object" (p. 47) and *thinking* as "the internalized conversation of the individual with himself via significant symbols and gestures" (p. 47) lays the groundwork for thinking about race as an identity within an individual. Although this identity process happens within individuals, it remains social in nature because it is the internalization of the dispositions of the "generalized *other*" (society) that creates the ability to take oneself as an object. For race theory, this means that people can be self-reflexive about what race they identify themselves to be, but that they cannot choose without restrictions and awareness of them. For example, mixed-race Japanese Americans could identify themselves as such, but the current racial framework constrains this identification. Most mixed race people know this and think of themselves in social life not as they are but as the current racial frameworks will allow them to be.

One example of this process can be seen in the language used to describe "mixed" people. By using the term mixed, multiracial people are using the discursive resources that are available to them within the existing definition of race. This term may seem contradictory because it seems to reify racial categories in the process of desiring to deconstruct them. However, if mixed-race people are seen as "thinking" in a Meadian sense, they are using the racial frameworks that exist to take themselves as objects and form a racial identity. In this way, their racial "selves" are constructed.

The second face of race as a social construct focuses more explicitly on presentation of the racial self in interaction with other individuals. Erving Goffman put forth the idea that the self is not a possession of the actor, but rather the product of the dramatic interaction between the actor and the audience (see Goffman, 1959; Lyman & Douglass, 1973). Racial identity in this sense becomes "impression management." Lyman and Douglass wrote: "From the ethnic actor's perspective, ethnicity is both a mental state and a potential ploy in any encounter, but it will be neither if it cannot be invoked or activated" (p. 349). Thus mixed-race African Americans can think they are black racially and can use this to strategize to get what they want, but this identity may be limited if others do not "legitimate" or "authenticate" their racial identity. In this sense, racially mixed people are never fully authenticated because they do not see themselves as fitting into the existing racial order nor are they recognized as such by others. The classic example of this is the mixed-race encounter. This is the social situation where someone asks a mixed-race person, "What are you?" What they are really asking is what racial category do you see yourself in and how does that fit with what I see you as. In this sense, race is created not only within individuals but also between individuals in interaction with one another (Williams, Chapter 12, this volume).

The third face of race as a social construct is that race is interactively created not only by individuals but also by groups. Race in this sense is "done" collectively. Blumer and Duster (1980) argued that racial groups create images of their own group and others via complex interaction and communication among the group's members. The groups interpret their "runs of experiences," which leads to a formation of "judgments and images" of their own group and others (p. 222). For example, Asian Americans have come together as a racial group and have formed definitions of what it means to be "Asian American," as well as what it means not to be Asian American. In this sense, they are drawing the "color line" and creating boundaries between racial groups. This is why erasing and redrawing color lines is so difficult, because on both sides of the line, people have a vested interest in keeping the lines right where they are.

This brings up the fourth face of race as a social construct. These racial groups are relational and hierarchical. Race as relational means that there are racial categories that are mutually exclusive; that is, people can belong to one and only one category. These categories are positioned in systematic connection with one another and thus only have meaning in relation to each other (Barrett, 1987, as described in Glenn, 1992). In addition, power is not equally distributed among these racial groups; they are arranged hierarchically. For example, Shinagawa and Pang (1988) argued that intermarriage can be "hiergamy" in that people of color can become socially mobile by "marrying up and out" (p. 112). If Japanese Americans marry whites (and more so if the male is white), they are not only marrying out of their racial group but also marrying "up" into a "white" racial group. The assumption made here is that there is a racial hierarchy with people of color at the bottom and whites on top.

These four faces of race as a social construct enable racial formation to take place as a process. This chapter uses existing theories to frame a new theoretical technique. It takes Omi and Winant's (1986) racial formation theory but adds to it a symbolic interactionalist twist that tries to keep in mind how social structures can and do constrain social action. But how then does this play out in reality?

HAPA ISSUES FORUM:
RACE IN ACTION

Our starting point to understand this complex social process is the Hapa Issues Forum (HIF). This is a student/community group of multiracial Japanese Americans that was formed to address the changing demographics of the Japanese American community, primarily the high out-marriage rate and the presence of many multiracial children (Shinagawa, 1994). The actions of HIF and the reactions of the larger Japanese American community are a microcosm of the process of redefining race.

The "traditional" Japanese American community has responded to their changing demographics in three ways. Some have been quick to sound the alarm that these trends are a threat to the Japanese American community, declaring, "the Japanese American community . . . thriving today 'will be no more in 2050' in the face of rising intermarriage" (quoted in Hirabayashi, 1993, p. B-15). Others feel that this is not a cause for alarm, but instead the natural path for Japanese Americans who have "made it" and are socially mobile in today's society. Others have taken a more dynamic stance regarding the change and have assembled panels and workshops to "discuss" what this means for the Japanese American community (Honda, 1993).

In turn, hapas who wish to define themselves in relation to the Japanese American community also have three responses to changing demographics. In the first response, some simply do not see themselves as Japanese American at all. These people are not represented in HIF because they do not see the need for the group and do not participate. The second response is to branch off and try to have a mixed-race community, that is, to join with other "mixed" people. This has not happened explicitly with the HIF. For example, forum members support the movement to put a mixed-race category on the U.S. Census (Fernández, Chapter 2, this volume) and on public school entrance forms (Graham, Chapter 3, this volume), but they do not take this as one of the organization's primary goals. The third is the HIF response, which is to try to join/transform the Japanese American community as it exists today to make it more inclusive.

But how is the HIF attempting to redefine Japanese America? Members are actively challenging and reconstructing race via the four faces of race. First, members of HIF "live" their political agenda every day. Underlying participation in the organization is a common bond of wanting to "resist" and "redo" racial categories. In this sense, there is a high level of agreement among members that they have experienced the "dissemblance" in having to "choose" one race or the other, on college entrance forms and so on. They actively identify themselves as hapa in their everyday life. Via an internal process, members have taken the existing racial frameworks and internalized them to such an extent that they realize they are standing between racial categories as they exist now but that they have the "right" to individually assert their identities as mixed people.

With the second face, forum members try to encourage people who interact with them one on one to see them as they are: hapa. One of the co-founders put it this way:

> I am applying to law school and I checked "other" and I walked my application over . . . and handed it in and the guy at the desk asks, "Why'd you check *other*?" and I said, "Well, you know I am not this and I am not that." He said, "it's not going to help you any and they are just going to lump you into this big mass." So . . . I just put Japanese and a little asterisk and put hapa.

In this instance, he "thought" (had an internalized conversation with himself and took into consideration what he wanted to express using existing racial categories) and put *other*. He then has an interaction with another individual who urges him to put something else (not *other*) because it has no legitimacy. He then strategizes that he can get what he wants (admission to law school) by putting Japanese American, but even so, he wants to assert his own identity and writes in hapa-Japanese American and Caucasian; his "true self identity" is presented. *The issue is not that mixed-race people are trying to "get something," but instead that there is flexibility within impression management.*

With the third face, HIF is a unique organization and the first of its kind by and for mixed-race Japanese Americans. It is collectively involved in creating an image of hapas primarily in relation to the traditional Japanese American community. In this sense, HIF is unlike other mixed-race groups (e.g., Multicultural Interracial Student Coalition or MISC, on the University of California, Berkeley, campus) in that it forms its identity as a group in direct relation to the Japanese American community.

Therefore, members recognize the fourth face of race as a social construct too. The HIF pamphlet reads,

> We seek to insure that upon arrival at the Twenty-First century, hapas will play a pivotal role in a revitalized Japanese American community. .... [We want the Japanese American community to] focus on the future by accepting the reality that hapas are becoming a significant part of the community and to insure that representation and recognition is forthcoming. (Unpublished material)

Also, there is this statement from the newsletter, in an article entitled, "Race and Ethnicity: Hapas and the Japanese American Community": "The Japanese American community must learn to acknowledge that hapas are part of the community, and hapa definitions of identity and experiences of race form an integral part of the Japanese American experience."

HIF makes it explicitly clear that the organization believes it has a right to represent hapas in relation to the Japanese American community. The forum argues, using its increasing numbers as a criterion for being heard, that this is a way to "save" the Japanese American community from "extinction." HIF markets its members as "new blood" to invigorate the existing Japanese American community and argues that they will ensure that the historical experiences, culture, and traditions of Japanese Americans get passed on to future generations.

What is HIF actually doing, then, to redefine what it means to be Japanese American? First, the organization exists; it developed as individuals came together around commonalities in their experiences with the existing racial order, the traditional Japanese American community, and the larger society. Members are actively working to increase understanding about hapas, both within the traditional Japanese American community and society at large via the newsletter *What's Hapa'ning?* as well as meetings and participation in Japanese American "things," such as the Cherry Blossom Festival. In addition, HIF had a conference in March 1994 entitled, "What Does the Future Hold for Japanese Americans?" The purpose of this conference was to bring people from the

Japanese American and larger communities to the UC Berkeley campus to "open a meaningful and lasting dialogue about the role hapas will play in the Japanese American community" (from HIF program).

It is clear that HIF sees itself primarily in relation to the Japanese American community, but members are also acutely aware that they can "change" the contours of that community. They speak of changing the "rules" within the traditional Japanese American community, such as "having so many players with Japanese last names" on a team in the Japanese American youth basketball league and/or stipulating that the Cherry Blossom Queen must be "so much" Japanese.

In all of the preceding examples, it is clear that HIF seeks to challenge the existing definition of Japanese American, but more than that, members are openly contesting not only racial boundaries but also the meaning of race itself. They stand in defiance of racial frameworks now embedded in state and other social institutions. They take the census and refuse to check a box or fill in their parts; just leaving the ethnic question blank asserts their "right" to identify and be identified as hapa (many do not like the *other* option because they feel it means "nothing"). In this sense, HIF is changing not only what makes one a member of the Japanese American community, but also changing the nature of membership as well. In other words, in this new definition of community, it is perfectly legitimate for them to have multiple allegiances to multiple communities. The changing face of Japanese America is a double process. The actual physical face of the average Japanese American will be mixed, and the face of the community that is Japanese America will also change. HIF is an important agent in the change of racial meanings within the Japanese American community. Members have used individual experiences to form a group identity that collectively puts pressure on the existing racial frameworks to change.

But why does HIF have the power to be heard? First of all, the Japanese American community traditionally has been one of the largest within the Asian American community. At present, with low immigration (4,000 a year in the 1980s), high out-marriage (as high as 50% by some counts), and low birthrates, Japanese Americans are declining in numbers under present criteria for defining "Japaneseness" (O'Hare & Felt, 1991). Therefore, part of the power of HIF comes from a community that is willing to listen to its mixed-race members. In other words, some traditional Japanese Americans welcome the participation of hapas as a way to increase their numbers and political pull. Second, the size of the Japanese American population as a whole is small compared to the general population, so instead of seeing its population die out, many want to see hapas incorporated and the definition of Japanese American expanded so that the label will continue to exist in a larger social context. This means that hapas are not being rejected by the community, because the community cannot afford it. If HIF is successful, the Japanese American community may have to change its face to "save face."

THE AFRICAN AMERICAN EXAMPLE

It is impossible to understand the contemporary role of mixed-race African Americans in the black community without first understanding the history of racial mixture within that community. Unlike the Japanese American community, the African American community has long included multiracial individuals. Since the first African men and women were brought to this continent, they have mixed with both Native Americans and whites (Wilson, 1992). From the colonial period to the Civil War, although some interracial unions involved free individuals, the majority of interracial contact occurred within the context of slavery. The relationship of the children of these unions, known as mulattoes, to the black community varied by region. In the upper South, mulattoes tended to be of parents who were both servants and were not considered as occupying a social position higher than that of blacks. In the lower South, mulattoes tended to be the children of wealthy planters, and many of them were given their freedom, along with access to education and other social goods. They developed into an elite class, tending to associate with and marry each other or whites. They are described as being the forerunners of the black elite (Degler, 1971; Williamson, 1984). Some mulattoes were born to free individuals, thus, they were also free and able to set up mulatto communities outside of the African American community. The majority of mulattoes, however, were born to slaves and given the legal status of slave. Under such a system, mixed-race people shared the same legal, if not social, status of the majority of blacks (Williamson, 1984).

The slave system provided the institutional apparatus to keep the races socially separate—not only blacks from whites, but mixed-race people from whites—in an effort to maintain white control over resources (Davis, 1991). The abolition of slavery dismantled that apparatus, but in its place came legal standards, such as the one-drop rule, that served the same purpose. The one-drop rule, a legal standard that designated people with any black ancestry as black, effectively blocked access to the white category, while taking away a mixed-race or mulatto category. The legacy of the one-drop rule is that most people who today identify as African American have some non-African ancestry. Jack D. Forbes estimates that 99% of the African American population has some degree of mixture (quoted in Wilson, 1992). In effect, to be African American means being racially mixed.

The high degree of racial mixture within the African American population makes it necessary to distinguish between two understandings of the term *mixed-race African American*. The first understanding refers to being of mixed racial ancestry, however remote to the individual. One can be of mixed racial ancestry and have parents who identified and were identified as African American, as is the case with most African Americans. The second understanding refers to being "immediately" mixed, that is, of an African American parent and a nonblack parent. Individuals of the former category are, by their own definition if not in popular understanding, African American. Their multiracial ancestry is not a unique experience within the African American community.

For our purposes, the term mixed-race African American refers to the second understanding. The experience of today's immediately mixed African Americans differs in important ways from that of African Americans of multiracial heritage. The majority of today's immediately mixed African Americans have been born in the post Civil Rights Era, part of a biracial baby boom beginning in the late 1960s, in a social and political climate characterized by relatively more tolerance for cultural diversity than in previous generations. This is the first generation of mixed-race African Americans to grow up in a nation where it was legal in all 50 states to marry interracially. As such, many mixed-race people have been raised in intact families, with access to and personal knowledge of all sides of their cultural heritage. For those who were not raised in intact families, often the nonblack parent has raised the children, and as such, these mixed-race people may feel little connection to the black community.

Although the biracial baby boom emerged in the context of an integrationist cultural attitude, at the same time a counter-ideology of black cultural nationalism put forth new standards of what it meant to be black and new criteria for authenticity. Black cultural nationalism, dedicated to finding unity in shared blackness, simultaneously subordinated difference within the community and, as a result, silenced expression of issues such as sexism and multiraciality. Immediately mixed African Americans, by virtue of having access to other cultural groups, were stereotyped as sell-outs (Cleaver, 1968/1992; Haley, 1964; Spickard, 1989). Claims of an authentic "blackness," in which one's African lineage predominated over all others, reinforced the logic of the one-drop rule: in order to maintain membership in the black community, one must identify as black *only*. According to such logic, which persists today, claiming a mixed identity is saying that one does not want to be black. In effect, the African American community has appropriated the one-drop rule; although it may have once served as a source of strength to form a community by emphasizing unity in shared blackness, this may become a tool of oppression for today's immediately mixed.

The unique demographic, political, and social experience of immediately mixed African Americans has direct implications for how they interact with the African American community to change the face of race. Because so many immediately mixed African Americans have access to all their communities, their experience runs counter to old ways of thinking about what it means to be African American. It is no longer possible to assume affiliation with the black community simply because one appears to be of African ancestry. Similarly, appearance is not as reliable an indicator of social standing as once believed. Immediately mixed individuals are not necessarily of the black elite; therefore light skin is a less strong predictor of class privilege. The legal and social climate from which the one-drop rule arose has changed considerably, thus calling into question its usefulness for negotiating race today.

The relatively tolerant history of multiraciality within the African American community makes the focus of efforts of mixed-race African Americans to dialogue with the African American community somewhat ill-defined. The absence of a group designed to dialogue primarily with the African American community is telling of the nature of the debate. HIF seeks inclusion in the Japanese American community and was organized specifically to dialogue with that community. Mixed-race African Americans do not need the rhetoric of inclusion and thus have not organized to dialogue directly with the African American community.

For some mixed-race African Americans, inclusion has been forced upon them or is conditional upon acceptance of a black-only identity or a prioritizing of identities. As such, groups of mixed-race African Americans have coalesced around the need to convey members' experiences as both/all (i.e., black *and* white) rather than either/or (black *or* white). It is only in this historical period that talk about claiming multiple racial identities is even an option. Although this is not the first historical period in which the ascription of an identity as African American has been challenged (passing, triracial isolates), mixed-race African Americans are challenging what such an identity means in unique ways. *The task for mixed-race African Americans in redefining race is to broaden prevailing notions of what it means to be African American, so that identifying with one's nonblack heritage does not preclude identification with one's black heritage.* The task is not to be recognized as a separate and distinct group, but to be recognized as both/all, with access to all sides of one's heritage. This is quite different from the efforts of "triracial isolates"— mixed-race European, African, and Native people—who seek to be recognized as culturally distinct kin groups or tribes (Blu, 1980; Greenbaum, 1991). They do not want to be a part of the African American community; mixed-race African Americans do. As such, mixed-race African Americans assert a multiracial identity, not to reflect internalized racism but to strive for a sense of wholeness.

Another contributing factor to the lack of direct dialogue between mixed-race African Americans and the African American community is that the community itself is diffused geographically. The Japanese American community is geographically concentrated on the West Coast, thus making it easy to locate and target participants for dialogue. The African American community is dispersed, and, more important perhaps, feels no demographic imperative to seek out mixed-race African Americans to participate in its political community or to act as culture bearers for the next generation. (According to the U.S. Census, 7.3% of all African American marriages in 1992 were interracial.) That lack of urgency may affect the ability of mixed-race African Americans to be heard.

The different histories of the Japanese American and African American communities shape the nature of group participation of hapas and mixed-race African Americans. Hapas, rejected by the Japanese American community, form groups focused on getting that community to include them. Mixed-race African Americans, included in the common understandings of blackness but with an accompanying silencing of other parts of their heritage, form groups focused on validating that experience. Mixed-race African Americans who are involved in mixed-race group activity tend to be involved in "umbrella" groups, that is, groups whose membership encompasses people of a variety of different heritages, such as UC Berkeley's MISC or Harvard's Prism. By definition, these groups are not focused on dialogue with only one group (i.e., the African American or Japanese American community). Because there has been little room to articulate an identity as mixed within the African American community, mixed-race African Americans have coalesced outside that community in coalition with other multiracial people in order to create a space in which to affirm their experiences. The racial eclecticism of these groups makes their goals more amorphous. Groups such as MISC provide social support for their members and describe the "mixed" experience to the general community, rather than to a particular racial/ethnic community. Although groups exclusively for mixed-race African Americans may exist, they are the exception rather than the rule. As such, the analysis of the re-creation of race in the African American community is not as neat as the Japanese American example. Rather than being able to focus on one group (like HIF, specifically formed for the purposes of engaging the wider Japanese American community), we must focus on mixed-race African Americans involved in a variety of mixed-race groups.

Mixed-Race African Americans:
Doing the Four Faces of Race

On the first face of race, mixed-race African Americans who were interviewed were well aware of the existing racial framework. When asked their "race," each offered a response that used the categories of the existing racial framework in novel ways. When asked his racial/ethnic identity, a member of MISC at UC Berkeley said,

> Given [my involvement in] a mixed-race group, as of now I'm mixed. I don't go much further than that. . . . I could say I'm half-black and half-white but that, I believe, is misleading because it's black but it's not black American, [which is] what people think of.

Suzanne, of European and African descent, described herself as "multiethnic":

> Now I'm also starting to say African American and European American because people don't understand "multiethnic." They want to know color, they want to know why I look the way I look.

Turning to the second face of race, Tarik, like the hapas in HIF, claims a multiracial identity. His household was picked by a company gathering television and radio ratings data. When the representative asked his race, he answered "mixed." Unsure of what that meant, the representative called back for clarification. Although Tarik refused to choose a racial classification, he did tell her he was Haitian and Iranian and proceeded to educate her on what being mixed-race meant.

This instance reflects a dialectic between an identification by others and Tarik's self-identification. Aware that his identification as mixed-race is confusing, Tarik specified his ethnic ancestry in terms with which the representative was more familiar, all the while maintaining a self-identification as multiracial. Although Tarik realized that because he revealed his Haitian ancestry, the representative will probably list him as black, by presenting and actively seeking to educate on mixedness, he was able to challenge the prevailing notion of race as a mutually exclusive proposition.

On the third face of race, the focus of HIF is to gain entry into the Japanese American community, and the goal of MISC is to offer a place for mixed-race people to meet, share experiences, and educate the wider society. Even though the groups may have different goals, their members, through their interactions with each other, discover and create a shared sense of "we" (a mixed-race group identity). A member of MISC argued that there is a mixed-race identity and likened it to the collective identity of other groups of color:

[W]hat connection can I have with someone who's half-Asian? It's the same connection I feel that blacks have. Because blacks, depending on where you live, are very different in their upbringing. A Los Angeles African American and an Alabama one and a New York [one], I mean they have a connection but is their culture really the same? Are they eating the same stuff? I would argue no. But people talk about a "black culture." I think people could talk about a "mixed-race" culture. Because a lot of what black culture is has to do with being black, has to do with other people's perceptions of you and how you have to deal with them and how you have to fight that off. Well, that's the same thing I see for mixed-race people. Our connection if anything *is* having to deal with people's intolerance and having to deal with questions and stares and weird experiences. Just like for a black American.

Gary, a member of HIF, agreed:

I think [a mixed-race group identity] exists already. I mean people have only just now become aware of it. I mean like you [a person of African American and Irish ancestry] and I can talk about similar experiences and we're from different cultural backgrounds.

Gary believes there is something unique to the experience of being mixed-race that is common among mixed-race people regardless of heritage, yet he wonders whether this is more characteristic of "activists" as opposed to those who are not.

I think that especially people who are real active in it, I mean there's this bond beyond just [being mixed-race]. I mean, yeah, we're both mixed-race and stuff, but even more than that, we're both active in working on it. So in that respect it's easy in that there already is that mixed-race culture I guess among activists.

For Gary, group activity involving multiracial issues creates and strengthens a consciousness of a mixed-race collective identity that is not dependent on shared ethnic ancestry. Such a notion underscores the idea that identities are socially constructed.

On the fourth face of race, in addition to being involved in umbrella groups with amorphous goals, mixed-race African Americans are in dialogue with the African American community. The educational efforts of groups such as MISC serve as both a forum for multiracial people and a dialogue with monoracial groups. A central objective of those efforts is to gain recognition for an identity as both/all rather than either/or. The assertion of such an identity at once recognizes and challenges the relational nature of American racial categories through its rejection of mutually exclusive membership rules—rules that have been especially salient in the African American community.

Suzanne is involved in a group focused on getting a multiracial classification on state and federal forms. Multiracial classification represents a very tangible challenge to the racial binary that ignores multiraciality in the African American community. Although Suzanne is sensitive to the perceived threat that a multiracial classification poses to the African American community—and well-aware of the hierarchical nature of racial categorizations—she believes binary thinking must be challenged:

> I think most of us are very willing to talk about it in our own voices, to the point of tears, to say now look, I am not trying to do this to take advantage of something. [I understand that] the one-drop rule has operated as a source of strength in the African American community. What needs to be talked about now is how the one-drop rule may be oppressive. We have to understand that opening up borders does not mean that people will be fleeing some sort of identity in order to hold onto another one. There are many of us [who] want to work in all of our communities, but we also need to understand how those minority group identities and the philosophies behind them may be very oppressive.

CONCLUSION

The four faces of race theory puts forth a new paradigm within the existing theoretical literature on race, allowing for a more dynamic model of racial formation. The above examples illustrate how multiracial people operate within existing paradigms while at the same time create new possibilities for moving beyond current understandings of race. We have attempted to show how meanings of race are socially created through interaction between and within individuals and groups.

To say that race is relational is to say that race gets its meaning in relation to other groups. It is the interaction of racial groups (in this case, mixed-race and monoracial) that negotiates those racial meanings and, in turn, affects all other faces of race. This is a potentially radical change in the conceptualization of race and its meaning, not only for multiracial groups, but for the monoracial groups with which they interact: Japanese American, African American, and European American. In redefining race, the task for hapas and mixed-race African Americans is to broaden prevailing notions of Japaneseness and blackness, such that identifying with one side of one's heritage does not preclude identifying with the other. The task is not to be recognized as a separate and distinct group, but to be recognized as both/all, with access to all sides of one's heritage.

Although this case study has studied one small slice of a very complex process, it does shed some theoretical light on how race is remade not only individually, but collectively as well. We have explored this process in two communities—one in which multiraciality has only recently but quite rapidly become an issue, the other in which multiraciality has been a constant reality. Despite these differences, the social actions of hapas and mixed-race African Americans are oriented in similar ways: toward a monoracially defined community with an emphasis on expanding notions of the requirements for membership in that community. We argue that the basis for this similarity is the comparable positions of marginality that hapas and mixed-race African Americans occupy within the current racial framework. By being neither black, Japanese, nor white but in-between, multiracial people experience the social constructedness of race in a way that allows them to see the possibilities of shifting from being "between" to being "all."

15

Without a Template

The Biracial Korean/White Experience

BRIAN CHOL SOO STANDEN

A bus ride from elementary school to my house. Young children screaming, running, and clamoring onto the giant orange-yellow beast. My sister was boarding three or four kids ahead of me. As she passed one particular child, my attention became focused on them. His gaze fell upon her. His eyes signaled

AUTHOR'S NOTE: First I want to thank my mother, Kim Chong Suk, and my father, Roger Brian Standen, for all of their love and support. I would also like to thank my sister, Sandra Kim Standen, for the emotional support and encouragement that she has provided me throughout the years.

Special thanks to the Asian American Committee on Education and to Dr. Lerita Coleman, Psychology, University of Colorado at Boulder, for providing the resources and funding for this project. I would also like to thank my committee for providing me with the tools and advice necessary to do research: Dr. Olivia Arrieta, Center for Studies of Ethnicity and Race in America, University of Colorado at Boulder; Dr. Lerita Coleman, Psychology, University of Colorado at Boulder; and Dr. Deward Walker, Center for Studies of Ethnicity and Race in America, University of Colorado at Boulder.

Finally, I wish to thank Michael Edward Jung Yul Eastman, Yuichiro Hara, Dr. Lane Hirabayashi, Center for Studies of Ethnicity and Race in America, University of Colorado at Boulder; Dr. Deborah Hollis, Library, University of Colorado at Boulder; the Olbert family; William Takamatsu-Thompson; and all the participants in the study, without whom the research would not have been possible.

245

recognition. His lips parted and formed a single word: "Chink!" I began to shake from the surge of adrenaline. I pressed forward. His actions would not go unanswered. Finally, I stood next to his sitting form. I reached deep inside my anger and released all of my strength through my foot and into his shin. I looked at his face, noting that he was somewhat overweight. My lips parted and formed a single word: "Chunk!"

It strikes me as rather odd that this particular memory now exists so clearly in mind. This was not the first, nor last, racist epithet hurled at me or my family. In fact, I buried the memory and the pain of that event for years. Then, I did this research.

Through this research, the significance of the event crept back into my consciousness. It symbolized my first recollection of being defined by those around me; it symbolized my first recollection of defining those around me. I knew that being Asian was not valued. I knew that being overweight was not valued. I knew that women were not valued. Yet I was able to act upon these values, although I did not have the means to conceptualize nor articulate them.

In my reflections on this event I began to understand. The assumptive, assimilative nature of mainstream suburban culture creates the image of a homogeneous, monocultural, male-dominated, hierarchical society. This understanding was the driving force of my research. I wanted to discover insights without assumption, without predefinition, without a template. ⚭

The number of studies on the biracial experience, as a whole, is meager at best and nonexistent with regard to biracial Korean Americans. Most studies have focused on psychological aspects of the biracial identity of people who combine African American and white backgrounds. However, a few studies have been done that focus on Amerasian people. These studies have either centered around Japanese/white individuals (Kich, 1982; Mass, 1992; Murphy-Shigematsu, 1986; Williams, 1992) or Japanese/African American individuals (Hall, 1980; Thornton, 1983; Williams, 1992). Although these studies represent groundbreaking achievements in understanding Amerasian people, the biracial experience is not a singular phenomenon. Just as a Japanese individual would not accurately be termed Chinese, so it may be that a biracial Korean American is not accurately termed a biracial African American or even a biracial Japanese American, although many experiences may, on the surface, be similar (King & DaCosta, Chapter 14, this volume). A full understanding of the biracial experience requires an examination of ethnic group out-marriage and the identity children of these unions develop.

Popular culture assumes the biracial individual's development will be problematic. This idea finds its roots in the "forced choice" dilemma (C. C. I. Hall, 1980, 1992). Classically, the dilemma has been between the dual heritages of the individual as described by Stonequist (1937). Maria Root (1992d) points out that "our tendency to think simplistically about complex relationships has resulted in dichotomous, hierarchical classifications systems" (p. 4). Because race has been constructed around the idea of "either/or," biracial people are caught between categories that may not fully describe their identity. In fact, this is the basis for the idea of a "marginal" position within a societal context. However, occupying a marginal space in U.S. society does not translate into identity problems (C. C. I. Hall, 1992; in this volume: King & DaCosta, Chapter 14; Root, Chapter 1; Weisman, Chapter 10).

Grove (1991) conducted a study on biracial Asian and white identity. College students attending a New England liberal arts college constituted the sample. Grove's study found no statistically significant difference between the identity status of Asian/white individuals and Asian *or* white participants.

Kich (1992) developed a significant model of Amerasian identity, based on a sample of 15 biracial adults, ages 17 to 60, of Japanese heritage. Kich recognized that "for biracial people, positive identification of themselves as being of dual or multiple racial and ethnic heritages has not been accepted or recognized in any consistent manner over the last several centuries" (p. 305).

However, identifying oneself as biracial is not always a sign of healthy self-acceptance. Sometimes it is indicative of a new "forced choice" dilemma. Rather than having to choose between their dual heritages, biracial people are put into a position that accuses them of being in denial for not accepting a biracial identity. Instead of a linear model with a singular identity resolution, a specific description of the factors that play into identity development and the subsequent resolutions is needed.

METHOD

The purpose of this study is to take a more specific ethnographic view of the biracial population with regard to how biracial Korean/white individuals negotiate a racial identity within the larger context of mainstream society. An interdisciplinary approach that combines elements of social psychology and symbolic anthropology was used. The researcher determined four sites that appear to be critical elements in the positive expression of a biracial individual's racial heritage: father, mother, peer group, and mainstream society; these were specified for information gathering.

The method of the study was based in part upon gathering life-history information, documenting participants' perceptions and opinions concerning their own culture or their racial identity. Langness and Frank (1981) described life history as giving "voice to persons in a range of societies—many of them members of subgroups shuffled about in the continual struggle of class interests and shifting national alliances" (p. 1). Using this method with a biracial Korean/white sample, the study provides a humanistic and a person-centered ethnography.

In addition to the life-history approach, the posture of the methodology was also influenced by Maria Root's (1992a) work on the methodological issues inherent in studying multiracial people. She submitted that qualitative research designs associated with disciplines such as anthropology and ethnography accommodate the small samples typically found when working with specific multiracial groups and that use of semistructured interviews and structured interviews were appropriate methods for studying multiracial groups (p. 186). Furthermore, she suggested that an important aspect of the initial research done on multiracial groups is that the researcher also be multiracial in order to place interpretation of results into the multiracial context (p. 188).

Using a structured interview format while allowing for the freedom of expression associated with life-history work, a test audio-recorded interview was done with a woman of Japanese and Jewish descent. From this initial interview, information about the questions themselves, as well as about the manner in which they were asked, were considered before conducting the actual study interviews. Eight audio-recorded interviews were conducted on a nonrandom sample of biracial Korean/white college students. The eight participants were contacted through previously established relationships within the Asian American community. The sample was limited to those people whose mother was a first-generation Korean immigrant and whose father was white. These limitations were imposed to control the context of the family structure as well as to provide a similar basis among the participants for analysis.

Each participant consented to the interviews, and each was assured of complete confidentiality. The names used in supporting results were changed in order to maintain this assurance. Participants cooperated in 90 to 120-minute interviews and responded to broad-based, open-ended questions about their thoughts regarding their parents, peer groups, racial identity, and mainstream society. In some instances, the researcher met with the participant before the actual interview took place to introduce himself and to establish rapport for facilitation of the future interview. Also, during and after some of the interviews, off-tape discussions of specific issues took place in which the researcher related his personal experiences with the participant. This technique was only used as a last resort when participants were experiencing extreme difficulty with the interview. The overall purpose of these techniques was to establish or sustain the trust between the researcher and the participant. The structure of the questionnaire was followed closely to maintain some control over variable presentations of the interview material.

RESULTS/DISCUSSION

The Sample

After the audio portion of the interview was completed, the participants filled out a demographic profile. This data defined the various financial and geographic contexts in which the participants previously and currently exist. Four males and four females between the ages of 19 and 23 were interviewed. The average yearly income of the participants was $0 to $9,999 (five responses) and $10,000 to $14,999 (two responses). One respondent said she was dependent on her parents. The average yearly income of the participants' parents varied from $35,000 or more (four respondents), to $30,000 - 34,999 (one respondent), and $20,000 and $24,999 (one respondent). One respondent said she lived with grand-parents, whose average annual income was between $0 and $9,999; an-other indicated that he was financially independent.

Occupations of the participants included student (3), bartender (1), busser (1), and sales (1); one was currently unemployed, and another did not answer the question. Two of the participants had received bachelor's degrees, and the rest were at different levels in a college or university. Occupations of the participants' parents varied. Although 5 out of the 8 mothers were housewives/homemakers, two respondents indicated that their mothers were employed in unskilled jobs; one mother was deceased.

The occupations of the participants' fathers included landscaper, chief executive officer, mechanic, auto sales/maintenance, law enforce-ment (2), and landman. One participant listed the occupation of her grandfather as a retired railroad worker. Out of the eight participants, six currently resided in suburban areas, one lived in an urban area, and another lived in a city—nonurban. All participants currently resided in the Colorado Front Range region (either in the Denver/Boulder metro-politan area or in Colorado Springs).

Participants were asked to rank the importance of race in daily interactions, using a 5-point scale ranging from 1 = *not important* to 5 = *very important*. Half of them said race was not important, one fourth said race was somewhat important, and the final fourth said race was very important. When asked about the importance of being Korean on a 5-point scale with similar parameters, all participants said that being Korean was very important. Fewer said that being white was important: 25% said being white was not important, 25% said it was somewhat important, and 50% said that being white was very important.

Ethnic Cues and Clues

Participants were asked, "What term would you use to identify yourself, in terms of racial, ethnic, cultural background and/or nation-ality?" The question was posed in this manner to obtain the richest responses. Participants answered the question similarly. Terms such as Jewish Korean American, Asian American, Asian American more spe-cifically Korean American, half-Korean and half-white, and half-Korean and half-Caucasian were included. With the exception of one answer, all specifically included an Asian heritage in general or more specific Korean heritage. Surprisingly, only three respondents indicated affiliation with being white in addition to being Korean. Amanda had trouble with the term white because her Jewish ethnic background played a prominent role in her identity formation.

On first glance, it seemed apparent that individuals in the sample were asserting and adopting a Korean or more generally Asian identity. However, for some, the terms merely described their ethnic heritage. For example, when asked why she identified herself with the terms half-Korean and half-white, Jane said,

> I don't know, that's just how I've always responded to that [laughs]. If anyone ever asked that's how I would say it.

Amanda answered in a similar manner:

> And why? Well . . . I guess I'm Jewish from both my parents. . . . My mother converted to Judaism for my father, and my mother is Korean so that makes me half Korean and half American and completely Jewish.

For other members of the sample, such as Sue, the terms had more of a consciously chosen meaning:

> I wanted to identify more with my Asian half than my white half so I started calling myself Asian American.

Malcolm saw the assertion of an Asian American identity as largely political:

> Actually, Asian American . . . in particular context depending on where you are at. To other Asian Americans, probably hapa . . . [to] best describe sort of the interracial, multiracial background that I have and sort of helps me identify within that community as someone that's unique.

Jane's and Amanda's answers exist as pragmatic explanations of their racial heritage. Sue's and Malcolm's answers, on the other hand, have an element of manipulation that shapes the term Asian American to fit their specific cases.

Lyman and Douglass (1973) described a process of ethnic impression management in which, on an individual level, "Ethnicity is an acquired and used feature of human identity, available for employment by either participant in an encounter and subject to presentation, inhibition, manipulation, and exploitation" (p. 350). Moreover, ethnicity exists as a kind of flexible characteristic that can be used as a "maneuver or stratagem in working out their own life chances in an ethnically pluralistic social setting" (Lyman & Douglass, p. 350).

At the heart of this theory is the idea that situational cues lead to a choice in identifying one's racial identity and that these "situations seem to dictate an appropriate ethnic choice so that an individual responds by casting himself in the apparently appropriate role" (Lyman & Douglass, 1973, p. 355). Following this theory a Japanese American individual can be simultaneously Asian, Asian American, Japanese, Japanese American, Nisei, son of immigrants from a specific geographic location, and American (Lyman & Douglass, 1973). Alternately, biracial Korean/white individuals can simultaneously be Korean, white, Asian, American, Asian American, Korean American, or hapa depending on the situation.

How do biracial Korean/white individuals express their different racial identities? Lyman and Douglass (1973) differentiated between what they term ethnic cues and ethnic clues. *Ethnic cues* "are those aspects of appearance and behavior . . . which can be assumed to be vested with ethnic significance but over the projection of which each actor has little control" (p. 361). Often, ethnic cues are translated as phenotypic characteristics and the associated stereotypes of behavior that follow. In contrast, *ethnic clues* are pieces of information that a person consciously manipulates to present a specific ethnic identity. The clues discovered in this study were the different terms, such as Asian American, Korean American, and half white/half Korean, that were used by the participants. Each term was a clue to the ethnic identity of the individual (in this volume, see Weisman, Chapter 10, or King & DaCosta, Chapter 14). Although it appears that the term is simply an answer to a question, in the context of the interview, choosing a term was the way participants could express their racial identity. Therefore, the slight differentiations in terms they used are linked to different interpretations of the same context.

Korean Ethnicity

Malcolm explained that to "most everyone," he identified himself as Asian American, but "to other Asian Americans, probably hapa," because it helps him "identify within that community." Malcolm's racial identity changes with the context of a given situation. He may identify himself as Asian American or hapa, depending on how he construes the construction of the situation. Moreover, other participants displayed a similar type of strategy with regard to how and when they would identify themselves.

For example, when asked about when he finds himself thinking about being Korean, Tom answered:

> Well, like I was saying, a lot of times it's just when social situations and circumstances present themselves, when there's issues that come up and . . . when, sometimes when I just reflect on the past and . . . when I think about, my daughter . . . about who I am. . . . how I want to present myself to my family and as far as my future.

Within this statement alone, Tom indicated several different contexts in which his Korean identity exists: in a past, present, and future context; in a family context; and in social contexts. Tom's Korean identity has a continual presence in his thinking about social issues, cultures, and his goals.

Similar context-based answers also appeared when other participants were asked about when they find themselves thinking about being Korean. One of the contexts that occurred several times was when participants were around other Koreans, especially family, as Jane noted:

> I think about it when someone asks me . . . and I think about it when I'm with my family, on like my mom's side of the family.

However, the type of identity expressed is not strictly limited to Korean or Asian. Sue mentioned one incident in which she defined herself as being white:

> I don't know if this would count, but me and two of my friends went to a black student . . . dance about a month ago. We were one of the few . . .

right then, I was about to say one of the few white people, so in that way,
I identify myself as a white person.

Responses to being asked "What are you?" depended on who was
asking. Shawn, for example, drew a clear distinction between how he
would respond to whites asking the question (negatively) and how he
would respond to Asians asking the same question (positively). Another example of the participants' identity being specifically defined
within a context comes from Lisa's experiences in one of her college
courses. In the course, she felt that white people were unjustly berated
by the students and the instructor. Indeed, she felt that her specifically
white identity was suppressed.

What do all these different, contextually based racial identity expressions demonstrate about the biracial Korean/white population? It suggests that racial identity among biracial Korean/white people exists as
a fluid and malleable construction. It is not static and confined to a
particular definition. Rather, it changes with each situation, depending
upon specific elements (C. C. I. Hall, 1992; Root, 1990; Stephan, 1992;
Williams, 1992, Chapter 12, this volume).

Wilson (1984) described a concept that provides insight into the fluid
nature of the biracial Korean/white identity. Discussing *situational ethnicity,* she elaborated on its theoretical implications, pointing out that
"at the small-group level, it means that in any given social situation, the
nature and scope of ethnicity will be defined by the participant actors
within boundaries delineated by social setting" (p. 50). Another pertinent aspect of Wilson's essay is the distinction between a micro- and
macrolevel context. Within the microlevel, interactions with other individuals and within different groups constitute the parameters. The
macrolevel encompasses the individuals' relative position within the
framework of mainstream society.

The critical distinction between the micro- and macrolevels places
fluid racial identity and more rigid racial identity into their respective
contexts. As Wilson (1984) described it,

> Society appears to be divided into a limited number of structured ethnic
> entities. . . . Yet as soon as ethnicity is analyzed within a social situation—
> at close quarters—it becomes apparent that these patterns are neither fixed
> nor always clearly defined. (p. 52)

Thus, for the biracial Korean/white individual, on a microlevel, racial identity is fluid and allows for the expression of many different, specific racial identities depending on the context of the situation. On the macrolevel, the amount of fluidity and interpretation allowed is greatly diminished.

Two questions in this study explored the macrolevel context for identity. The first question asked people how they saw themselves in the context of mainstream society. Two individuals saw themselves as progressing to some higher status in mainstream society. With those two exceptions, all other participants felt as though they were not a specific part of mainstream society or they were alienated from it.

Institutionalized forms were discussed as representations of mainstream society's racial categories. Participants were asked what they indicated as their identity or racial background on school applications, job applications, or census forms. Interestingly, these were often seen in terms of possible benefits to the individual, especially school applications. Six out of the eight participants said that they put down Asian American or Asian/Pacific Islander on the forms. One participant said she put down "White. White and sometimes just a little Korean." One participant said that he checked two boxes, Caucasian and Asian/ Pacific Islander (see also King & DaCosta, Chapter 14, this volume). When asked if what they checked accurately described their racial identity, the views were varied.

Some participants felt that Asian/Pacific Islander did not describe their racial identity accurately, but they put it down for scholarship opportunities. One participant felt that it did not describe anything. Two participants felt that it did not accurately describe their racial identity because they could not indicate anything more specific than Asian/Pacific Islander. Malcolm's views about the accuracy of the categories examine the nature upon which the categories are perpetuated:

> I think people choose to label themselves how they see fit. I was in a 7-11 one day and there was this Asian woman, she obviously looked Asian, you know, features-wise. She had a Southern accent and she was from Texas. So I said, "You know, it's very interesting that you're Asian American with a Southern-twang accent." She said "I'm not Asian. I'm Texan." [Laughs] So, I thought this is the ultimate in the political irony of things.

C. C. I. Hall (1992) noted similar difficulties with rigid classification among the African American/Japanese participants in her study. More specifically, the difficulties centered around the "please choose one" ethnic identity question. She described age as part of the developmental process and a possible factor in the conceptualization of racial identity as something beyond an "either/or" concept. In this study, one of the main factors surrounding the participants' views of themselves may be the influence of college and subsequent exposure to multiple conceptions of self.

Forms are one kind of ambiguous representation of mainstream racial categories. Although the categories are confining, some negotiation of the forms to the person's perceived benefit does take place. Thus institutional forms are a combination of micro- and macrolevel contexts. They are limiting in that they are not accurate descriptions of a biracial Korean/white identity, but they can be interpreted in terms of possible advantages and disadvantages.

Phenotype

The participants had no specific appearance that led the researcher to distinguish a single phenotypic category, of the sort that currently exists on forms. However, the researcher often had a nondescript "feeling" about being similar in appearance to the participants. Unfortunately, it could not be determined whether this was the result of knowing that the participants were biracial Korean/white or if it was an ability to spot those people who appeared similar to the researcher, regardless of prior knowledge (C. C. I. Hall, 1980, 1992). As Hall (1992) said, "it is difficult to explain to a 'nonmember' what the salient characteristics are in determining another member, but it appears that many mixed individuals experience the same phenomenon" (p. 260).

With an often ambiguous phenotypic appearance, biracial Korean/white people are inevitably asked to say "what" they are. All participants in this study had been asked "What are you?" at one point or another. The pervasiveness of racial ideology can be seen in such a question. Omi and Winant (1986) suggest that "comments such as 'Funny, you don't look black,' betray an underlying image of what black should be" (p. 62) and that such comments contain beliefs about particular racial groups. Moreover, the writers go on to state that "rules shaped by our perception of race in a comprehensively racial society determine the 'presentation of self' " (p. 62). At this level and within a personal context, race takes on another set of meanings—meanings that shape a person's racial identity. The ambiguous appearance of a biracial Korean/white individual obscures the strictly defined and socially accepted definition of Asian physical characteristics, as well as white physical characteristics.

Cultural Access

The amount of access that the participants had to Korean cultural practices and customs was rather limited. The main hindrance they suffered was lack of fluency in the Korean language. Although many of the participants were familiar with some words and often recognized the language, none had a clear and strong use of the language. Furthermore, all participants indicated that the language used in their homes was English.

The bulk of their knowledge of being Korean came from folk practices. These included taking shoes off when entering the house, eating Korean foods, and celebrating a child's first birthday. When asked what his mother told him about being Korean, Shawn said,

> It was mostly like stories, like her experiences. And what is like proper Korean custom. Like how to greet your elders, mostly. . . . Well, I had the traditional first Korean birthday and I did the whole get-up in the first birthday outfit.

Another way that the participants access Korean culture is symbolic, through terminology used to indicate racial identity (Asian American, Korean American, etc.) and a specific cultural identity. In a similar manner, participation in Korean organizations and events serves not only as actual expression but also as symbolic expression of a Korean cultural identity. Although the participants may not have had a specific working definition of what being Korean is, through these symbolic interactions they placed themselves within an abstract Korean identity.

Yet, there may be more to the Korean cultural understanding of the biracial Korean/white individual. On a socialization level, each participant was in part socialized in a Korean manner from each of their mothers. For example, Malcolm said,

> You know. . . . every time I go home, it's like "Are you hungry?" I went to my mom's house last night, 10:30 at night, my mom's awake she says "You want me to make you some egg rolls?" 10:30 at night, I'm like "Mom, I don't need any egg rolls." . . . The point is there are cultural things that we experience on a daily basis that we don't get at other people's house[s].

In this manner, the participants expressed a diversity of ways in which they experienced and identified with being Korean. The socialization process, with a working definition of Korean cultural values, is an area that warrants further research with this population.

CONCLUSION

An important aspect of the sample and of understanding the macrolevel context in which participants formed their identity is that the participants represent a combination of dominant and subordinate groups within U.S. society. Their parents represent two disparate societies that have come together through the U.S. involvement in Korea. Although not all participants in the sample explicitly said that their fathers were in the U.S. military, it is through the military presence of the United States in Korea that the possibility of the couples' meeting existed.

In order to understand the identity of the biracial individual, the specific group relations in terms of history—political, economic, and social—must be examined to place the individual within his or her specific context. Further research is required on relations between Korea and the United States, the lives of Korean Americans in the United States, and the Asian immigrant experience. Such research will contribute to an accurate description of biracial Korean/white people's experience within the U.S. racial paradigm. Thus the conclusions presented here are specific to the biracial Korean/white population in the Colorado Front Range region. Although some of the ideas and theories presented in this study may be applicable to other biracial and multiracial groups, it must be acknowledged that different groups have different experiences.

The construction of the biracial Korean/white racial identity is a complex and tangled mesh. In a microlevel context, identity is fluid, providing for a "best-fit" racial identity depending on the specifics of the context. However, a rigid racial identity within the macrolevel context requires biracial Korean/white people to choose a specific single identity. However, what is true about both contexts is that the identities within them are specific to them. Understanding biracial Korean/white racial identity is placing the terms and the individuals in context so that they are given dimension and depth.

Moving away from biracial identity as a psychological malady or as a marginalized position within the societal context provides a more accurate picture of the way in which biracial people operate. Rather than imposing a template upon the experience, the experience should speak for itself in its many forms. Conceptions such as denial of racial heritage need to be closely scrutinized for presuppositions about what a biracial person experiences. Viewing racial identity on a microlevel as fluid and malleable is a more correct conception of how biracial Korean/white people act. Racial theories that necessitate blood as racial identity need to be reexamined in light of such movement in and out of various racial contexts.

PART IV

Gender and
Sexual Identity

16

In the Margins of Sex and Race

Difference, Marginality, and Flexibility

GEORGE KITAHARA KICH

As a preadolescent, I lived with my family in an apartment building in Chicago on a short, dead-end street that served as a courtyard for our neighborhood. Families of many racial and ethnic backgrounds lived there; it was an enclave of languages and accents, smells and tastes, body shapes and movements. I think I was happy. Catholic school demanded that I act a certain way in order to be acceptable there, but in the neighborhood, I could be everything I felt I was. In terms of race and ethnicity, we were all so different that my being mixed race and from Japan was just another way of being like everyone else.

Those years were spirals of energy, discovery, and experimentation with boundaries and identities. I realized somewhere in this ferment that sex was something that was possible among all the genders, and more important, that my curiosity and excitement about these possibilities had to be dampened

AUTHOR'S NOTE: I want to thank my colleague Margo Okazawa-Rey, EdD, for our initial conversations on this topic. Don McKillop, PhD, has been an invaluable friend and support; his understanding of sexual identity has been an important resource for me and my thinking. I especially want to thank my wife, Mary Ann Leff, MFCC, for both her clinical insights and her personal presence.

263

because other people did not see it the way I did. At first, I did not understand the strength and pervasiveness of what I would later learn to call male conditioning and heterosexism. Shame and guilt reinforced my adolescent doubts, compounded by moving to the foreign white suburbs, driving me underground.

Years later in college, loving men and women and meeting other biracial people, I could experience the truth of my multiple identities, even though I still was not able to articulate them. As I discovered the words for me (*biracial* and *bisexual*), I felt freed up to recognize both myself and the nature of choice in a developing identity. Over the years, I have worked hard at integrating these areas of identity, organizing and layering them, mapping shared terrain, ideals, and goals. I am now in a happy and enduring, monogamous, heterosexual marriage, aware and accepting of myself and my multiple identities. &

As an exploratory presentation and discussion of the intersection of biraciality and bisexuality, this chapter is based on the assumption that developmental processes for those who are both biracial and bisexual have necessitated complex and conscious decisions about the expression of these *other*ed racial and sexual identities.

The complex experience of an *other*ed life tends to lose validity and coherence due to the shaming and reification of a majority society and its rules. Therefore, in using language and concepts to map out the various territories of an *other*ed life, we run the risk of shadowing the experience with pathology or elevating it with idealization. Recognizing the reality of multiple identities resurrects a fuller sense of self from the homogeneity and reductionism of the "melting pot" myth.

This chapter is about the intersection between two aspects of our multiple self-maps: our sexual identity and our racial/ethnic identity, and in particular, the experience of identifying as both bisexual and biracial. In order to explore the territory of this complexity, we must choose a quadrant, a temporary center of focus, to allow a recognition of foreground and background, the inner depths and the borders. This chapter focuses on several themes:

1. the twinship of the experience of the identities of biraciality and bisexuality, especially in terms of being different from the ideologies of various

majorities (European Americans, monoracial groups, heterosexuals, gays/ lesbians, etc.);

2. marginality and one's relationship to the monoculture; and

3. flexibility, or holding ambiguity, paradox, and contradiction as a way of life.

Within each of these themes, biracial and bisexual identities will be discussed.

For the purposes of this chapter, the term *biracial* will be used to include all mixed-race and multiracial people. *Bisexual*, however, is more complex to define. It usually implies two broad dimensions: (a) self-acceptance of the possibility of sexual or intimate attraction to people of both sexes to equal or varying degrees and (b) a wide range of behavioral and relational choices, such as active mixed-gender sexual partners, or a heterosexual or gay or lesbian relationship choice with a self-recognition as bisexual, or celibate with a self-recognition as bisexual, among others. Bisexual as a label seems to hold many possibilities: "One of the beauties of 'bisexuality' is that it can permanently embrace the 'choose not to label' category; it can challenge our obsessive need to order and categorize society to make it static" (Colker, 1993, p. 128). Some people recognize that they are bisexual after an encounter or sexual feelings with someone of the same sex. Others have always known that they were bisexual.

Although the population of biracial/bisexual people might indeed be small, this analysis of each identity position can be a way of understanding and overcoming the process of *othering*. Moved by denial, ethnocentrism, and prejudice, people and institutions categorize some people as outsiders, as *other* than normal, standard, or acceptable. Deconstructing the identity and relational modes of biracial and bisexual identities can be a way to understand the nature of living flexibly in the margins. Fluidity of self-experience can be seen as one way to creatively understand and manage the "marginal lifestyle." A discourse on aspects of biracial and bisexual experience of self can help us understand the possible nature of cognitive and interpersonal flexibility for all people. The movement between the poles of insider and outsider perspectives, something we all share in various circumstances, can then be understood in terms of its influence on our ability to hold and understand differences and similarities, in ourselves and others.

DIFFERENCE

Identity, as constructed within a politics of difference, refers to the articulation and reintegration of aspects of a self that have historically been made invisible, oppressed, or marginalized. However, different kinds of sociomoral reasoning—for instance, hypothesized as having to do with women's ways of caring and knowing (Gilligan, 1982; Gilligan, Ward, & Taylor, 1988; Mirkin, 1994)—raise the possibility that a personal and social identity can be framed and experienced in multiple dimensions. When difference (expressed through identities that are racial, ethnic, cultural, class, gender, sexual, etc.) is subjugated and repressed, the fullest and conscious expression of one's self becomes impossible. The sense of self becomes subject to the will of a dominant majority that cannot tolerate differentness and the ambiguity, openness, and dialogue that is required of it.

When a majority group assumes the power of instituting norms from which minority groups are seen to deviate, differences between these groups become institutionalized. Difference is then perceived as a deficit, or as a failure to meet the standards of the majority (de Monteflores, 1986, p.73).

However, the negativization of difference occurs because of the social ideological context of a totalitarian heterosexist and white supremacist homogeneity. Simply because we are not all alike, acknowledging difference more emphatically allows us to recognize our similarities without fear of losing other important aspects of ourselves.

Ethnic/Racial Identity

The degree of biological variability and difference between members of the same race has been found to be greater than between people of so-called different races. Researchers have recognized the socially defined and mutable nature of race, either as complicated by multiracial people or via lack of a scientifically rigorous definition (Wright, 1994; Yee, Fairchild, Weizman, & Wyatt, 1993). The biracial or multiracial person's embodied, racialized identity and experience is contextual, ambiguous, and political (Root, 1992d). The biracial person's process of developmental self-valuation is a major journey through these self and society interactions: awareness of differentness, struggle for acceptance, self-acceptance and assertion of an interracial identity, and an ongoing reevaluation and expression of a transforming ethnic/racial self in relationship to others (Kich, 1982). In this context, the very process of the biracial person's identity development becomes the reframing of differentness as deficits to a valuing of one's alterity as positive (Weisman, Chapter 10, this volume).

The inevitable and highly determining influence of parents, and subsequently partners and other relationships, can become the grounding for the biracial person's ability to resist the urge for a premature closure of his or her racial/ethnic identity. Support and acceptance occurs through providing structures and contexts for understanding race and differentness and through expressing comfort and openness in communicating about race, ethnicity, and culture. It is in this process that the initial ability to accept difference and to tolerate ambiguity occurs. Recontextualizing the problem of difference and ambiguity as the perceivers' confusion opens up the possibility of experiencing one's racial/ethnic identity as a process: a mobile, developmentally varying construct, requiring self-analysis and ongoing dialectic revisions. In parallel, a developing sense of self as sexual also emerges, co-influenced by family, society, and self-perceptions.

Sexual Identity

Along with locating oneself on racial and ethnic landscapes, sexual identity is charted among the landmarks of biology and behavior, of self-awareness and relatedness, and of belongingness and differentiation, within which everyone navigates.

Writers in many areas of discourse separate and reassemble the multiplicity of sexual identity in many ways: for instance, as deeply interwoven between genetic and social learning dynamics (Money, 1987; Money & Ehrhardt, 1972); as being rooted in and constructed by "cultural schemas" separate from ourselves (Bem, 1993, p. viii); as requiring the recognition and inclusion of different cultural experiences (Anzaldúa, 1990; "Dimensions of Desire," 1994; hooks, 1984; Lim-Hing, 1994; Takagi, 1994); and as compelling a revisioning of male power and intimacy dynamics (Kupers, 1993; Pederson, 1991). Self-definition plays a significant role, especially in terms of the valuing of different ways of knowing the self, both as sexual and as more than sexual:

Although I have lived monogamously with a man I love for over 27 years, I am not now and never have been a "heterosexual." But neither have I ever been a "lesbian" or a "bisexual." What I am—and have been for as long as I can remember—is someone whose sexuality and gender have never seemed to mesh with the available cultural categories, and that— rather than my presumed heterosexuality—is what has most profoundly informed not only my feminist politics but also [my] theoretical analysis. ... not that I am attracted to both sexes, but that my sexuality is organized around dimensions other than sex. (Bem, 1993, p. vii)

Bem does not elaborate further; however, her statement is an example of sexuality as a fundamental aspect of overall identity that can be reconfigured and reintegrated as a unique and personal assertion.

McKillop's (1994) conceptualization about sexual identity is useful in understanding bisexuality. He separates out components of sexuality that had previously been merged. He examines sexuality as an interacting constellation of five distinct identities: gender, body image, sexual scripts, gender role, and sexual orientation. Also, in recognizing both biological determinants and social factors in each of the five areas, McKillop described two dimensions for each area: innate sexuality (biological, no choice) and sexual behavior (learned, choices possible). What is important here is that sexuality can be understood as having multiple components involving a range of biological givens and personal choices. His schema clarifies what sexual identity a particular person has, what aspects could be seen as chosen or not, and it strengthens the idea that sexual identity is more fluid than previously defined. Gender-role identity, for instance, includes the degree to which a person has or uses "feminine" or "masculine" traits, roles, and behaviors. Within this, a person has innate masculinization or feminization aspects that are due to hormonal or genetic factors over which a person has no choice. However, a person does have control over the type of social or cultural role-based sexual behavior (e.g., behaviors ascribed to males or females, the centrality of sex in relationships, etc.). In terms of sexual orientation identity, the degree and object of one's attraction involve no choice, but what we decide to do with that attraction involves behaviorial choices.

The bisexual self-label as one's sexual orientation identity may include sexual behavior with both men and women, or with no one, or with exclusively one gender (Klein & Wolf, 1985; McKillop, 1994; Weinberg,

Williams, & Pryor, 1994). A person who is bisexual in orientation may choose any gender-role identity, for instance, either identified along socially prescribed traditional norms, masculine if a man, feminine if a woman, or androgynous. The deepening and expansion of sexual identity proposed by McKillop's (1994) model allow a revaluing of "different" sexual identities and experiences, clarifying what is possible to choose and what is not. As a result, the idea that sexual identity is a process, something that develops and emerges over time and experience, is both strengthened and clarified.

Weinberg et al. (1994) describe a stage model developed via intensive interviews with bisexuals. The model describes the sequence by which the interviewees became aware of their sexual identity and understood and accepted themselves as bisexual (sexual orientation identity). This process is reminiscent of other developmental sequences for racial/ethnic identity formation in the movement from less coherent, confused, and questioning positions, to a clearer and more resolved identity (Atkinson, Morten, & Sue, 1989; Kich, 1982; Root, 1990; Sue & Sue, 1990).

> They had experienced a period of considerable confusion, doubt, and struggle regarding their sexual identity . . . having strong sexual feelings for both sexes that were unsettling, disorienting, and sometimes frightening. . . . Following this initial period of confusion, which often spanned years, was the experience of finding and applying the label. . . . For many who were unfamiliar with the term bisexual, the discovery that the category in fact existed was a turning point. . . . Usually it took years from the time of the first sexual attractions to, or behaviors with, both sexes before people came to think of themselves as bisexual. The next stage then was one of settling into the identity . . . characterized by a more complete transition into self-labeling . . . the consequence of becoming more self-accepting. [There was] continued uncertainty [and] even after having discovered and applied the label "bisexual" to themselves, and having come to the point of apparent self-acceptance, they still experienced continued intermittent periods of doubt and uncertainty regarding their sexual identity . . . [based on] the lack of social validation and support. (Weinberg et al., 1994, pp. 26-37)

The developmental transitions experienced by the research sample reflect the bisexual person's response to initial personal and social confusion, conflict, and dissonance about sexual orientation differences. Developmental perspectives allow an understanding that this process is transitional to an ongoing reaffirmation and self-acceptance as a whole, complete person who is bisexual. However, identity does not remain static. Transitions continue as social forces and personal relationships change. Interestingly, research about biracial identity development mirrors these steps, as well as the experience of ongoing adaptation to a changing world (Kich, 1982; Root, 1990).

Two theories that have emerged from a long-standing debate about the nature and rationality of bisexuality are the conflict model and the flexibility model (Zinik, 1985). These models

> encapsulate the opposing views on the issues of choice and decision-making: The conflict model explains bisexuality as characterized by indecision and the inability to choose a sexual/gender preference; the flexibility model characterizes bisexuality as the conscious decision to adopt a dual orientation, as a free choice. (p. 13)

"Open gender schemas" (Weinberg et al., 1994) could also account for the experience of conscious free choice for bisexuals:

> In putting together their sexuality, they seem to be able to build upon and respond to a wider range of gendered signals than heterosexuals and homosexuals do. . . . An open gender schema allows persons to be extremely adaptable in meeting their sexual needs as their situation changes. (p. 288)

The dichotomizing of conflict and flexibility, although useful as a temporary theoretical strategy to understand opposing interpretations, can be discarded in favor of a normalizing and dialectical understanding of developmental processes. Both conflict and flexibility occur, being necessary attributes of growth and change. We learn as we grow, and constraints on the experience of differentness undermine our ability to develop skills to handle conflict with emotional and cognitive flexibility.

MARGINALITY AS CENTER

Marginalization is a process, an everyday activity "by means of which certain people and ideas are privileged over others . . . ignored, trivialized, rendered invisible and unheard, perceived as inconsequential, de-authorized, 'other' or threatening, while others are valorized" (Tucker, 1990, p. 7). In the history of the enforcement of marginalization, the marginalized were indeed the outsiders, without recourse to acceptance or freedom. Marginalizing works because (a) the dominant group targets the marginalized *other* as being the embodiment of negativism, of being the dissident or the outlaw, the ones who do not fit in to the categories of acceptance and solidarity (Dollimore, 1991); and (b) because they get away with it. An alienating and deadly social and personal position—the outsider's voice and experience easily turn into internalized oppression. An intersubjective and interactionist reconfiguring of the marginal position (Weisman, Chapter 10, this volume) can allow a repositioning of self as central to each person's drama of race and gender.

In the postmodern era, being different as a way of life recognizes that living in the cultural margins allows fundamental access to both the perspectives of the insider and of the outsider. Traversing the realms of race and sex, being biracial and bisexual, brings with the marginality a wide array of experiences and knowledge. Essed (1990) stated one aspect of this experience:

> Everday racism implies that people of color can, potentially, experience racism every day. As a result, people of color learn to systematically observe the behavior of whites. They develop expertise in judging how whites behave toward them. They also gain insight into the white delusion of superiority and the ideology defining people of color as inferior. They have daily opportunities to test new insights, because they have contact with all sorts of whites every day. (p. 259)

However, biracial and bisexual people have experienced oppressive responses from all sides, being marginalized by dominant majorities of every context: straights, gays/lesbians, European Americans, and other monoracials. Monoracial European Americans and people of color have historically positioned biracial people as both idealized and disturbed. Similarly, bisexuals have been castigated by both heterosexuals and gays/lesbians as indecisive, untrustworthy, and irresponsible.

Interestingly, both insider and outsider positions can be reframed as a source of positive learning for marginalized peoples. As an insider, a person benefits from acceptance, shared language and meanings, and the solidarity and sense of community engendered by a common fate. As an outsider, the marginalized person experiences the dynamics of boundary maintenance and inclusion/exclusion processes, from which a critique of marginalization is possible (Ferguson, Gever, Trinh, & West, 1990; hooks, 1984). Marginalization *is* oppressive and victimizing. However, when not overcome directly, people who are marginalized can use their ambiguous appearance, for example, both to pass into the mainstream (Bradshaw, 1992; Daniel, 1992b; de Monteflores, 1986) and to create separate and private communities and traditions (Spickard, 1989) as sites of resistance and assertion (Daniel, 1992b; hooks, 1990).

The task has been to reframe the notions of marginality-as-negative by creating and articulating a presence in the center of the discourse, a temporary centralizing of the contents of the difference. By dissecting the binary standard and seeing beyond the reified limitations of the dominating groups, it can be seen that others experience a marginal status and thereby hear a chorus of shared voices. Furthermore, as solidarity emerges among all the marginalized, the very definitions and placement of the center are called into question:

> As historically marginalized groups insist on their own identity, the deeper, structural invisibility of the so-called center becomes harder to sustain. The power of the center depends on a relatively unchallenged authority. If that authority breaks down, then there remains no point relative to which others can be defined as marginal. The perceived threat lies partially in the very process of becoming visible. It becomes increasingly obvious, for example, that white American men have their own specificity, and that it is from there that their power is exercised. No longer can whiteness, maleness, or heterosexuality be taken as the ubiquitous paradigm, simultaneously center and boundary. (Ferguson, 1990, p. 12)

Bisexual identity and biracial identity are achievements created through the discourse between the margins and the center of complex sexual and racial/ethnic psychologies and politics (Heyl, 1993; Hutchins & Kaahumanu, 1991; Klein, 1978/1993; Lukes & Land, 1990; Root, 1992b; Singer, 1976; Weinberg et al., 1994). Thus the rearticulation of difference, as expressed personally and in relationship through sexuality and race, brings the marginal experience back into the center. In this way, bisexuality and biraciality as voices have begun to speak, centering themselves as the basis of their own experiences, not in contrast or against other standards.

AMBIGUITY, INTERPERSONAL COMPETENCE, AND COGNITIVE FLEXIBILITY

Social and personal categories are designed to make identifying each other easy. However, when categories are reified, the variability and richness of our lives can be dismissed and lost. But because ambiguity is part of the territory of being either biracial or bisexual, resolving difference involves asking and answering more questions, sometimes taking longer to resolve misperceptions and misunderstandings among people with different languages, appearances, and behaviors. It requires making an effort to actively learn from each other, as the same and as different. However, perceptions and past experiences provide either an openness to accept and be curious about the mystery and enticements that ambiguity provides or leave a dread and fear of the unpredictability and dangerousness of the unknown. Ambiguity can result in anxiety and foster denial and lack of communication. Fear is mixed with an inability to understand each other's differentness, an apparent inability to find mutual understanding step by step, and a mistrust in each other's willingness to stay with the process. The fear and dread of rejection, of being dis-identified, of having to organize an enraged yet coherent explanation for existence, mix with the internalized oppression that the marginalized person experiences, a self-doubt that results in an ambiguity to themselves. When people alienate themselves from their true selves and their true self-reflections, in order to safely relate to the dominant group, the alienation takes on a life of its own. The self-oppression that results creates a fog of emptiness, fear, and ambiguity to self.

People without the experience of resolving ambiguity, of moving from marginal status to center, or of expanding definitions beyond traditional constraints in order to really see what in fact exists often cannot adapt competently to marginality or to ambiguity, much less to a person who embodies ambiguity. The dominant majorities often are not able to discover in themselves the wish to inquire, to be curious about differences or the struggle to resolve marginalizing experiences. Marginalization itself is the dominant majority's attempt at disowning and projecting self-awareness, ambiguity, anomalies, and contradictions onto the stranger, the unknown and seemingly unknowable person.

In terms of confronting people with identities as bisexual or biracial, ambiguity and the anxiety that attends it are usually things that the dominant majority people experience. Their intolerance is derived from projections of fear and dread, from an inability to expand rigid categories, and from the unconscious hope that demonizing the *other* will contain their dread. When marginalized people believe the dominant majority's projections—that they are indeed the savage and untameable Calibans (Takaki, 1993), the embodiment of the foreign *other* in Shakespeare's *The Tempest*—they fall into the denial, stereotypes, and confusions that maintain the image of their own inhumanity. The dominant majority do not see the biracial and/or bisexual person as simply exercising ways of expressing an identity, along a spectrum of identities that the dominant majority person often sees in a disjointed, fragmented, and frightened way. De Monteflores (1986) stated that "the valuing of one's difference, as a member of a rejected minority, can lead to the valuing of difference itself, which is perhaps one of the most important contributions which minorities can make to the larger society" (p. 75). She described several processes that enhance the revaluing of difference: taking on the struggle of understanding boundaries; confronting and transforming deficits into strengths; creating safety in community and solidarity; and recognizing and revaluing oneself as special. The management of difference and the openness to ambiguity challenge and foster emotional and cognitive flexibility.

The intolerance of ambiguity (Frenkel-Brunswik, 1949) in emotional or interpersonal expressions may be seen either as a premature closure of perceptions due to fear, anxiety, or cognitive overload or as an inability to access multiple sides of ambivalences, either of feelings, questions, or opinions. Frenkel-Brunswik found that children tested in several cognitive and personality domains who manifested "extreme racial prejudice" also scored high in such areas as "intolerance of ambiguity," "distortion of reality," and "rigidity" (p. 122). She said, "Basically, therefore, avoidance of ambiguity and related mechanisms, directed as they are toward a simplified mastery of the environment, turn out to be maladaptive in the end" (p. 135).

A person's degree of emotional/cognitive/social flexibility (the ability to tolerate and to manage increased levels of complexity and differentiation) may be understood as a developmental consequence of a healthy adaptation to life. Prior work on biracial identity alludes to this as a developmental achievement, having necessitated a dialectic of resistance, self-acceptance, passing, and self-renewal (Bradshaw, 1992; Daniel, 1992b; Kich, 1992). Interpersonal competence, manifesting as *relational competence* (Surrey, 1991) or as *intercultural competence* (Samovar & Porter, 1988), both speak to the same context of the possible achievement of an ability to live in the margins, as well as to move relationally with others that reframes a sense of oneself as having been an exile or a sojourner (Said, 1990). People learn and develop competencies as they journey over the difficult terrains of their racial and sexual lives. Flexibility of constructs, relational competence, and adaptability are potentially the skills of living with difference and in the margins.

> Relational competence can be defined as the interest and capacity to stay emotionally present with, to enlarge or deepen the relational context to create enough "space" for both or all people to express themselves, and to allow for possible conflict, tension, and creative resolution. Recognizing the growth and change in people, ongoing connection implies a process of attunement to change, that is, staying "current" in relationship. Western society discourages this possibility. It highlights and encourages separation and individuation, does not emphasize the importance of ongoing connection, and has not given enough support or educational experience to the skillful engagement of differences, conflicts, and powerful feelings in relationships. As a result, this relational pathway of development is obscured; its potential remains unacknowledged and undeveloped. (Surrey, 1991, p. 171)

No longer bound by linear and centrist definitions, people who have traversed the margins and the center have the opportunity to reevaluate and reorganize themselves, the processes of interconnectedness, and the power dynamics of social and political discourse.

BISEXUALITY AND BIRACIALITY

What is there to learn about people's "use" of a bisexual orientation and a biracial identity? These are personal and relational choices about the ways in which they are mediating and managing their sexual, racial, and ethnic identities, as well as ways of maintaining ties to multiple communities (in this volume: see Twine, Chapter 18; Weisman, Chapter 10). *If the achievement of an identity of any kind is entrenched at the expense of another category of people, then the personal and interpersonal competencies necessary for mutually empowered relationships have not been accounted for.* This error occurs when the dominant majorities counterposed against each level of identity do not own their own projections and do not recognize their marginalizing power.

The difference, *other*ness, marginality, and ambiguity of the lives of people who are biracial and/or bisexual powerfully reflect back to the dominant majority groups a mixture of mystery, fear, and/or enlightenment. However, to biracial and/or bisexual people, the task is to see past the distorted and cloudy mirror of the majorities, through the crucibles of the struggles, experiences, and relatedness of the chorus of the marginalized. If the ambiguity that comes from the struggle can be tolerated and there is a generosity toward reconnection, then the marginalized can reflect back, as an archaeological returning or re-membering to the "monopeoples" of the world, their own shadowed, buried, altered, and disowned projections. As the centers of liminal coherence, the ambiguous and marginalized must create and subsequently communicate core identities that are named, vitalized, and accepted by themselves, expressing through their own stories a view of experience and relatedness that the dominating majorities could never see by themselves.

17

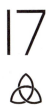

(Un)Natural Boundaries
Mixed Race, Gender, and Sexuality

KAREN MAEDA ALLMAN

I used to wonder why I have so often felt preoccupied with issues of boundaries and of identity. Why am I still startled when someone asks, yet again, *What are you?* Are you (fill in the blank racial/ethnic group, usually an incorrect one)? It can't be! Are you sure? Are you a woman first or a person of color/Asian American first? If this is a lesbian group, why do you keep talking about race? We are all women here!

An Asian American professor, one with whom I had often spoken about our shared experiences with racism on our campus, once told me, "You can pass for white any time." I had to stop myself from immediately running to look at myself in the mirror, and I must confess that I spent a lot of time scrutinizing my appearance in the following weeks. Had my features suddenly shifted, perhaps in the middle of the night, when I was sleeping? She seemed to think that my Asian heritage was something hidden within me, a secret that only she could see, and that racism was something I could choose to experience or not. I wondered if perhaps my lesbianism somehow "whitened" me in her eyes, and I wanted to tell her that lesbians, too, wondered "what" I was, had never heard of Asian lesbians, marveled over my command of English, and wondered if my mother was a "war bride" or a "geisha." How does one negotiate a multiple situated identity if race, gender, and sexual orientation are taken for granted as so separate and boundaried? ⚭

Reading the growing bodies of literature that could be counted as part of lesbian and gay studies, or, arguably more inclusively, queer studies, (which also embraces the bisexual and transgendered), I am impressed with the overlap of issues and authors with those literatures counted as women's studies and ethnic studies. The co-editor/contributors of one of the most influential (mostly lesbian) women's (women of color) studies, *This Bridge Called My Back: Writings by Radical Women of Color* (1981), Cherrie Moraga and Gloria Anzaldúa, both identify as lesbians, as women of color, and, albeit differently, as people of mixed racial heritage. My having to use these parentheses, almost as disclaimers, reminds me yet again of these perpetual questions:

1. Is a lesbian a "real" woman?
2. Are all of the "women" white? and
3. Are you a "woman" first or are you (fill in your race, please choose one) first?

Speaking as a lesbian, living out the possibilities and problems of a gendered identity, and attempting to attend to a mixed racial/cultural heritage may seem fatiguingly complex, and yet that is what many of us do as a matter of everyday life. It is often the stuff of the background, unremarkable until we bump up against some invisible boundary of action or thought, including that which would deny the interconnectedness of sexuality, race, and gender identities within ourselves as individuals and as peoples.

I will argue within this chapter that race and gender are not fixed or natural properties of individuals, but, rather, social constructs with real world consequences. Race and gender are mutually co-constructive, shifting and historically situated idea systems that not only shape how individuals and groups perceive themselves and others, but also aid us in organizing and trying to make sense of ourselves as embodied beings.

Sexuality, including sexual practices, desires, and orientations, provides a means and direction through which the boundaried hierarchies of genders, races, and classes can be transgressed, maintained, or both.

I will use the term *compulsory heterosexuality*, following Rich (1986), throughout this chapter as a sort of shorthand in the interests of the reevaluation of what is taken for granted about sexuality (and its relationship to race and gender) in general. Pointing to the "compulsory" in compulsory heterosexuality moves attention from heterosexuality as natural and unremarkable and directs attention to the exercise of power required to maintain heterosexuality as everyone's norm and the considerable political interests that are supported by maintaining a compulsory heterosexuality (versus a freely and joyously realized one).

I propose that race, gender, and sexuality exist as a sort of unstable triad; shifts in one create disturbances in the other two. Transgressing racial boundaries, therefore, would not only potentially destabilize notions of racial purity but also threaten exposure of the racialized, historicized character of gender roles. Proscriptions against "race mixing" often coexist with calls for adherence to "traditional" gender roles and an emphasis on heterosexual, procreative sex only within the institution of marriage. Groups of women, especially those organizing together across racial lines for political, social, or cultural purposes, may find themselves facing homophobic attacks for not placing the interests of men (especially men of their own racial group) first and risk being called traitorous and "unnatural" as women, or lesbians (Pharr, 1988).

RACIALIZED GENDER

Fujinuma (personal communication, 1994) noted that, historically, Western feminist models that attempt to examine the interrelationships of race, gender, class, and sexuality typically use additive models, as if the constructs existed independently. In contrast, anti-Orientalist, postcolonialist critics such as Nandy (1983) and Said (1978) hypothesize and critique a Western imperialist model in which the Western European (white) male colonizer sees himself as standing above the potentially exploitable, colonized *other* (all women; men of color). Fujinuma instead

proposed a fused model, in which multiple allegiances might be acknowledged, the simultaneity of oppressions explored (Lorde, 1984),
and oppressive hierarchies analyzed and dismantled. Glenn (1992)
similarly posited the relationality of gender and race, noting that each
is "positioned and gain[s] meaning in relation to the other" (p. 34). She
theorized a systematic relationship between, to use my own personal
example, Asian and American and woman in relation to myself, and
Asian American woman in relation to Asian American man, African
American woman, and so on. I propose that this relationship is co-
constructive, with one driving and being driven by the others.

Three basic assumptions underlie the arguments that I am making:

1. the sex/gender system is profoundly and interdependently racialized
   and racializing;
2. race is also thoroughly engendered and engendering; and
3. compulsory heterosexuality depends upon rigidity in gender roles and is
   reinforced by the promotion of racial purity.

The Sex/Gender System

The use of the term *sex/gender system* splits matters of the body or the
physiological sexed body from those of the psychologically, socially,
culturally engendered psyche (de Beauvoir, 1953). Although the split-
ting of sex from gender may serve a progressive end by removing some
of women's destiny from biology, and thus from the realm of the natural
and inevitable, current scholarship indicates considerable overlap.
Lacquer (1990), for example, argued that our ideas about gender shape
what we think is sex. I will use gender throughout as a sort of shorthand
for a system of representation of the relations between the socially
constructed, (mostly) permanent classes of men and women (de Lauretis,
1987). This system of representation is, however, articulated through race,
another system of representation of the relationships between socially
constructed classes of people. Both systems are projected upon the
bodies of individuals, and both systems have profound, real world
effects on the lives of actual people.

How is gender racialized? Many feminist and nonfeminist discussions of women's roles draw implicitly upon the spirit of what Welter
(1966) identified as the "cult of true womanhood" (p. 156), a Victorian

era domestic feminine ideal. Purity, piety, domesticity, and submission are identified as her "cardinal virtues"; she is living out her nature. Asexual and frail, this stereotyped "true woman" existed as the reverse of the stereotypes of the hypersexualized, tough, hard-working African American woman slave mammy (Collins, 1990). This true woman must be white and class privileged, implying that women who were not, perhaps were not women at all. During the movements for universal and women's suffrage, white men argued that voting would overtax the weak, delicate natures of (white) women, inspiring Sojourner Truth's famous "Ain't I a Woman" speech. Unfortunately, white men and women on both sides of the suffrage debate seemed not to think so, a problem that has remained into the present, as demonstrated by the title of a recent anthology of African American women's writing: *All of the Women Are White, All of the Men Are Black, But Some of Us Are Brave* (Hull, Scott, & Smith, 1982).

Takaki (1979), writing of roughly the same period, noted that part of the responsibility of white women, as appropriate to their gender and race, was to keep themselves separate from social spaces in which interracial exchanges might occur, especially those in which the white women might meet men of color of roughly the same social status. He wrote of the anxieties of white, class-privileged men among the faculty and student body of Harvard Medical School upon the admission of three men of African descent and one white woman. White, male, class (and implicitly heterosexual) privilege was in part based on and justified by the absence of these *others* from the social space of Harvard and the professional space of medicine, which as a discipline itself sanctioned and naturalized the era's theories of (white) female and black (male) inferiority through supposedly scientific studies based on differences in cranial capacity and the like (see Gould, 1981, for further discussion). According to evidence presented by Green (1983), the supposed desexualized white "true woman" was even used to demonstrate the "natural" superiority of the white race, white women having evolved past the allegedly lower, base, and sexual "natures" of African American and Native American women.

Takaki (1979) suggested that the mixing of white women and black men also increased white male anxieties about miscegenation. White, class-privileged, male identity depended on a special relationship as the protector and keeper of white womanhood; as Hurtado (1989) noted, white women retained privilege through their relationship with white men. Takaki (1979) further observed that, if black men, as well as white men, could aspire to "manhood" (as opposed to black manhood), co-mingle in the same professional and social circles, and also pursue relationships with white women, and if white women could aspire to the same professional and social circles, possibly pursuing sexual and other intimate relationships with men of African descent, the foundations of white supremacy and male superiority would be shaken.

Morrison (1992) and Collins (1990) have explored the ways in which people of African descent have served a symbolic purpose as a repository for what was disowned and projected from white psyches, particularly sexuality. Thus hypersexualization of African American women and men (and other people of color) serves to excuse and justify the rape of African American women by white men (and sometimes men of color, as a function of internalized racism and sexism). Passive, desexualized, white women, following this logic, must be protected from the dangerous, uncontrolled sexuality of nonwhite men. The white woman's sexuality and relationship choice are not her own but rather belong to white men, perhaps as compensation for her "protection." White women's (white men's, African American women's and men's, etc.) role expectations are in this way bound by racial, gender, and heterosexual imperatives.

Engendered Race

The interconnectedness of race, gender, class, and sexuality does not only occur between black and white, nor do notions of "race" always remain stable, even within historical time periods, if other interests take precedence. The following example describes shifts in racial classifications of women versus men, class privileged versus not, within what was once considered a racially homogeneous group. Once again, (hetero)sexuality is deployed in the interests of drawing and redrawing engendered and racialized boundaries.

Casteñeda (1991) used the writings of primarily and specifically Anglo American male writers to illustrate the gradual shift of (again) 19th-century male Anglo American views of women of Mexican descent during the U.S. colonization of what is now California. During this time period, according to Casteñeda, women of Mexican descent, formerly viewed as "racially inferior Mexicans," became marriageable "Spanish ladies." Mexicanas and Mexicanos of *mestizo* descent (probably a mixture of indigenous Native American, European, and African descent) were at first considered both racially and morally inferior by the new European Americans, who were, not coincidentally, interested in land acquisition. Mexicana women, unlike European American women, were able to own and inherit property and thus enjoyed considerable economic power at the time; as prospective marriage partners, they provided access to the land. These land-owning, class-privileged women gradually came to be seen as somehow more "illustrious, moral, and chaste" (p. 35), more favoring the "European," than the men of their own communities. These elite women, the "Spanish ladies," were thus desirable as mates for Anglo men, whereas the men, elite or not, remained Mexican. Casteñeda noted that the elite women, while assuming the privileges of white womanhood, were also expected to live within the bounds of the "cult of true womanhood," including loss of economic and political power, desexualization, and separation from their own histories, cultures, and communities.

Collins (1990) noted that, although the stereotypes—or as she terms them, controlling images—may change with the passage of time, new controlling images build upon old ones. Controlling images, invested with the power to limit the affected person's choices, perpetuate distorted information and render invisible and/or exceptional that which does not fit the image. These examples from the past do not apply in the same way to the present, yet the effects of these differing histories of racialized genders, inflected by class, maintained through sexuality continue to inform our understanding of ourselves as relationally raced and gendered beings.

MIXED BLOOD/LESBIAN INTERRUPTIONS

I have discussed the importance of traditional heterosexual roles in maintaining separation of genders and the purity of races. Moraga (1983) has written that women's betrayal of each other on the basis of race has its roots in both sexism and heterosexism. She notes that, as the child of an interracial marriage between a Mexican American woman and a white American man and as a lesbian, she is seen by members of her own culture, Chicana(o) as, as the latest in a long line of female race traitors. The historical/mythological figure, Malintzin Tenepal, much reviled translator and mistress to Cortes, has carried the blame for having given over her own body, and thus symbolically and physically that of the race, leading to the destruction of indigenous Mexican culture. Moraga describes her association with the Malintzin through her own femaleness. Chicana women are related to Malintzin much as Christian women are linked to their own mythic ancestress, Eve. I cannot help but remember Casteñeda's Spanish ladies, as well.

As a mixed Chicana lesbian who is defying subservient gender roles, including reappropriation of her own sexuality, Moraga (1983) is obviously not placing her own community's men first, and she recalls having been accused of "contributing to the genocide of her own people" (p. 113). She is both evidence and perpetuator of that original transgression. Part of her own loyalty to *la raza* is the expectation that she will surrender her own will and sexual self to the men of her race; not doing so opens her up to charges of selling out to the white man, either directly, or by implication (lesbianism supposedly caused by corrupting influences working in the service of white men in the interests of destroying communities of color).

Chicanas, like many other groups of women, are thus discouraged from placing a premium on their relationships with women, including their own mothers and daughters, much less women from other races or cultural groups. Subscribing to subservient gender roles and relinquishing ownership of one's sexuality to the men of the group are constructed as prerequisites to full membership in the racial group. Love for one's race translates into love and support for the men of the race first, whereas love for women, of the race or not, sexually or otherwise, becomes suspect, something taken or stolen that rightfully belongs to the men of the race, indirectly aiding the (white) oppressors.

Hemphill (1992), a gay African American poet/activist, argued against Black Nationalist claims that whereas white male homosexuality is evidence of the degradation and inferiority of the white race, black male homosexuality is a result of the oppressive condition of white racism. He urged us to resist linking (intraracial, compulsory) heterosexuality with black identity, progressive antiracist struggles, and the survival of the black community, noting that for black men to love themselves and to love other black men is a radical act in itself. He asked us not to reduce the complexities of sexuality and sexual desire to a mere reaction to oppression. Considering the continuing hypersexualization of African Americans and the circular logic that allows for the use of this stereotype as proof of a supposed moral weakness, are African American gay men, not unlike Victorian era African American women with class privilege, being asked to "rise above" and deny their sexual selves in the interests of class mobility and the general uplift of the race?

Interestingly, Katz (1990) closely identified the construction of *homosexuality* and *heterosexuality* with the Victorian period, before which homosexual and heterosexual behavior existed, but homosexuality and heterosexuality as identities, as understood today, did not exist. According to Katz, heterosexuality was at first a term of sexual pathology, descriptive in the 1890s of people drawn to nonprocreative sexual activity with either opposite gender or both genders. The norm, against which the pathology of heterosexuality was constructed, was that of an orientation toward procreation and away from "unnatural lust," just as current heterosexual norms are interdependent with the discourse on the pathology of homosexuality. It is not surprising when people of color, already historically the recipients of white peoples' projections about sexual deviance, strive to avoid further associations by trying to embody the norm as much as possible.

Wong (1992) noted that, in the literature of Chinese-born American immigrants, "heterosexual fulfillment" marks the immigrant male subjects's acclimatization to a new homeland. The current controlling image of the desexualized (feminized), unassimilated Asian man exists, of course, in relation to the hypersexualized, exotic, and available Asian woman, as well as to the images described earlier in this chapter. Wong described the portrayal of immigrant experience in America as a gender-role reversal in which, given the association of masculinity with power within both Chinese and "American" cultures, being less Americanized and less in control over one's situation is less masculine. White American women are portrayed as sexual, aggressive, and wielding power over the less Americanized Chinese men. Strength or displays of sexuality in Chinese women are portrayed as threatening and emasculating to Chinese men; as evidence of treachery and the "unnatural" distribution of power. Successful adjustment entails reaffirmation of proper masculine roles through a return to traditional gender roles through male success in work; male dominance; and fulfilling, procreative heterosexuality.

Gay and lesbian Asian Americans—like African Americans, Chicanas(os), Arab Americans, Native Americans, and other gay people of color—may face criticism from their communities of origin regarding suspicions that homosexuality is a sort of foreign, (white) American problem, or a result of continued oppression, a stagnation within the above-mentioned gender-role inversion, standing in the way of full adaptation to the immigration process, evidenced by heterosexuality and the production of a family. Considering the close relationships between gender roles and expectations of heterosexual behavior, it is not surprising that often the two are confused. Dominance is linked with masculinity; loving and supporting men is linked with female gender roles—if a woman does hard, physical, nondomestic work, or chooses to love women, does that make her a "man"? If a man chooses nondomination-based models of masculinity or chooses to love men, does this make him a "woman"? Perhaps, as Pharr (1988) argued, homophobia, the fear and hatred of those who engage in same-sex love, and heterosexism, the institutionalization of compulsory heterosexuality, instead work in tandem to reinforce racist sex roles and limit the choices and possibilities of all.

MIXED-RACE LESBIAN IDENTITY

Mixed families contain opportunities for many permutations, confusions, and working out of racialized gender roles, engendered racial identities, and multiple sexualities. Will the children, as is hypothesized, identify with the race of the similarly gendered parent? Will "looks" determine monoracial or mixed identities and alliances? Moraga (1993) wrote that her sex is "brown" and her brother's is "white." Here she was speaking of the lines of power and of relative privilege in her family: identifying with and mirroring a (white and male) father. She later contrasted with her own mixed-blood, lesbian identity this (heterosexual) brother, who plainly and unquestioningly identifies with white maleness and its associated privileges, the (heterosexual) blondest brother who sports a *Viva la raza* tattoo on his arm. To what degree might inhabiting a lesbian identity lessen the necessity, benefits, and appeal of a monoracial, traditionally engendered presentation of self?

Mixed women, already arguably more marginal to identifiable racial groups, might feel more pressure to submissiveness to males and to compulsory heterosexuality in order to demonstrate affiliation and identification with a particular racial group, whether people of color or white/European American (Twine, Chapter 18, this volume). Mixed women, especially lesbians, may, however, have more opportunities to experience the overtness of the power relations that reinforce what have been represented as "natural" roles for women and men.

Mixed-race women who are lesbians exist in at least a triply marginalized space, inhabiting the ground on which the boundaries between groups are constantly contested and reconstructed. We face the pressures toward conformity to conflicting racialized gender roles, toward choosing one race. We are identified as "confused," and, in a sort of self-fulfilling prophecy, our gender nonconformity and incorrect sexuality are identified as evidence of our racial confusion (Pinderhughes, 1995). We are also pressured within our lesbian communities to conform to an unspoken white lesbian norm, not unlike the normative whiteness of "woman" discussed earlier. The importance of "choice," of "please choose (the correct) one," although often projected onto the bodies and into the psyches of mixed-race people, is probably of most interest to those who have most at stake in maintaining all boundaries as "natural" and fixed.

Mixed-race lesbians may be suspicious of any kind of identity politics based on single-group membership, whether based on race, gender, or sexual orientation. Too many opportunities exist to exclude us, to declare us as suspect *others*. Sometimes I feel anxious, lest I be associated with the "Oppressor" because I am lighter complected and because I know that white men, like my father, are not always the oppressors. I feel anxious because I am Japanese American, and Japanese are supposedly "taking over the world," or at least the United States. I worry that, because I am an Asian woman, sometimes reticent, that my reticence may be used as evidence to support stereotypes of "Oriental" women's "natural" passivity, submission, and obedience to men and that I may be perceived as one of a group that is supposedly selling out to men or to some kind of "model minority" stereotype. Will my lack of reticence be considered "un-Asian" by Asians and non-Asians alike, even though I know that my mother, like most Asian women I know, does not fit that stereotype? I am dismayed that not only straight, white people, but other lesbians, other people of color, and particularly lesbians of color, will believe these things about us. I am also given many opportunities to continue to build upon my critical consciousness as insider/outsider (Trinh, 1991), to examine my own participation and self-interest in projecting onto some *other*.

I feel discouraged when I experience white women's unwillingness to give up the reflection of white male privilege, even while claiming a feminist or a lesbian identity. Even when male privilege is disavowed, the maintenance of white privilege depends upon sharing of white racial identity and assumptions of white privilege with that other half of the race. I can only commit myself to a feminist scholarship and activism, for example, that exists to end sexist oppression for all women, not just white women by default and women of color as our issues overlap (hooks, 1984). I continue to be concerned about and interested in the ways in which interracial politics and the continuing pathologi-zation and marginalization of lesbians within feminism continue to work against the elimination of sexism.

Efforts to put issues concerning lesbianism at odds with issues con-cerning race similarly privilege an assumption of normative whiteness within the term lesbian and involve tacit acceptance and shared invest-ment in white privilege among (white) lesbians and white heterosexual women and men. Lesbian writings or events may completely ignore nonwhite or mixed-race lesbians, marginalize our experience into a somehow completely separate, unrelated "lesbian of color" category, or selectively use our perspectives only as they support a "normative" white lesbian experience or agenda. Many lesbian of color texts address this problem, the most famous of which is probably *This Bridge Called My Back* (Moraga & Anzaldúa, 1981), but the discussion can also be followed within such lesbian journals as *Sinister Wisdom*, particularly regarding recent discussions of the still poor representation of the writings of lesbians of color in recent lesbian or lesbian/gay anthologies.

A published conference talk and discussion by film theorist Teresa de Lauretis (1991) provides one example. She analyzed what she identifies as one of the first independent movies with a lesbian them, *She Must Be Seeing Things*, but does not mention that the women involved are a black/white interracial couple. When conference participants and panelists asked her to address this, she said that she had written on the topic of race at other times, that she did not think the film was about race, that the film was not made by a woman of color, that the film did not "really deal with her as a black lesbian," partly because this character is also Latina, that the film did not overtly deal with racial difference, and so on. Finally, she remarked that she was disturbed that "the specificity of lesbian sexuality must remain unspoken or unspeakable even in the context of a gay and lesbian conference" (p. 272). Clearly, to de Lauretis, attention to interraciality (and perhaps to some trading upon some obvious stereotypes of both black and white women within the film) can only confuse and distract. Interraciality can only be a part of lesbian sexuality if it is not remarked upon, or perhaps if it is absent. Curiously, the bulk of her analysis rested upon discussions of fantasy and of the unconscious. Yet race, which seems very much in the realm of projection and of the fantastic both within the film and within our lives in general, because it is not directly spoken of, can only be erased.

Anzaldúa (1987) has said that her lesbianism left her raceless and countryless, that queers comè in all races, are all to a degree cast out and disavowed, yet all are potential lovers of each other. Identifying and reclaiming her identity as *mestiza*, she encouraged Chicanas(os) and the rest of us to affirm our disowned parts, whether racial, gendered, or homosexual, to develop a new, border consciousness that can deal with ambiguities and contradictions and can heal the splits between us. We can all identify as mixed, affirming the mixed heritage of races and cultures previously constructed as monoracial or monocultural. Perhaps, she states, the lines between races, genders, homo, and hetero do not have to be so jarring. Moraga (1993), a first-generation mixed-race woman, also lesbian, seemed sympathetic, but more ambivalent about being named the one to bear this new mestiza species, "both a product of rape and the mother of the next generation" (p. 128). Anzaldúa invited us to explore the boundaries between us, and Moraga reminded us that someone already lives there on that ground on which these painful relations between people are being contested . . . again.

Meeting at the Boundaries

Moraga (1993) noted that none of her relationships have ever been raceless and attributes this to being a mixed-race person. I would add that relationships are never raceless, although racial issues may remain unconscious or unspoken. If racial difference can be eroticized, so can racial similarities. The attraction of the maintenance of white privilege, of avoidance of questions about one's loyalty to one's particular racial/ethnic group, of one's ability to fit in, may all be affirmed by a relationship constructed as monoracial, whether between two lesbians (or gay men, heterosexuals, or bisexuals). Dating interracially may bring such issues to the surface. Mixed-race lesbians, for whom most, if not all relationships may be interracial, are simply provided with more opportunities to deal consciously with issues of race.

Cornell (1992) invited us to reconsider the role of the unconscious in "imagining difference" and producing sexual desire. The controlling images described earlier in the chapter are often, I suspect, produced not through conscious deliberation, but rather appear as self-evident social facts. The metaphor of color, standing in for race and for difference, cannot be understood as free from the chains of signifiers that give it meaning: historical situations involving labor relations, engendered meanings, projected desire. Meanings of gender, also apparently self-evident, also exist in relation to historical relations of racialized genders, classes, sexualities. These relations and the meanings ascribed and linked to them remain visible in the traces of the metaphor of "true woman" and her legacy, the ways in which woman and lesbian continue to be understood as white. Reproduction of this metaphor involves the systematic erasure of the links of this chain into the unconscious, where the connections are still recognized but are difficult to articulate directly. Much work remains in bringing these pieces into consciousness. I remain optimistic about the development of a "borderlands" consciousness, about the exploration of an *other*ness that is an empowering and not alienating critical difference, and about engagement with those trying to negotiate boundaries and connections with me, and not through me.

18

Heterosexual Alliances

The Romantic Management
of Racial Identity

FRANCES WINDDANCE TWINE

Growing up on the Southside of Chicago as the daughter of a black American mother and a lighter skinned father of Native American (Creek Nation) and African heritage during a turbulent period of overt racial conflict and anti-black racism, I learned at an early age (and in very violent ways) about the enforcement of racial and ethnic boundaries. My extended family consisted of a multiracial, multinational, multicultural, and multigenerational group of unhyphenated northern blacks, southern-born black Creoles from Louisiana, enrolled members of the Creek Nation of Oklahoma, Anglo Americans, and Scottish immigrants.

When I left my childhood home of Chicago to live in New York City, New Orleans, and later San Francisco, I found that my experience of being racialized and growing up "black" within a multiracial household was regionally and generationally specific. I had a very different interpretative framework than my African-descent peers who had grown up in multiracial families in suburban communities in other regions of the United

291

States. My interests in the maintenance and enforcement of
racial, ethnic, and cultural boundaries eventually led me to
graduate training in anthropology at the University of California
at Berkeley. ⚠

> Di moin qui vous laimein, ma di vous qui vous ye.
> *Tell me whom you love, and I'll tell you who you are.*
>
> > Creole proverb as translated by
> > Lafcadio Hearn, 1885.

In recent years a body of literature on the politics of multiracial identity
and multiracial classification has emerged (Gibbs & Hines, 1992; Kich,
1992; Root, 1992b; Spickard, 1992; Tizard & Phoenix, 1993). However,
this literature has generated little empirical data on the role that heterosexual romantic partners assume in the negotiation and assertion of
shifts in the racial identity of young adults of multiracial heritage in the
contemporary United States. Cultural anthropologists, sociologists, and
historians have addressed the role that the regulation of heterosexual
romance has played and continues to assume today in the establishment
of racial identities and in the maintenance of the racial order (Blee, 1991;
Dominguez, 1986; Frankenberg, 1993; Fredrickson, 1981; Twine, Warren,
& Ferrandiz, 1991). Thus, given the significant role that the regulation
of heterosexual romance has assumed in the construction, enforcement,
and maintenance of racial boundaries and bounded racial identities, the
examination of heterosexual romantic choices among individuals of
multiracial heritage demands more attention from scholars.

This chapter will examine several interrelated issues, including:

1. the role of heterosexual romance in the transformation of racial identities
   among young adults of mixed African descent;
2. the enactment and management of racial identities through the selection
   of romantic partners; and
3. the racial politics of desire.

By analyzing and mapping the romantic histories of several young
adults of multiracial heritage, I will explore the role that *heterosexual*
romantic partners play in racial identity shifts and in the "grounding"
of a monoracial identity.

THE BERKELEY CAMPUS: THE EMERGENCE OF A
MULTIRACIAL STUDENT POPULATION

This chapter is based upon empirical research conducted between Fall 1990 and Spring 1991 on the Berkeley campus of the University of California. It examines how racial identities are "managed" in the context of romantic relationships. There are no exact published figures on the number of students of multiracial heritage in the UC system. However, since 1990, students of multiracial heritage have become more visible in campus politics. In 1990 I began interviewing undergraduate and graduate students who self-identified as being of multiracial heritage on the Berkeley campus for a graduate student research project. One of the goals of this research project was to evaluate whether the Civil Rights Movement, which had forced the dismantling of antimiscegenation laws banning interracial marriages and facilitated the relocation of some segments of the middle-class African American community to the suburbs, had generated more public space for the assertion of a multiracial identity among individuals of known African ancestry.

METHOD

The data for this chapter come from structured audiotaped and videotaped interviews conducted in 1990 and 1991 with 25 undergraduate and graduate students on the UC Berkeley campus. I asked for volunteers to participate in this study by announcing my research in several large introductory classes in anthropology, sociology, and peace and conflict studies. Students who were interested identified themselves as being of multiracial heritage. A total of 25 students who ranged in age from 18 to 27 and had origins in the states of California, Colorado, New York, Texas, and Hawaii were interviewed. All of my informants had grown up in multiracial family networks. No attempts were made to interview a representative sample, because no sampling frame was available; no published data identifying the number of students of multiracial heritage were available. My sample consisted of young adults who had one black and one nonblack parent including the following: 3 of European Jewish heritage; 4 of Asian (Chinese,

Japanese, Korean) parentage; and 11 of European American heritage including Anglo, German, and Spanish parentage.

As a graduate student instructor, I worked with a large number of undergraduates and soon found myself becoming actively involved in an organization founded by two undergraduate students whom I had taught in an introductory course. During this time I decided to transform my research interest in racial identity formation into a graduate research project. During the initial stages of my research, I met two undergraduates, both the daughters of North American black fathers and nonblack mothers, who had recently founded a student organization called Multiethnic Interracial Students Coalition (MISC), the first student organization in the UC system specifically designed to address the needs and concerns of students from multiracial backgrounds.

I regularly attended the MISC meetings and requested permission to interview some of the members of the group. As a result of my participation in MISC, the number of interviewees began to snowball. I also gained access to nonmembers of this organization through friendship networks so that my sample was not limited to active participants of the student organization. All students were asked the same set of questions about their individual and family history and the formation of their racial identity before and after their participation in the Berkeley community. I audiotaped the first set of interviews. After completing 25 interviews with students of multiracial heritage, I selected a sample of my informants and requested permission to conduct a videotape interview for a film project that I was coproducing on the experiences of students of multiracial heritage. My research formed the basis for a film that I coproduced with Jonathan W. Warren and Francisco Ferrandiz, entitled *Just Black?: Multiracial Identity* (Twine et al., 1991).

THE RACIAL ORDER
AND THE POLITICS OF DESIRE

In both the academic and the popular press, we can find evidence of how romantic choices are "read" as indications of racial identity and racial allegiances (Blauner, 1988; Frankenberg, 1993; Funderburg, 1994). "A biracial person's choice of lover and spouse serves for many observers as yet another racial litmus test. The choice is seen as an affirmation of the biracial person's own racial affiliation" (Funderburg, 1994, p. 197) Individuals who claim a multiracial identity are a threat to the racial order in the contemporary United States (Davis, 1991; Nakashima, 1992), because they challenge the belief that individuals belong to mutually exclusive and distinct racial categories. As Nakashima argued, "American culture is forced either to adjust the system to make room for persons or to adjust the person to fit the system" (p. 164). The experiences of the Berkeley students whom I interviewed demonstrate how the selection of romantic partners enables some young adults of multiracial heritage to adjust themselves to the current racial order. The consequences of their need to make themselves "fit" the current system are reflected in the conscious decisions that young adults of multiracial heritage often make regarding who constitutes an appropriate and desirable romantic partner.

One of the questions I posed to my interviewees was whether there had been any changes in their friendship networks or romantic partners during the past several years. Most identified changes in the types of people they found desirable. Shifts in their racial identities paralleled shifts in their romantic partners. Shifts in racial self-identification were often partially expressed and grounded in romantic choices. This can be illustrated by the experiences of Alex, the 21-year-old son of an African American mother and a white Jewish American father. Alex reported experiencing a dramatic shift in his identity during his first 3 years on the Berkeley campus. Prior to his attendance at UC, he described a pattern of rejecting black women in dating and social life. He self-identified as "biracial" before coming to Berkeley and had attempted to assert a biracial identity as "black and Jewish." He said that he had been unsuccessful in this endeavor and had "given up" his white Jewish identity in favor of a monoracial African American identity.

> It was strange to try to be black and it was strange to try to be Jewish. . . . In the time period around junior high school, I was really ashamed of being black. I couldn't relate socially to the kids that I knew were black. I didn't talk to them. . . . Like every other adolescent, I was interested in [romantic] relationships with girls. It was hard when I [was attracted to] white girls because I had to think about my racial identity . . . and that affected my ability to enjoy my social life. . . . But we didn't date black girls.

Alex drew a clear link between his dating relationships and his racial identity. He was very conscious of the politics of desire and how his racial identity affected his desire for certain types of girls in junior high school. Alex went on to describe how he rejected his African American mother's attempts to encourage him to date black girls. Dating a black girl was in conflict with his attempt to assert a biracial identity as a (white) Jewish American and African American male. Alex recognized that demographics were not the single most important factor in his selection of white girls at his predominantly white high school. He argued against a demographic justification by clearly stating that he made a conscious decision to reject *all* of the black girls who expressed romantic interest in him.

> But I think that it's not just a coincidence that I never dated any black girls in high school. Looking back I definitely avoided it. I remember a [black] girl in my high school who had her mother ask my mother if I would be her escort for the cotillion. . . . I do realize that I was running away just because it would have been dating a *black* girl. And she was pretty too, nice, stylish, popular. Irrelevant. Totally irrelevant.

As someone who currently self-identifies as black and had embraced a monoracial identity, Alex interpreted his behavior during this period as his attempt to flee from a monoracial black identity because he wanted to assert a biracial identity at that time. His dating behavior, like that of other individuals who are biracial cannot be easily coded by race and whose appearance is racially ambiguous in some contexts, reveals that he was conscious of the importance of his romantic partner in coding him racially. Alex's partner provided the ground upon which he publicly asserted a black racial identity. His partner provided cues to others as to his racial identity and allegiances in cases where his physical appearance did not provide sufficient cues.

The strategies used by Alex to distance himself in high school from individuals who were black echoed those described by Jasmine, the daughter of a Japanese woman and a black American man. In Jasmine's descriptions of her romantic relationships during junior high and high school, a pattern of rejection by African-descent men emerged. All of her boyfriends were of exclusively or predominantly European ancestry. African-descent men did not express interest in her. She interpreted this as motivated by their desire to avoid a public affiliation with someone of salient African ancestry.

> Black guys at my school wouldn't go out with me. And I couldn't figure out why until I grew up. Because by them dating me, they were identifying themselves as black. By going out with white women, they were identifying themselves as something else. . . . I remember them saying I don't want to go out with that nigger.

The importance of dating as an expression of racial self-identification was mentioned by everyone interviewed. Romantic partners functioned as one important expression of group membership. Because racial identities are socially constructed, identities only have meaning within the context of a system of relationships. The desire for a position of racial neutrality and social acceptance (within a specific group context) influenced the dating behavior of individuals from multiracial families when they were in a predominantly white suburban context, but the criteria for social acceptance changed once they began to attend UC Berkeley (Twine, in press). In their attempt to socially construct a different racial identity, they selected partners who were "marked" racially, that is individuals who were recognized as belonging to the racial category with which they now identified.

Ayana, the daughter of an Anglo American mother and an African American father, also identified her racial identity shifts as linked with her dating relationships. In order to shed the monoracial identity that she had acquired at home from her father, she "did things in order to counteract that identity." Ayana described a change in the men she found attractive in college at the same time that she was relinquishing a monoracial identity and asserting a biracial identity.

> I became aware of a [shift in my identity] when I started college in Los Angeles. I would only [date] certain types of guys. I went from being really immersed in this [black only] social work to dating this [mixed-race] guy. . . . My present boyfriend is interracial. He's Japanese, Indian, and black. . . . But let me just say this and I'll summarize my history. I think that the type of men that I chose [to date] has definitely changed to being more out-casted men.

The men that Ayana dated reflected the racial identity that she embraced; she enacted that identity in her desire and selection for men of specific racial backgrounds. Her dating history reflected a shift from a preference for monoracial African American men to a preference for African-descent men of multiracial heritage that paralleled her shift in identity.

THE POLITICS OF ROMANCE: RACIAL IDENTITY ENACTED THROUGH ROMANTIC EXPERIENCE

For Alex, asserting a monoracial identity as an individual of multiracial heritage required him to privilege his social connections to individuals publicly recognized as black. Furthermore, it required him to restrict his romantic relationships to women identified as black. The restriction of one's romantic relationships to a specific group is not unique to individuals of multiracial heritage. However, *it takes on added meaning in those cases in which racial identity is contested, ambiguous, and multiple.*

> My change in racial identity . . . came since I've been in college. My desire to *live* as an African American came first as a personal need and then as an intellectual thought. When I got here, it was like a switch. . . . At 18 years old you get to start over with who you're going to associate with. . . . What is it like to live as a black person? I think living as a black person . . . well, personally it is being around black people. That's my personal definition. It's that almost all of my friends are black. My girlfriend is black. I've only dated black women since I've been in college.

The above quote demonstrates that Alex is ambiguous in appearance, and his recently acquired monoracial black identity requires him to perform certain types of cultural work in order to demonstrate to both himself and the black community that he is unequivocally located socially in the black. His allegiance to the black community is expressed partially through his romantic allegiance to brown-skinned women who are integrated into the black campus community and, more important, publicly recognized as black.

Jessica, the 24-four-year-old daughter of an Anglo American woman and an African American father, grew up in an exclusively white suburban community. She described her pre-Berkeley racial identity as neutral. She had shifted from a neutral racial identity in high school to a biracial identity in college. When asked how she was categorized by others, Jessica reported that when, as a child, she visited her relatives in a Spanish-speaking area of Los Angeles, she was often taken for a Mexican American, so the social context was crucial in how she was racially identified. To offset her ambiguous physical appearance, Jessica described how she consciously selects the social events that she will attend in her efforts to clarify her biracial identity as an African-descent woman.

> People always think I'm Hispanic. They think I'm Mexican or sometimes they think I'm Polynesian. Black people know I'm black though . . . when I'm in a black environment, people know [that I have a black parent]. Especially if I'm at a black conference or I'm in a black organization or at a black meeting.

Jessica went to these black conferences and meetings with men who were recognized as members of the black community. Heterosexual romance provided an arena in which she learned the expectations that the middle-class black community had of women recognized as *culturally black*. Romance provided an avenue to a publicly recognized black social identity. Her shift from a racially neutral or off-white identity to a biracial identity precipitated a shift in the types of men she found desirable. After returning from a year abroad in Africa, she began to see herself as biracial, which precipitated a shift in her romantic partners of choice.

> And when I came back [from Africa], I started dating predominantly black men. Actually since I've been back, I haven't dated any white men. And so there's been a big shift in the men I've seen. And the boyfriend I have currently is black.

Like other students of African descent who had been raised by European American or Asian American parents, Jessica described having had to "work hard" at establishing and maintaining ties to the

African American community in order to assert a biracial identity. She identified her black boyfriend as one of her most important links to the black community. Dating men identified as black was important to her in part because her physical appearance did not clearly "locate" her in the black community. Her long, straight black hair and light skin resulted in her being identified as nonblack in many situations. She described being mistaken for Mexican American, Polynesian, and white in various contexts. Thus, for Jessica, her membership in the black community was communicated to the public by her dating men who were recognized as black men exclusively and by participating in black events. Jessica self-identified as biracial; her black boyfriend helped her to establish a context in which she could be read as biracial instead of as white, Mexican, or Polynesian, all groups to which she was perceived to belong. As she explained,

> I consciously try to connect [to blacks] . . . like my boyfriend. His family is a working class black family. And I feel very accepted and embraced when I'm with his family and his community.

The desire to establish a biracial identity for individuals who appear to be monoracial or racially ambiguous partially hinges on their romantic affiliations because they experience shifts in their racial self-identification. Moreover, there is often a contradiction between their racial self-identification and the racial identity ascribed to them by others. Mimi, the 26-year-old, brown-skinned daughter of a Chinese father and an African-descent mother now identifies herself as "black and Asian." Mimi, who was born in Jamaica, grew up in Canada and Texas. Her Chinese father prohibited her mother from ever discussing her multiracial heritage and kept her African ancestry hidden. Her shift from a monoracial Chinese identity to a biracial identity occurred during her first year at Berkeley, but the ground was laid for this shift when she became integrated into a black friendship network on her job the year before attending Berkeley.

> He controlled our family situation. I didn't know anything about my mother's family until very recently. He didn't want us to know anything about our black blood. So the whole time I was growing up I was led to believe that I was only Chinese.

Although Mimi and her siblings teased their mother about her "hard" hair and were conscious of the fact that their mother kept her hair chemically straightened, and although their maternal aunts were of salient African descent, this was never discussed. Mimi used language that was very similar to Alex's in describing her racial identity as lived experience and as involving a shift from dating whites to blacks exclusively.

> But now and for the past 5 years when people ask me I tell them first that I'm Jamaican by birth but in terms of race I always say I'm Asian and black. . . . I guess at one time [becoming a biracial black Asian] was a conscious effort to seek out the company of black people but now it's just a way of life.

ROMANTIC ACCESS TO A
RACIALIZED CULTURAL IDENTITY

As a woman whose physical appearance and cultural training do not declare her African American heritage, Mimi has learned to "work" at asserting a biracial identity by actively cultivating friendships and romances with black men. When asked how she asserts a biracial identity, she revealed her constant anxiety about not having the same cultural knowledge as individuals who had been socialized as black and grown up in African American family networks.

> I'm 24 years old. I feel like I ought to know more [about African American history and culture] than I do now . . . even in social situations when we're having discussions, I'm afraid [a monoracial black] will find out that I don't know about black history and say that I'm not really black. I feel all the time that I'm scrambling to catch up—to get to speed with everybody else, in terms of what I should know [about being black].

The anxiety of not having the cultural information to claim a biracial identity was echoed by several women who were attempting to assert newly acquired multiracial identities. Their ability to make identity claims that did not correspond to their physical appearance or cultural training was based on their ability to function within racially closed social spaces where monoracial blacks could pass judgment on their rights to membership in the black community. Their black romantic partners were crucial in both providing them with cultural information and giving them access to these communities. For my informants, the heterosexual romantic arena proved to be an important avenue for the acquisition of the cultural capital deemed necessary by the black campus community to function effectively. They acquired this cultural fluency (and identity) partially through their heterosexual romantic liaisons, which gave them access to cultural information that they had not received in their homes. The adopted daughter of two Anglo American parents and the biological daughter of a black American man and an Anglo American woman, Whitney described how crucial her relationship with her boyfriend had been in giving her access to the cultural information upon which her new monoracial black identity was based.

> It was really after I met Raishan, that he and his family started [teaching me to be black]. That's when I started learning [about black culture]. . . . His family really takes pride in their black heritage. . . . when I first went to their house, his dad showed me [around the home]. The first thing he said to me was, "You can tell that this is a black family's house and I want to show you why." And so he showed me.

Both Mimi and Whitney talked about how much they "learned" from black male partners, which enabled them to assert a black identity with confidence. The issue of what cultural knowledge is necessary in order to be taken seriously when one's appearance does not signify that one is of predominant or exclusive African ancestry concerned several of my informants. Thus heterosexual romance provided a safe place for them to culturally retrain themselves as they shifted their racial identity.

THE SEXUAL PLEDGE OF ALLEGIANCE

The issue of sexual allegiance is a crucial one when an individual is attempting to maintain ties to multiple communities. The problem of dual allegiances arose in interviews, particularly with individuals of African and European ancestry. Like individuals from monoracial families, they had been carefully taught to express their allegiance by restricting their sexual relationships with members of those racial groups with whom they self-identified. Like other informants, they used romance to assert their racial identity. Some informants experienced conflicts with their parents when they began to exclusively date men of African descent who self-identified as black, as they shifted from a biracial identity to a monoracial black identity. Tehmina, the 23-year-old daughter of a second-generation Russian-Jewish American mother and black American father, described how her mother responded to her preference for black men.

> And my mom is wondering "[When] are you going to date a white person?". . . She feels hurt because she sees me identifying with my African American cultural heritage . . . especially when we have a conversation about who I'm dating and almost everybody I bring home is black. Almost everybody. And all the pictures on my wall. Almost everybody is black.

Prior to her attendance at UC Berkeley, Tehmina had self-identified as "Caucasian," which was an expression of her cultural connection and allegiance to her Russian Jewish American mother (biological) and her Anglo American stepfather. She had had no contact with the relatives of her black American father, and he did not participate in her upbringing. Her identity began to shift at Berkeley, and at the time of this interview she self-identified as a black Jewish American and restricted her dating to men who were publicly recognized as black. During the interview she talked about her history of being rejected as a desirable partner by her white male peers in high school because she was not seen as attractive. She felt that because she was now a member of the black campus community and not the white Jewish campus community, she must demonstrate her allegiance to the community by not dating nonblacks. When she discussed her current boyfriend, she emphasized the disapproval that she might receive from the black campus community if she did not place emphasis upon the African heritage of her Puerto Rican boyfriend, who is of multiracial heritage. Tehmina reflects upon the response of the black community to her dating.

> Something that I noticed when I told [black students] that [my boyfriend] is Puerto Rican is that I had to back it up with "He's Afro-Puerto-Rican." He "acts black" and "looks black," too.

Like Tehmina, informants who had recently acquired a monoracial black identity or a biracial identity often emphasized the African heritage of their romantic partners. Several students reported only dating multiracial people of African heritage in order to assert a biracial identity. An example of this can be taken from an interview with Arthur, the 23-year-old son of a German American mother and an African American father. He asserted his biracial identity and heritage by dating primarily women of multiracial heritage. His preference was for individuals who, like himself, were from multiracial families, although he denied that he had strong preferences for any specific racial mixture.

[In high school] I dated all different ethnicities, different [racial] backgrounds. It didn't matter. That was how I was raised. And I dated who I thought was attractive and who I found interesting. But most of the people that I was attracted to were diverse [multiracial] like me.

CONCLUSION

My research among undergraduates at UC Berkeley who were the product of multiracial families revealed that my informants' romantic relationships directly corresponded to shifts in their racial identity. Such shifts were accompanied by shifts in preferred dating partners. Thus their romantic relationships served as one marker of their racial identity. One theme that emerged in all of the interviews was the central role of heterosexual romance in the management and negotiation of racial identities, particularly for individuals who cannot be easily coded by race because of their ambiguous physical appearance.

Whether they shifted from a multiracial to a monoracial identity or vice versa, all informants identified their attraction to romantic partners from a preferred racial background as an expression of their allegiance to a specific racial community.

19

Ambiguous Bodies
Locating Black/White Women in Cultural Representations

CAROLINE A. STREETER

On the commuter train one evening, a black woman asks me for a quarter. I recognize her from the street. Practically toothless and no doubt aged beyond her years, she is drunk, as she is whenever I see her. I tell this woman that I don't have a quarter (not true).

She stops in the aisle, scrutinizing me. "Your mama white?"

"Umhmm," I nod in confirmation.

"What's your daddy?"

AUTHOR'S NOTE: A heartfelt thanks to my colleagues Herb Green, Kendra Wallace, Kimberly McClain DaCosta, Dorian Harding-Morick, Rebecca O'Ríain, and Cynthia Nakashima for reading drafts of this chapter and giving me invaluable critical input. Special thanks to Maria P. P. Root for her patience. My teachers Barbara Christian and Saidiya Hartman asked me provocative questions and made incisive evaluations that improved the writing and the analysis. An anecdote told to me by Jayne Ifekwunigwe about a conversation between her and Troy Duster provided the inspiration for the epigraph in the conclusion. Although their work is not quoted directly, Norma Alarcón's lectures and the writings of Homi K. Bhabha and Stuart Hall have profoundly influenced my thinking about race, mixed race, ethnicity, culture, and the politics of representation.

"He's black."

"Hmmph." She moves on down the aisle.

I sit there wondering for the millionth time, so what does that make me?

Now, if that woman had asked me "So, what does that make you?" I would have responded with words like "both," "mixed," and "biracial" to describe myself. Nevertheless I am left with the knowledge that at the age of 33, my sense of racial/ethnic identity can be unsettled by a stranger. This kind of interrogation makes me feel undermined, as if I had no sense of "self," despite the availability of words to "label" my identity.

The vulnerability that I experience is related to the tension between the value placed in Western culture on having a whole, or "unitary" self and the growing body of literature from people who possess marginalized subjectivities, which express the realities of fragmentation. "Wholeness" is not a natural state, but the result of an act of will (Harris, 1991, p. 249). I experience this phenomenon on a daily basis, constantly renegotiating the variety of intersecting identity realms that make me who I am.

A second striking aspect of my encounter with the street woman is that it illuminates how we relate to an *other*, which involves constructing "them" as an object of difference. The awareness of being so constructed was articulated by W. E. B. Du Bois (1903/1975) as *dual consciousness* for African Americans—the possession of both a self-concept and a heightened perception of how others see one. How I view myself with regard to blackness and whiteness is an experience of being "not quite the same, not quite the other" (Trinh, 1991, p. 74). The simultaneous sense of being insider and outsider. Boundaries—both those that are internalized and those that are exteriorized—are perpetually shifting and contingent. This chapter grew out of my desire to create a narrative that would begin to explore how racialized boundaries are represented in words and images. &

One of the most compelling transformations in discourses about race has been the recent attention given to mixed-race issues in both academic dialogues and the popular media. This inclusion raises the question of how to theorize about mixed race as well as how to talk about it on *Oprah*. As an academic *and* a pop culture vulture, I know that theory and talk-show banter are not mutually exclusive; in fact, in the field of cultural studies, they are "mutually co-constructive." In this chapter, I intentionally oscillate between the language of critical theory and the common modes of expression used to talk about race in popular literature and media. I am putting these discourses into dialogue to discuss biracial black/white women and their representational role in maintaining racial boundaries. Thinking about race in the United States always entails a consideration of the relationship between "blackness" and "whiteness." This relationship is mediated by the black/white woman, a figure I analyze in selected texts and media images.

In my use of terminology, I implicitly assume that in the United States, black people have African heritage and white people have European heritage (admittedly, a generalization that does not include everyone socially defined as black or white). Thus I use terms to indicate race interchangeably with terms that denote ethnicity, particularly when discussing communities. I use the terms biracial, black/white, multiracial, and mixed race interchangeably. The idea that race is a social construction is a given in this discussion. Thus the notion that monoracial is a distinguishable category from multiracial is implicitly problematic and is one unresolved tension that drives my narrative.

Why is the black/white woman pivotal to the enforcement of racial boundaries? The maintenance of racial difference within the context of compulsory heterosexuality relies on woman's role as both biological and cultural reproducer (Allman, Chapter 17, this volume; Butler, 1993). Multiracial people generate social uncertainty about the status of race as a unitary category. The institutionalization of hypodescent and antimiscegenation laws indicates the extent of social anxiety engendered by the possibility of slippage between the racial categories of white and black. I call black/white women *ambiguous bodies* in order to point to the undefined gulf that exists in this in-between space between blackness and whiteness. The term *ambiguity* denotes both instability and multiple meanings. I argue that the control of what the ambiguous body of the black/white woman shall signify is crucial to the continued coherence of race as ideology. The twin specters of hypodescent and antimiscegenation laws compose the pillars of the metaphoric gate that separates whiteness from blackness. The black/white woman is the symbolically charged gatekeeper of this boundary. Although laws about racial categories and interracial relationships have changed, the authority of hypodescent and the miscegenation taboo remain evident in contemporary discourses about race.

This chapter also maps convergences in critical theory, history, politics, and popular culture to speak about the crucial relationship between social constructions and individual agency. Although cultural representations are powerful, black/white women are not simply the passive recipients of social inscriptions of race/ethnicity, gender, or sexuality.

LINGUISTIC BINARIES
AND RACIALIZED BODIES

A number of destabilizing theoretical trends and voices from the academic margins are influential in my ideas about ambiguous bodies. Michel Foucault (1980) has observed that " 'truth' is linked in a circular relation with systems of power which produce and sustain it, and to effects of power which it induces and which extend it" (p. 133). Foucault's critical insight about the conditional status of truth is extremely helpful in an interrogation about race and racialization. The postmodern critique of theoretical traditions that rely on binary models of analysis has resulted in a profound questioning of dualisms such as male/female, black/white, true/false—and the role of dualisms in perpetuating problematic power dynamics. The pioneering work of women of color in elaborating theories of knowledge based on multiple consciousness similarly questions the usefulness of binary oppositions (Anzaldúa, 1987; Moraga, 1981). In this sense, the work of theorists such as Foucault complements that of feminists of color, who remind us that "the master's tools will never dismantle the master's house" (Lorde, 1981, p. 98). Women of color have also critiqued theories that "rank oppressions" (Moraga, 1981, p. 29), signaling a departure from looking at any single category as the "primary" construct of an identity and paving the way for increasingly complex analyses.

Judith Butler's (1993) *Bodies That Matter: On the Discursive Limits of "Sex"* is a recent example of how a variety of different theoretical influences converge in contemporary texts. Her critical framework for thinking about how subjects come into being is influential in my analysis of the importance of language in the racialization of black/white women. Butler's theorization of the sex/gender system emphasizes the importance of the production of meaning in spoken and written language, or the power exerted by the signifying domain in the emergence of sexed/ gendered beings. Butler employs a term, *performativity*, to describe the relationship between language and the creation of the lived "realities" that we inhabit. Performativity is "that reiterative power of discourse to produce the phenomena that it regulates and constrains" (p. 2). As Butler contended, this is not the same as saying that discourse causes difference. Discourse is formative of the parameters of identification and determines the "cultural intelligibility" (which could be understood as social acceptability) of an identity.

Butler (1993) proposed that the production of (heterosexual) "male" and "female" subjectivities relies on the enforcement of socially regulated norms of sex/gender. Can we similarly propose that there are "norms of race"? Butler suggested that "the symbolic domain, the domain of socially instituted norms, is composed of racializing norms . . . they exist not merely alongside gender norms, but are articulated through one another" (p. 182).

Thus may the question of the black/white woman's signification be posed. How might socially instituted norms of gender and race converge in that ambiguous body that dwells in the space between blackness and whiteness?

THE DRAMA OF "PASSING" IN THE
AFRICAN AMERICAN LITERARY TRADITION

The practice of "passing" involved a person of mixed race whose phenotype prevented the detection of nonwhite ancestry. Rendering blackness "invisible" was, in a racially segregated society, the only way to gain access to a variety of privileges and economic opportunities (Daniel, 1992b).

The figure of the tragic mulatta(o) (usually a woman) within the genre of the passing narrative was a literary device used by African American novelists to "talk back" to the prevailing racial ideology of the late 19th and early 20th centuries (Brown, 1864/1969; Chestnutt,

1900/1968, 1901/1969; Fauset, 1929; Harper, 1892/1987; Johnson, 1912/ 1960; Larsen 1928/1986b, 1929/1986a; Toomer, 1923/1988; Webb, 1857/ 1969). The mulatta was tragic because of her mixed blood; she belonged nowhere, a fact that damaged her psyche and rendered her vulnerable to marginalization in both black and white communities. The passing narrative clarified the extent to which the social definition of blackness condemned people to an alienated condition.

How have literatures from writers of other ethnicities negotiated the racialization of mixed people? A number of compelling discourses subvert the dominant construction of race as a polar relationship between black and white. This is particularly true in the western United States, where the interrogation of traditional paradigms of race and ethnicity is increasingly persistent. Chicana writer Gloria Anzaldúa's (1987) conceptualization of *mestizajé*, Gerald Vizenor's (1981, 1990, 1991) formulation of "trickster discourse," and Leslie Marmon Silko's (1977, 1991) fiction are exemplary types of writing that grapple with the meaning of ethnicity and the politics of cultural difference in the context of racial hybridity.

The fact that the passing narrative is the prevailing way in which the topic of mixed race is addressed in black literature attests to the particular process of racialization experienced by Americans of African descent. Novels in the African American literary tradition illuminated the heightened importance of class mobility for mulattas who passed. Harlem Renaissance novelist Nella Larsen was particularly adept at portraying the dilemma of the mulatta excluded from the elite black middle class. Because social mobility in the black middle class of the early 20th century was the purview of men, a mulatta's access was strictly dependent on marriage. Yet she could be compromised in this endeavor by the stigma of mixed blood, which in African American communities frequently signified a predisposition to lax morals (also the case in white communities; Nakashima, 1992). This judgment stems from both sexual stereotyping and the association of mulattas with poor whites (Gwaltney, 1980). Allusions equating black/white women with prostitutes are made in both fiction and social science literature (Gwaltney, 1980; Larsen, 1929/1986a; Toomer, 1923/1988). Thus, when the mulatta did not meet black bourgeois standards of acceptability, her economic and social mobility became dependent on her ability to pass successfully enough to marry a white man.

Interestingly, the marriage between a black/white woman and a white man puts norms of heterosexuality into conflict with the maintenance of (white) racial purity. The passing mulatta's ability to enter into unions with white men also gave her access to the privileged status of white womanhood, thus threatening the status of the "cult of true womanhood" (Carby, 1987). The mulatta's access to white men through marriage posed a dual threat to the black community. This miscegenation represented a double loss of both her body and her capacity to produce black children. For the black/white woman who identified as white, female agency was pitted against norms of racial identification, giving rise to considerable tension vis-à-vis African American communities. This effect persists in extant discourse, an issue that is explored next in my analysis of contemporary material.

A LATE 20TH CENTURY MEDIA MULATTA

Despite the fact that the ethnic landscape of the United States has always included groups that are not African American or European American, the contemporary discourse of race in the mainstream media tends to ignore other groups. Recent manifestations of racial/ethnic conflict such as the rebellions/riots of Los Angeles clearly contradict the dominant binary model (Gooding-Williams, 1993). However, the representation of ethnic conflict as largely a phenomenon of tensions between blacks and whites still dominates our newspapers, airwaves, and television screens. In a climate in which the legibility of race is restricted to black and white, people of mixed race tend to be imagined as black/white biracials. Under these conditions, reinscriptions of the tragic mulatta and reenactments of the passing narrative become the normative, conventional subtexts that drive the media's representations of black/white women.

For most contemporary Americans, the nation's "origin story" of racial conflict is not situated in the encounters between Europeans and Native Americans, but in the southern United States, where the legacy of slavery has indelibly marked history and where the definitive battles of the civil rights movement were waged. Thus, when in February 1994 an Alabama high school principal attempting to ban interracial dating at the school prom allegedly labeled black/white teenager ReVonda Bowen a "mistake," the nation's dominant narrative of race relations was mobilized in the media. The tiny town of Wedowee, Alabama (population 800), became emblematic of the perceived vulnerability of relations between the (two) races. As Connie Chung put it, "Three decades of racial progress seemed to evaporate in one instant" (Sherriffe, 1994). A close reading of the media coverage of this event demonstrates that the language used to talk about race has undergone significant shifts in the late 20th century.

In coverage of the controversial events at Wedowee, it was reported that Principal Hulond Humphries considered canceling the prom because he was concerned about racial tensions at the school; apparently he feared that interracial dating would cause fighting to break out among students at the dance (Stephens, 1994). I read Humphries's linkage of racial tension with interracial dating as an invocation of the miscegenation taboo. The principal's encoded rhetoric is clarified because ReVonda Bowen, a black/white teenager, was singled out as illustrative of the results of miscegenation.

Principal Humphries's language and the media's reporting of the event indicate important shifts in the national discourse about race that are the result of the 1967 U.S. Supreme Court ruling on the aptly titled *Loving v. Virginia*, which repealed the last of the antimiscegenation laws in the United States. The legalization of miscegenation, or consensual relationships and marriages, is indicative of the Supreme Court's judgment that it is inappropriate to enforce racial boundaries through the control of citizens' private sexual activities and reproduction. The term miscegenation is so anachronistic that it is rarely used, and it was absent from media coverage of the events in Wedowee. Yet, the centrality of interracial relationships to the controversy indicates the deeply rooted effects of the miscegenation taboo.

Who would benefit from the observance of the taboo, or for whom do interracial relationships cause racial tension? Historically, white communities in the United States have benefited from institutionalized racial boundaries. Moreover, the social visibility of race mixing is confined to black communities. Traditionally, black communities have "absorbed" mixed-race people according to the logic of hypodescent (the one-drop rule), as well as interracial couples/families, due to segregation. ReVonda Bowen planned to attend the prom with her white boyfriend. In the eyes of Principal Humphries, they would be a "mixed couple," despite the fact that Bowen's father is white. Here it is clear that Bowen is rendered black through the logic of hypodescent.

A community's stake in policing racial boundaries is complex because of the masking effect of the rhetoric; neither white nor black communities are ever homogeneous. In fact, Bowen's racialization as black reflects the prevailing view held by both white and black observers. As I will detail in a later example, African Americans also commonly deploy the one-drop rule in the racialization of black/white people. Yet the consensus in Wedowee was generalized by the media along racial lines, with most white citizens supporting Humphries and most black citizens condemning him. The point is that effects of the miscegenation taboo and the reification of hypodescent reflect a profound power differential between blacks and whites. The fact is that these social conventions are successful in keeping white communities "pure." In Wedowee, the official school prom was boycotted by black students, who held an alternative prom at which mixed couples (and mixed people) were welcome. When the flexibility of the boundary between black and white is visible only in the black community, it is the black community that gets "polluted," as it were. The white community is left "intact."

What role does the black/white woman assume in this context? Significantly, ReVonda Bowen's racial image is reminiscent of an optical illusion: at times mixed, at times black (although emphatically not white). Bowen's initial question in response to Humphries's ban on interracial dating—"What race should my date be?"—emphasized the problematic in-between position of the tragic mulatta; that is, where does she belong? Simultaneously, the question becomes transformed by its contextualization in the late 20th century. From Bowen's contemporary perspective as a black/white woman, the miscegenation taboo puts her in an untenable position. Her question implied that she is bound to transgress the taboo regardless of whom she dates. Bowen's intimation of a biracial self-concept was clearly a post-1967 manifestation and also a direct challenge to the logic of hypodescent. However, the dominant discourse about race in the popular media was unable/unwilling to accommodate the nuances of biracial positionality.

The responses to Bowen indicated that she is stigmatized both for being mixed and for being black. However, we must interrogate the stigma of being black/white—what constitutes it? Is Bowen not more pejoratively "marked" by her African American than her European American heritage? An editorial piece (Tucker, 1994) about Wedowee reflects on the "silver lining" of the controversy—the fact that Bowen was elected class president at her high school is regarded as an optimistic sign that Bowen could be popular in spite of her interracial heritage. Might this author actually be expressing surprise that she could be popular in spite of her blackness?

Although the response in Wedowee was not absolutely divided along racial lines, the media's documentation of white folks rallying around Humphries and black folks rallying around Bowen racialized the debate, excluding the both/and or in-between perspectives. Interestingly, the reaction of another biracial student, a woman of Indian and white descent, was noted in newspapers. The student, Tawanna Mize, was reported as having been hurt by the principal's remarks (Weaver, 1994). Yet it was also reported that Mize did not take offense at Principal Humphries's comments because she thought they were taken out of context; she did not think he intended to insult Bowen. Mize's perspective was not widely reported in the press. Moreover, the apparent contradiction in her remarks is intriguing and should be pursued. This omission further reinforces the idea that only African Americans and European Americans matter in Randolph County.

MODERN MULATTAS
ON DAYTIME TELEVISION

During the past 2 years, daytime television talk shows have given an unprecedented amount of airtime to the subject of biraciality. If the audience members on these shows are a barometer of the national mood, it is clear that people are interested in the phenomena of mixed identity, multiracial families, and the increasing recognition of the multiple racial heritage of the American population. Multiracial issues have seemingly acquired "a place at the table" in the public discourse about race and ethnicity. However, the resurrection of the passing narrative in the media genre of the talk show indicates a regressive streak in the way racial boundaries are being discussed. Discussions focus almost exclusively on African Americans, European Americans,

Table 19.1 Characteristics of Biracial Women on *Sally Jessy Raphaël*

	Jeananne	*LaToya*	*Nathalie*
Age:	early 20s(?)	early 20s(?)	15
Age when told she was biracial:	17	5 or 6(?)	always knew
Currently identifies as:	black	white	white
Was raised as:	white	black	white
Mother (also on show) is:	Nancy (white)	Alice (black)	Karen (white)
Father was:	absent & black	absent & white	absent & black
Raised by:	mother & (white) stepfather	black female relatives	mother
Community background:	white	black	white
Schools:	white	black	mixed
Class background:	middle	working	working
Current class seems to be:	middle	middle	working
Stated reasons for current racial identification:	economic opportunities, identifies with black community	economic opportunities, identifies with white community	economic opportunities, identifies with white community
Is racial/ethnic identity challenged by family/schools/community?	Yes, challenged by whites when identified as white; also told by blacks that she should choose between black or white, told she could not be biracial as a black fashion model	Yes, challenged by blacks who accused her of feeling superior because she is biracial	Yes, challenged by blacks who accused her of feeling superior because she is biracial; also challenged by whites who disbelieve her ethnicity

and the biracial person's transgression (or not) of the boundary that distinguishes black from white.

The theme of ambiguous bodies can be further explored through a close reading of an episode of the talk show *Sally Jessy Raphaël* titled "I Don't Know Who I Am" (1993). This episode featured three black/white women—Jeananne, LaToya, and Nathalie—who were either white or black-identified (see Table 19.1). Reading the talk show as a text allows us to study what happens when biracial women come into contact with the representational apparatus that popular culture deploys to talk about race.

Of the many recent talk show broadcasts on biraciality, I was interested in this one because it featured women who appeared with their mothers. In the case of people who are "immediately mixed," with parents from two socially defined racial groups, the child's multiracial identity stands in contrast to the parent's monoracial one. This allows us to glimpse a variety of ways in which people identify, how they are being racialized, and how the relationship with a parent can affect that process. The information that I compiled in Table 19.1 confirms contemporary theory about multiracial identity formation (Kich, 1992; Root, 1992b), namely that self-identity may differ from parents' identity (or that of other family members) and is likely to change over a lifetime. The three women's recognition of their biracial heritage, combined with their decision to assert a monoracial identity, indicates the kind of slippage or cognitive flexibility (Kich, Chapter 16, this volume) that has become recognized as common in multiracial people.

Like the case of ReVonda Bowen, the show reflects significant shifts in the public discourse about race that are the result of profound social changes in the United States. The episode's title—"I Don't Know Who I Am"—conjures up the tragic mulatta stereotype. But the host's introduction gives a contemporary spin to the mulatta's dilemma. Sally Jessy Raphaël said that her biracial guests identify as black or white because they have decided that articulation of a mixed identity is problematic. Their racial identification actually poses a challenge to the authority of hypodescent. As detailed in Table 19.1, their chosen identity is the result of their life experiences, and it reflects their aspirations for the future.

The phrase that Sally invoked repeatedly—that her guests have "chosen one race over the other"—encourages reflection on what "choosing a race" might mean in a post-1967 context. The political history of the civil rights movement is an important context for understanding this notion of choosing race. The passage of civil rights legislation was the result of mobilization in African American communities, as well as coalitions across ethnicities. This push for political power was dependent on African Americans uniting across differences of class, color, religion, and ethnic heritage (Williamson, 1984). To a great extent, then, the success of the civil rights movement was based on the number of citizens who identified as African American. The strategy of organizing around the identity marker of race was effective in a segregated society that used the one-drop rule to exclude and disenfranchise black citizens.

In light of this recent history, racial passing is still a potent accusation when made by African American communities. How does the *Sally Jessy Raphaël* show reinscribe the passing narrative? The drama of passing was enacted through audience members' responses. On the level of representation, the way that the action was structured aids and abets this. Most of the audience members who spoke were African American, and the camera dwelled on black faces. The first guests to appear were LaToya and Nathalie, who both identify as white, with their respective mothers Alice (black) and Karen (white). The disapproval directed at the young women by the audience was definitive; they accused white-identified LaToya and Nathalie of "turning their backs on the black race."

In a post-civil rights era context, where African American access to political and economic power is linked to numbers, the one-drop rule functions to empower black communities by establishing their constituency. However, another legacy of the civil rights movement can be in direct conflict with this aspect of black empowerment. The generation of black/white people known as the "biracial baby boom" (Root, 1992d, p. 3) has not experienced the historical imperative to identify as black. Moreover, many have been raised in the multiethnic households and communities of a desegregated society, a fact that results in different kinds of relationships to black communities.

Thus the black community's fear of losing numbers is one subtext that informs the visceral response on the part of black audience members to "passing for white" guests LaToya and Nathalie. The imperative for women like them to "switch back" is linked explicitly to gender and sexual identity (Allman, Chapter 17, this volume). If they identify as white women and partner with white men, they will have white children, representing further attrition for African American communities. Nevertheless, both LaToya and Nathalie live as white women in communities that have accepted them as such. Their identification with whiteness is not based on phenotype alone; evidence that the traditional passing narrative is being subverted.

When the third biracial woman, Jeananne, and her white mother, Nancy, joined the guests, the traditional passing narrative began to unravel completely. Jeananne was black-identified, significantly due to economic considerations; she worked as a fashion model for black publications. She also remarked that her motivation to identify as black was encouraged by the lessening of the stigma faced by African Americans. Whereas her mother avoided telling her about her biracial heritage in order to protect her from discrimination, for a grown-up Jeananne "it's not the same to be black in the '90s as it was in the '60s . . . its easier."

What makes Jeananne, LaToya, and Nathalie ambiguous bodies? All three are classic examples of mixed women; their phenotype makes them hard to categorize racially or ethnically. However, in the context of African American history, all three would likely be able to pass the paper bag, blue vein, and comb "legitimacy tests" of the late 19th and early 20th centuries (designed to preserve the status of mulatto elites; Williamson, 1984). I believe that this accounts for some of the hostility that was directed at LaToya and Nathalie; their identification with whiteness was perceived to be a self-conscious deployment of phenotype. The audience was quick to challenge them (to remind them of "their place" in a racist society). An African American woman audience member reminded LaToya and Nathalie that private social institutions in the United States might reject them on the basis of phenotype. Her comment highlights the distinction between institutionalized racism, extant in mainstream society, and colorism in African American communities.

The tensions engendered by colorism in black contexts are frequently played out on the bodies of black/white women. Because colorism is expressive of a standard of beauty that values a white phenotype (light skin, straight hair, narrow features), particularly in women (although not exclusively), it is an instance of the convergence of norms of gender and race. The effects of colorism in black communities privilege mulattas, albeit in insidiously heterosexist ways (Russell et al., 1992; Walker, 1983). For example, Alice Walker wrote that a light-skinned woman is considered a "prize" for the African American man; she is seen as a weak woman who is easily dominated (p. 305).

The pointed absence of condemnation of multiracial, black-identified Jeananne is puzzling given the way in which her success as a fashion model could be interpreted as evidence of colorism, not to mention opportunism. However, Jeananne affirms the political and moral imperative to identify as black, a legacy of civil rights movement activism.

The *Sally Jessy Raphaël* show framed her identity as noncontroversial. In contrast, LaToya and Nathalie were criticized for avoiding blackness in order to achieve material gain.

White-identified LaToya and Nathalie have suffered the effects of colorism. Both described being criticized by black people for "thinking they are better" because of the way that they look. By the same token, their physical appearance was invoked to remind them of their "place." An African American woman from the audience opined, "You say you're going to live as white women? Not with that (skin) color and that nappy hair."

The insistence by African American audience members on LaToya's and Nathalie's blackness is disturbing on a number of levels. The audience's contestation of the (white) racial identification of the ambiguous body has the unsettling ventriloquist effect of black people articulating norms created to uphold a racial hierarchy. Moreover, on *Sally Jessy Raphaël*, the exercise of African American authority over racial boundaries becomes a type of entertainment (a rather cynical effect).

The discourse on *Sally Jessy Raphaël* exposed a compelling way in which black/white women's observance of heterosexuality problematizes the maintenance of racial boundaries. Ambiguous racial identity conflicts with the miscegenation taboo. In order for norms of racial purity to complement norms of heterosexuality, black/white women must marry black men. This tension is explicitly addressed by Jeananne's mother, Nancy. She told her daughter at the age of 17 that she was biracial "because I was terrified that she'd marry a white man and have a black baby." A similar anxiety is characteristic of the passing mulatta in African American literature. In Nella Larsen's (1929/1986a) novel *Passing*, the mulatta Clare Kendry expresses this same fear:

> I nearly died of terror the whole nine months before Margery was born for fear that she might be dark. Thank goodness, she turned out all right. But I'll never risk it again. Never! The strain is simply too—too hellish. (p. 197)

Not surprisingly, biracially identified guests are rare, or in the minority on talk shows. From the start, it is clear that the selection of guests is designed to support the idea that biracial identity is deviant and unsustainable. However, what is worth noticing (and what I maintain is new in the discourse) is the complex type of self-identification that

we saw on the part of the women on *Sally Jessy Raphaël*. They acknowledged both biracial heritage and a current monoracial identification.
Their racial identities were contingent on personal experiences, as well
as being expressive of their aspirations. Although the three shared little
apart from their heritage, what is striking is the extent to which their
racial identity has been fluid, changing, and flexible, inscribed by
myriad influences. The narrow focus of the show's stated topic was
actually subverted by its own content.

CONCLUSION

Is the zebra black with white stripes
Or white with black stripes?
The trickster answers,
Essentially striped.

I have mapped some narrative shifts that deal with the tragic
mulatta, the miscegenation taboo, hypodescent, and the passing narrative to interrogate discourses that have been relevant to the racialization
of the black/white woman in the United States. Racial inscriptions of her
ambiguous body have followed consistent trends. However, I have situated these narratives in their historical and sociopolitical contexts to
illuminate some dramatic shifts that are uniquely possible in our time.

The contradictory project of negotiating the language of race to
articulate multiracial realities is a significant tension in scholarship
about mixed race. In other words, discourse is simultaneously a trap
and an enabling condition.

Being constrained by terminology puts one in the tricky position of
inhabiting a perpetually complex stance. Namely, we critique our system of analysis even as we use it to communicate. Such a conflation of
the positions of subjectivity/objectivity, or insider/outsider is employed
in a growing variety of critical discourses (such as postmodern, queer,
feminist women of color, and critical race theories) that challenge
binaristic theoretical models (Butler, 1993; Lugones, 1994; Trinh, 1991;
P. J. Williams, 1991). I believe that mixed-race scholarship has something
to gain from all of these, as well as something to contribute.

PART V

Multicultural Education

20

Making the Invisible Visible

The Growth of Community
Network Organizations

NANCY G. BROWN

RAMONA E. DOUGLASS

The impetus for my involvement in the multiracial movement began as a personal exploration in order to be the best possible parent to my multiracial children. Within a short time, however, my enthusiasm to dialogue with and educate others grew. I undertook the challenge of co-founding Multiracial Americans of Southern California (MASC), thereafter becoming its president for 7 years. I felt then, as I do now, that my husband and I were capable of parenting our African American and European American children in a way that would allow them to fully acknowledge both sides of their heritage, despite society's rules and attitudes.

As a psychotherapist and parent, I believe it is humanly possible to embrace duality as it pertains to race, just as we incorporate and use the many facets of ourselves simultaneously. It is most important to remember that if interracial unions had never been illegal, and if race differences had never been used as divisive forces, there might never have been a multiracial movement. I see the movement as an imperative step and catalyst in the process to engage people at all levels to rethink their notions about race and its connection to all other forms of oppression in our society. &

Nancy G. Brown

I have been a part of the Civil Rights Movement in America since the early 1970s. My interracially married parents were activists in the 1960s and challenged the racial status quo by coming together as a family in 1947. I had no choice as a multiracial child in this society, and later as a multiracial adult, but to champion the cause of interracial families and their multiracial offspring. When I joined Chicago's Biracial Family Network (BFN) in 1985, it was with the understanding that I would become an active, articulate, and persistent voice for multiracial people throughout this nation. As a member of BFN's board of directors for 7 years, its president for 1 year, and later as the vice-president and president of the Association for MultiEthnic Americans (AMEA), I have diligently worked to raise public awareness on issues of race and ethnicity in our own communities, as well as with those who question our right to self-identification. It is my belief that the only way we can expect our goals, challenges, history, and triumphs to be accurately assessed or recorded is to do it ourselves. I hope that what we have chosen to detail in this chapter will provide a practical guide and chronology for interracial community groups today, tomorrow, and for many generations to come. &

Ramona E. Douglass

In June 1967, the U.S. Supreme Court under Chief Justice Earl Warren handed down a landmark decision that would forever alter the face and fabric of American race relations. The celebrated case of *Loving v. Virginia* firmly eradicated the last vestiges of our nation's antimiscegenation laws, which had tarnished our historical growth and development since 1661 (Hollis, 1991).

It took more than 300 years for Americans to truly have the right to the pursuit of happiness, the right to choose their life partners—not on the basis of race or ethnicity, but by personal preference and love. Since that time, interracial marriages and their developing families have grown in numbers so staggering that by 1990, estimated marriages between blacks and whites had tripled in less than three decades. According to 1990 census statistics, 6% of African American households nationally had nonblack spouses (Wright, 1994). In Fall 1993, *Time Magazine* published the results of a survey on interracial families; it purported that 65% of Japanese Americans and 70% of Native Americans married out of their ethnic communities. More than 2.5 million Americans have defied ethnocentric notions to cross racial barriers and marry one another (U.S. Bureau of the Census, 1992). Equally significant were the birthrate figures for multiracial children, which reportedly have increased in the last two decades to more than 26 times higher than any other measured group (Smolowe, 1993).

The reasons for this visible surge of cross-cultural energy are multifaceted. Out of the secrecy and shame that marred many an interracial union prior to the *Loving* decision has come a new proud legion of vocal, diverse, and increasingly politicized multiracial/multicultural families. The repeal of America's antimiscegenation laws may have freed one generation of interracial couples to live and love as they see fit, but it has yet to unshackle the seeds of those unions—its multiracial offspring—from being perceived through the eyes of many Americans that are colored by racist notions.

There is still a racial myth on the books of our legal, legislative, and administrative branches of government, purporting that one drop of black blood, or one discernible black ancestor, makes someone black. It is a notion not born out of science or logic, because it applies to no other culture, in no other nation in the world; it is born out of oppression and the slave trade. Unfortunately, what was originally enacted by European Americans to ensure the racial "purity" of the "haves" versus the "have nots" has recently been embraced by some segments of the oppressed culture as a red badge of courage or sign of black nationalist loyalty.

The issue is not whether or not to embrace one's African American culture. The tragedy in racial rigidity and the "one-drop rule" lies in the negation, obliteration, or depreciation of any other racial/ethnic strain that a multiracial child might lay claim to. In our public school systems, in the media, or on state and federal forms, multiracial children continue to be denied the dignity of self-identification. The "eyeball test" is still being used in many classrooms across America by teachers whose own racial baggage may further depreciate the self-esteem of the young minds entrusted to their care.

Textbooks that color our history with a Eurocentric brush may sprinkle the public educational system with a dab of so-called multiethnic studies—a little African American studies here, a few women's studies there—in progressive classrooms, in a few select schools. However, multiculturalism in the 1990s still struggles over the notion of a distinct group whose sense of racial and cultural affiliation reaches across diverse ethnic racial and religious lines, making a powerful statement of its own.

It is in this historical context that the first interracial/multicultural networks were born in the late 1970s and early 1980s. In order to fully assess the impact of these networks in the interracial/multicultural community during the past 15 years, one must address the psychological metamorphosis that has occurred alongside the legal changes affecting interracial marriages and multiracial identity for adults, children, and the family unit as a whole.

Interracial families, and multiracial individuals specifically, growing up prior to and just after the *Loving* decision, were encouraged to conceptualize their blended heritage as something not to be acknowledged or shared with others. They were programmed to think that their birth should have never happened and that they possessed a trait making them seem different and strange. Thus what ultimately developed was a shame-based perception of self. With the internalization of these negative self-concepts, many multiracials chose to funnel their energies and personal images into one monoracial/monocultural identity that society at large would accept. This stance, although expedient, often fostered a sense of powerlessness and invisibility on the part of the individual.

It has often been hypothesized that multiracial people experience racial identity confusion when attempting to interact with the various components of their racial/ethnic lineage (Gibbs, 1989; Root, 1992b). In actuality, more often than not, there have been compelling external rather than internal factors that have historically forced multiracials to choose one racial/ethnic group instead of claiming or incorporating all of their rightful heritage. However, once multiracial people have been allowed to, or have chosen to celebrate and embrace their total identity, the result has been twofold: (a) greater physical and psychological comfort with themselves and (b) improved capability in navigating the varied terrain of race and ethnicity.

With the ban lifted on interracial marriages, the advent of school desegregation, and other civil rights enactments in the late 1960s/early 1970s, more people from differing racial/ethnic backgrounds had the opportunity to interact in the workplace, the halls of education, and in some enlightened/integrated communities. Drawn together by like interests and concerns, interracial couples, single parents with biracial/multiracial children, and transracial adoptive families sought mirror images of themselves and similar life circumstances. Forming a basic support network satisfied a number of group and individual needs, providing a sense of community, networking, and racial/ethnic dialogue; it offered a platform upon which educational forums could be built. It encouraged individuals, couples, and families to affiliate, participate, and identify themselves in an atmosphere of health and safety.

FORMING A MULTIRACIAL
SUPPORT GROUP

Every organization has its own unique character born out of the goals and personal needs of its founding members. But despite regional variations on a common theme, any group hoping to sustain itself past an initial meeting and an exchange of "war stories" needs to take into consideration a number of steps formulated to ensure future stability and success.

The process of forming a multiracial support group requires four major processes: research, creating an initial meeting, the first meeting and beyond, and local versus national activities.

Research

When researching, investigate other multiracial support organizations. Determine their location, their organizational structure, and why and when they were formed. Where available, get a sample of their bylaws or articles of incorporation. Organizations frequently engage in newsletter exchanges, which provide a wealth of information for starting a support group. *New People Magazine* provides a listing of all current groups that includes pertinent names and addresses.

Define the potential participants. Multiracial adults and children, as well as interracial families, both biological and adoptive, are all potential members. There are others, not directly involved in interracial situations, who appreciate the level of dialogue these groups tend to engage in. So include them in your research.

Network with others who share your interest in starting a group. At least one to three people have discussed the idea. Now it is time to develop a plan to create your initial meeting.

Creating Your Initial Meeting

Think of ways to publicize your meeting; these may depend on available resources such as time and money. You can create a flyer and hang it in community areas including schools, religious institutions, community organizations, medical offices, and recreational departments. Another option would be to take an advertisement in a newspaper or find other sources of free announcement listings. Include meeting place, date, time, and a brief statement describing the purpose of the gathering. Potential meeting places may be someone's home or office or the free community rooms of libraries, banks, or malls, which need to be reserved in advance.

When describing the purpose of the initial meeting, remember to use words that identify the individuals whom you are seeking to interest. Inviting "families" runs the risk of excluding single adults or couples without children. It is equally important to consider the needs of families with children and to make decisions about the inclusion of small children at meetings.

Take care when publicizing personal phone numbers and addresses. There are many people who still have very negative attitudes toward interracial/cultural relationships, and personal safety for members of a group should have a high priority.

Some organizations, before holding an initial meeting, attempt to draw interested parties in advance by first securing a post office box, then writing letters/flyers to interested persons, organizations, community affairs departments, or local radio and television. The benefit is that this allows a screening process by which an individual's motivation for participation in the group can be assessed, similar to the process an employer might use to assess a job applicant or volunteer. Most beginning groups don't have the luxury of screening their volunteers, but they do pay attention to individuals who may have personal agendas that conflict with the group's mission.

The First Meeting and Beyond

Several areas are important to address as you begin meeting with your initial group. We outlined eight tasks to consider in this process.

1. Upon arrival, welcome each person and introduce each new participant. An easy ice-breaking strategy is to conduct a "go around" where everyone does a self-introduction including their name, how they learned about the group, and what their goals/expectations might be. This helps to create a group focus or mission statement.
2. Attempt to prioritize people's goals and wishes be they social, educational, or political. Identify short- and long-term goals for each area.
3. Identify concrete activities of interest to the group.
4. Look at available peoplepower and resources needed to organize and carry out these activities.
5. Pick a name for the group.
6. Decide on an organizational structure: nonprofit, association, chapter, or affiliate of another organization. The benefit in becoming a nonprofit organization is to be able to solicit grants, accept tax-exempt contributions, and apply for tax-exempt status with the Internal Revenue Service.
7. Issues of leadership, positions, terms of office, and voting procedures should be defined. Guidelines to assist in this process are available at nonprofit management agencies that exist in most major cities. Standard positions usually include a president, vice-president, secretary, treasurer, and newsletter editor. Other possible positions oversee membership, social activities, education, fund raising, and public relations.
8. Decide on a logo and consider getting business cards. You may want to get your logo copyrighted.

Steps 1 to 8 may take as many as 10 meetings to accomplish. You may find people who initially commit and later drop out, while new people continue to come. There is usually a stable core of individuals that gets established by the sixth meeting. The organizer(s) need to have an understanding of the stages of group process and communication

(Bennis, 1969). The basic tasks and structure to be determined are (a) frequency and structure of meetings, (b) meeting chairperson, (c) written or verbal agenda, and (d) method of communication between meetings. All of the above eventually get resolved as needs surface in the group. A cohesive group will evolve at some point with identifiable goals and shared vision.

Local Versus National Activities

Contact the major national organizations such as AMEA or PROJECT RACE for information on becoming a member or affiliate. These two groups had grassroots beginnings and rely on local eyes, ears, and resources to promote programs that benefit multiracial individuals and interracial families across the country. Other local groups will also engage in newsletter exchanges, which can help keep your membership appraised of activities and opinions that may be of future value or interest. Many groups around the country offer major conferences that members of your organization may want to attend. This type of networking greatly decreases isolation and helps to bring people together as a part of a very real, ever growing "multiracial movement."

Five significant organizations across the nation, in our opinion, have set the tone and character of the interracial/multicultural movement. These are:

I-Pride, San Francisco
The Biracial Family Network of Chicago
The Interracial Family Circle of Washington, DC
Multiracial Americans of Southern California
PROJECT RACE, Roswell, Georgia

A sixth organization, AMEA, arose out of the interracial community's desire to seek a multiracial category on the U.S. Census and from a belief that coming together as a federation of local grassroots organizations with a nationally unified multiracial/multicultural agenda would cause the racial/ethnic power brokers in this country to take notice of the growing numbers of interracial families and multiracial individuals across the nation. Many other organizations have evolved in the last decade, drawing from the expertise and experiences of these key groups.

In an effort to gain a better understanding of each organization's goals, history, leadership, and outstanding accomplishments, we formulated a questionnaire that was sent to key people in each group. Written responses or follow-up telephone interviews filled in the details needed to give an accurate overview of the developing interracial community network system.

Six questions were posed to the organizations mentioned above, (excluding AMEA, which will be profiled later in this chapter) and those questions were as follows:

1. Who were the founders of the organization and when was it formed?
2. Why was the organization formed? Name some specific issues that precipitated its formation.
3. Who was the organization's first president? Who is the current president?
4. Does the organization have a mission statement or specific goals? Give a brief description.
5. How do the goals of the organization today differ from its beginning?
6. What has been the organization's most significant accomplishment and its greatest challenge?

I-Pride. Chronologically, I-Pride is the oldest interracial support network in the United States today. All of the groups surveyed seemed to have a specific community need or goal that compelled them to form an alliance or bond around a particular issue or concern. For I-Pride, it was the question of racial classification in the Berkeley public school system, which had historically required that multiracial/multiethnic students racially label themselves in one racial/ethnic group or default to the deprecating term *other*. A high proportion of mixed-race children were already in the school system, and similar families were established in the San Francisco Bay area. A group of concerned teachers, social workers, therapists, and parents banded together and proclaimed these options unacceptable. I-Pride was formed in February 1979 and incorporated in October 1982. Its first president was George Kitahara Kich, who was elected at the time of incorporation.

Carlos Fernández, an attorney and I-Pride's longest-term president, joined in 1984. Jan Faulkner, one of I-Pride's principal founders, can be credited with introducing him to the organization when they met at an international party. Faulkner also has the distinction of being Fernández's fourth-grade teacher. Fernández later became the primary catalyst for the formation of AMEA. Under his leadership, I-Pride became one of AMEA's charter members in 1988.

I-Pride's primary goal is education about interculturalism and interracial identity. In particular, it seeks to combat the ever-present racism toward interracialism. The membership continues to strive for the unification of their growing community with an eye on mutual support and public recognition.

Biracial Family Network. Cognizant of some of the interracial rumblings coming out of California, Irene Carr, a white mother in the Midwest whose youngest biracial son was struggling with identity and assimilation issues within the black community, sought guidance from Julie Whitten, one of I-Pride's founding members, on how to start an interracial support network. The Biracial Family Network of Chicago (BFN) began as a parents' discussion and support group, drawing from six mothers with biracial children. BFN's first meeting was held in Hyde Park, at Irene Carr's home on September 13, 1980. The founders of the organization included Irene Carr, Alice Culbert, Doris Dubin, Gloria Goodman, Kay Macke, and Mary Lou Todd. BFN became more than a mother's group, as other types of people expressed an interest in the organization. In 1984, BFN's first affiliate group, the Biracial Family Network West, was formed in Oak Park, Illinois, for members living in Chicago's western suburbs. Later, the MultiEthnic Unity Effort of Lake County, the Interracial Family Network of Evanston, Illinois, and the Biracial Family Network of Fort Wayne, Indiana, were formed by members originally affiliated with the Hyde Park group.

In 1985, the BFN incorporated, and in 1986 it acquired nonprofit status. The multiracial issue and the growing numbers of biracial/multicultural adults who began joining its organizational ranks in the late 1980s gave BFN a new focus and direction. Former President Irene Carr (personal communication, 1994) states that "the original goal has evolved from promoting integration to combating racism." In 1989, BFN drew media attention with the production of a 1-hour documentary on the organization, coproduced by two multiracial adults: jazz stylist Paul Serrano and then-publicity chair Ramona Douglass. The documentary was aired several times in 1989 and 1990 on Chicago Access Cable. Many requests for talk show appearances and or calls for the expertise of BFN members soon followed, along with requests from authors and researchers doing books/studies on multiracial identity and interracial families. In 1988, BFN became a charter member of AMEA, thanks to the diligent efforts of founding mother and former president Carr.

BFN published an anthology on multiracial identity titled *Interracial Identity: Celebration, Conflict, or Choice?* Initiated in 1991 and completed in 1992, this book had been the brainchild of Margo Ruark Hearst, its editor. Hearst, a European American mother of a biracial child, was concerned about the paucity of literature available to the average interracial/multicultural family interested in seeing and reading about constructive, positive images of itself. Her dream was to be able to pass on those images to other families in BFN and to the multiracial community at large. With the aid of BFN's Task Force of Book & Media Productions, grant proposals were written and submitted; there was a call for papers from the national interracial community, and the response was impressive. By the time the book was finally compiled and edited, there were contributions from the fields of child psychology, sociology, the arts, educational development, and so on. By 1994, the anthology was in its third printing, and it was being used by interracial study groups, as well as college courses on multiculturalism, child development, gender/ethnic studies and social psychology across America.

Interracial Family Circle. The Interracial Family Circle of Washington, D.C. (IFC), formed in 1984, had beginnings similar to I-Pride and BFN. It was born out of a sense of isolation that interracial couples were feeling in our racially fixated society. Six interracial families of black/white origin decided that it would be helpful for multicultural families to have a place where they could socialize together, share common goals and concerns, and provide support for one another in the District, northern Virginia, and Maryland. Later the group grew to include not only couples with and without children, but single parents with biracial children, biracial and multiracial adults, and both single and married individuals with adopted or foster children.

In 1992, under the leadership of President Edwin Darden, the IFC took on the monumental task of hosting the 25th anniversary of the

Loving decision. This celebration marked 25 years of freedom from the repressive and oppressive miscegenation laws that were challenged and eventually dismantled in 1967. On June 13, 1992, more than 200 interracial families from 30 states assembled in Chevy Chase, Maryland. Thanks to the dedication and diligent planning of Edwin and Lori Darden, the guest and speakers list read like an honors page in interracial history. The keynote speakers were the ACLU attorneys (Bernard Cohen and Philip Hirschopf) who argued the *Loving* case before the U.S. Supreme Court. Mildred Loving herself, accompanied by her daughter, son-in-law, and grandchildren, were also in attendance. Richard Perry Loving, Mildred's deceased husband, was acknowledged with a posthumous award, and the mayor of Chevy Chase honored this event with a city declaration.

There were panels on the media, the multiracial category, the embracing of a multiracial identity, and parental reactions to the interracial involvement of their children. Panelists and participants included some of the most noteworthy spokespersons in the multicultural movement: Carlos Fernández, then AMEA's president; Nancy Brown, president of MASC; Ramona Douglass, president of BFN and central vice president of AMEA; celebrated writer and reporter, Itabari Njeri; Ruth and Steve White from the *A Place For Us Ministry;* as well as Carol Coccia, Marybeth Seader, census officials, and more. As Edwin Darden (personal communication, 1994) put it, this was

> the first national conference in history to gather all three segments of the interracial community . . . interracially married and involved couples, individuals of biracial or multiracial descent, and transracial adoptive families. . . . There was an emotional connection between the participants . . . who came together for 2 days . . . virtual strangers . . . yet with a lot in common—a shared history over space and time. We knew each other's story intimately and could relate to the joy and pain. . . . It was an exciting, breakthrough event, which I hope will be remembered and revered as an historic occasion that marked an anniversary and also stressed our togetherness/positive feelings of community.

Multiracial Americans of Southern California. Multiracial Americans of Southern California (MASC) was co-founded by Nancy G. Brown, RN, MN, a partner in an interracial marriage with two multiracial children, and Levonne Gaddy, LCSW, a multiracial adult. Gaddy had learned about the existence of I-Pride through giving community talks on interracial issues, and at one of these she met Nancy Brown. Together, in 1987 they developed a core group that was interested in creating a multiracial support network. The initial group included Gaddy, Brown and her husband, two multiracial adults, one partner from an interracial marriage, and a single parent with a racially mixed adopted son. This diversity led to MASC's broad mission statement, which was to meet the educational, cultural, and social needs of racially blended couples, families, and individuals. The major impetus was the passionate argument against forcing multiracial adults or children to choose one identity over another, thus denying a part of the person and one of the parents. This reflected some of the issues that several members of the founding group were grappling with. Other goals in the formation of MASC were (a) eradicating stereotypes about our relationships and children, (b) celebrating our unions/families, (c) educating and networking with similar organizations, and (d) raising public consciousness about our existence and issues.

MASC was also a charter member and co-founder of the national group AMEA. Nancy G. Brown, who served as MASC's first president from 1987 to 1994, remains on its board of directors and is an active public speaker for the organization. She is also vice president of AMEA, having served on its board for a number of years.

MASC's greatest accomplishment has been conducting an annual Kaleidoscope educational conference every year since 1987. This event occurs each October, California's diversity month. Several well-known educators and writers in the multiracial field originally spoke on these issues at Kaleidoscope and are now helping to create a new generation of students and researchers willing to take a more accurate look at interracial marriages and multiracial identity.

MASC has been a much-used resource for institutions of higher learning, radio, television, and authors of new books on this topic. In the opinion of one of its founders, "individuals drawn to MASC tend to be exceptional people who have been able to transcend issues of race and talk about them objectively." According to Brown, "We believe that through the discourse in which we are engaged, bridges between people and attitudes will be built."

PROJECT RACE. PROJECT RACE (Reclassify All Children Equally) was founded by Susan Graham and Chris Ashe in Fall 1991. The organization has acted as a national advocacy network for multiracial children and adults through education, community awareness, and legislation. Its main goal, as stated by President Susan Graham (personal communication, 1994), "is for a multiracial classification on school, employment, state, federal, census, and medical forms requiring racial data."

PROJECT RACE has had many significant legislative accomplishments, beginning with Ohio's Am. Sub. H.B. No. 154, in 1992, and Illinois' S.B. 421-Public Act 88-71 in 1993. In 1994, a model piece of multiracial legislative work was accomplished in Georgia, namely, Senate Bill 149. What set this bill apart from the Ohio and Illinois bills was the fact that this legislation clarified many questions that the others did not answer. The previous legislation affected only public school forms. Georgia's bill added a "multiracial" category not only to the public school forms, but to all state agency forms, as well as all employment forms and applications (Graham, Chapter 3, this volume). Graham, (personal communication, 1994), who is a European American mother of a biracial son and daughter, believes that these grassroots success stories have sent a "very strong message to Washington: We are serious and we are successful in our political efforts across the nation."

The passage of the Georgia model prompted greater publicity on the question of a separate category for multiracial children and also resulted in the introduction of new legislation in three more states. Both PROJECT RACE and AMEA had the privilege of testifying before the Congressional Subcommittee on the Census in June 1993. For PROJECT RACE, the critical event came after the hearings, when it was asked in 1994 to represent multiracial people at a meeting of federal government agencies at the National Academy of Sciences in Washington DC. According to Graham (personal communication, 1994), "it was at this meeting that we were able to fully discuss our future needs on the federal level and gain needed support for the civil rights of multiracial children and adults."

Across the board, the item most often cited as the biggest challenge for the multiracial support networks was the maintenance of their very existence. They are all nonprofit and volunteer. The lack of access to grant money has been a major stumbling block, and limited funds are available to expand the scope of work and services provided by these organizations. When grants are received, too often the groups are forced to adjust their services to meet the grant criteria. As with all volunteer organizations, the work tends to be a labor of love done by a dedicated few. Given that premise, it is truly amazing and wonderful that these groups have not only survived but continue to grow in number and scope.

Association of MultiEthnic Americans. The limited resources described above, along with the desire to give interracial families a national voice, played a significant part in the formation of AMEA. On November 12, 1988, the Organizing Committee of the National Association of Multi-Ethnic Americans met in Berkeley, California, and with 14 charter member organizations from across the nation, AMEA was born. Those original networking groups included:

Interracial Family Alliance (Atlanta, Georgia)
Interracial Club of Buffalo (New York)
Biracial Family Network of Chicago (Illinois)
Honor Our Ethnic Youth (Eugene, Oregon)
A Place for Us Ministry (Gardena, California)
Interracial Family Alliance (Houston, Texas)
Multiracial Americans of Southern California (Los Angeles, California)
Interracial Connection (Norfolk, Virginia)
Parents of Interracial Children (Omaha, Nebraska)
Interracial Families, Inc. (Pittsburgh, Pennsylvania)
IMAGE (San Diego, California)
I-Pride (San Francisco, California)
Interracial Network (Seattle, Washington)
Interracial Family Circle (Washington, DC)

At that founding meeting, Carlos Fernández (I-Pride) was elected president; Ramona Douglass (BFN), vice president; Reggie Daniel (MASC), secretary; and Sara Ross (HONEY), treasurer.

AMEA was approached by its founding executive committee as a new business venture and proceeded on the basis of a 2-year and 5-year plan. The first 2 years were essentially AMEA's start-up phase, aimed at determining whether it could sustain itself, at uncovering strengths and weaknesses, at gauging what role it should play on a national scale, and at publishing a national newsletter. A basic statement of purpose was drafted, defining AMEA as an educational organization that promoted "a positive awareness of interracial and multiethnic people and families." Within the context of a 5-year plan, AMEA wanted to launch an education and/or legal defense fund; create a multicultural resource center or institute; staff a political action committee to lobby for changing official forms; and establish an AMEA hotline/switchboard to disseminate information and provide solutions to interracial/multicultural problems that arise across the nation (Fernández, 1990).

By September 1994, AMEA had:

1. incorporated with 501c3 (nonprofit) status pending;
2. established a national 800 number: 1-800-523-AMEA;
3. testified before Congress, through its Political Action Committee (PAC), on the necessity for creating a multiracial/multiethnic category on all federal forms;
4. created an educational/legal advisory board with connections to prestigious institutes of learning across the country; and
5. formed alliances with other national advocacy groups such as PROJECT RACE to monitor both local/state and federal activities affecting our interracial communities.

To give greater accessibility to the national and international multiracial network, AMEA has gone on-line with Internet, thanks to the support and interest of Silicon Graphics, Inc., out of Mountain View, California. Tim and Jacqueline Fuzell-Casey have donated their time and computer literacy to AMEA in an effort to bring us all closer to our dream of a bulletin board/database and electronic National Resource Center. The AMEA Internet address is amea@sgi.com.

After 6 years of dedicated service as president of AMEA, Carlos Fernández stepped down from that post and passed the mantle of leadership over to Ramona Douglass at the close of the annual meeting, hosted by Pittsburgh's Interracial Families, Inc., June 3 to 5, 1994. Douglass has been a vice president of AMEA since its inception in 1988, is a multiracial adult, and has also served 7 years on her local interracial community group's board of directors (BFN/Chicago) in the capacities of president, vice president, and publicity chair. She was also responsible for creating BFN's first Biracial Adult Support Group in 1989. At the same meeting, Nancy G. Brown (MASC) was elected vice president; Jan Carpenter (IMAGE) remained secretary after 6 years, and Jo Myrtle Wolf (BFN) was voted in as treasurer.

AMEA today is gaining national media recognition as a secular, nondenominational organization open to people of all faiths as well as various racial/ethnic backgrounds. In addition to affiliate local membership groups, our ranks have been joined by individual members, fledgling student groups, and others interested in promoting positive images in the multiracial/multiethnic community. Carlos Fernández has remained a vital part of AMEA's board of directors and is now acting as a director and coordinator of legal and civil rights.

EYE ON THE FUTURE

Looking at the future viability of local and national multiracial network organizations, it is hoped that through the resolution of our own internal issues on race, we can set the tone and be the bridge for society in general as it grapples with the question of how do diverse cultures and races learn to function harmoniously. The mechanics of this process include the following:

1. acknowledging that racism (as well as all the other "isms") is still a problem that prevents us from living and working together harmoniously;
2. accepting the premise that racism is just one form of oppression that is detrimental to all human beings, whether they are the direct or indirect recipients;
3. identifying the interpersonal and societal mechanisms that have contributed to learned racism on an individual basis; and
4. finding the courage to engage in the intellectual and emotional process of defining for ourselves, stripped of our own layers of bias, how we feel about ourselves, our own unique culture, and the choices we make in relating to other human beings.

Seminars and conferences sponsored by interracial organizations include MASC's Kaleidoscope; BFN's ongoing participation in Dialogue Racism workshops; the IFC-hosted *Loving* Conference in Washington, DC; Pittsburgh's *Interracial Families, Inc.* Town Meeting; *New People Magazine*'s 1993 conference, "Every Side Is Our Side," and their 1994 conference, "No More Fear." These are just a few examples of how the interracial community is determined to examine itself, affirm its strengths, and eradicate its weaknesses. What we have to offer one another is support, courage, and a mutual sense of responsibility. We as individuals, family units, and diverse communities are living proof of the human ability to transcend cultural and ethnic differences. We must show first ourselves and then the world that each of us has the capacity to truly love and rationally dialogue with one another, no matter what color we are, what language we speak, or what faith we adhere to. That is a gift worth sharing.

Challenging Race and Racism
A Framework for Educators

RONALD DAVID GLASS

KENDRA R. WALLACE

I first became conscious of racism during my elementary school years. My family was one of the small number of Jewish families in a rural Ohio county. When I was perhaps 10, our temple was attacked and defaced with swastikas and anti-Semitic slogans. At the consolidated K to 12 public school, there were few blacks or nonwhites: my siblings and I were the only Jews. Playground attacks by other students coupled with classroom denunciations by teachers made clear my own status in their eyes.

I began to openly challenge racism expressed by students or teachers before starting high school in the early 1960s, and soon my parents had introduced me to civil rights movement demonstrations. My commitments to struggle for social justice deepened in my resistance to the war in Vietnam and became the foundation of my professional development as a philosopher of education. Focusing on the formation of liberating

AUTHORS' NOTE: We wish to thank Julie Duff, Denis Phillips, Tara Washburn, and Pia Wong for their helpful comments on an earlier draft. All remaining deficiencies remain our own responsibility.

educational practices, I have worked over many years with a broad variety of organizations, including those serving indigenous communities in North America and the highlands of Guatemala, communities of Korean Americans and African Americans, and also urban communities of the indigent and homeless.

Meanwhile, my own family has become more mixed. I am Jewish, primarily of Romanian and Russian descent but with Scottish and Native American (Lenape) roots, as well. I live with my wife, Merle, who is Jewish of Polish and Russian descent, and our son, Benjamin, 3, who is of mixed African, Mexican, and English American descent, and also my teenage children, Hannah and Daniel, whose mother is Quaker of Danish and Swedish descent. So these matters occupy an increasing space in daily life.

In this article, I have shared some of the insights gleaned from these roots and experiences, hoping to invite you into deeper commitments along with me to challenge the oppressions of race and racism. &

Ronald David Glass

My interest in developing this chapter stems out of many experiences. Growing up in an interracial family, I was raised knowing that I was a part of more than one community and was encouraged to affirm my biracial identity. I lived in Minnesota as a child and had connections to all facets of my heritage, as well as to other biracial children of the same background. When my family moved from Minnesota to California, being both black and white was difficult for most of the kids at school to understand, except for the biracial kids who I became friends with over the years. There was dissonance between the school culture and my home environment, so I learned to do some tricky moves to successfully walk the tightrope of ethnicity at school.

As a biracial educator, I'm interested in how schools can rethink their treatment of human diversity. I know people will always subject me to "authenticity tests" by virtue of my physical appearance, my experiences, and my self-identification. These legitimacy tests reflect very real tensions within and between social groups—tensions that can make going to school a very treacherous and uncomfortable journey for multiracial children in different parts of the United States.

I believe that schools can play a more active and supportive role in dealing with the diversity that children bring into the classroom. The ways in which human diversity and social inequalities are dealt with in U.S. schools generally fail to get at the heart of racism, and in fact, can work to reinforce it. I hope this chapter can contribute to the development of educational projects that support more liberating conceptions of diversity, and commit students and staff to critical dialogues about their ongoing relationships with racism, with inequalities, and with each other. ⚬

Kendra R. Wallace

From the very beginning of this discussion, we want to caution that care be taken in talking about race. This is true not just because race is an emotionally explosive subject, nor because race is a theoretically contested notion, nor because race continues to play a daily role in the suffering of millions of innocent people, including vast numbers of children. It is true especially because it can be so easy to speak of race and to forget about racism, to speak glibly of harmful social realities without taking responsibility for transforming injustice.

We examine how educators can help to dismantle racism and to reconstruct commonsense meanings of race. We argue that recent multicultural educational approaches are inadequate because they often reinscribe essentialist notions of race and fail to challenge the structures of racism. We argue for an education geared strategically and directly to the actual struggles that are at the core of racial orders, and we suggest a framework of values to ground such an education.

In sketching an outline for an education capable of challenging race and racism, we will draw on perspectives advanced by people who do not fit neatly within the racial and social orders and on educational practices born of movements for social justice. From these contexts, we intend to suggest a point of departure toward a vision of identities, relationships, and institutions no longer limited by racist hierarchies and interpretive frameworks. By calling attention to the importance of fixing a point of departure and a future destination, we do not mean at all to overlook the middle passage. The conflicts that are certain to mark this passage toward justice cannot be successfully navigated without continual critical attention both to the defining power of racial orders and the human creative power to transform culture and history. We offer a framework that meets these demands and provides numerous sound pathways for practice.

ON RACE AND RACISM

Race cannot be ignored as a conceptual framework because of its theoretical inadequacy for capturing the phenomenon of race or because of its simplistic use of reified notions for historically dynamic meanings and practices. Nor can the politics of race be transcended by a mental act of some sort (like a change in belief or an act of will) or wished away in a fantasy of color blindness. Nor can race be subsumed within nationality or ethnicity. Race matters (West, 1993), and we argue for a focus of attention on the continuing significance and changing meaning of race (Omi & Winant, 1986, 1993) to be linked with projects engaged in contesting that very significance and meaning.

A conscious politics needs to accompany every use of race. There are tremendous difficulties in analyzing the social geography of the United States, when despite the complete lack of moral, social, or scientific merit in the concept of race, it has persisted and entered every social institution. "Society is so thoroughly racialized that to be without racial identity is to be in danger of having no identity. To be raceless is akin to being genderless" (Omi & Winant, 1993, p. 5). It seems that all our talk and action gives meaning (of one sort or another) to race, creating the illusion that race exists outside the social constructions of which it is a part. Even radical social scientists and/or feminists can fall into an objectivism about race (Omi & Winant, 1993; Roman, 1993), or racialized minority groups can regard whiteness with the same objectivist gaze turned on them (hooks, 1992). It is hard to remove from our understanding a materialist bias that leads us to engage race as if it were somehow more basic than the social constructions of racism, as resident in a person's biology. But, to put it simply, no bodily feature or capacity, from skin color to intelligence, can be uniformly mapped onto racial categories. Racism and race cannot be cleanly separated from one another.

By inventing references that point to the open, dynamic, political character (that is, the formation) of race, we can see more clearly the ideological struggles at the core of racism. This is critical, for example, for grasping the differences between self-identifications and imposed definitions. Whether race is being used as an organizing schema to resist racism rather than to further exploitation or used in self-referentially identifying ways rather than imposed as a limiting label, it can equally suffer from the defect of seeming to express natural, given, and defining human conditions. This defect can contribute to contradictory results. Thus, in those cases where race is invoked to resist racism, as in the civil rights and black power movements of the 1960s, political dialogue can be opened to broader democratic participation, and many more individuals can pursue self-realization through a wider range of choices, even as a bankrupt conceptual structure that contributes to oppression (race) is reinforced and kept in play in political discourse.

Advances against racism and the fixity of race have not eliminated racial categories as "self-evident" markers. But an even stronger challenge to race can come from people at the margins to all racial centers; that is, from people expressive of multiracial existence and evident human variation, who resist efforts to be subdued and brought within racial orders. The multiracial offspring of the 1960s' movements, along with new waves of immigrants, contribute to the highly contested multicultural environment of today's cities and schools. Racialized experience continues to play a central role as personal and group identities sort themselves along evolving gradients. It is this fluid sociohistorical formation that needs to be the focus of our efforts.

History lives on in the struggles of the day, so the historical roots and logic of racism must be unearthed in order to combat it more effectively. A number of researchers have analyzed various racial classifications or formations and agree that deeply rooted religious views of racial existence and significance began to give way (without ever disappearing altogether) in the 19th century to views influenced by a scientistic explanatory framework (Banton, 1987; Biddiss, 1979; Gossett, 1963; Miles, 1989, 1993; Omi & Winant, 1986). Instead of God, science, in the guise of social Darwinism, seemed to ordain the existing hierarchical social order as the natural order expressing pregiven destinies. Educators then and now were far from alone in believing that "shared behavioral norms, and the social and economic differences between human groups—primarily races, classes, and sexes—arise from inherited, in-born distinctions and that society, in this sense, is an accurate reflection of biology" (Gould, 1981, p. 20).

The U.S. mythos, which since its inception has been deeply secured in notions of the racial superiority of whites, became linked to the idea that the social and natural orders were being continually perfected through human works. Evolution entered the talk of every domain of social life, from business, to education, to sports, to sex, to national politics (Hofstadter, 1955/1959). Few doubted the United States would prevail in this competition of the survival of the fittest, because its capitalist ethos so closely matched what science "proved" was natural law. Social Darwinism got expressed in reform movements embodying not only this "optimistic" view of steady progress but also a more decidedly pessimistic outlook. These latter movements were cloaked in discourses of human improvement and included a diverse blend of liberals and reactionaries. Alarmists called for state intervention to prevent the degeneration of the best humans, being caused by medical and social programs allowing the "weak" and "misfits" to reproduce at threateningly high rates: The undesirables should be prevented from reproducing, and the desirables should be encouraged to breed. Calls for forced institutionalization or sterilization were linked with attacks on voluntary birth control among the "fittest" segments of the population, and thus to attacks on the women's liberation movement (Proctor, 1988).

We find elements of early religious racism, of biological deterministic racism, and both pessimistic and optimistic forms of social Darwinism reflected in some present-day rhetoric (Omi & Winant, 1986). We continue to hear officials worry about the reproductive excesses of poor and minority communities and the resulting degradation of our student population and schools, calling for a reintroduction of eugenics into public policy. Many educators remain blindly infatuated with scientistic rationales for policies with unconscionable costs in damaged lives.

Some researchers and educators still attempt to restore the scientific status of race and to prove the inherent superiority of certain races by assigning numbers for performances on tests of one sort or another (Herrnstein & Murray, 1994). Testers are ever ready to count and time prescribed performances, and the debates continue unabated over the validity of this research and the significance of the bell curves that chart these numbers (Cronbach, 1975; Gould, 1981). Lane (1994) and Ryan

(1994), for example, demonstrate that Hernnstein and Murray's (1994) arguments rely on tainted research conducted by white supremacists and eugenicists with explicit ties to historical racist movements, including World War II Nazis. Academic, school, and policy authorities repeat time-worn views in present-day jargon, rearticulating racist world-views and failing to acknowledge the fundamental fallacies embedded in this work: namely, the distortion of complex human realities by simplistic reifications ranked along a single scale (Gould, 1981), and the masking of politics with pseudo-objective lenses and veils.

These explanatory narratives and institutional forces persist despite corrections at the level of theology, science, law, or even majority view, and they give way (and then but in part) only to organized challenges to the racist lived practices that have shaped communities for generations. Racial formation takes place not just at the macrolevel, but at the human level at which history is made day-to-day. Racial contradictions and tensions are already clearly visible in the lives of young children (Troyna & Hatcher, 1992) and continue to be elaborated in identity formation and social activities throughout people's lives (Frankenberg, 1993; Nash & Weiss, 1970; Wellman, 1993).

In the face of such persistent forms of life, a strategic praxis is required; that is, we require a long-term struggle with flexible tactics that focuses on self-change as well as institutional and social change. To undermine race as an organizing principle for thought and action while at the same time deploying race in the struggle to dismantle racism, we need a strategic form of education linked to transformative action, which can situate the lived contradictions of race and challenge the institutions of racism. We will offer a values framework and action plan that can provide a basis for the required educational praxis. Although our discussion will focus on public schools, they alone, even if they were to implement our recommendations, cannot be the instrument of social change. Nonetheless they can play a significant role in the formation of a citizenry that would have the collective strength to make profound transformations.

ON RACE, RACISM, AND EDUCATION

This section explores the limits and the possibilities of addressing racism through multicultural education. Although public education has formulated many responses to the challenges posed by its diverse population, current discourses around race within schools can be characterized by a general fixation on "cultural differences" tied to essentialist constructions of identity. That is, they assume that existing cultural or racial manifestations are naturally given, unchanging, and all-defining. Such discourses effectively focus attention away from an examination of power and racial formation and toward a preoccupation with the cultural *other* as perceived from a Eurocentric standpoint. We develop this criticism and present ideas for developing a more critical, antiracist, and emancipatory pedagogy.

Since the vast expansion of public education at the start of the century, U.S. schools have generally approached multicultural issues from an assimilationist perspective. School culture embedded the values and norms of the white Protestant middle class. Immigrants were expected to part with their languages and customs and become generic Americans indistinguishable from other citizens. Public schools legitimated and secured a specific cultural perspective, which simultaneously marginalized the experiences and identities of students from subaltern or nondominant groups. Although many immigrant groups recognized this structural inequality with concern, and some struggled for control of their local schools, the response was more often to maintain the home culture through independent community institutions rather than to challenge the content or structure of public schooling (Tyack, 1974).

The transition into the mainstream generally eluded immigrants of racialized minority groups, regardless of their desires for assimilation. On the other hand, those of white European descent could invoke ethnicity selectively after two or three generations, once linguistic and cultural competencies and access to social institutions had been successfully established (Waters, 1990). Racial or ethnic identity remained something regarded as extrinsic to being "American," reinforcing the illusion that the mainstream had evolved beyond particular racial or ethnic affiliations.

However, after the U.S. Supreme Court's 1954 Brown decision and later in the 1960s, the Eurocentric foundations of the public educational system began to crack under sustained criticism from politically organized African Americans and later from other groups. They demanded equal educational opportunities and greater accountability for the academic success of every student regardless of cultural background (Banks, 1988). Generally, public schools responded with a liberal compromise that focused on increased representation among the staff or within the curricula.

Although this was a significant advance, such ameliorative measures left untouched most of the core structures and ideologies of public education, such as academic ability tracking, and schools continued largely to reproduce the existing race, gender, and class positions and relations of their students. Emphasizing interpersonal and individualistic aspects of the inequalities and injustices of racism, liberal multicultural education was incapable of transforming the racial order even within the schools, let alone in society at large (McCarthy, 1988).

The main impediments blocking the capacity of schools to challenge racism and enable students to engage in critical emancipatory projects can be discerned in three multicultural approaches currently found in schools: *cultural understanding, cultural competence, and cultural emancipation approaches* (McCarthy, 1993). We use this tripartite framework because it embeds an account of the politics of the educational context and is compatible with the view we develop, but other, not mutually exclusive frameworks for analyzing multicultural education are available. For example, Banks (1993) offered an historical cataloguing of approaches, whereas Sleeter and Grant (1987) provided a thematic categorization.

The cultural understanding approach emphasizes the improvement of intercultural relations and promotes positive interactions between individuals primarily by encouraging knowledge of one's own cultural origins and respect for others from diverse backgrounds. For example, students might be encouraged to share their family's distinctive foods and holidays and trace these to past times and various other parts of the world. Proponents believe that by instilling in students a greater tolerance and respect for human diversity, they will foster a pluralist society marked by increased racial harmony and equality. But this approach downplays the tensions generated trying to balance the goal of national social cohesion with pluralism and a respect for cultural diversity (Lynch, 1986), and it also fails to address embedded conflicts between groups.

The second approach, *cultural competence*, encourages pluralism by viewing cultural diversity as a given resource to be preserved and tapped in order to foster cross-cultural competency. Beyond knowing one's own racial or ethnic identity and respecting others, one is expected to develop a knowledge and understanding of other cultural groups (McCarthy, 1993). For example, students might be required to write a report on a famous person of an ethnic group other than their own, or teachers might add a special segment to their regular curriculum during Black History Month.

We believe that both of these approaches move in constructive directions. However, they assume that the origins of racism and injustice are within an individual's value system or knowledge base and thus fail to take into account the systemic dimensions of racism and to situate these within broader historical struggles. Racial, ethnic, or cultural identities, which are the outcome of conflicted negotiations within inequitable power relations, are mistaken for natural differences or for individual choices. Static, homogeneous cultural groups are assumed to be competing on equal footing in a neutral public arena.

Cultural understanding and cultural competence approaches in multicultural education cannot adequately address the tension between a cultural relativist position that treats each group as inherently distinct and incomparable and a cultural universalist position that treats the public arena as embodying transcendent values that permit each group its independence while providing a level playing field for fair competitions. These approaches cannot deconstruct the myths of meritocracy and individual achievement. When racial differences are both essentialized and naturalized, the ideological battles actually giving rise to these differences and their associated explanations of human diversity are ignored (McCarthy, 1993; Omi & Winant, 1986, 1993; Winant, 1994).

In the 1970s, these approaches became marked by an effort to replace race with culture. As race, culture, and ethnicity became interchangeable and subsumed within the single concept of culture, not only was racism obscured, but again humans were regarded as occupying discrete and static locations by virtue of birth. These locations were often depicted as bipolar (e.g., white-black, dominant-subordinate, center-margin). Over time, "in fact, race and ethnicity have been generally reduced to a discourse of the *other*, a discourse that, regardless of its emancipatory or reactionary intent, often essentialized and reproduced the distance between the centers and the margins of power" (Giroux,

1992, p. 113). What is suppressed is heterogeneity and the contradictions and multiplicities of particular identities or cultures.

Both cultural understanding and cultural competence approaches to multicultural education ignore the lengthy debates within anthropology over adequate formulations of the meaning of culture by failing to expose and problematize the historically evolving underlying relationships between identity and power (Roseberry, 1992). The liberal response to the challenge of racist school practices once again results in reinforcing racism when identities are seen as created and manipulated across a series of perceived "cultural" borders that reconstitute differences. This does not undo racism but actually supports it by attributing the source of human differences to mutually exclusive racial and cultural variables—a *differentialist racism* (Balibar, 1991). Both approaches find support from a proliferation of theories that attempt to explain the disparate experiences of "minority" students by, for example, appeals to cultural "learning styles." That is, rather than explaining an African American male's poor performance on a written exam as the result of systematic exclusion from certain educational opportunities or lack of assistance in acquiring certain writing skills, the teacher may explain the performance by invoking a conception of African American culture as oral. Well-meaning educators are in fact racializing student experiences by mistaking effects for causes, and treating African American culture as having no history or capacity for writing. That is, they attribute the effects of inequitable power relationships (practices, discourses, and representations) in the school and society to inherent cultural variables (Giroux, 1992).

Cultural emancipation, the third major approach to multiculturalism, relies on deepened curricular reform to boost the success and economic progress of subaltern racial groups (McCarthy, 1993). Proponents argue that more relevant and less alienating schooling for minority students will increase student engagement and academic achievement and thus will lead to more job opportunities for minority youth and ultimately to greater economic and social power for disadvantaged groups. However, this faith in the redemptive qualities of the educational system ignores the degree to which a capitalist economy constrains schools and individuals so that inequitable class, gender, and race relations are largely reproduced, and it precludes the possibility of meaningful employment for everyone regardless of educational attainment. This approach reflects a "particular naiveté about the racial character of the job market . . . [and] the structural and material relations in which racial domination is embedded are underemphasized" (McCarthy, 1988, p. 269).

What is needed is a more relational analysis of schooling that shows the links between social structures, what real people such as teachers do, and the interactive (and sometimes contradictory) effects of race, gender, and class relations (McCarthy, 1988; Weis, 1988). Racism is not simply a consequence of cultural ignorance, nor is it simply a secondary feature of capitalist ideology. Racial formation occurs within a highly contested and contradictory political, economic, and cultural milieu, of which schools are but one part. In this context, schools create differences—or inscribe a "politics of difference"—that are not predictable at the individual level. Race, class, and gender are not unproblematic natural states, but are "structuring principles" that inform how groups interact (McCarthy, 1988) and provide the norms and standards within which individuals make choices about their own identities.

McCarthy (1993) outlined a critical emancipatory multiculturalism that would include a systematic critique and reconstruction of Eurocentric school knowledge, which situates knowledge production within an ideological matrix of interests and power. He called for a nuanced discussion of contradictions, discontinuities, and multiplicities that inhere in racial identity at both group and individual levels to be at the core of the new paradigm. These recommendations are closely aligned with antiracist pedagogy that has been developed in the British context and that locates the source of racism and inequality within the power dynamics of the state and its informing ideologies (Anthias & Yuval-Davis, 1992; Brandt, 1986).

When we begin to see the dynamics of the discontinuities, contradictions, and multiplicities of race, we can engage race as a *consequence* of racism. That is, because racial identities or cultural representations are produced and legitimated within schools (and other social institutions) structured by profound power imbalances, and because race, in and of itself, has no existence outside these particular, historical signifying practices, then an adequate oppositional pedagogy must embody not only a challenge to racism but new conceptions of identity and difference that challenge race itself.

We do not want to be mistaken that the challenge to race that we propose is akin to color blindness. Color blindness can be a form of defensiveness among teachers (Sleeter, 1993), or part of a more general color or power evasiveness (Frankenberg, 1993) that has the effect of denying racism. Color and race cannot be ignored: They have to be seen through in order to see what is behind them. Neither running from race (race or color blindness) nor running to race (as in the race infatuation seen in some elements of nationalism or Afrocentrism) can come to grips with racism. Only by seeing racial formation is one enabled to intervene historically both in self-identity development and in structural transformation. By seeing racial formation, we can see more clearly how to be subjects and not objects of history and thus how to make new racial futures.

In the next section, we suggest some ways that the lived negotiations taking place within and across race, gender, class, ability, and other groupings can become an explicit focus for curricula at every level. Moreover, we will outline an education that should enable people to engage in these negotiations with a clearer sense of the obstacles they face and a stronger knowledge of transformational action, ways of consciously creating a world more just and less racist.

CHALLENGING RACE AND RACISM

To challenge race and racism, educators must move away from an infatuation with fixed racial identities and toward a thoughtful reconsideration of racism as a "total social phenomenon" that obscures the ideological foundations of identity (Balibar, 1991). Educators need to be critically suspicious of the discursive practices central to racism: all categorizations of social groups, assumptions about natural divisions between people, and assignments of traits based on origins in group differences (Miles, 1989, 1993; Wetherell & Potter, 1992). We need to problematize the seeming naturalness or commonsense reality of race, which plays such a dominant role in the everyday lives of students, teachers, administrators, and nearly every other school community member. It is worthwhile to recall that the naturalization of race is sometimes articulated even by antiracist activists (Frankenberg, 1993).

We can take some direction from developments within an emerging multiracialist movement. Even multicultural educators have paid little attention to the experiences of multiracial people, who constitute a growing portion of the population with critical insights into the contradictions and discontinuities of the racial order because of their unique place within it (Funderburg, 1994). People of immediately bi- or multiracial background often occupy a position of *cultural hybridity* (Bhabha, 1990). This enables some negotiation within the multiplicity of subject positionings established by racial canons without policing the borders of identity along fixed and imaginary lines (Shohat, 1992). The introduction of a "third space" (Bhabha, 1990) can contribute to a reorientation of racial geography that may permit the construction of identities more resistant to the deformations of racism (Hall, n.d.). It can open spaces that defy unjust hierarchies or refuse debilitating limits on self-understandings and social relations. Articulating a multiracial position undermines the fixity of race as a concept while taking into account the importance of race as a structuring force.

With the vision possible from this "third space," school faculty, staff, students, and parents can be challenged with an image of a diverse learning community committed to respectful relationships not predicated on race. This image helps provide a glimmer of hope where despair can easily prevail since racism is so tightly woven into the fabric of everyday life. A critical hope that reveals new possibilities is not incidental but is rather indispensable to radical change (Freire, 1994). In order to realize the hoped-for future, action needs to be guided by values aimed at recreating school culture and preparing people for the struggles attendant to overcoming racism.

We outline five core values that are crucial to challenging race and racism. The first value is *community*. Every school needs to be understood as one community composed of many communities, each with its own multiplicities, contradictions, and historically evolving identity. The diversity within a school contributes to its excellence by providing an array of sustaining heritages from which to draw in enabling every member of the community to realize his or her fullest potential.

The second value is *mutual respect*. The dignity and rights of every person and community within a school must be respected, or a genuine learning community is impossible. This means that every voice is invited into the dialogue for reasoned debate and decision making and that free speech is joined with attentive listening. It also means a commitment to nonviolence in word and deed, and to the safety and caretaking of every person and of the environment. Only in a respectful community of communities will people be supported and able to explore and develop their unique identities without being forced into the existing racial, class, and gender orders.

The third core value is *truth seeking*, the commitment to an education that enables the critical investigation of the world, society, and each student's life. Truth seeking is a form of understanding that grasps the limits and historical nature of knowledge. Thus it is not a matter of establishing truths so much as it is the stimulation of curiosity, the shaping of research skills, and the formation of virtues such as honesty, openness, and courage. The commitment to truth seeking is particularly important because oppressive orders rely so heavily on misinformation and distortions of reality for their justification.

Compassionate responsibility, the fourth core value, is vital to the formation of a school culture that can challenge race and racism. Every person has been and continues to be negatively marked by race, gender, and class ideologies, regardless of how vigilant his or her efforts to avoid or transcend these oppressions. They operate at cultural, institutional, and individual levels, to some degree invading every domain of existence from the most public to the most private. In an important sense, no one is guilty for this terrible state of affairs: Guilt is personal and cannot be inherited. At the same time, everyone is responsible for the horrors of the present age because our actions either carry forward or try to transform the past. This means being compassionate and not blaming when racism is manifest in any way, so that schools can be places to heal from the damage done. It means not seeking to assign guilt, but seeking to invite and enable responsibility, both in the sense of capable of response or empathy toward suffering, and capable of being accountable for suffering caused and for our human obligation to alleviate unnecessary suffering.

Finally, the community needs to direct its respectful, knowledgeable, compassionately responsible actions toward the realization of *justice*, the fifth core value. There is no denying that injustices riddle U.S. history, even as its founding ideology championed justice for all, and there is no denying that this contradiction is reflected in every community and school. An injustice suffered by one is an injustice to all; justice demands that past inequities be redressed and present inequities fairly faced. By studying and celebrating the long history of struggles for justice (participated in by every community in some form at some moments in history), schools can nurture citizens committed to resolute nonviolent transformation of the injustices discovered in the school and society.

These values and the vision of a new society they engender will reach far beyond the school and challenge the racial, gender, and class order of the society. Resistance will be strong and varied, both from those in (Sleeter, 1993) and outside the schools. The relations and institutions in which power and privilege have been structured for centuries cannot be wished away, scientifically reasoned away, or even made to go away by lives given in opposition to them. In fact, the need for profound struggles to establish or maintain a just society would not vanish even if racism and other oppressions suddenly disappeared. Conflict occurs even where relations are shaped by caring, loving commitments to protect, nurture, and train children (Ruddick, 1989). Confrontation to the level of organized civil disobedience could be expected even in a well-ordered and substantially just society, although it would need to meet some key conditions: The civil disobedience actions would have to be a last resort, nonviolent, and public (no secret actions), with the activists willing to suffer the consequences of the rule of law (Rawls, 1971). From interpersonal to interinstitutional domains, within the closest relations and spiritual bonds, deadly force can emerge.

Therefore we argue that an education to challenge race and racism should prepare people for nonviolent struggle at least as well as soldiers are prepared for armed struggle, taking as a minimal measure the numerous such nonviolent campaigns in U.S. history (Cooney & Michalowski, 1987). Nonviolent theorists and practitioners have developed more than 200 specific methods of struggle, ranging from personal noncooperation to general strikes and boycotts, which can make the costs of maintaining an unjust status quo very high (Gandhi, 1940; Sharp, 1973). Not only can the conduct of everyday affairs be rendered virtually impossible, but active nonviolence can be extended to national defense, a capacity perhaps needed because the institutions and cultural formations sustaining racism and other relationships of domination are themselves global (Boserup & Mack, 1975).

We can learn much from the role education has played in past campaigns for social justice. In the United States, struggles for women's, labor, civil, housing, and other rights have demonstrated that movement building requires an education grounded in democratic values, building from the existing strengths and knowledge of the community and structured around small-group critical dialogue linked to transformative action (Adams, 1975; Altenbaugh & Paulston, 1980; Freire, 1970; Reed, 1981; Tjerandsen, 1980). Education capable of challenging race and racism must build on the successful efforts of the past and then invent itself anew in order to overcome the ever-changing social formations that seek to sustain unjust hierarchies of power and privilege.

CONCLUSION

We alone as individuals or collectively as educators cannot overcome race and racism, but we have important roles to play. Schools are key institutions in the re-creation of society, and educators cannot abdicate their responsibility in helping to shape a more just future. Although we cannot detail how particular educators need to engage the challenge to race and racism in their specific situation, we hope that we have given enough concrete suggestions to help people move further along this path regardless of their present location.

- Each of us can reduce the number of educational contexts in which race is permitted to be a factor in explanations and analyses.
- We can foster a critical awareness of racial formation, of the historical production of representations and identities.
- We can discourage educational self-interpretations and ascribed identities that invoke or impose race while encouraging those not defined by relations of domination, such as interests or skills.
- We can encourage antiracist and antisexist commitments that strive to disrupt the racial and gender orders of oppression as found in the classroom, school, and society.
- We can openly question our use of race precisely in those moments when racialized language seems to be our only recourse in describing educational situations.
- We can follow a professional practice grounded in the core values of community, mutual respect, truth seeking, compassionate responsibility, and justice and work to establish a school culture expressive of these values.

- And finally, we can prepare students (and ourselves) for the protracted struggles ahead if racism is to be overcome and race is to fall into insignificance.

As educators, it is up to us to make education make a difference. To challenge race and racism is to challenge ourselves and the institutions within which we live: It is only through our own lives that justice can be realized.

Being Different Together in the University Classroom

Multiracial Identity as Transgressive Education

TERESA KAY WILLIAMS

CYNTHIA L. NAKASHIMA

GEORGE KITAHARA KICH

G. REGINALD DANIEL

In the spring of 1992, the University of California, Santa Barbara's Asian American Studies program (now a full-fledged department) offered the first course ever on Asian-descent multiracials. Half of the students in the class were multiracial and transracially adopted. Another 10% consisted of monoracially identified European Americans, and the remaining 40% were monoracially identified Asian Americans. All of the multiracial students were a mixture of Asian and European ancestries, except for one student who was Filipino and Mexican. On the first day of class, students introduced themselves and explained why they were interested in taking the course. A Euro American student prefaced her remarks by stating, "As you can tell, I'm obviously white." She was immediately challenged by her multiracial classmates. One multiracial student asked her to explain what "obviously white" meant. As this Euro American student attempted to articulate the taken-for-granted assumptions of racial designations in American society, describing skin color, physical features, geographical origins, and so on, another multiracial student pointed out to her that many of the Eurasians in the class in fact looked "more obviously white" than she did, according to the phenotypical standards of "race" to which this Euro American student subscribed. One multiracial student after another easily poked holes in this Euro American student's loosely threaded explanation of race. The multiracial students indicated how many of them possessed lighter complexions, lighter hair and eye coloring, and more phenotypical characteristics associated with European ancestry than did this self-professed "obviously white" woman. For the next 10 weeks, this Euro American female student was put on the defensive by the multiracial and transracially adopted students in the class. For the first time in her life, she was forced to interrogate her taken-for-granted assumptions about race and to question her social location in American society, not only in relation to monoracially identified groups of color, but also in relation to multiracial peoples with European ancestry.

We have come to realize from our years of teaching race relations and multiracial identity that these kinds of conflicts and confrontations are critical, if not necessary. It is only through these classroom experiences that both students and professors are able to interrogate interactively and integratively our own theoretical, conceptual understandings of the world around us; grapple with painful, perplexing contradictions; connect them to our everyday lives; and engage in the transformative power of transgressive education (hooks, 1994). &

A "critical mass" (Root, 1992b, 1994b) of multiracial students, faculty, and staff personnel in higher education has allowed for a multiracial and multiethnic studies "field" to emerge. This chapter highlights the importance of the growing number of courses by, for, and about biracial and multiracial peoples offered on university campuses and the role that ethnic studies has played in fostering a multidisciplinary, education-as-empowerment framework within which biracial and multiracial student activism, scholarly research, and teaching are taking place. This chapter discusses the value and necessity of integrating the study of racially and culturally blended peoples into academic curricula at the college and university level. We raise questions of pedagogy and methodology of teaching courses about such a complex group of peoples who neither had a social script to follow nor a legitimate space of academic inquiry in which to write and construct one until now (Natasha Hansen, personal communication, October 1994).

THE PROBLEMS OF CURRENT
CROSS-CULTURAL AND MULTICULTURAL STUDIES

General cross-cultural or multicultural education courses in the social sciences, literature, humanities, law, medicine, and fine arts typically have not included modules or lectures on multiracial peoples, or even on interracial marriages. A major unstated focus of these courses is often to educate and enlighten Euro Americans about the impact of race, ethnicity, and culture. These courses, although well-intentioned, often have an underlying paternalistic view about peoples of color. They legitimize the separation and inequality across racial and ethnic groups; they foster learning about *other* peoples' cultures; and they assume, if not perpetuate, the notion of race with distinct borders. Curiously, the fact of interracial relationships is all too often missing. Subsequently, multiraciality is erased out of textual and experiential existence.

In multiculturally sensitive fields, there are often options and even requirements for taking a class on one or two of the major "ethnic" groups in the United States, which almost always means a topic on a racial minority group. For example, in the state of California, one of the academic requirements for state licensure as a psychotherapist is to take a graduate course in "cross-cultural mores and values, including a familiarity with the wide range of racial and ethnic backgrounds common among California's population" (Board of Behavioral Science Examiners, 1990, p. 6). Courses and textbooks used to fulfill this requirement (e.g., Atkinson et al., 1989; Chin, De La Cancela, & Jenkins, 1993; Dana, 1993; Ho, 1992; McGoldrick, Pearce, & Giordano, 1982; Sue & Sue, 1990; Vargas & Koss-Chioino, 1992) are generally surveys, attempting to do too much in too little space and time. They often carry the cross-cultural load for the rest of the curriculum.

The texts and course materials in multicultural or cross-cultural education have often been criticized for

1. being too reductionistic and anthropologically distanced (e.g., studying "the Natives" or "the exotic *other*");
2. presenting materials without a social and political framework;
3. failing to recognize diversity within groups and ascribing cultural practices and beliefs across members of a group; and/or
4. focusing on clinical case examples that simplistically limit or expand the possibilities for change for the racial or ethnic client.

Moreover, the implication for students of these cross-cultural or multicultural classes (and even ethnic studies classes, as we shall explain later) is that (a) the historical separation of the races is normal, (b) that the differences between cultures are insurmountable, and (c) that there exists such a thing as a "bona fide" monoracial group. Furthermore, students are not challenged to think about how race is constructed. Thus, taken-for-granted, faulty notions of race (Williams, Chapter 12, this volume) are pedagogically duplicated and legitimized.

Except for brief references—usually to make the claim that race is a faulty concept, but nevertheless a significant one because of its sociological application—there is little or no mention of interracial relationships, marriages, and families or the biracial offspring and the complexity of their identities and social locations in traditional studies of race and ethnic relations. However, U.S. history of race and ethnic relations is embedded in a history of laws and regulations concerning interracial contact, sexuality, and economics, mostly in the forms of restriction and prohibition (Tenzer, 1990). Understanding personal, family, and community dynamics without an understanding of this history presents students with an ahistorical view of entrenched and deterministic racial and ethnic conflict. For instance, many students are surprised and dismayed to understand that the antimiscegenation laws in the United States were ruled unconstitutional by the U.S. Supreme Court as recently as 1967. Upon learning about the U.S. antimiscegenation laws, a biracial Eurasian student at UC Santa Barbara, who took a course on multiracials of Asian descent titled, "The World of Amerasians," wrote in her journal entry,

I am appalled! In some states, my parents' love for each other was illegal when they first got married—speaking of "forbidden fruit." There was a time when my siblings and I could have been treated as illegal products of an illegal union. I always thought I was different from "full-blooded" Asians because being part-white, [that] my history was not one of racial discrimination. After I read about these laws, I called my father and asked him what it was like. This is the first time my father and I ever really talked about my parents' marriage from a racial perspective.

By reading how blood quantum laws were instituted by the U.S. government, students learn concretely how race came to be employed as one of the single most significant markers of status, privilege, and power. For example, on learning how multiracial individuals and intermarried couples were incarcerated in concentration camps along with monoracially identified, intramarried Japanese Americans during World War II, the structural manipulation of racial definitions is illuminated. Furthermore, by studying the realities of interracial families, students can understand more easily the contradictory context in which racial and ethnic identities are constructed in a society that is embedded in the paradox of the "melting pot myth." That is to say, the "melting pot truth" has only been extended to Euro American individuals, whose multiple European identities have been allowed to (or perhaps forced to) "melt" together, join forces, and then reap the personal, economic, and legal rewards of such a privileged identity. The study of interracial relations, sexuality, and marriage, as well as the treatment and placement of the biracial offspring, therefore can provide critical insight into how and why race became such an effective tool to differentiate, rank, and offset groups of people. Race-difference paradigms, which dominate the literature on race relations, are directly challenged by introducing the study of multiracial peoples.

Most texts intended for use in general cross-cultural or multicultural education classes do not explicitly state this, yet they appear to be directed at training and increasing the awareness of Euro American teachers, therapists, and professionals as they interact in an increasingly multicolored world. Current personal realities become engaged with the need for class time focused on helping students to process their feelings, their perceived realities, and their current judgments. For instance, reading the history of the slavery process in the United States often generates feelings of guilt on the part of Euro American students, sparking debates about current responsibility for the consequences. Some Euro American students sometimes express distanced and somewhat paternalistic views of the *other* as having been the unfortunate victims of prior racism, without understanding the systematic, personal, and institutional processes of cumulative disempowerment and continued dehumanization of peoples of color. The impact of modern racism requires a deeper level of self-awareness, sensitivity, and critical thinking.

If there are students of color in these classes, sensitivity to their presence and their reactions to materials presented in class or in the texts becomes important. They may become inadvertent spokespersons for their entire group. As representatives of their groups, students of color in these classes are treated as the norm for all members of their group, the exception to the norm of their group, or even the scapegoat for the covert and overt hostility by other class members. When the majority of the students in the class are Euro American, the "outsider" perspective of students of color often becomes the focus of class discussions. As a necessary introduction for Euro Americans to the racialized realities, ethnic rituals, and worldviews of peoples of color, these sessions can sometimes provoke impatience on the part of students of color as they ask why do we have to take on the role of educating white people.

Furthermore, within this type of classroom context, the multiracial person disappears into a monoracial projection fostered by teachers, fellow students, or both. Unless interracial themes, histories, and concepts are presented as part of the course, either the credibility of the multiracial individual as a person of color is questioned and resisted or, if he or she possesses European ancestry, it is not acknowledged due to a hypodescent mentality that devalues ancestries of color and then locates biracial individuals into the lower status racial group. The dynamics of modern racism, which creates invisible minorities and then discounts the racism that produced their realities, are again repeated with multiracial students.

If peoples' heritages are treated as if they are monoracial without understanding the consistent and persistent, yet unsuccessful campaign by the American government to prevent interracial unions, then the idea of race and its racist origins are never fully interrogated. That is to say, race continues to be treated as biologically based (i.e., genetic, natural), rather than as a socially constructed, politically maintained category (Omi & Winant, 1986). Both students of color and Euro American students, whose understanding of their social realities in American society may be different, are invested in the race-difference paradigms that legitimize their separate and unequal social locations. For many students, questioning the differences among the concepts of race, ethnicity, nationality, culture, and heritage become a confusing emotional process. By studying the history of interracial blending, by interacting with people from different backgrounds in the form of casual classroom contact, or by engaging in intimate interpersonal friendships and companionships across racial boundaries in the present, students and teachers personally realize the importance of interracial relationships in comprehending the highly racialized world in which we live and operate.

In cross-cultural and multicultural studies, students recognize that these courses are about so-called "monoracial" peoples and about how they are supposed to relate to these different peoples. However, when students are introduced to the extent of the legacy of racial and cultural blending in American history and its effects on present-day multiracial trends, they gradually begin to see how their own family genealogies connect with others. They not only wonder about the facts of their own histories, but they become curious as to why these facts seem to have remained hidden. If and only when the shared family histories of these students who have been forcibly socialized to experience separate racial statuses are recognized, appreciated, and nurtured can false, rigid, and unequal boundaries be transgressed and transformed. At a time when cross-cultural and multicultural education continues to duplicate the same racial and cultural hierarchies that it proposes to defeat, the implementation of topics on multiracials becomes necessary to provide effective conceptual tools for understanding the complex structure of race relations and their day-to-day impact within the realm of interpersonal experiences.

ETHNIC STUDIES AS MODEL FOR
MULTIRACIAL AND MULTIETHNIC STUDIES

The university has privileged dispassionate, apolitical, and depersonalized inquiry and deemed it "quality" education. The struggle for the inclusion and integration of the voices and experiences of marginalized peoples into academia has always been and necessarily remains political, personal, and passionate. Peoples of color, multiracial individuals, gays, lesbians, and bisexuals, women, members of the working class, people with disabilities, and those who belong to all of these groups have been forced to create and sustain their own analytical and personal spaces within university contexts. In an academic world that has often been hostile to marginalized populations, ethnic studies programs and departments have become locations of analytical and personal refuge for students and faculty of color, at times even referred to as an "academic ghetto."

Ethnic studies on college campuses, unlike the "traditional" disciplines, arose out of a student and community empowerment movement in which students of color and their Euro American allies organized, rallied, and protested under the threat of guns, police batons, and punitive administrative actions. As a result of the grassroots mobilization of students, community members, and supportive faculty and staff, many colleges and universities have come to include the histories and experiences of non-Anglo Protestant groups into their curriculum and language references. About 25 years have passed since colleges and universities first began implementing ethnic studies classes, programs, research centers, and departments. The action-oriented, bottom-up, multidisciplinary educational model of ethnic studies has allowed for a critical and transgressive self-interrogation of its fields in order to explain its scholarship and membership. As a result, ethnic studies, perhaps more so than any other field in higher education, has been at the forefront of including the histories and experiences of multiply marginalized groups such as multiracial peoples.

Scholars interested in doing research and teaching in the area of multiracial identity have often found institutional support in a variety of ethnic studies settings. Indeed, several courses on multiracial individuals, groups, and families have been offered sporadically by individual instructors interested in this subject matter within various departments, and others have included topics relating to biracial children, interracial dating and marriage, and multiracial populations in general social science, literature, humanities, and ethnic studies courses. However, the only two regularly offered courses on multiracial peoples built into the core curriculum are (a) UC Berkeley's "People of Mixed Racial

Descent" course, first designed and introduced into the ethnic studies curriculum by Dr. Terry Wilson in the late 1970s, and (b) UC Santa Barbara's "The World of Amerasians," introduced into the Asian American studies department curriculum and institutionalized by its chairperson, Dr. Sucheng Chan. Both of these courses on multiracial peoples are offered through ethnic studies departments. Moreover, both courses have served as a catalyst for the formation and revitalization of multi-racial student organizations such as UC Berkeley's MISC and UC Santa Barbara's Variations. Out of these courses and groups have also come student-published journals, such as *Voices of Identity, Rage,* and *Deliverance* (No Collective, 1992) from UC Berkeley and *Inside/Out: Poetry and Prose by People of Mixed Heritage* (Littlejohn, 1994) from UC Santa Cruz and student-produced documentaries like Deidre Natsuno Howard's *And We Are Whole* and Erika Schmitt's *Variations on Race* from UC Santa Barbara.

Other ethnic studies courses have also inspired multiracial students to become agents of identity proclamation and change. Several of the multiracial individuals who took Jere Takahashi's Japanese American history class at UC Berkeley formed the Hapa Issues Forum, which now meets regularly, puts out a newsletter, and organizes a yearly conference on issues facing Asian descent multiracials. When Professor Ronald Takaki introduced his graduate teaching assistant, Cynthia Nakashima, to his comparative race and ethnic relations class at UC Berkeley as a scholar doing research on mixed-race identity, a biracial student of European and African ancestries and another of African and Pilipino ancestries approached Nakashima and together they started the Students of Interracial Descent (SID), which has since become Multiethnic/Interracial Students' Coalition (MISC). Students are now organizing multiracial associations on college campuses, putting on forums and conferences, and conducting groundbreaking research on multiracial populations and identity development, in turn further encouraging faculty to continue teaching courses on these topics. For example, when Dr. Terry Wilson proposed and taught the first course ever on multiracial people at UC Berkeley in the 1970s, it was designed as a seminar. Each year, the enrollment increased due to its extraordinary popularity. In 1990, when 480 students showed up, Dr. Wilson changed it to a lecture course, which now takes in about 250 students. In Fall 1994, when Cynthia Nakashima taught this course, she had five teaching assistants—all of whom were mixed-race women of various blends doing groundbreaking multiracial research from a variety of disciplines.

Ethnic studies has functioned as an ideal intellectual environment for the discourse on multiraciality due to its interdisciplinary approach. Ethnic studies' lack of disciplinary borders is compatible with the examination of multiracial individuals—by definition, a group that crosses many sociopolitical boundaries. The deconstructionist and post-modern leanings among ethnic studies scholars have also been methodologically and theoretically useful for questioning cultural constructions and presumptions of social boundaries as they relate to multiracial peoples. For example, with tremendous support from UCLA's Asian American Studies Reading Room coordinator, Marjie Lee, Steven Masami Ropp, an active member of Hapa Issues Forum and a UCLA graduate student, has spearheaded the compilation of an extensive, multidisciplinary, selected bibliography project on Asian descent multiracials, *Prism Lives, Emerging Voices*. Ropp has designed this bibliographical project so it could "facilitate multiracial scholars to consider works from a multitude of academic fields, seek out broader level connections and constructs in terms of theory and structure, and to develop this growing field on multiracial identity and experience" (Ropp, Williams, & Rooks, 1995, p. 1).

In examining multiracial peoples' experiences and identity development, ethnic studies has also had its limitations and shortcomings. The administrative and pedagogical thrust in ethnic studies programs mirrors the dominant assimilationist, race-difference paradigms—even when these programs harshly criticize the paradigms and take into account power relations between racial minority groups and the superordinate Euro American group. It is no surprise that much of the emphasis on intergroup relations in ethnic studies' research and teaching therefore has been on minority-majority relations. Ethnic studies programs are often designed to examine their own group or intraracial and panethnic dynamics in relationship to the superordinate Euro American group. The question of whose educational needs ethnic studies should meet is debated in terms of how it would be beneficial to the students of that program's specific racial, ethnic affiliation or to Euro Americans. We might want to ask why it is never assumed or expected that African American students should take Asian American studies, that Asian/

Pacific Islander American students should take Chicano/Latino studies, that Native American students should take black studies, or that all students should take a class on multiracial populations, and so on.

The divisions among the various ethnic studies programs across university campuses (in which budget and planning, faculty hiring, and curricula and course offerings are directly involved) pose a major problem for understanding the social realities of groups that defy single racial and ethnic identifications. For example, when examining the histories, literary character analyses, or identity development of Afro-Asians or black Native Americans, should one implement a class on these groups from within black studies, Asian American studies, Chicano/Latino studies, or Native American studies? Ideally, courses on multiracial populations would be cross-listed in and offered from within all ethnic studies. However, at a time of budget cuts and freezes, when ethnic studies programs are often among the financially hardest hit, each program would rather protect and preserve courses dealing with topics specifically about its own group, understandably. Thus the challenges that often face the multiracial individual in a zero-sum, either-or society also confront students and faculty trying to foster a multiracial consciousness in an either-or ethnic studies setup, coupled with the competition for seemingly ever-dwindling resources.

For now, the ethnic studies avenues open to scholars interested in teaching and doing research on multiracial identity are as follows:

1. To work with supportive ethnic studies faculty and implement courses on multiracial peoples within specific ethnic studies programs and departments, such as the courses on multiracial people taught at UC Berkeley and UC Santa Barbara;
2. To incorporate topics of interracial marriage and multiracial peoples into general ethnic studies courses already offered; and
3. To bridge and coalesce the all-too-often socially and politically disjointed ethnic studies programs by offering courses on interracial relationships and multiracial populations that are cross-listed, such as the courses on multiracial identity taught by Dr. G. Reginald Daniel at UCLA through the center for both Latin American and Afro-American studies and funded by the Counsel on Educational Development, or Dr. Vicki Mays's course on interracial relationships at UCLA, cross-listed in psychology and Afro-American studies.

When the critical mass of multiracial students, staff, and faculty grows in numbers and departmental influence and administrative clout, a "multiracial/multiethnic studies" department may not be unimaginable.

METHODS OF TEACHING
BIRACIALITY AND MULTIRACIALITY

There are two ways in which the study of multiracial populations has been introduced and integrated into college and university courses. The first is to include this topic in the general courses on race and ethnicity, such as Asian American history, comparative race relations, African American women's experience, introduction to Chicano studies, contemporary Native American and Euro American relations, Chicana/ Latina literature, cross-cultural psychology, cultural anthropology, methods classes, and so on. Dr. G. Reginald Daniel, who has taught, "Betwixt and Between: Multiracial Identity in Global Perspective and Close Encounters: Racial and Cultural Blending in the Americas" at UCLA has said,

> Ideally the topic on multiracial identity not only should be dealt with in courses dealing specifically with the topic in order to give students a more detailed and in-depth analysis, but also should be incorporated into general courses on race and ethnicity. My fundamental goal is to provide all students with an examination of the multiracial experience in the larger world arena in order to facilitate an understanding of the complex issues surrounding the newly emerging multiracial consciousness in the United States. By so doing, I feel it may be possible to define ways of nurturing this consciousness in manner [sic] that could help move race relations toward a broader basis of cooperation and collaboration. (Daniel & Collins, 1994, p. 2)

Kevin Yoshida, a biracial Euro American and Japanese American student, was pleasantly surprised when he took the general sociological survey course on race and ethnic relations at Santa Monica College in Spring 1992. This course included readings from *Racially Mixed People in America* (Root, 1992b) throughout the semester, along with other general race relations texts and a specific discussion on intermarriage and multiracial identity the last 2 weeks of the course. After taking this course, Yoshida, (personal communication, 1992) remarked,

This was one of the only courses I've taken in college that has allowed me to connect my multiple identities and understand my humanity in its fullness. I am biracial Japanese American and white; I am fluently bilingual in English and Spanish. I am a gay man of color. I am a multiracial, international person. I am many things simultaneously. This course legimitized who I am and how I live.

Leslie Hunter, a binational, biracial woman of African American and Honduran ancestries, took the same general sociology course on race and ethnic relations at Santa Monica College 2 years later in Spring 1994. For a group project assignment, Hunter volunteered to work on the topic of black-Latino conflict in Los Angeles. During the week that multiracial identity was covered, Hunter generously and openly shared her personal experiences with the class. Although she often felt each of her parent groups treated her as the *other*, she articulated that being both African American and Latina—at times simultaneously and at other times situationally—best described who she is. Until Hunter mentioned her African ancestry, most students in the class simply assumed she was Latina.

The voices and faces of students like Yoshida and Hunter directly contest faulty notions people have about how biracial people should look, act, and be named. Personal testimonies like those articulated by Yoshida and Hunter in class and in their writings bring to life the theoretical models that seem abstract to most students and show how teaching about multiraciality can have personally transformative experiences for multiracial students and the students they encounter in the classrooms.

Scholars such as Dr. Sucheng Chan (UC Santa Barbara), Dr. Jere Takahashi (UC Berkeley), Dr. Ronald Takaki (UC Berkeley), Dr. Robert Blauner (UC Berkeley), Dr. Melinda Micco (Mills College), Dr. Darrell Darrisaw (Carleton College, Minnesota), Dr. Amy Mass (Whittier College, California), Dr. Maria Root (University of Washington), Dr. Christine Hall (University of Arizona), Dr. Paul Spickard (Brigham Young University-Hawai'i), and others have used guest lecturers and panels of speakers and included readings on multiracial individuals in one or two class sessions of the course as a method of integrating this subject matter into their courses. Other scholars, including Root, Hall, Mass, and Spickard, as well as Dr. Jack Forbes (UC Davis), Dr. Gerald Vizenor (UC Berkeley,

UC Santa Cruz) and Caroline Streeter (Stanford) have also taught specific courses on multiracial peoples and/or have woven the discussion of multiraciality throughout their general courses as well.

A far more challenging and ideal way to include multiraciality on a regular basis is the total incorporation of racially mixed people into the curriculum. Cynthia Nakashima includes mixed-race issues throughout her introduction to Asian American history course at UC Berkeley. For example, Nakashima begins by looking at early intermarriage rates and interracial families in the context of Asian male labor immigration (i.e., the Chinese, Filipinos, and South Asian Indians) and European American hostility. The gender imbalance caused by the restriction of Asian female immigration may explain why out-marriage frequently occurred among some Asian men in the United States and not others (e.g., Chinese men and Native Hawaiian women in Hawai'i; Chinese men and African American women in the American South; Filipino men and Euro American and Mexican women in the West Coast; South Asian Indian men and Mexican women in California, Chinese and Japanese men with Euro American women on the East Coast, etc.). Nakashima also examines the dominant racial ideology and the corresponding laws regarding miscegenation between Euro Americans and Asians as an important and telling aspect of the viewing of Asians as racial *others* in the United States. Ethnicity, gender, geographical location, and class are accounted for when Nakashima interrogates the intermarriage patterns of early Asian immigrants and Asian Americans in the United States (Gulick, 1914; Leonard, 1992; Posadas, 1989; Spickard, 1989). She also discusses the impact of antimiscegenation laws on the numbers and racial combinations of intermarriages and points out that a sizable number of second-generation Asian Americans may have been mixed race because there were so few Asian women at the time.

World War II has had a significant impact on the lives of Asian Americans (Chan, 1991). Nakashima also lectures on how World War II was important for interracially married couples and for multiracial, Asian-descent Americans as well because:

1. Racial ideology had begun to turn away from biological determinism and away from hybrid degeneracy.
2. Internment of Japanese Americans tested the line between Asian and European American; interracially married families were interned, al-

though gender and race of the parents qualitatively altered the life experiences of internees.

3. World War II and U.S. military dominance in Asia created the "war bride" and Amerasian phenomena.
4. U.S. military presence in Hawai'i also brought Asian Americans in Hawai'i together with servicemen of various racial and ethnic ancestries.

Following World War II, the structural and demographic changes in the United States also affected interracial families and Asian-descent multiracials. During the 1960s civil rights and racial/ethnic power movements, the last of the antimiscegenation laws were struck down, and the biracial baby boom began. Post-1965 issues are around mail-order brides, sex tours, the homecoming act for Vietnamese Amerasians, and the withdrawal of U.S. bases in the Philippines leave thousands of Pilipino Amerasians behind. Nakashima's approach to integrating mixed-race issues throughout general ethnic studies can also be adapted to including discussions on women of color and gays, lesbians, and bisexuals of color in these courses.

Finally, one could design and organize a complete course on multiracial identity in which an interdisciplinary ethnic studies approach is taken, such as the courses taught by Dr. Jack Forbes (UC Davis), Dr. Terry Wilson (UC Berkeley), Dr. G. Reginald Daniel (UCLA), Teresa Kay Williams (UC Santa Barbara), Cynthia Nakashima (UC Berkeley), Dr. Melinda Micco (Mills College) or a more single-discipline course on this subject matter, such as the courses taught by Dr. Gerald Vizenor in literature (UC Berkeley), Teresa Kay Williams in sociology (UCLA), and Dr. George Kitahara Kich in graduate level cross-cultural psychology. These courses have a profound impact on both monoracially identified and biracial and multiracial students. Having entire courses on this subject matter give academic legitimacy to multiracial peoples by locating their identities into the structure of knowledge. They teach students that the realities of multiracial groups illuminate the salience of race and ethnic relations in an ever-transforming world community and give them analytical tools to question, challenge, and transgress take-for-granted, normalized assumptions upon which this salience rests.

Multiracial students have become accustomed to not having their identities and realities affirmed in academic disciplines. "Learning about one's culture" or "finding one's roots" is often done through monoracial exploration of one heritage over another. Natasha Hansen, a first-year graduate student, expressed her amazement when she stumbled across a course on multiracial identity offered by UCLA's sociology department in Fall 1994. Hansen explained,

> Frantically searching for a third course to take in the schedule of classes, I was pleasantly surprised to come upon a course titled, "Within, Between, and Beyond Race: Racially Mixed People in the U.S." Actually, I was not pleasantly surprised, I was shocked. Because I am a black and white biracial woman, I have become accustomed to being socially located on the margins. This being the case, being able to take a class that focuses on and centralizes my plural racial identity seemed unbelievable.

Treacy White, a biracial Japanese Euro American woman described her reactions upon taking a course on multiracial people of Asian descent at UC Santa Barbara in Spring 1992, when the first course on this topic was offered. She has written in her first journal assignment,

> I don't know where to begin! Should I begin with how excited I am about this class? Should I begin with asking myself who I am? Or should I begin with my own experiences as being biracial and Amerasian? No. I think I will begin with my reactions to all the things I've learned from Maria P. P. Root's [1992b] book thus far.
>
> I have to admit that as I opened this book I found myself getting excited. Never have I read any literature about people like myself. It feels good to know that my kind of racial background has been acknowledged and has actually spurred interest in people. As I read chapter one I was actually nodding my head in agreement with what Root was saying. Being half Japanese and half white, I have always had qualms about committing myself to one or the other culture. I don't think I am Asian enough to say I am Asian American and I am not completely white so I can't say that I am. So what am I? I do not want to divide myself. I don't want separate what makes me a complete person, but society seems to allow me only to be one or the other. Now it seems that some people are finally saying I don't have to deny part of my heritage.

Lee Corbett, a Korean American man adopted into a Euro American family, became an outspoken campus activist after taking a class on the multiracial identity of Asian-descent Americans at UC Santa Barbara. He is one of the several founding members of UC Santa Barbara's multiracial organization, Variations, which grew out of the political

quest of the students who took this course. In a personal letter he wrote
to the instructor years later, Corbett reflected,

> That was the first class that presented models that captured the struggles
> I went through as a multiethnic, Asian American man adopted into a
> European American family. Your class has been invaluable for my own
> personal and intellectual growth.

Examining the racial and cultural multiplicity embodied by multiracial
individuals permits many monoracially identified students to make
connections with their multiple realities. Que Dang, a UC Santa Barbara
graduate, had taken a course on multiracial people of Asian descent as
an elective for her Asian American studies' major in Spring 1993. Dang
explained what she had gained from taking this course:

> That was the only Asian American Studies class I took in which I was not
> part of the numerical majority. Most of the students were biracial, but at
> the same time, I could relate to the racial and cultural duality of biracial
> people because I was born in Vietnam and came to the U.S. at the age of
> two and being a refugee in a country that thinks of itself as an immigrant
> nation. I have also dealt with the bicultural struggles of being Vietnamese
> and being American within my family. At the time I took the class, I was
> dating someone African American. Our visual, phenotypical differences
> were an issue for the people around me perhaps more so than when I've
> dated European American men. I saw the class as pertaining to my
> prospective children. I'll most likely marry someone who is not Vietnam-
> ese so the class gave me insight on what I may expect when I marry and
> have children.

Euro-American students who can move beyond the notion of "studying
other people's fascinating cultures" can also participate in a liberating
educational process that transgresses the invisible power dynamics
between themselves and students of color in the classroom. Myra
Mayesh has taken the general sociology course, "Race and Ethnic
Relations," at Santa Monica College in which multiracial identity models were treated as central to understanding intergroup dynamics. After
taking this course, Mayesh recognized how she too could understand
her many selves in relationship to her racial status in American society.
Mayesh has explained,

This course has been one of the most enriching experiences, yet one of the most academically challenging courses I've taken . . . As a European American woman, I have only had to see my gender in relationship to my sexual orientation and perhaps socioeconomic status. Not only has this course challenged me to look at my racial status, gender, sexual orientation, and class in relationship to one another, but by looking at multiple racial realities as both black and white—rather than black or white—it provides a model for my other dualities.

As these students' statements illuminate, there are benefits to being an "insider majority group member"; one possesses the shared values, assumptions, and even similar physical appearances with the majority of the class, including the instructor. Being an insider majority group member gives students the sense that they are part of a larger collective.

Students of color who take ethnic studies courses often express how comfortable it is sitting in a classroom filled with co-ethnics and taking courses taught by professors of color, who speak their same consciousness. Although the disadvantages are numerous and perhaps obvious (e.g., alienation, exclusion, invisiblity, etc.), there are also advantages to being an "outsider minority group," a racially and culturally marginalized member in the classroom setting. Students of color, multiracial students, female students, gays, lesbians, and bisexual students are accustomed to sitting on the sidelines in terms of class participation, course materials, texts, and so on. Euro American students, who often experience being an outsider minority group member when they take ethnic studies classes, learn for the first time what it is like when your group is not addressed by the course materials or, when covered, is not always portrayed in an accurate or flattering way. Euro American students hear some students of color angrily refer to them as "whites" and "white people" as they experience their individuality dismissed and humanity objectified. Euro American students learn what it feels like to be marginalized in text and in physical presence within this artificial setting of the classroom.

Being forced to occupy an outsider minority group position allows students to see themselves in relationship to the contextual majority group whose human existence, perspective, and worldview are validated at the expense of theirs. Multiracial students often experience being insiders and outsiders simultaneously in these settings, where fellow classmates and instructors alike have no clue as to what being biracial and multiracial entails.

In *Teaching to Transgress*, bell hooks (1994) explains how teaching and learning can be transformative acts, restoring for us the vision of education as a form of liberation. The classroom must been seen as an important revolutionary site, where critical thinking can and must be nurtured. hooks stated this powerfully:

> The classroom with all its limitations remains the location of possibility. In that field of possibility we have the opportunity to labor for freedom, to demand of ourselves and our comrades an openness of mind and heart that allows us to face reality even as we collectively imagine ways to move beyond boundaries, to transgress. This is education as the practice of freedom. (p. 231)

As attacks are waged on affirmative action programs and multiculturally focused curricula with accusations that "politically correct cops" are "closing the American mind" (Bloom, 1987; D'Souza, 1991), universities are in desperate need of more courses that provide safe spaces for healing, understanding, and compassion among monoracially identified students of color, monoracially identified Euro Americans, and multiracial students of various sexual orientations, socioeconomic statuses, and physical abilities. The new and exciting emergent field of multiracial studies has the potential to fulfill the promise of education that transgresses boundaries, that inspires critical thinking, that dismantles hierarchies, that moves and transforms the world.

CONCLUSION

The university has traditionally been an exclusive location, as the ivory tower metaphor implies, where knowledge has been produced and transmitted. All members of the society take part in creating knowledge, but only those with MAs and PhDs next to their names are credited with this task, thereby excluding the nonformally trained from the material rewards of producing and transmitting knowledge. It is through our conscious efforts as students, professors, and activists to continue the inclusion and incorporation of all members of our society into the production of knowledge and to connect what is studied in our classrooms to the everyday lives of our students that we can reclaim a university from which all can benefit, not just an exclusive group of well-trained professionals. The study of multiracial populations through multidisciplinary research methods and rigorous analytical thinking provides us with insight into the social realities of individuals who live along and across ever-expanding borders.

In addition to immigration, economic restructuring, and increased structural intergroup contact at primary and secondary levels of inter-action, multiracial populations are contributing to the much-debated demographic changes in the United States. Multiracial people should not simply be seen as mere interracial and intercultural ambassadors put on this earth to bridge the gaps between and across groups because this view absolves the monoracially identified populations from their responsibilities of cooperation and coalition building. Rather, we should be asking how biracial and multiracial peoples process their personal and social selves in a variety of contexts; how they gain entry into and negotiate membership into various groups; how they are perceived and treated by subordinate and superordinate groups; and under what conditions newly recognized identities are mounted and sustained. What do these boundary-defying populations tell us about how boundaries are constructed, maintained, violated, and deconstructed? How do the studies of biracial and multiracial identities fit into the structure of knowledge?

Students who have been asking these questions have been at the forefront challenging the increasingly volatile racial climates on college campuses. In order to network with other biracial and multiracial students who are navigating the uncharted waters of this new multira-cial consciousness, students at Kansas State, Harvard, Yale, Brown, Stanford, New York, Michigan, University of Southern California, UC Berkeley, UC Santa Cruz, UC Irvine, UC Santa Barbara, and other campuses have formed multiracial student associations. Some biracial students in these multiracial organizations have also jointly retained mem-bership in traditional racial and ethnic student organizations (Black Stu-dent Union, Asian Pacific Coalition, MECHA, American Indian Students Association, etc.).

These organizations, along with courses on multiracial topics, are crucial to the social and political institutionalization of an identity that would otherwise remain individually based. Multiracial identity has

been seen as temporary and transitional—a stage in development before people either become an appendage to the subordinate racial group
through social customs and hypodescent laws or become part of the
superordinate group through straight-line assimilation into the core
society. The emergence of university courses and student organizations
by, for, and about biracial and multiracial people strongly indicates that
this identity deserves social and academic legitimacy and institutional
sustenance. What multiracial studies in higher education can offer is the
abolition of hierarchies and transgression of boundaries that separate
us from the totality of our humanity and divide us from one another.

23

Multicultural Education

FRANCIS WARDLE

I first became interested in multicultural issues for biracial children when my oldest child, then 4, returned from an argument with a little boy whose family had just come from Mexico. She was frustrated because he told her, in a very negative way, that she was black, and he was not. "How can he say that, when he's darker than me?" she wanted to know.

But the foundation of my interest in multicultural education was set by my family and the Bruderhof communities in which I was raised. Later in high school, I created my own multicultural reading program by studying books about Althea Gibson, Paul Robeson, and Dick Gregory. In college I continued my interest by enjoying the music of (and playing on the college radio station) the great black singers Paul Robeson, Marion Anderson, and Roland Hayes.

In 1976 I traveled with an earthquake relief group to the highlands of Guatemala. I worked and lived with the Mayan people and with the international members of the relief group. Some years later, I joined the dance group Fiesta Mexicana in Kansas City, Kansas, and performed at local festivals and fiestas.

But clearly the strongest influence on my study of multicultural issues has been my wife, a strong, independent woman who has set her own goals and defined her own success. &

Recently, the educational magazines, *Instructor, Sesame Street Parents, Scholastic Early Childhood Today,* and *Learning* included articles on multicultural education.[1] The *Learning* article even included a pie chart showing the percentage of each ethnic group in major U.S. cities. None of these articles acknowledged the existence of biracial children (Wardle, 1994d). Ramirez and Ramirez's (1994) book, *Multiethnic Children's Literature,* totally omits any books about multiracial people, interracial families, and biracial children; *Valuing Diversity* (McCracken, 1993), *Anti-Bias Curriculum* (Derman-Sparks, 1989), and *Multicultural Education in a Pluralistic Society* (Gollnick & Chinn, 1994) provide no discussion and support of our population; and *Roots and Wings* (York, 1991) includes an activity that requires all children to select a traditional reference group for their ethnic identity, thus forcing biracial children to choose the identity of one parent and reject the identity of the other.

TV's Sesame Street Race Project, which is passionately and justly committed to supporting the racial and ethnic identity of minority children, does not include biracial children in the program because, according to Dr. Lovelace, it would be just too difficult to do (Wardle, 1994d).

It is curious that books and programs so dedicated to celebrating the diverse heritage of this country, and teaching about the struggles of people to define their rights and freedoms, totally ignores the rich history of mixed-race people. It seems logical that these writers and educators would be highly sensitive to the issues surrounding people of mixed racial and ethnic heritage. Clearly, the omission of biracial and multiracial people in traditional multicultural curricula is a deliberate attempt to highlight the history and struggles of single racial groups while perpetuating the notion of the abnormality of multiracial people. Multiculturalists are more concerned with preserving the racial politics of this country than meeting the needs of all our children—especially biracial and multiracial children.

TRADITIONAL MULTICULTURAL MODELS

Traditional multicultural models view multicultural education as a process whose major aims are to help students of diverse cultural,

ethnic, gender, and social class groups attain equal educational opportunities. Furthermore, multicultural education as traditionally defined
aspires to help all students develop positive cross-cultural attitudes,
perceptions, and behaviors (Banks & Banks, 1989).

> Multicultural education is the educational strategy in which students'
> cultural backgrounds are used to develop effective classroom instruction
> and school environments. It is designed to support and extend the con-
> cepts of culture, cultural pluralism, and equality into the formal school
> setting. (Gollnick & Chinn, 1994, p. 3)

These traditional models of multicultural education view the child
as the product of culture. Culture forms the prism through which
members of a group see the world, create shared meaning, think, feel,
and behave (Bowman, 1989; Gollnick & Chinn, 1994). Because culture
in America is synonymous with race (Wilson, 1984), children are then
viewed as the product of the culture of their ethnic community: African
American, Native American, Asian, Hispanic, or European (Derman-
Sparks, 1989; McCracken, 1993; Wilson, 1984; York, 1991). Individual
identity and positive self-esteem are based on pride in one's cultural
group's history, achievements, solidarity, and loyalty (Derman-Sparks,
1989; Matiella, 1991; McCracken, 1993; U.S. Department of Human Services, 1991). Variability within racial groups is minimized or totally ignored.

Conventional models for multicultural education require teachers to
expose children to the five traditional cultural groups' values, celebra-
tions, histories, traditions, and art forms. It enables teachers to help each
child connect with his or her heritage, and to feel positive about the group to
whom he or she belongs. Multicultural curricula then provide books and
other materials to reflect each of these groups (Ramirez & Ramirez, 1994).

A NEED FOR A NEW APPROACH

The conventional model for multicultural education does not allow
us to support the history, identity, and healthy development of biracial
children. By dividing our country's population into five traditional
groups, we always force biracial children to reject a significant part of
their heritage (Bowles, 1993). Furthermore, most multicultural publications create the false dichotomy of white people in one camp and people

of color in the other. Again, this artificial battlefield places the biracial child in a position of conflicting loyalties and psychological stress (Bowles, 1993; Wardle, 1992). Another problem with the traditional model is that it is incorrect and misleading to teach students that this country is comprised of five distinctly different, unified, homogeneous groups. Where does the Guatemalan Mayan Indian who is a recent immigrant to this country fit in? What about the historical and bitter conflict between the Koreans and Japanese? We should just place them both in the Asian American group? Clearly, the conventional multicultural model is not authentically multicultural (Wardle, 1994a). Also, a model that continues to stress single racial and cultural groups, and how people are different from each other, is destructive to all children, because children need to learn how to live and work together and because research suggests activities that stress differences cause conflict (Lewit & Baker, 1994; Powlishta, Serbin, Doyle, & White, 1994; Spencer & Markstrom-Adams, 1990).

An example of the real problems the conventional model creates for biracial children occurred recently in Denver. The biracial son of one of my friends was requested by his teacher to bring to school a photograph and information about a grandparent. This activity was part of the school's Black History Month curriculum. The child brought to school material about his white/Caribbean Indian grandfather—a prominent citizen in his day, and a person of whom the child was justly very proud. The teacher rejected the child's contribution to the class.

We must change the way we look at people in this country (Brandt, 1994). Rather than place people in sociopolitical groups (to the pleasure of sociologists, demographers, politicians, and traditional multiculturalists), we must view each person as an individual affected by a variety of influences, including, but not limited to, race, ethnicity, and family. Thus a true multicultural curriculum must respond to, reflect, and support the unique set of experiences every child brings to our programs (Wardle, 1994a).

MULTICULTURAL CURRICULA
MUST SUPPORT BIRACIAL CHILDREN

Why is it essential that multicultural education include biracial children? Many researchers have demonstrated the need for minority children to have a clear sense of racial or ethnic identity to develop a strong self-image (Jacobs, 1977; McRoy & Freeman, 1986; Phinney & Rotheram, 1987; Ruiz, 1990). Race and ethnicity are ambiguous, sociopolitical concepts that have no scientific or biological base (Spencer & Markstrom-Adams, 1990), and we need ultimately to eliminate racial classifications entirely (*Federal Register,* June 9, 1994, pp. 59, 110). However, minority children still do require educational programs designed specifically to support their healthy development. Biracial children must be included in this approach because they are both minorities and children whose full identity has, and is, often denied. Biracial children's needs are clearly different from those of white children or other minority children (Brandell, 1988; Gibbs, 1987; Jacobs, 1977; McRoy & Freeman, 1986; Wardle, 1987, 1988). Thus a multicultural curriculum must respond to the unique needs of these children.

Many authors and researchers suggest the most effective way for all minority children to succeed in this society is for them to develop a truly bicultural or multicultural competence (Banks, as quoted in Brandt, 1994; Cross, 1985, 1987, 1991; Gollnick & Chinn, 1994; Jones, 1985; Spencer, 1984). Biracial children provide a natural and obvious model for this approach. A multicultural education model should capitalize on the strengths of these children. Furthermore, the work of Spencer and Cross demonstrates that the best way to develop the strong identity of all minority children, including biracial children, is to provide positive individual experiences that develop sound personal identity, along with reference group orientation (Cross, 1985, 1987, 1991; Spencer, 1984).

By omitting our children in current multicultural curricula, it is easier for schools and other institutions to move toward ethnic and racial segregation (ethnocentric curricula, opposition to transracial adoption by the National Association of Black Social Workers and many professionals, popularity of the Nation of Islam spokespeople, etc.) (Benjamin-Wardle, 1994a; Hollis, 1993; Wardle, 1994c). This is not only unhealthy for our society in general, but it is very detrimental for biracial children. It requires them to select a single racial/ethnic identity group, reinforcing one of the worst myths in our society (Benjamin-Wardle, 1991; Jacobs, 1977; Wardle, 1992). This myth states that for biracial children to develop into healthy, secure individuals, they must be raised with the identity of one of their parents, preferably the parent of color. If they are not raised in this way, they will become confused, messed up, and dysfunctional (Bowles, 1993; Brandell, 1988).

Biracial children challenge the assumption that races must be kept separate. They also show that interracial marriage can be successful and that racial differences in this country are not as extreme as many portray them.

SUPPORTING BIRACIAL
IDENTITY DEVELOPMENT

This chapter takes the position that the best way to raise healthy, mature, happy biracial children is to raise them with a pride and acceptance of their total heritage.

> While issues have up until now mandated that biracial children be viewed as black, this stance has not taken note of the psychological meaning of disowning part of oneself. The resulting confusion and identity crisis this poses for biracial children can no longer be put on hold. (Bowles, 1993, p. 427)

For biracial children to grow up with a healthy and secure identity, all aspects of their genetic heritage and ecological environment must be supported (Wardle, 1987, 1988, 1993b).

However, this affirmative position is contrary to much of society, and to almost all professionals—especially social workers and psychologists (Bowles, 1993; Melina, 1990; Powell, 1988). Thus part of a multicultural curriculum that includes biracial children must also provide information, support, and resources to help interracial families deal with this societal conflict about how to raise their children. Even if interracial families choose to raise their children with a single identity (a black-white child as black, a part Native American child as Native American), children must be taught about their full genetic and cultural heritage. Children need this information because mature mental health is dependent on accurate self-knowledge. Biracial children also need a strong ego and techniques to defend themselves, because single-race children harass biracial children by questioning their ethnic and racial purity and loyalty.

The future of the interracial movement is dependent on adults whose childhoods include rich, supportive, positive biracial experiences. Efforts toward a multiracial category (Graham, Chapter 3, this volume), national and local interracial organizations (Brown & Douglass, Chapter 20, this volume), and all the books in the world will go for naught if we do not raise secure, independent, multiracial adults who can withstand the societal, political, and academic need of this society to insistently separate people into exclusive sociopolitical groups.

More and more biracial children are being raised with a solid biracial identity (Benjamin-Wardle, 1991; Brandell, 1988; McRoy & Freeman, 1986; Wardle, 1987) and view themselves as biracial or multiracial (Benjamin-Wardle, 1991; Erkut, Fields, Almeida, Deleon, & Sing, 1993). Are we, in our curricula that claim to support diversity and the accurate identity of every one of our children, going to ignore the biracial student's own self-identity?

SUPPORTING BIRACIAL CHILDREN
IN A MULTICULTURAL CURRICULUM

How should the history of multiracial people, including persecution and denial, and the current set of experiences of the biracial child be covered in a multicultural curriculum? Developmentally appropriate considerations (Bredekamp, 1987) are particularly important to multicultural curricula, because it is so easy to provide a tourist approach (Derman-Sparks, 1989) that trivializes culture and actually teaches stereotypes. Young children are very aware of physical differences and are beginning to learn societal biases based on skin color. However, they do not understand the politics of race until adolescence. Thus multicultural education must match information, ideas, and concepts to the developmental needs of children, from early childhood to college (Wardle, 1987).

Multicultural education that recognizes and supports biracial children is based on two basic assumptions. The first is that biracial children have the inalienable right to their true identity. They need their entire heritage to be recognized and supported. And they need to be viewed as normal, well-adjusted individuals. Second, schools and professionals have an obligation to support, nurture, and celebrate biracial children, their families, and history. The program must support the heritage of both sides of a child's background (Wardle, 1987). And the program needs to provide experiences and processes that enable biracial children to develop strong individual identities (Brandell, 1988; Erikson, 1963; Wardle, 1989).

WHAT A MULTICULTURAL CURRICULUM MUST INCLUDE

Central to a multicultural curriculum must be the acknowledgment that America's and the world's people are not divided into exclusive cultural boxes; that there is far more variability within groups than between them (Wardle, 1992). The goals of a multicultural curriculum that includes biracial children should (a) support and celebrate each child's total heritage, (b) enable all children to be comfortable and successful around a vast range of diversity, and (c) enable teachers to maximize their effectiveness with each child (Wardle, 1994b). The specifics of this curriculum are listed below.

Correct Inaccurate History

- Cover the history of biracial/multiracial people in this country (Spickard, 1989).
- Cover the history of biracial/multiracial people in the world (Winn, 1994).
- Read books that discuss various aspects of this issue (Frederic Douglass' autobiography; James Earl Jones's autobiography, etc.).
- Explore the evolution of racial categories on census, medical, and government forms (Lewit & Baker, 1994).
- Expose students to the rich history of people overcoming all sorts of differences to marry and successfully raise a family (national origin, language, income, social status, religion, and race).

Explore Racism Against Biracial People

- Expose all students to the history of racism against multiracial people.
- Regard as racial harassment any student, teacher, or visiting speaker who advocates against a biracial student's right to self-determination and/or against celebrating both parents' heritages.

This harassment appears in a variety of innocuous forms. Many discussions about interracial marriage strongly suggest people select mates from outside of their group for ulterior, dishonorable reasons (even the term *out-marriage* implies rebellion and nonconformity). It is popular today to discuss racial pride and solidarity by claiming those who marry outside their group, and biracial children who claim both sides of their heritage, are disloyal, confused, and lack racial pride. It is also popular and acceptable to accuse biracial children, and interracial parents who raise their children as proudly biracial, of being ashamed of their minority heritage.

- Explore the politics behind the strong opposition by minority groups, many professionals, and adoption agencies toward transracial adoption (Benjamin-Wardle, 1994c; McRoy & Hall, Chapter 5, this volume).
- Explore the politics behind the strong opposition by minority groups, many minority professionals, and adoption agencies toward raising biracial children with a proud biracial identity (Bowles, 1993; Melina, 1990; Powell, 1988).
- Examine why we have five broad ethnic and racial categories, themselves quite ad hoc and arbitrary, and how they have developed their own constituencies, lobbies, and vested interests (Editorial, *San Jose Mercury News*, August, 17, 1994, p. 11b).
- Explore the politics and pressure groups behind the strong opposition to a multiracial category (Graham, Chapter 3, this volume).

Explore the Problems of Single-Race Groups

- Explore the need for humans to select exclusive groups based on arbitrary criteria; explore different ways people create exclusive groups; examine the power of those people who belong to groups, as opposed to those kept out.
- Study historical and current conflicts between racial groups that illustrate the dangers of breaking people into racial/ethnic camps.
- Discourage school/college groups that are defined exclusively by race (Benjamin-Wardle, 1994a); examine positive and inclusive methods for students to both develop a sense of ethnic and racial pride and to communicate that secure identity to others.
- Study the sameness of people across groups, and the variability within groups.

Support the Biracial Child's Self-Esteem

- Expose all students to multiracial heroes, such as Alexander Dumas, Maria Talchief, Frederic Douglass, James Audubon, and Betty Okino (Benjamin-Wardle, 1992; Wardle, 1993a).

- Provide students with visual images of multiracial people, interracial families, and biracial children.
- Cover the current status of multiracial people throughout the world (Mestizo, Creoles, Hawaiians, Brazilians) (Winn, 1994).
- Provide a vast range of positive activities that allow biracial students to explore their entire heritage and total personality (Jacobs, 1977; Wardle, 1987, 1989).
- Explore how biracial children in white homes can achieve a strong racial identity and attachment with their white parents (remember, biracial children with one white biological parent have some genetic and cultural heritage similar to their white parent).
- Empower biracial children to view themselves as possessing the ability to choose groups they wish to belong to, and, in some circumstances, to bridge the gulf between racial groups (Wardle, 1994c).

   Biracial students need tools to assist them in bridging this gap, just as they need tools in defending themselves against insensitive teachers, social workers, psychologists, and peers (Wardle, 1991a).
- Help students develop a strong personal identity without having to put down other groups, to join exclusive, race-defined organizations, or to develop a them-versus-us mentality.

Explore All Forms of Diversity

- Use a range of disciplines, for example, art and biology, to show how mixing colors, genetics, and so on is a natural, positive, dynamic process (Wardle, 1991b).

   The notion of purity (in these cases 100% pure-bred animals and primary colors) is very limiting. Pure-bred animals are highly subject to disease, and limiting artistic activities to primary colors reduces almost all creativity.
- Give historical examples of powerful groups that were defined around ideas, visions, art forms, and politics, rather than by race (the Fabian Society, Impressionists, early 20th century art and classical music movements, etc.).
- Provide resources for the student (*New People, Interrace, Interracial Voice*, conferences, a list of local advocacy groups, adoption agencies that support transracial adoption, The Center for the Study of Biracial Children, A Place for Us Ministry, etc.).
- Encourage other forms of diversity in education, such as providing full bilingual instruction, starting at preschool (Benjamin-Wardle, 1994b; Wardle, 1993c).

- Explore the concept that, in a free society, people have the right to marry whom they choose, and raise their children as they choose, without criticism and harassment from others.

Provide Antibias Activities

- Provide antibias activities to enable students to engage in practices that make their schools and colleges better places for biracial and multiracial students (Banks & Banks, 1989; Derman-Sparks, 1989; Gollnick & Chinn, 1994; Wardle, 1994a).
  An antibias activity for school-age children could be to persuade their school district to eliminate the federal forms that require biracial children to choose the heritage of one parent and deny that of their other parent; or to adopt a form that includes a category for all children (but not an *other* category). Another approach might be for students to request the elimination of race/ethnic-specific student groups in their schools and colleges (Benjamin-Wardle, 1994a).

Provide an Inclusive Multicultural Curriculum

- Provide activities and content that stress how this country is made up of diverse peoples with rich and compelling histories, and that its future success is dependent on these peoples working together productively; stress the societal need to help people work together for the common good, and for multiracial people to fit comfortably within the overall demographic mix (Wardle, 1994a).

Closely Examine Language Used to Study and Discuss Biracial Children

- Carefully select words that support the normalcy and dignity of a biracial identity.
  Maladjustment, cultural margins, hidden agendas, ambiguity, racial conflict, identity dilemma, and marginality, are all commonly used words in discussing biracial children. They reinforce the negative images and myths many people have about biracial children. For example, the phrase *identity dilemma* supports the popular and professional notion that all biracial children are terribly confused about their identity. Students should carefully explore how words are used to divide people and maintain societal boundaries.

- Closely examine words used to discuss interracial marriage.
    Out-marriage, disloyalty, miscegenation, and cultural loyalty all com-
    municate that interracial marriage is somehow unnatural and engaged in
    by people who lack a secure and healthy identity.
- Explore language that is accurate and positive and that enhances the
    healthy development of interracial families and biracial children.

CONCLUSION

Multicultural education is a critically important movement that influences students of all ages. It is essential that our programs support
each child, expose children to ideas and people who are different, and
correct some of the inaccuracies of history. In so doing, however, accurate depictions of people of mixed heritage must be included. And the
total ecological and genetic heritage of biracial children in our programs
must be fully and positively supported. If we refuse to include this
population we are dishonest and hypocritical. Further, continued omission of biracial children and multiracial people in our multicultural
programs casts doubt on our sincerity in meeting the needs of every
child we serve.

NOTE

1. The articles are as follows:
    "The Multiracial Connection," *Instructor Magazine, 103*(6), 37-54, published in
        February 1994
    Sesame Street Parents
    "Multicultural Holidays," *Scholastic Early Childhood Today, 9*(3), 44-52, published in
        November/December 1994
    "American Pie—A Multicultural Snapshot," *Learning '94, 22*(6), 29-36.
    Federal Register, June 9, 1994, pp. 59, 110.
    Editorial, *San Jose Mercury News,* August 17, 1994, p. 11b.

PART VI

The New
Millenium

24

2001

A Race Odyssey

CHRISTINE C. IIJIMA HALL

I began my odyssey/journey in the early 1970s because I wanted to understand multiracial people and share my findings with mental health professionals, parents, teachers, and other interracial individuals. I was unsure of the path I would follow to achieve this goal, but one of the routes was my dissertation. There had been a few "wanderers" before me so I had some direction. There were also others researching simultaneously, but I did not know of them because we were all taking different paths toward the same search for truth. Many of us have met up at different junctions at different times and new journeyers join the search every day, continuing (and beginning) at different points.

I am pleased to write this chapter for Dr. Root's new book. I read all the manuscripts for this book so I could write this final chapter. I was excited to see how far we have come in understanding ourselves as a group. I look forward to the new millennium of additional research, writings, political activism, and demographic changes in the United States and the world. ⚛

odyssey: an intellectual or spiritual wandering or quest
(*Merriam Webster's*
Collegiate Dictionary, 10th ed.)

An intellectual or spiritual voyage can begin with (quest) or without (wandering) a goal. Many times, the traveler has a goal but is unsure of the path and begins to wander, looking for a path (or paths) that may lead to the goal. History and research have shown that different individuals seek the same goal through various methods and paths. Similarly, the authors included in this current volume and others are on an intellectual or spiritual wandering/quest to understand and learn about a "new people" through varied paths. I will briefly review the past and recent work on multiracial people, then discuss where I think we will be heading in the new millennium.

THE FIRST JOURNEYS

The multifaceted aspect of interracial identity allows for journeys to begin from the psychological, sociological, anthropological, political, spiritual, medical, and other perspectives. It is important for all these paths to be explored. Thus research on interracial identity has emerged from many disciplines. The studies are not necessarily in conflict; they are all reality from different perspectives. It is hoped, however, that the investigators use the past interdisciplinary research/literature rather than beginning their journeys anew. The markings left by earlier travelers will accelerate their journey.

The journey to interracial identity and understanding began centuries ago (see Spickard, 1989, for an excellent historical review). The need to discover from where we came was the first part of the journey. Spickard (1989) outlined the immigration and fraternizing patterns of many ethnic groups in the United States. The contemporary history (after 1940) begins with information regarding interracial marriages, which included data on courtship and marriage, as well as the stability and frequency of marriages. Early research included work on interracial marriages by Walters (1953), Connor (1961), Gordon (1964), Monahan (1970), Stuart and Abt (1973), Tinker (1973), and Kikumura and Kitano (1973).

The history of lack of social support for mixed marriages is well documented in antimiscegenation laws and in other publications. The prevailing view of interracial marriages in the early research and literature was negative. In an effort to discourage miscegenation, potential partners were asked: What about the children? Subsequently, research, writings, and other forms of media focused only on the negative aspects of mixed race individuals; for examples, see *Imitation of Life* (Sirk & Stahl, 1934), *Pinky* (Zanuck & Kazan, 1949), and Teicher (1968). However, as mixed people came of age and as others became sensitive to the issue, another perspective began to emerge in the literature and research in the 1960s. Personal stories of interracial identity and experiences could be seen in novels such as *Passing* and *Quicksand* by Nella Larsen (1929/1986a, 1928/1986b) and in books that included personal accounts of interracial marriages and children, such as *Marriage Across the Color Line* (Larsson, 1965). Although some early psychological and sociological research existed (Park, 1937), most of this literature has emerged since the late 1970s (Chang, 1974; Dien & Vinacke, 1964; Hall, 1980; Kich, 1982; Moritsugu, Forester, & Morishima, 1978; Piskacek & Golub, 1973; Root, 1990; Strong, 1978; Thompson, 1967; Thornton, 1983; Wagatsuma, 1976).

Dissemination of the information uncovered by this research was difficult, however. Many scholars have reported that editors of professional journals, magazines, documentaries, and books felt the issue of multiracial individuals was not relevant enough for wide appeal (personal experience and conversations with Root, Kich, Thornton). Thus many dissertations and other research remained unpublished and unknown. In early 1990, Dr. Maria P. P. Root (1992b) brought the "mothers and fathers" of interracial research together and produced the first research-oriented book on interracial marriages and interracial individuals—*Racially Mixed People in America*. The book contained never-before-published research and theory on racially mixed identity and experiences.

The current volume, also edited by Root, now brings many of the pioneer researchers back for further analysis of mixed identity, but it also brings together a new generation of researchers, theorists, and community activists. In reviewing the chapters of this new book and in observing the past 30 years, I find the path followed by this journey of interracial identity much more distinct.

THE JOURNEY OF SELF-DEFINITION

One of the first steps to exploring identity is to define oneself and to establish terminology. Most of the authors in this book define what is meant by race, ethnicity, culture, biracial, and multiracial. Most also agree that race is a sociopolitical construct rather than biological reality. Many ethnic people in the United States are attempting to move away from racial terminology because it is used for oppression. However, the current authors and others are somewhat forced to use racial terminology because it is so commonly used in the United States and will probably not be eliminated in the near future. "Although a multiracial identity choice might (indeed, has already begun to) achieve legitimacy, complete devaluation of the concept of race is not likely to take place in the absence of promotion by the country's majority group (Weisman, Chapter 10, this volume, p. 162). The United States is so "racialized that to be without racial identity is to be in danger of having no identity" (Omi & Winant, 1993, p. 5; cf. Glass & Wallace, Chapter 21, this volume).

Therefore, multiracial researchers use new terminology that includes racial terms such as biracial, multiracial, Amerasian, Eurasian, Afroasian, and racially/culturally blended. A fear remains among most authors, however, that by using such racial terminology, we may be validating the concept of racial segregation that has misclassified us and classified our ancestors for political and economic reasons. From another perspective, perhaps we should define ourselves before others define us. Most authors chose the latter perspective of defining ourselves before others define us inappropriately. This self-definition provides us the "dignity of self-identification" (Brown & Douglass, Chapter 20, this volume, p. 325).

THE PERSONAL JOURNEY:
A SEARCH FOR SELF AND ACCEPTANCE

The search for knowledge about oneself and others with whom to identify is another part of the journey. Thornton (Chapter 7, this volume) explained that the direction and motivation for his research was shaped from his personal need to discover and understand himself. As he became more comfortable with himself as a person, the direction of his work on identity changed. Thornton's experience shows that ethnic identity is a dynamic process (McRoy & Zurcher, 1983) that is influenced by experiences, maturity, and external forces such as other individuals, social issues, and political movements.

One major external force that has influenced the lives and racial identity of racially mixed people is the lack of acceptance from particular ethnic groups. Most of the research and literature reiterates that racially mixed people experience prejudice from their mothers' and/or fathers' racial groups. Many of these monoracial groups believe that membership within the group is exclusive and that alliances with another group "dilute" the affiliation with the group. However, multiracial research has shown that most racially mixed people do not feel this "dilution" or dichotomization of choices. For example, Mass (1992) found that many Japanese/white individuals felt just as Japanese as monoracial Japanese individuals. In addition, the black/Japanese participating in my dissertation felt equally black and equally Japanese, but they also believed they were part of a new race rather than part of the black or Japanese races. Although this may appear contradictory, perhaps mixed individuals feel very much a part of both groups culturally, but "racially" feel that they are part of a new race. Subsequent research by others has shown that mixed-race people tend to feel this same "simultaneous membership" (Root, 1992a; Thornton, Chapter 7, this volume; Williams, 1992).

An additional characteristic common to many racially mixed individuals is "multiple fluid identities" or "situational identity" (Root, 1992a; Williams, 1992; in this volume, Daniel, Chapter 8; Thornton, Chapter 7). This phenomenon refers to the ability to move between (or among) and/or identify with multiple ethnic groups in different situations. For example, Zack (Chapter 9, this volume) found this phenomenon with her sample of black and Jewish individuals. She discovered that black/Jewish white people may feel more Jewish among blacks than they do among Jews and feel more black among Jews than among blacks. Daniel (Chapter 8, this volume), Standen (Chapter 15, this volume), Sung (1990), and Wilson (1984) also discussed this situational ethnicity, in which an interracial individual may feel more one race than the other or feel equally both depending on the situation. Thus research has shown that simultaneous and multiple group membership is possible for racially mixed individuals.

Society as a whole, however, still seems incapable of allowing multiple-group membership. Multiracial individuals are forced to choose alliances between/among the many groups to which they belong. These groups may neither consistently nor completely accept mixed-race people as legitimate sisters and brothers, particularly if the person *identifies* as mixed race.

This nonacceptance may stem from a criterion for admission/membership: shared common experience. Many monoracial group members require "proof" that multiracial individuals have experienced, for example, the black, Asian, white, Hispanic, Native American, or Jewish, "experience," such as discrimination, slavery, or the Holocaust (Zack, Chapter 9, this volume). The question is rarely posed to monoracial people, even though their experiences vary tremendously. The few "in-group" individuals who encounter this similar need for validation are light-skinned blacks and blacks adopted by white families (Hall, 1980). Although these people are monoracial, their identity and affiliations are questioned due to their physical or background difference. What tends to be forgotten is that people of color in the United States experience discrimination regardless of their hue, socioeconomic level, and neighborhood (Haley, 1964). Research by Cauce et al. (1992) showed that biracial individuals were similar to monoracial people of color in terms of life stresses, psychological distress, behavior problems, and self-worth. In fact, greater stress may be possible because multiracial people contend with racism from multiple sources including their own (biological) groups. The pain from this multiple racism and nonacceptance is stated very poignantly in the personal interviews conducted by Williams (Chapter 12, this volume).

The research world is also inflexible in understanding the multiracial experience. Thornton (Chapter 7, this volume) showed that much of the multiracial identity research tends to follow monoracial paradigms. Rather than approaching the identity of interracial individuals as a new area of study, researchers attempt to adapt traditional research paradigms to fit this new population. Allman (Chapter 17, this volume) reviewed this issue and found that traditional additive models (which view various constructs independently) are obsolete and that a fused model (which acknowledges multiple, dependent allegiances) is more appropriate. Thornton (Chapter 7, this volume) agreed that many variables in ethnic research are enmeshed and virtually inseparable. Thornton did mention, however, that some researchers have appropriately customized the monoracial research paradigm to the multiracial world. For example, Poston (1990) did an excellent job of outlining the stages of identity development of racially mixed people by adapting William Cross's (1978) model of Nigrescence.

COLLECTIVE JOURNEY:
THE SEARCH FOR OTHERS

Individuals soon begin seeking others similar to themselves. This collective can provide social and political support. Brown and Douglass (Chapter 20, this volume) discussed the history and the need for support groups for interracial couples and their families and also interracial individuals. The groups provide a family and personal support network where children can play together; families can have dinners together; and parents can learn more about prejudice, child rearing, extended family issues, and racial classification issues.

Racially mixed baby boomers were probably the most active in establishing and using these groups for political purposes. With support from these groups, racially mixed people can become more active in "refusing to accept marginality" (p. 154) and "defining a place where (we) belong" (p. 154) (Weisman, Chapter 10, this volume). Graham (Chapter 3, this volume) discussed further use of these groups to move forward with political agendas. She discussed confronting school boards, the Bureau of the Census, the medical world, and other groups to recognize the existence of a new group of people. In addition, Carlos Fernández (1992b), one of the most visibly active person's on mixed people's rights, has testified in Washington, DC, for inclusion of a racially mixed category on the census questionnaire.

FUTURE PATHS AND DIRECTIONS

With the changing demographics in the United States and abroad, I have no doubt that the issue of interracial people and their identity will become a more prominent topic. For example, within the last 2 years, *Time* magazine has featured two cover stories on racially mixed people.

Several books on interracial marriages and interracial individuals can be found in bookstores, and the topic of race and genetic differences is out of the closet again with the popular acceptance of the new book, *The Bell Curve*, and the recent statement by the president of Rutgers University about the genetic inferiority of people of color.

Research

The United States is obsessed with race for oppressive reasons. Racial differences are viewed as biologically rather than culturally determined. These differences are then given value at the sacrifice of people of color. That is, if the majority group possesses a specific characteristic, any group that has a characteristic different from this must be inferior. This perception of race has hindered much of our ability to research race from another perspective. Researchers of color have found it necessary to explore racial/cultural differences in a defensive mode by proving the differences among groups were minimal and/or the result of environmental factors. (Feminist research followed a similar path.) The current trend in research is to explore the differences *within* a group and view these differences as positive or negative characteristics of a particular ethnic group, rather than to compare these differences to the white population. An understanding of these positive and negative group characteristics is used to promote the survival and success of that particular group. It is exciting to see ethnic research conducted to further the advancement and achievement of people of color, rather than being conducted as reactive research proving our worth in society.

The majority of this work is being conducted by researchers of color. Some researchers (predominantly white males) have believed this "insider" approach nullifies the researcher's objectivity. This is an inaccurate assumption. Female, ethnic, interracial researchers are professionals who are aware of methodological controls to reduce bias. Actually, the biased research tended to be conducted by external researchers (Guthrie, 1976). Thus, when Thornton (Chapter 7, this volume) reveals his personal feelings and other "internal" researchers discuss individual rights or use the word "I" or "we," people should not falsely believe that these researchers are not objective professionals. Individuals who are members of the researched group may in fact be more suited for researching their own group. They understand the experiences of the group and are able to conduct appropriate research. Researchers from outside the group may have a tendency to view a social experience from their point of reference and therefore misinterpret an action or bypass a major issue of that group entirely. Many researchers external to a group understand this phenomenon and seek "informants" (group members) to better understand a group. Eliminating the middle person, many ethnic and female researchers have begun to conduct their own studies due to inappropriate research being conducted on their group. Root (1992a) believes that much of the initial interracial research should, in fact, be conducted by multicultural individuals for these reasons.

As ethnic people, we must continue to research ourselves. As mentioned earlier, in order to proceed with our journey, we must follow the markings that have been left by such forefathers and foremothers as Wagatsuma (1976), Strong (1978), Hall (1980), Kich (1982), Thornton (1983), Spickard (1983, 1989), Murphy-Shigematsu (1986), and Root (1990). We must learn and build a solid theory of, and data on, ethnic identity historical information. The existing research is not extensive, so it is still possible to read all the relevant material. However, because most of this information is in thesis and dissertation form, the pieces are lengthy. The trade-off is in the richness of information dissertations and theses allow. Although this information may be time consuming to use and difficult to obtain, these hurdles must be passed when dealing with an emerging topic.

To enable greater access to this information, we must ensure that dissertations, theses, and other research are published in books and journals. However, this has been difficult for a couple of reasons. As stated earlier, many publishers and journal editors still do not believe the topic of interracial identity is relevant and do not publish our works. Sage Publications has been very receptive to ethnic and feminist literature in the past and is the company that published the first contemporary edited book on the multiracial experience (Root, 1992b). Also, ethnic students still have limited access to mentors to teach them the publishing game. We need to reach out to young professionals and walk them through the intimidating path to publication.

We must also extrapolate and generalize the results of research on one group of mixed people to another group. That is, research on black/ Asians can be used to help with research on white/blacks, white/Asians,

Hispanic Asians, or other mixtures. There are many common issues encountered by mixed people. (Of course, different mixtures may encounter different problems, especially minority-majority mixtures versus minority-minority mixtures). In fact, many of the ethnic identity works done by black, Hispanic, and Asian researchers (Cross, 1978; Helms, 1990a; Ramirez, 1983; Sue & Sue, 1971) cross reference each other, respect each other, and build from each others' research. Theories can only be built by working with established foundations and subsequent work. This also includes research from other countries and religions, as discussed by Weisman (Chapter 10, this volume) and Zack (Chapter 9, this volume).

We must also use oral history and interviews—qualitative, in addition to quantitative work. Although excellent quantitative work like that of Lynda Field (Chapter 13, this volume) is imperative, qualitative work is also necessary to ensure a broad understanding of mixed-race people. Teresa Williams's (1992; Chapter 12, this volume) work with young Asians and Latino mixed people is excellent. In her current chapter, respondents eloquently told us what life is like in the 1990s for the Generation X interracial people. Cindy Nakashima's (Chapter 6, this volume) reference to novels such as *Passing* and *Quicksand* are also important. Novels, although they may not be considered qualitative data by some, are rich with interpretations and emotions of individuals and convey the reaction of society toward these individuals.

Who is Mixed?

For the older generation of biracial researchers, the answer to the question of who is mixed was easy. Interracial people were those whose father's race was different than their mother's—black/white, Japanese/white, Japanese/black, and so on. King and DaCosta (Chapter 14, this volume) call this "immediately mixed"; Wardle (Chapter 23, this volume) calls this group "biracial" (versus multiracial, a person with several racial heritages). However, this new generation of mixed people now includes individuals who are children of interracial mothers and interracial fathers. Many are one-quarter Asian, one-eighth Hispanic, and so on. Are you still interracial if at least one parent is mixed race? Daniel, Graham, Weisman, and others (Chapters 8, 3, and 10, this volume, respectively) pointed out that there are very few "pure raced" individuals in the United States, especially among blacks. Will this "hypodescent, one-drop" rule apply to interracial group inclusion also? This question has not been a prominent one in the United States as yet. When a critical mass of multiracial people emerges, I have no doubt that guidelines of inclusion will be established for economic and sociopolitical reasons.

Economics may force an answer to the question of who is mixed race. The economic element is primarily based on affirmative action and employment issues. If a person is "only" one-eighth black, does this person still qualify for financial aid, scholarships, college admission programs, and so on? One group that is currently experiencing this is the Native American community. Due to the fact that many people were identifying themselves as Native American for particular benefits, the federal government instituted a requirement for each tribe to "validate" membership in the tribe. "Official" Native Americans are required to show paperwork when seeking health benefits, scholarships, and the like. Because the number of other mixed-race people is not yet at a critical mass, this dilemma is a not pressing one. However, as numbers increase, the issue may become more prominent.

The political/social ramifications of determining mixed-race membership involve the terms of acceptance by various ethnic groups, as mentioned earlier. With which group do you identify? Which groups accept you? If the racially mixed groups begin to fractionate, we may resemble a particular social strata in Japan. Japan has shown a hierarchy among mixed-race people (Thompson, 1967). In Japan, Japanese white individuals have much greater status than individuals who are Japanese mixed with any other racial group. In the United States, the majority of out-marriages among Japanese and Chinese Americans are with Caucasians. This could stem from a cultural preference for Caucasians or perhaps a numerical or propinquity phenomenon. That is, because there are more whites in the population, there is a higher probability of this combination (Spickard, 1989). Will mixed-race people who are part white have a higher social status (which aids in economic status) than those who do not have white "blood"?

We hope not to resemble Japan with these hierarchies of racially mixtures. However, an episode of the 1960s television show, *Star Trek*, comes to mind when I think of this possibility. Frank Gorshin appeared as an alien who was colored black on one side of his face and white on the other side. His arch enemy was a man who had similar coloring. Captain Kirk cannot comprehend the vicious anger between these two men. Frank is angered by Kirk's lack of observation and points out that his enemy is black of the right side of his face and white on the left side, whereas he (Frank) is black on the left and white on the right.

As mixed people, we must be cautious about creating a racial hierarchy within our own group. Rather, I hope that we will become the true "metropolitan" people touted by Park (1937), who can move among any group and act as a "bridge" for future race relations.

I will briefly touch on a final issue of who is mixed. The decision of what constitutes an interracial adoption is a driving force for a legal definition of who is racially mixed. In Ruth McRoy and Zurcher's (1983) study on transracial adoptees, they included the adoption of a mixed-race, black/white child into a white family as an interracial adoption. Most social service agencies also agree with this classification. Currently, however, many white families argue that a mixed black/white child can also be classified as white. I have also interviewed a Hispanic woman, married to a white man, who was attempting to adopt a Hispanic child. The adoption agency, however, classified this adoption as an interracial adoption and was thus searching for an all-Hispanic household as an alternative. McRoy and I (Chapter 5, this volume) discuss the pros and cons of transracial adoptions, but the discussion of what constitutes a transracial adoption will continue in the legal realm.

PHYSICAL APPEARANCE

Deciding who is racially mixed may be difficult philosophically, but it will also be difficulty physically. I am able to recognize a mixed-race person fairly easily. Like other ethnic or racial groups, I suppose we are good at identifying "one of your own." Many white people tend to identify us by stereotypical features, a system in which all multiracial people look alike. However, all black, Asians, Hispanics, and so on are different; the within-group differences are quite strong. These differences also include linguistic, cultural, or historical differences, such as Japanese from Hawaii, blacks from the Caribbean islands or New York, Russian Jews versus Polish Jews, and so on. This ability to see over and beyond the stereotypical features is similar to the ability of Alaskan Natives to see different types of snow—we know how to differentiate among the many physical features and cultural characteristics. However, as the combination of mixtures becomes more complicated (an eighth of this, a quarter of that, etc.), it will becomes more difficult for us to determine the "membership" of mixed-race people.

Identification of membership is important to different people for different reasons. As I stated previously, U.S. history records that identification of racial membership has been used for oppressive reasons. However, for many of us, it is necessary to find others similar to ourselves. I am guilty of watching people and wondering about their racial background. I, however, do this out of pride in seeing others like myself. I watch television, movies, advertisements, sporting events, plays, and so on, and I get excited when I see a mixed person and try to determine "what they are." Recently I saw Alisa Gyse-Dickens in a black musical stage production and recognized her as the black/Japanese woman from the old television show, *A Different World*. Her stage credits included a tour with *Miss Saigon*. Her mixed-race background allowed her to expand her repertoire of ethnic roles.

I have much pride when I see a multiracial person succeeding. I take personal pride when I see highly visible people such as entertainers Alisa Gyse-Dickens, Mariah Cary, Keanu Reeves, and Amy Hill, as well as athletes Tiger Woods and Greg Louganis. I also feel much sadness when I hear of a crime committed by an interracial person. This collective response of happiness and sadness occurs among racially mixed people, just as it does with other ethnic or racial groups.

Racial Classifications

This collectiveness among mixed-race people will be very important in the future. The journey to group identification and acknowledgment will probably be the most prominent and difficult journey in the new millennium. Currently, individuals and groups are battling the "system" for inclusion of mixed-race categories on the national census forms. Many are frustrated with lack of inclusion and are choosing to identify as *other*. Fernández (1992b) has found that California is leading the way for the change; *other* is the fastest-growing racial identification category in the state among those frustrated with the "check one" choices. Root (Chapter 1, this volume) also reminded us that the *other* category grew 45% and now numbers 9.8 million people. Most pleas to have a multiracial category have been emotionally based in terms of trying to convey the psychological importance of culture/ethnic identity. We also need to address the issue as a pragmatic/bureaucratic and financial one. If people continue to choose *other*, the United States will soon have unusable "dirty" data; we will not have accurate counts of specific racial/ethnic groups.

Although many believe that U.S. Census data should not include race categories, the elimination of the racial membership question will probably not occur within the near future. Because the racial category question, the term *race*, and the belief in race will exist for a while, there is a need to educate current and future generations of children about racism through our schools and through societal change (Glass & Wallace, Chapter 21, this volume). With the current trend toward a more conservative definition of race (white and nonwhite), Wardle (Chapter 23, this volume) believes that all efforts toward a multicultural category and all the books and organizations will mean nothing unless we raise multiracial (and other) adults to deal with social, political, economic, and academic discrimination.

Racism Continues

It is important to educate young children about the inappropriateness of race and its resulting racism. Children begin to use race as a means of inclusion and exclusion at an early age, reflecting the adult world. Within the last 2 years, I have been asking parents of mixed-race children to describe the 1990s experience of mixed-race youth. They tell me that discrimination is strong. Their children are not accepted by white groups, and they are also ostracized and taunted by monoracial children of color. Mixed-race children are no longer nonentities. Young people are very aware of the terms biracial and mixed race, and most know at least one person who fits this category. Mixed-race people are becoming a viable group to subject to discrimination.

In addition to the discrimination, parents have also told me of an alarming situation. Young people are being asked to choose alliances to specific ethnic groups for purposes of gang recruitment. Children, in general, are dodging the need for gang membership; however, many are forced to seek refuge in gangs for protection. Multiracial youth are being asked to choose between different racial gangs or become targets of several gangs. As a mixed-race baby boomer, my issues were ones of identity and acceptance; today's children are fighting for their lives.

Children mimic the behaviors of adults. A greater acceptance of racial discrimination appears to be on the rise in the 1990s. Recently, the United States has seen an increase in conservative elected officials, an inappropriate use of freedom of speech rights for pejorative oratory, the passing of Proposition 187 in California, and the current threat to affirmative action laws. Mixed-race people will experience the same increased discrimination as any other racial group. Mixed-race people will also simultaneously experience discrimination from their own biological racial groups. Forecasts for the 21st century predict that people of color will represent more than half of the United States. If biracial youth are currently being discriminated against by youth of color, the pattern most likely will continue into the new century. Interracial people will become the new discriminated against "minority" in the United States. As a means of survival, many of these multiracial people may deny their racially mixed membership and begin "passing" as monoracial individuals.

A True Multiracial Identity

The future also points to the reality of a formal multiracial identity. In addition to mixed-race people experiencing simultaneous membership in their various ethnic/racial groups, they are also acknowledging themselves in the new category of multiracial. Research has shown that a healthy identity is maintained by membership in an appropriate referent group (Kich, 1982; Mass, 1992; Weisman, Chapter 10, this volume). Thus, in addition to having referent groups comprising multiple monoracial groups, a multiracial person maintains a healthy multiracial identity through membership with a group that identifies as multiracial. The emergence of such groups as the *Multiracial Americans of Southern California, I-Pride, Hapa Issues Forum,* and so on have helped multiracial people with their journey to find referent groups.

CONCLUSION

As stated throughout this book and in this concluding chapter, the future of mixed-race people may go in either a positive or negative direction. The multiracial people of tomorrow may be discriminated against as the "new minority," be accepted as the new ambassadors of peace because they are able to bridge many groups, or represent the majority of people in the United States. Through technology, the United States is no longer an independent entity. The world is growing smaller every day. I hope the United States acknowledges that the ethnic, racial, religious, and other discrimination and oppression can only lead to the destruction of an entire nation or world.

Appendix 1
Executive Office of
Management and Budget

Statistical Directive No. 15[1]

**Race and Ethnic Standards for Federal Statistics
and Administrative Reporting**

This Directive provides standard classifications for recordkeeping, collection, and presentation of data on race and ethnicity in Federal program administrative reporting and statistical activities. These classifications should not be interpreted as being scientific or anthropological in nature, nor should they be viewed as determinants of eligibility for participation in any Federal program. They have been developed in response to needs expressed by both the executive branch and the Congress to provide for the collection and use of compatible, nonduplicated, exchangeable racial and ethnic data by Federal agencies.

1. Definitions

The basic racial and ethnic categories for Federal statistics and program administrative reporting are defined as follows:

a. *American Indian or Alaskan Native.* A person having origins in any of the original peoples of North America, and who maintains cultural identification through tribal affiliation or community recognition.

b. *Asian or Pacific Islander.* A person having origins in any of the original peoples of the Far East, Southeast Asia, the Indian subcontinent, or the Pacific Islands. This area includes, for example, China, India, Japan, Korea, the Philippine Islands, and Samoa.

c. *Black.* A person having origins in any of the black racial groups of Africa.

d. *Hispanic.* A person of Mexican, Puerto Rican, Cuban, Central or South American, or other Spanish culture or origin, regardless of race.

e. *White.* A person having origins in any of the *original peoples* of Europe, North Africa, or the Middle East [emphasis added].

2. Utilization for Recordkeeping and Reporting

To provide flexibility, it is preferable to collect data on race and ethnicity separately. If separate race and ethnic categories are used, the minimum designations are:

a. *Race*:
   - American Indian or Alaska Native
   - Asian or Pacific Islander
   - Black
   - White

b. *Ethnicity*:
   - Hispanic origin
   - Not of Hispanic origin

When race and ethnicity are collected separately, the number of white and black persons who are Hispanic must be identifiable, and capable of being reported in that category.

If a combined format is used to collect racial and ethnic data, the minimum acceptable categories are:

American Indian or Alaska Native

Asian or Pacific Islander

Black, not of Hispanic origin

Hispanic

White, not of Hispanic origin

The category which most closely reflects the individual's recognition in his community should be used for purposes of reporting on persons who are of mixed racial and/or ethnic origins [emphasis added].

In no case should the provisions of this Directive be construed to limit the collection of data to the categories described above. However, any reporting required which uses more detail shall be organized in such a way that the additional categories can be aggregated into these basic racial/ethnic categories.

The minimum standard collection categories shall be utilized for reporting as follows:

a. *Civil rights compliance reporting.* The categories specified above will be used by all agencies in either the separate or combined format for civil rights compliance reporting and equal employment reporting for both the public and private sectors and for all levels of government. Any variation requiring less detailed data or data which cannot be aggregated into the basic categories will have to be specifically approved by the Office of Federal Statistical Policy and Standards for executive agencies. More detailed reporting which can be aggregated to the basic categories may be used at the agencies' discretion.

b. *General program administrative and grant reporting.* Whenever an agency subject to this Directive issues new or revised administrative reporting or recordkeeping requirements which include racial or ethnic data, the agency will use the race/ethnic categories described above. A variance can be specifically requested from the Office of Federal Statistical Policy and Standards, but such a variance will be granted only if the agency can demonstrate that it is not reasonable for the primary reporter to determine the racial or ethnic background in terms of the specified categories, and that such determination is not critical to the administration of the program in question, or if the specific program is directed to only one or a limited number of race/ethnic groups, e.g., Indian tribal activities.

c. *Statistical reporting.* The categories described in this Directive will be used at a minimum for federally sponsored statistical data collection where race and/or ethnicity is required, except when: the collection involves a sample of such size that the data on the smaller categories would be unreliable, or when the collection effort focuses on a specific racial or ethnic group. A repetitive survey shall be deemed to have an adequate sample size if the racial and ethnic data can be reliably aggregated on a biennial basis. Any other variation will have to be specifically authorized by OMB through the reports clearance process (see OMB Circular No. A-40). In those cases where the data collection is not subject to the reports clearance process, a direct request for a variance should be made to the OFSPS.

3. Effective Date

The provisions of this Directive are effective immediately for all *new* and *revised* recordkeeping or reporting requirements containing racial and/or ethnic information. All *existing* recordkeeping or reporting requirements shall be made consistent with this Directive at the time they are submitted for extension, or not later than January 1, 1980.

4. Presentation of Race/Ethnic Data

Displays of racial and ethnic compliance and statistical data will use the category designations listed above. The designation "nonwhite" is not acceptable for use in the presentation of Federal Government data. It is not to be used in any publication of compliance or statistical report.

In cases where the above designations are considered inappropriate for presentation of statistical data on particular regional areas, the sponsoring agency may use:

(1) The designations "Black and Other Races" or "All Other Races," as collective descriptions of minority races when the most summary distinction between the majority race and other races is appropriate; or

(2) The designations "White," "Black," and "All Other Races" when the distinction among the majority race, the principal minority race, and other races is appropriate; or

(3) The designation of a particular minority race or races, and the inclusion of "Whites" with "All Other Races," if such a collective description is appropriate.

In displaying detailed information which represents a combination of race and ethnicity, the description of the data being displayed must clearly indicate that both bases of classification are being used.

When the primary focus of a statistical report is on two or more specific identifiable groups in the population, one or more of which is racial or ethnic, it is acceptable to display data for each of the particular groups separately and to describe data relating to the remainder of the population by an appropriate collective description.

Note

1. Directive No.15 supersedes section 7(h) and Exhibit F of OMB Circular No. A-46 dated May 3, 1974, and as revised May 12, 1977.

Appendix 2
AMEA Proposed Revised
OMB Minimum Reporting Standards
With Multiracial, Multiethnic Categories

I. *Race and Ethnicity Separated Format*
  a. Race:
    1. American Indian/Alaskan Native
    2. Asian/Pacific Islander
    3. Black
    4. White
    5. Multiracial (persons of more than one of the listed groups only)

  For respondents in this category, specify races of parents.

    1. American Indian/Alaskan Native
    2. Asian/Pacific Islander

    3. Black
    4. White
  b. Ethnicity
    1. Hispanic origin
    2. Not of Hispanic origin
    3. Multiethnic (parent[s] of Hispanic and non-Hispanic origin)

II. *Race and Ethnicity Combined Format*
    1. American Indian/Alaskan Native
    2. Asian/Pacific Islander
    3. Black, not of Hispanic origin
    4. Hispanic
    5. White, not of Hispanic origin
    6. Multiracial/Multiethnic (persons of more than one of the listed groups only)
For respondents in this category, specify races/ethnicities of parents.

    1. American Indian/Alaskan Native
    2. Asian/Pacific Islander
    3. Black, not of Hispanic origin
    4. Hispanic
    5. White, not of Hispanic origin

(Association of MultiEthnic Americans 6/93)

References

Achenbach, T. M., & Edelbrock, C. S. (1983). *Manual for the Child Behavior Checklist and revised child behavior profile.* Burlington: University of Vermont Department of Psychiatry.

Achenbach, T. M., & Edelbrock, C. S. (1987). *Manual for the youth self-report profile.* Burlington: University of Vermont Department of Psychiatry.

Adams, F. (1975). *Unearthing seeds of fire: The idea of Highlander.* Winston-Salem, NC: John F. Blair.

Adler, P. S. (1974). Beyond cultural identity: Reflections on cultural and multicultural man. In R. Brislin (Ed.), *Topics in cultural learning* (Vol. 2, pp. 23-40). Honolulu: East-West Center.

Adoptive Families of America (AFA), (1994), Position statement on transracial adoptions, St. Paul, Minnesota.

Alexander, A. L. (1991). *Ambiguous lives: Free women of color in rural Georgia, 1789-1879.* Fayetteville: University of Arkansas Press.

Alipuria, L. (1990). *Self-esteem and self-label in multiethnic students from two Southern California state universities.* Unpublished master's thesis, California State University, Los Angeles.

Allen, R. L. (1990). *Black awakening in capitalist America: An analytic history* (African World Press ed.). Trenton, NJ: Africa World Press.

Almaguer, T. (1994). *Racial fault lines: The historical origins of white supremacy in California.* Berkeley and Los Angeles: University of California Press.

Almquist, E. (1989). The experience of minority women in the United States. In J. Freeman (Ed.), *Women: A feminist perspective* (4th ed., pp. 414-445). Mountain View, CA: Mayfield.

Alonso, W., & Waters, M. (1993). *The future composition of the American population: An illustrative simulation.* Paper presented at the winter meetings of the American Statistical Association, Fort Lauderdale, FL.

417

Altenbaugh, R. J., & Paulston, R. G. (1980). Work people's college and the American labor college movement. In R. G. Paulston (Ed.), *Other dreams, other schools: Folk colleges in social and ethnic movements* (pp. 198-213). Pittsburgh, PA: University of Pittsburgh.

Anderson, M., & Fienberg, S. E. (1995). Black, white, and shades of gray (and brown and yellow). *Change, 8*, 15-18.

Anthias, F., & Yuval-Davis, N. (1992). *Racialized boundaries: Race, nation, gender, colour, and class and the anti-racist struggle.* London, UK: Routledge.

Antonovsky, A. (1956). Toward a refinement of the "marginal man" concept. *Social Forces, 44*, 57-67.

Anzaldúa, G. (1987). *Borderlands/La frontera: The new Mestiza.* San Francisco: Spinsters/Aunt Lute Foundation.

Anzaldúa, G. (Ed.). (1990). *Making face, making soul: Creative and critical perspectives by women of color.* San Francisco: Aunt Lute Foundation.

Appadurai, A. (1993). Patriotism and its futures. *Public Culture, 3*(5), 411-429.

Appiah, A. (1990, October). "But would that still be me?" Notes on gender, "race," ethnicity, as sources of "identity." *The Journal of Philosophy, 87*(10), 493-499.

Appiah, A. (1992). *In my father's house.* New York: Oxford University Press.

Atkinson, D., Morten, G., & Sue, D. (Ed.). (1989). *Counseling American minorities: A cross-cultural perspective* (3rd ed.). Dubuque, IA: William C. Brown.

Bachrach, C. A. (1991). On the path to adoption seeking in the U.S., 1988. *Journal of Marriage and the Family, 53*, 705-718.

Bailey v. Fiske, 34 Maine Reports 77 (1852).

Balibar, E. (1991). Is there a neo-racism? In E. Balibar & I. Wallerstein (Eds.), *Race, nation, class: Ambiguous identities* (pp. 17-28). London: Verso.

Banks, J. A. (1988). *Multiethnic education: Theory and practice.* Boston: Allyn & Bacon.

Banks, J. A. (1993, September). Multicultural education: Development, dimensions, and challenges. *Phi Delta Kappan*, pp. 22-28.

Banks, J. A., & Banks, C. A. M. (Eds.) (1989). *Multicultural education: Issues and perspectives.* Boston: Allyn & Bacon.

Banton, M. (1987). *Racial theories.* Cambridge, UK: Cambridge University Press.

Barrett, M. (1987). The concept of difference. *Feminist Review, 26*, 29-41.

Barringer, F. (1989, September 24). Mixed race generation emerges but is not sure where it fits in. *New York Times*, p. 14(N).

Barringer, F. (1991, March 11). Census shows profound change in racial makeup of the nation, *New York Times*, pp. A1, B8.

Bem, S. L. (1993). *The lenses of gender: Transforming the debate on sexual inequality.* New Haven, CT: Yale University Press.

Benet, M. (1976). *The politics of adoption.* New York: Free Press.

Benjamin-Wardle, M. (1991). 14-year old speaks out, proving that teens have concerns, too. *New People, 1*(6), 6.

Benjamin-Wardle, M. (1992). Betty Okino—a beaming biracial gymnast. *New People, 3*(1), 8.

Benjamin-Wardle, M. (1994a). Ethnic clubs exclude others. *New People, 4*(2), 6.

Benjamin-Wardle, M. (1994b). A French twist: Biracial—and bilingual. *New People, 5*(1), 6.

Benjamin-Wardle, M. (1994c). Suffer the little children. *New People, 4*(4), 6.

Bennett, J. Jr., (1982). *Before the Mayflower: A history of the Negro in America, 1619-1964.* New York: Penguin.

Bennis, W. G. (1969). *Organizational development: Its nature, origins, and prospects*. Reading, MA: Addison-Wesley.

Benson, S. (1981). *Ambiguous ethnicity: Interracial families in London*. London: Cambridge University Press.

Bentley, N. (1993). White slaves: The mulatto hero in antebellum fiction. In *American Literature, 65*(3), 501-523.

Berman, P. (1994, February 28). The other and the almost the same. *The New Yorker*, pp. 61-71.

Berzon, J. R. (1978). *Neither white nor black: The mulatto character in American fiction*. New York: New York University Press.

Bhabha, H. (1990). The third space: Interview with Homi Bhabha. In J. Rutherford (Ed.), *Identity: Community, culture, difference* (pp. 207-221). London: Lawrence & Wishart.

Biddiss, M. (1979). *Images of race*. Leicester, UK: Leicester University Press.

Blauner, B. (1988). *Black lives, white lives: Three decades of race relations in America*. Berkeley/Los Angeles: University of California Press.

Blee, K. (1991). *Women of the Klan: Racism and gender in the 1920s*. Berkeley/Los Angeles: University of California Press.

Bloom, A. (1987). *Closing of the American mind*. New York: Simon & Schuster.

Blu, K. (1980). *The Lumbee problem: The making of an American Indian people*. Cambridge, UK: Cambridge University Press.

Blumer, H., & Duster, T. (1980). *Theories of race and social action* (UNESCO Report). Poole, UK: Sydenhams.

Board of Behavioral Science Examiners. (1990). *Laws and regulations relating to the practice of marriage, family, and child counseling* (amended 1993). Sacramento, CA: Author.

Boserup, A., & Mack, A. (1975). *War without weapons: Nonviolence in national defense*. New York: Schocken.

Bourguignon, E. (1979). *A world of women: Anthropological studies of women in societies of the world*. New York: Praeger.

Bowen v. Randolph County Board of Education, Case No. 94-A-325, U.S. District Court, Middle District, Alabama (1994).

Bowles, D. D. (1993). Biracial identity: Children born to African American and White couples. *Clinical Social Work Journal, 21*(4), 417-428.

Bowman, B. (1989). *Educating language-minority children* (ERIC Digest). Urbana, IL: ERIC.

Boyd, H. (1995). Will Blacks and Jews ever come of age? *Crisis, 102*(2), 126-133.

Boyd, R. L. (1993). Differences in the earnings of black workers in the private and public sectors. *The Social Science Journal, 30*(2), 133-143.

Boyd-Franklin, N., & Garcia Preto, N. (1994). Family therapy: The case of African American and Hispanic women. In L. Comas-Díaz & B. Greene (Eds.), *Women of color: Integrating ethnic and gender identities in psychotherapy* (pp. 239-264). New York: Guilford.

Boykin, A., & Toms, F. (1985). Black child socialization: A conceptual model. In H. McAdoo & J. McAdoo, (Eds.), *Black children* (pp. 33-51). Beverly Hills, CA: Sage.

Bradshaw, C. K. (1992). Beauty and the beast: On racial ambiguity. In M. P. P. Root (Ed.), *Racially mixed people in America* (pp. 77-90). Newbury Park, CA: Sage.

Brandell, J. R. (1988). Treatment of the biracial child: Theoretical and clinical issues. *Journal of Multicultural Counseling and Development, 16*, 176-187.

Brandt, B. (1994). On educating for diversity: A conversation with James A. Banks. *Educational Leadership, 16*(5), 28-31.

Brandt, G. L. (1986). *The realization of anti-racist teaching*. London: Falmer.

Bredekamp, S. (Ed.). (1987). *Develomentally appropriate practice in early childhood programs serving children birth through age 8* (rev. ed.). Washington, DC: NAEYC.

Brittan, A. (1973). *Meanings and situations.* London: Routledge & Kegan Paul.

Brown, P. M. (1990, August). Biracial identity and social marginality. *Child and Adolescent Social Work, 7,* 319-337.

Brown, W. W. (1969). *Clotelle; or, The colored heroine, a tale of the southern states.* Miami, FL: Mnemosyne. (Original work published 1864)

Buck, P. S. (1930). *East wind, west wind.* New York: John Day.

Butler, J. (1993). *Bodies that matter: On the discursive limits of sex.* New York: Routledge.

Camper, C. (Ed.) (1994). *Miscegenation blues: Voices of mixed-race women.* Toronto, Canada: Sister Vision Press.

Carby, H. V. (1987). *Reconstructing womanhood: The emergence of the Afro American woman novelist.* New York: Oxford University Press.

Carson, C. (1992). Blacks and Jews in the Civil Rights Movement. In J. Salzman, A. Back, & G. S. Sorin (Eds.), *Bridges and boundaries: African Americans and American Jews* (pp. 36-49). New York: George Braziller.

Cartoof, V., & Klerman, L. (1982). *Adoption: Is it an option for pregnant adolescents?* Waltham, MA: Florence Heller School for Advanced Studies in Social Welfare.

Casteñeda, A. I. (1991). The political economy of nineteenth century stereotypes of Californians. In M. R. Ornelas (Ed.), *Between conquests: Readings in early Chicano history* (pp. 87-105). Dubuque, IA: Kendall/Hunt.

Cauce, A., Hiraga, Y., Mason, C., Aguilar, T., Ordonez, N., & Gonzales, N. (1992). Between a rock and a hard place: Social adjustment of biracial youth. In M. P. P. Root (Ed.), *Racially mixed people in America* (pp. 207-222). Newbury Park, CA: Sage.

Chan, S. (1991). *Asian Americans: An interpretive history.* Boston: Twayne.

Chang, D. (1956). *Frontiers of love.* New York: Random House.

Chang, T. (1974). The self-concept of children of ethnically different marriages. *California Journal of Educational Research, 25*(5), 245-252.

Chao, C. A. (in press). A bridge over troubled waters: Being Eurasian in the U.S. of A. In J. Adleman & G. Enguidanos-Clark (Eds.), *Racism in the lives of women: Testimony, theory, and guides to antiracist practice.* New York: Haworth.

Chestnutt, C. W. (1968). *The house behind the cedars.* Ridgewood, NJ: Gregg Press. (Original work published 1900)

Chestnutt, C. (1969). *The marrow of tradition.* Ann Arbor: University of Michigan Press. (Original work published 1901)

Child Welfare League of America (CWLA). (1958). *Standards for adoption service.* New York: Author.

Child Welfare League of America (CWLA). (1973). *Standards for adoption service.* New York: Author.

Child Welfare League of America (CWLA). (1987). *Report of the Child Welfare League of America National Adoption Task Force.* Washington DC: Author.

Chin, J. L., De La Cancela, V., & Jenkins, Y. (Ed.). (1993). *Diversity in psychotherapy.* New York: Praeger.

Chuan, W. B. (1993). Dissenting from the interracial movement: A Chinese-American perspective. In M. R. Hearst (Ed.), *Interracial identity: Celebration, conflict, or choice* (pp. 91-99). Chicago: Biracial Family Network.

Cleaver, E. (1992). *Soul on ice.* New York: Laurel, Stoke, Dell. (Original work published 1968)

Close, E. (1995, February 13). One drop of bloody history. *Newsweek,* p. 70.

Colker, R. (1993). A bisexual jurisprudence. *Law & Sexuality: A Review of Lesbian and Gay Legal Issues, 3,* 127-137.

Collins, P. H. (1991). *Black feminist thought: Knowledge, consciousness, and the politics of empowerment.* New York: Routledge, Chapman & Hall.

Comas-Díaz, L. (1987). Feminist therapy with Hispanic/Latina women: Myth or reality. *Women and Therapy, 6,* 39-61.

Comas-Díaz, L. (1988). Mainland Puerto Rican women: A sociocultural approach. *Journal of Community Psychology, 16*(1), 21-31.

Comas-Díaz, L. (1989). Puerto Rican women's cross cultural transitions: Developmental and clinical implications. In C. Garcia Coll & M. L. Mattei (Eds.), *The psychosocial development of Puerto Rican women* (pp. 166-199). New York: Praeger.

Comas-Díaz, L. (1991). Feminism and diversity in psychology: The case of women of color. *Psychology of Women Quarterly, 15,* 597-609.

Comas-Díaz, L. (1994a). Integrative approach. In L. Comas-Díaz & B. Greene (Eds.), *Women of color: Integrating ethnic and gender identities in psychotherapy* (pp. 287-318). New York: Guilford.

Comas-Díaz, L. (1994b). LatiNegra: Mental health issues of African Latinas. In R. V. Almeida (Ed.), *Expansions of feminist family theory through diversity* (pp. 35-74). New York: Haworth.

Connor, W. (1961). *An investigation of the marital stability of twenty American-Japanese couples in the Sacramento area.* Unpublished master's thesis, Sacramento State College.

Cooney, R., & Michalowski, H. (Eds.). (1987). *The power of the people: Active nonviolence in the United States* (2nd ed.). Philadelphia: New Society.

Cornell, D. (1992). What takes place in the dark. *Differences, 4*(2), 45-71.

Courtney, B. A. (1995, February 13). Freedom from choice: Being biracial has meant denying half of my identity. *Newsweek,* p. 16.

Cronbach, L. (1975, January). Five decades of public controversy over mental testing. *American Psychologist,* pp. 1-13.

Cross, W. (1978). The Thomas and Cross models of psychological Nigrescence: A review. *Journal of Black Psychology, 5,* 12-31.

Cross, W. E. (1985). Black identity: Rediscovering the distinction between personal identity and reference group orientation. In M. B. Spencer, G. K. Brookings, & W. R. Allen (Eds.), *Beginnings: The social and affective development of black children* (pp. 155-171). Hillsdale, NJ: Lawrence Erlbaum.

Cross, W. (1987). A two-factor theory of black identity formation: Implications for the study of identity development in minority children. In J. S. Phinney & M. J. Rotheram (Eds.), *Children's ethnic socialization: Pluralism and development* (pp. 117-133). Newbury Park, CA: Sage.

Cross, W. (1991). *Shades of black: Diversity in African American identity.* Philadelphia: Temple University Press.

Cruse, H. (1987). *Plural but equal: A critical study of blacks and minorities in America's plural society.* New York: William Morrow.

Dana, R. H. (1993). *Multicultural assessment perspectives for professional psychology.* Boston: Allyn & Bacon.

Daniel, G. R. (1988, October). *Multiethnic individual: An operational definition.* Paper presented at Kaleidoscope, the Annual Conference of Multiracial Americans of Southern California, Los Angeles.

Daniel, G. R. (1992a). Beyond black and white: The new multiracial consciousness. In M. P. P. Root (Ed.), *Racially mixed people in America* (pp. 333-341). Newbury Park, CA: Sage.

Daniel, G. R. (1992b). Passers and pluralists: Subverting the racial divide. In M. P. P. Root (Ed.), *Racially mixed people in America* (pp. 91-107). Newbury Park, CA: Sage.

Daniel, G. R. (1994). *Two parent ethnicities and parents of two ethnicities: Generational differences in the discourse on multethnic identity—a preliminary study.* Unpublished manuscript.

Daniel, G. R., & Collins, III, J. U. (1994). *Pluralism and integration: The dynamics of ethnic relations reconsidered.* Unpublished manuscript.

Davis, F. J. (1991). *Who is black? One nation's definition.* University Park: Pennsylvania State University Press.

de Beauvoir, S. (1953). *The second sex.* New York: Knopf.

Degler, C. N. (1971). *Neither black nor white: Slavery and race relations in Brazil and the United States.* New York: Macmillan.

de Lauretis, T. (1987). *Technologies of gender.* Bloomington: Indiana University Press.

de Lauretis, T. (1991). Film and the visible. In Bad Object-Choices (Ed.), *How do I look: Queer film and video* (pp. 223-276). Seattle, WA: Bay Press.

Del Valle, M. (1989). *Acculturation, sex roles, and racial definitions of Puerto Rican college students in Puerto Rico and the United States.* Doctoral dissertation, Department of Education, University of Massachusetts at Amherst.

de Monteflores, C. (1986). Notes on the management of difference. In T. S. Stein & C. J. Cohen (Eds.), *Contemporary perspectives on psychotherapy with lesbians and gay men* (pp. 73-101). New York: Plenum.

Derman-Sparks, L. (1989). *Anti-bias curriculum: Tools for empowering young children.* Washington, DC: National Association for the Education of Young Children.

Dickens, A. G. (1966). *Reformation and society in sixteenth-Century Europe.* New York: Harcourt, Brace & World.

Dien, D., & Vinacke, W. (1964). Self-concept and parental identification of young adults with mixed Caucasian-Japanese parentage. *Journal of Abnormal and Social Psychology, 69*(4), 463-466.

Dimensions of desire: Other Asian and Pacific American sexualities: Gay, lesbian and bisexual identities and orientations [Special issue]. (1994). *Amerasia Journal, 20*(1).

Doe v. LA Department of Health and Human Resources, 479 So. 2d 369, 371 (LA Ct. App. 1985), writ denied 485 So. 60 (1986), cert. denied 479 U.S. 1002 (1986).

Dollimore, J. (1991). *Sexual dissidence: Augustine to Wilde, Freud to Foucault.* New York: Oxford University Press.

Dominguez, V. (1986). *White by definition: Social classification in Creole Louisiana.* New Jersey: Rutgers, The State University Press.

D'Souza, D. (1991). *Illiberal education.* New York: Free Press.

Dubinin, N. P. (1965). Race and contemporary genetics. In L. Kuper (Ed.), *Race, science, and society* (pp. 68-74). New York: Columbia University Press.

Du Bois, W. E. B. (1975). *The souls of black folk.* New York: Macmillan. (Original work published 1903)

Dyer, K. J. (1976). Patterns of gene flow between Negroes and white. *U.S. Journal of Biosocial Science, 8*, 309-333.

Equal Employment Opportunity Commission. (Rev. 4-1989). Standard Form 100, OMB no. 3046-0007.

Erdrich, L., & Dorris, M. (1991). *The crown of Columbus.* New York: HarperCollins.

Erikson, E. (1963). *Childhood and society* (2nd ed.). New York: Norton.

Erikson, E. (1968). *Identity: Youth and crisis.* Toronto: Norton.

Erkut, S., Fields, J. P., Almeida, D., Deleon, B., & Sing, R. (1993). *Strength in diversity: Toward a broader understanding of racial and ethnic diversity in girl scouting.* New York: Girl Scouts of America.

Espín, O. M. (1984, August). *Selection of Hispanic female healers in urban U.S. communities.* Paper presented at the annual meeting of the American Psychological Association, Toronto, Canada.

Essed, P. (1990). *Everyday racism: Reports from women of two cultures* (Cynthia Jaffe, Trans.). Claremont: Hunter House.

Evinger, S. (1995). How shall we measure our nation's diversity? *Change, 8,* 7-14.

Falcon, A. (1993). The Puerto Rican community: A status report. *Dialogo: Newsletter of the National Puerto Rican Policy Network, 5,* 10-13.

Fanon, F. (1967). *Black skin, white masks.* New York: Grove.

Far, S. S. (pseudonym, Edith Maud Eaton). (1909, January 7). Leaves fom the mental porfolio of an Eurasian. *Independent,* pp. 125-132.

Farley, R., & Allen, W. (1989). *The color line and the quality of life in America.* Newbury Park, CA: Sage.

Fauset, J. (1929). *Plum bun, a novel without a moral.* New York: Frederick A. Stokes.

Ferguson, R. (1990). Introduction: Invisible center. In R. Ferguson, M. Gever, M.-H. Trinh, & C. West (Eds.), *Out there: Marginalization and contemporary cultures* (pp. 9-14). New York: MIT Press.

Ferguson, R., Gever, M., Trinh, M.-H., & West, C. (Eds.). (1990). *Out there: Marginalization and contemporary cultures.* New York: MIT Press.

Fernández, C. A. (1990, Fall). President's report. *Networking News: The Official Periodical of the Association of MultiEthnic Americans,* pp. 1-2.

Fernández, C. (1992a, June 13). *Historical summary of the antimiscegenation laws of the United States.* Paper presented at the Loving Conference, Washington, DC.

Fernández, C. (1992b). La Raza and the melting pot: A comparative look at multiethnicity. In M. P. P. Root (Ed.), *Racially mixed people in America* (pp. 126-143). Newbury Park, CA: Sage.

Field, L. (1992). *Self-concept and adjustment in biracial adolescents.* Unpublished doctoral dissertation, University of Denver, Denver, Colorado.

Folaron, G., & Hess, P. (1993). Placement considerations for children of mixed African American and Caucasian parentage. *Child Welfare, 72,* 113-125.

Forbes, J. D. (1984). Mulattoes and people of color in Anglo-North America: Implications for black-Indian relations. *Journal of Ethnic Studies, 12,* 17-61.

Forbes, J. D. (1988). *Black Africans and Native Americans: Color, race, and caste in the evolution of red-black peoples.* Oxford, UK: Basil Blackwell.

Foucault, M. (1980). *Power/knowledge: Selected interviews and writings, 1972-1977* (C. Gordon, Ed.). New York: Pantheon.

Frankenberg, R. (1993). *White women, race matters: The social construction of whiteness.* Minneapolis: University of Minnesota Press.

Franklin, A. J., & Boyd-Franklin, N. (1985). A psychoeducational perspective on black parenting. In H. McAdoo & J. McAdoo (Eds.) *Black children* (pp. 194-210). Beverly Hills, CA: Sage.

Fredrickson, G. (1981). *White supremacy: A comparative study in American and South African history.* London/New York: Oxford University Press.

Freire, P. (1970). *Pedagogy of the oppressed.* New York: Seabury.

Freire, P. (1994). *Pedagogy of hope*. New York: Continuum.

Frenkel-Brunswik, E. (1949). Intolerance of ambiguity as an emotional and perceptual personality variable. *Journal of Personality, 18*, 108-143.

Fuchs, L. H. (1990). *The American kaleidoscope: Race, ethnicity, and the civic culture*. Hanover, NH: The University Press of New England.

Fulbeck, K. (1994, July). Thought flights of a hapa artist: An essay of anger and frustration. *Cinevue, 9*(2), 8.

Funderburg, L. (1994). *Black, white, other: Biracial Americans talk about race and identity*. New York: William Morrow.

Gallup Poll. (1991, August). For the first time, more Americans approve of interracial marriage than disapprove. *Gallup Poll Monthly*, No. 311, pp. 60-64.

Gandhi, M. K. (1940). *The story of my experiments with truth*. Ahmedabad, India: Narajivan.

Garfinkle, H. (1967). Passing and the managed achievement of sexual status in an "intersexed" person. In H. Garfinkle (Ed.), *Studies in ethnomethodology*. Englewood Cliffs, NJ: Prentice Hall.

Gelles, T., & Kroll, J. (1993, April). *Barriers to same-race placement*. St. Paul, MN: North American Council on Adoptable Children.

Genovese, E. (1974). *Roll, Jordan, roll: The world the slaves made*. New York: Pantheon.

Gibbs, J. T. (1987). Identity and marginality: Issues in the treatment of biracial adolescents. *American Journal of Orthopsychiatry, 57*(2), 265-278.

Gibbs, J. T. (1989). Biracial adolescents. In J. T. Gibbs, L. N. Huang, & Associates (Eds.), *Children of color: Psychological intervention with minority youth* (pp. 322-350). San Francisco: Jossey-Bass.

Gibbs, J. T., & Hines, A. (1992). Negotiating ethnic identity: Issues for black-white biracial adolescents. In M. P. P. Root (Ed.), *Racially mixed people in America* (pp. 223-238). Newbury Park, CA: Sage.

Gibbs, J., & Moskowitz-Sweet, G. (1991). Clinical and cultural issues in the treatment of biracial and bicultural adolescents. *Families in Society: Journal of Contemporary Human Services, 72*, 579-592.

Giddens, A. (1984). *The constitution of society: Outline of the theory of structuration*. Berkeley: University of California Press.

Gilligan, C. (1982). *In a different voice: Psychological theory and women's development*. Cambridge, MA: Harvard University Press.

Gilligan, C., Ward, J. V., & Taylor, J. M. (Eds.). (1988). *Mapping the moral domain: A contribution of women's thinking to psychological theory and education*. Cambridge, MA: Harvard University Press.

Ginorio, A. B. (1971). *A study of racial perception in Puerto Rico*. Unpublished master's thesis, Department of Psychology, University of Puerto Rico, Rio Piedras.

Giroux, H. (1992). *Border crossings: Cultural workers and the politics of education*. New York: Routledge.

Gist, N. P. (1967). Cultural versus social marginality: The Anglo-Indian case. *Phylon, 28*, 361-375.

Glancy, D., & Truesdale, C. W. (1994). *Two worlds walking*. Minneapolis: New Rivers Press.

Glazer, N. (1983). *Ethnic dilemmas*. Cambridge, MA: Harvard University Press.

Glazer, N., & Moynihan, D. P. (1970). *Beyond the melting pot* (2nd ed.). Cambridge: MIT Press.

Glenn, E. N. (1992). From servitude to service work: Historical continuities in the racial division of paid reproductive labor. *Signs Journal of Women in Culture and Society, 18*(1), 1-43.

Goffman, E. (1959). *The presentation of self in everyday life.* New York: Anchor Press Doubleday.

Goldberg, M. M. (1941). A qualification of the marginal man theory. *American Sociological Review, 6,* 52-58.

Gollnick, D. M., & Chinn, P. C. (1994). *Multicultural education in a pluralistic society.* New York: Merrill.

Gooding-Williams, R. (Ed.). (1993). *Reading Rodney King, Reading urban uprising.* New York: Routledge.

Gordon, A. (1964). *Intermarriage: Interethnic, interracial, interfaith.* Boston: Beacon Press.

Gordon, L. R. (1995). *Bad faith and antiblack racism.* Atlantic Highlands, NJ: Humanities Press.

Gossett, T. F. (1963). *Race: The history of an idea in America.* New York: Schocken.

Gould, S. J. (1981). *The mismeasure of man.* New York: Norton.

Gould, S. J. (1994, November 18). Curve ball. *The New Yorker,* pp. 139-149.

Graham, R. (1990). *The idea of race in Latin America, 1870-1940.* Austin: University of Texas Press.

Green, A. W. (1947). A re-examination of the marginal man concept. *Social Forces, 26,* 167-171.

Green, H. (1983). *Light of the home: An intimate view of the lives of women in victorian America.* New York: Pantheon.

Greenbaum, S. (1991). What's in a label? Identity problems of Southern Indian tribes, *Journal of Ethnic Studies, 19*(2), 107-126.

Greene, B. (1990). What has gone before: The legacy of racism and sexism in the lives of black mothers and daughters. *Women and Therapy, 9,* 207-230.

Greene, B. (1992). Still here: A perspective on psychotherapy with African American women. In J. Chrisler & D. Howard (Eds.), *New directions in feminist psychology: Practice, theory, and research* (pp. 13-25). New York: Springer.

Greene, B. (1993). Human diversity in clinical psychology: Lesbians and gay sexual orientations. *The Clinical Psychologist, 46,* 74-82.

Grosz, G. (1993, January/February). 1993 guide to best and worst cities for interracial couples, families, and multiracial people to live. *Interrace,* pp. 31-34.

Grove, K. (1991). Identity development in interracial, Asian/white late adolescents: Must it be so problematic? *Journal of Youth and Adolescence, 20,* 617-628.

Gulick, S. L. (1914). *The American Japanese problem.* New York: Scribner.

Gupta, A., & Ferguson, J. (1992). Beyond "culture": Space, identity, and the politics of difference. *Cultural Anthropology, 7*(1), 6-23.

Guthrie, R. (1976). *Even the rat was white: A historical perspective of psychology.* New York: Harper & Row.

Guzman, M. E. (1986). *Acculturation of Mexican American adolescents.* Unpublished doctoral dissertation, University of Denver, Denver, Colorado.

Gwaltney, J. L. (1980). *Drylongso: A self portrait of black America.* New York: Vintage Books.

Hacker, A. (1992). *Two nations: Black and white, separate, hostile, unequal.* New York: Scribner.

Haizlip, S. T. (1994). *The sweeter the juice: A family memoir in black and white.* New York: Simon & Schuster.

Haley, A. (1964). *The autobiography of Malcolm X* (as told to A. Haley). New York: Ballantine.

Hall, C. C. I. (1980). *The ethnic identity of racially mixed people: A study of Black-Japanese.* Unpublished doctoral dissertation, University of California, Los Angeles.

Hall, C. C. I. (1992). Please choose one: Ethnic identity choices for biracial individuals. In M. P. P. Root (Ed.), *Racially mixed people in America* (pp. 250-264). Newbury Park, CA: Sage.

Hall, S. (n.d.). New ethnicities. *ICA Documents, 7*, 27-31.

Hall, S. (1992). New ethnicities. In J. Donald & A. Rattansi (Eds.), *Race, culture, and difference* (pp. 252-59). London: Sage.

Hamilton, J. A. (1989). Emotional consequences of victimization and discrimination in "special populations" of women. In B. Parry (Ed.), *Women's disorders: Psychiatric clinics of North America*. Philadelphia: W. B. Saunders.

Handlin, O. (1957). *Race and nationality in American life*. Boston: Little, Brown.

Harper, F. E. W. (1987). *Iola Leroy or shadows uplifted* (Hazel Carby, Ed.). Boston: Beacon Press. (Original work published 1892)

Harris, A. P. (1991). Race and essentialism in feminist legal theory. In K. T. Bartlett & R. Kennedy (Eds.), *Feminist legal theory: Readings in law and gender* (pp. 235-262). Boulder, CO: Westview.

Harrowitz, N. A., & Hyams, B. (Eds.) (1995). *Jews and gender*. Philadelphia: Temple University Press.

Harter, S. (1990). Causes, correlates, and the functional role of global self-worth: A life span perspective. In J. Kolligian & R. Sternberg (Eds.), *Competence considered* (pp. 67-97). New Haven, CT: Yale University Press.

Helms, J. E. (1989). Considering some methodological issues in racial identity research. *The Counseling Psychologist, 17*(2), 227-252.

Helms, J. E. (1990a). *Black and white racial identity: Theory, research and practice*. New York: Greenwood.

Helms, J. E. (1990b). Introduction: Review of racial identity terminology. In J. E. Helms (Ed.), *Black and white racial identity: Theory, research, and practice* (pp. 3-8). New York: Greenwood.

Hemphill, E. (1992). *Ceremonies: Prose and poetry*. New York: Plume/Penguin.

Henriques, F. (1974). *Children of conflict: A study of interracial sex and marriage*. New York: Dutton.

Hernton, C. (1988). *Sex and racism in America*. New York: Grove Weidenfeld. (Original work published 1965)

Herrnstein, R., & Murray, C. (1994). *The bell curve: Intelligence and class structure in American life*. New York: Free Press.

Hershel, A. J. (1992). What happens to them happens to me. In J. Salzman, A. Beck, & G. S. Sorin (Eds.), *Bridges and boundaries: African Americans and American Jews* (pp. 86-87). New York: George Braziller.

Herzog, K. (1983). *Women, ethnics, and exotics: Images of power in mid-nineteenth century American fiction*. Knoxville: The University of Tennessee Press.

Heyl, S. (1993). *Strengths and weaknesses: A collection of performance texts*. Unpublished master's thesis, University of California, Los Angeles.

Higham, J. (1975). *Send these to me: Jews and other imigrants in urban America*. New York: Atheneum.

Hirabayashi, L. (1993). Is the JA community disappearing? *Pacific Currents* (*Pacific Citizen's* year-end issue), pp. B15-16.

Ho, F., & Johnson, R. (1990). Intraethnic and interethnic marriage and divorce in Hawaii. *Social Biology, 37*, 44-51.

Ho, M. K. (1992). *Minority children and adolescents in therapy*. Newbury Park, CA: Sage.

Hofstadter, R. (1959). *Social Darwinism in American thought, 1860-1915* (Rev. ed.). New York: George Braziller. (Original work published 1955)

Hollis, D. (1993). It's a black thing, you wouldn't understand. *New People: A Journal for the Human Race, 4*(1), 15-21.

Hollis, Y. W. (1991). A legacy of loving. A special commemorative section. *New People Magazine: A Journal for the Human Race*, pp. 9-12.

Honda, H. K. (1993, April 16). Asian Americans talk about pressure of out marriage. *Pacific Citizen*, p. 3.

hooks, b. (1984). *Feminist theory: From margin to center*. Boston: South End Press.

hooks, b. (1990). Marginality as a site of resistance. In R. Ferguson, M. Gever, M.-H. Trinh, & C. West (Eds.), *Out there: Marginalization and contemporary cultures* (pp. 341-143). New York: MIT Press.

hooks, b. (1992). Representations of whiteness. In *Black looks: Race and representation* (pp. 165-178). Boston: South End Press.

hooks, b. (1994). *Teaching to transgress: Education as the practice of freedom*. New York: Routledge.

Houston, V. H. (1991). The past meets the future: A cultural essay. *Amerasia Journal, 17*(1), 53-56.

Hull, G. T., Scott, P. B., & Smith, B. (1982). *All the women are white, all the blacks are men, but some of us are brave*. New York: Feminist Press.

Hurtado, A. (1989). Relating to privilege: Seduction and rejection in the subordination of white women and women of color. *Signs, 14*(4), 833-855.

Hutchins, L., & Kaahumanu, L. (1991). *Bi any other name: Bisexual people speak out*. Boston: Alyson.

I don't know who I am. (1993, November 16). In M. Murphy (Producer) *Sally Jessy Raphaël*. New York: Multimedia Entertainment Inc.

Irons, P., & Guitton, S. (Eds.) (1993). *May it please the court*. New York: New Press.

Jackson, J., McCullough, W., & Gurin, G. (1988). Family, socialization environment, and identity development in black Americans. In H. McAdoo (Ed.), *Black families* (pp. 242-256). Newbury Park, CA: Sage.

Jacobs, J. H. (1977). *Black/white interracial families, marital process, and identity development in young children*. Unpublished doctoral dissertation, Wright Institute, Berkeley, California.

Jacobs, J. (1992). Identity development in biracial children. In M. P. P. Root (Ed.), *Racially mixed people in America* (pp. 190-206). Newbury Park, CA: Sage.

Jamoo. (1993). Passing for white: The outing of mixed-race people. In M. R. Hearst (Ed.), *Interracial identity: Celebration, conflict, or choice?* (pp. 79-88). Chicago: Biracial Family Network.

Jefferson, M. (1994, May). A spy in the house of race. *Elle*, pp. 74, 76, 78.

Jenkins, A. (1985). *Dialogue and dialectic: Psychotherapy in cross cultural contexts*. Paper presented at the annual meeting of the American Psychological Association, Los Angeles.

Johnson, D. (1992a). Developmental pathways: Toward an ecological theoretical forumulation of race identity in black-white biracial children. In M. P. P. Root (Ed.), *Racially mixed people in America* (pp. 37-49). Newbury Park, CA: Sage.

Johnson, D. (1992b). Racial preference and biculturality in biracial preschoolers. *Merrill-Palmer Quarterly, 38*, 233-244.

Johnson, J. W. (1960). *The autobiography of an ex-coloured man*. New York: Hill & Wang. (Original work published 1912)

Johnson, R., & Nagoshi, C. (1986). The adjustment of offspring of within-group and interracial/intercultural marriages: A comparison of personality factor scores. *Journal of Marriage and the Family, 48,* 279-284.

Jones, A. (1985). Psychological functioning in black Amerians: A conceptual guide for use in psychotherapy. *Psychotherapy: Theory, Research and Practice, 22,* 363-369.

Jones, L. (1994a). *Bulletproof diva: Tales of race, sex and hair.* New York: Doubleday.

Jones, L. (1994b, May). Mama's white. *Essence,* pp. 78, 80, 150-151.

Jorge, A. (1979). The black Puerto Rican woman in contemporary American society. In E. Acosta-Belen (Ed.), *The Puerto Rican woman* (pp. 134-141). New York: Praeger.

Kallgren, C., & Caudill, P. (1993). Current transracial adoption practices: Racial dissonance or racial awareness? *Psychological Reports, 72,* 551-558.

Kanuha, V. (1990). Compounding the triple jeopardy: Battering in lesbian of color relationships. *Women and Therapy, 9,* 169-184.

Katz, J. N. (1990). The invention of heterosexuality. *Socialist Review, 90*(1), 7-34.

Kerckhoff, A. C., & McCormick, T. C. (1955). Marginal status and marginal personality. *Social Forces, 34,* 48-55.

Kerwin, C. (1991). Racial identity development in biracial children of black/white racial heritage (Doctoral dissertation, Fordham University, 1991). *Dissertation Abstracts International, 52,* 2469-A.

Kerwin, C., & Ponterotto, J. (1995). Biracial identity development: Theory and research. In J. G. Ponterotto, J. M. Casas, L. A. Suzuki, & C. M. Alexander (Eds.), *Handbook of multicultural counseling* (pp. 199-217). Thousand Oaks, CA: Sage.

Kerwin, C., Ponterotto, J., Jackson, B., & Harris, A. (1993). Racial identity in biracial children: A qualitative investigation. *Journal of Counseling Psychology, 40,* 221-231.

Khanga, Y. (1993). *Soul to soul: The story of a black Russian American family, 1865-1992.* New York: Norton.

Kich, G. K. (1982). *Eurasians: Ethnic/racial identity development of biracial Japanese/white adults.* Unpublished doctoral dissertation, the Wright Institute of Professional Psychology, Berkeley, California.

Kich, G. K. (1992). The developmental process of asserting a biracial, bicultural identity. In M. P. P. Root (Ed.), *Racially mixed people in America* (pp. 304-317). Newbury Park, CA: Sage.

Kikumura, A., & Kitano, H. (1973). Interracial marriages: A picture of the Japanese Americans. *Journal of Social Issues, 29*(2), 67-81.

King, D. (1988). Multiple jeopardy, multiple consciusness: The context of a black feminist ideology. In M. Malson, E. Mudimbe-Boyi, J. O'Barr, & M. Wyer (Eds.), *Black women in America* (pp. 265-295). Chicago: University of Chicago Press.

King, M. L., Jr. (1992). What happens to them happens to me. In J. Salzman, A. Beck, & G. S. Sorin (Eds.), *Bridges and boundaries: African Americans and American Jews* (pp. 88-90). New York: George Braziller.

Kingston, M. H. (1989, December). The novel's next step: If someone could create the global novel, we'd all have a sequel. *Mother Jones,* pp. 37-41.

Klein, F. (1993). *The bisexual option.* New York: Harrington Park Press. (Original work published 1978)

Klein, F., & Wolf, T. (Ed.). (1985). *Two lives to lead: Bisexuality in men and women.* New York: Harrington Park Press.

Koss-Chioino, J. (1992). *Women as healers, women as patients: Mental health care and traditional healing in Puerto Rico.* Boulder, CO: Westview.

Kotkin, J., & Van Agt, A. (1991, Fall). Peoples beyond nations. *New Perspective Quarterly*, pp. 46-55.

Kovel, J. (1984). *White racism: A psychohistory.* New York: Columbia University Press.

Krieger, N. (1994). *Proposed "race/ethnicity" questionnaire and data code form.* Prepared for July 14, 1994, Office of Management and Budget hearings, San Francisco.

Kull, A. (1992). *The colorblind constitution.* Cambridge, MA: Harvard University Press.

Kupers, T. A. (1993). *Revisioning men's lives: Gender, intimacy, and power.* New York: Guilford.

Lane, C. (1994, December 1). Review of Herrnstein and Murray (1994). *New York Review of Books, 41*(20), pp. 14-19.

Lang, B. (1990). *Act and idea in the Nazi genocide.* Chicago: University of Chicago Press.

Langness, L. L., & Frank, G. (1981). *Lives: An anthropological approach to biography.* Novato, CA: Chandler & Sharp.

Laqueur, T. (1990). *Making sex.* Cambridge, MA: Harvard University Press.

Larsen, N. (1986a). *Passing.* New Brunswick, NJ: Rutgers University Press. (Original work published 1929)

Larsen, N. (1986b). *Quicksand.* New Brunswick, NJ: Rutgers University Press. (Original work published 1928)

Larsson, C. (1965). *Marriage across the color line.* Chicago: Johnson.

Laszlo, E. (1987). *Evolution in our hands: The grand synthesis.* Boston: Shambala, New Science Library.

Lauren, P. G. (1988). *Power and prejudice: The politics and diplomacy of racial discrimination.* Boulder, CO: Westview.

Lee, J. F. J. (1991-1992). *Asian Americans.* New York: The New Press.

Lee, S. (1993). Racial classifications in the U.S. census: 1890-1990. *Ethnic and Racial Studies, 16*(1), 75-94.

Lemmel, D. (1992). *Outside the colorlines: An analysis of the external influences contributing to the development of a a biracial identity.* Senior thesis, Bard College, Social Studies Department, Boston.

Lempel, L. R. (1979). *The mulatto in United States race relations: Changing status and attitudes, 1800-1940.* Unpublished doctoral dissertation. Syracuse University, Syracuse, NY.

Leonard, K. I. (1992). *Making ethnic choices: California's Punjabi Mexican Americans.* Philadelphia, PA: Temple University Press.

Lerner, G. (1986). *The creation of patriarchy.* New York: Oxford University Press.

Lewit, E. M., & Baker, L. G. (1994). Race and ethnicity—changes for children. *The Future of Children, 4*(3), 134-144.

Lieberson, S., & Waters, M. C. (1988). *From many strands: Ethnic and racial groups in contemporary America* (Report for the National Committee for Research on the 1980 Census). New York: Russell Sage.

Lim-Hing, S. (Ed.). (1994). *The very inside: An anthology of writing by Asian and Pacific Islander lesbian and bisexual women.* Toronto: Sister Vision Press.

Littlejohn, III, B. (Ed.). (1994). *Inside/out: Poetry and prose by people of mixed heritage: Vol. 1.* Santa Cruz: University of California, Santa Cruz.

Longres, J. F. (1974). Racism and its effects on Puerto Rican continentals. *Social Casework, 55,* 67-75.

Lorde, A. (1981). The master's tools will never dismantle the master's house. In C. Moraga & G. Anzaldúa (Ed.), *This bridge called my back: Writings by radical women of color* (pp. 98-101). Watertown, MA: Persephone Press.

Lorde, A. (1984). *Sister outsider.* Freedom, CA: Crossing Press.

Loving v. Virginia, 388 U.S. 1 (1967).

Lugones, M. (1994). Purity, impurity, and separation. *Signs: Journal of Women in Culture and Society, 19*(2), 458-479.

Lukes, C. A., & Land, H. (1990). Biculturality and homosexuality. *Social Work, 35*, 155-161.

Lyles, M., Yancey, A., Grace, C., & Carter, J. (1985). Racial identity and self-esteem: Problems peculiar to biracial children. *Journal of the American Academy of Child and Adolescent Psychiatry, 24*, 150-153.

Lyman, S. M., & Douglass, W. A. (1973). Ethnicity: Strategies of collective and individual impression management. *Social Research, 40*(2), 344-365.

Lynch, J. (1986). *Multicultural education: Principles and practice.* London: Routledge.

Lythcott-Haims, J. C. (1994). Where do mixed babies belong? Racial classification in America and its implications for transracial adoption. *Harvard Civil Rights—Civil Liberties Law Review, 29*, 531, 532.

Mar, J. B. (1988). *Chinese Caucasian interracial parenting and ethnic identity.* Unpublished doctoral dissertation, University of Masachusetts at Amherst.

Marger, M. N. (1994). *Race and ethnic relations: American and global perspectives* (3rd ed.). Belmont, CA: Wadsworth.

Martin, C. G. (1990). Orientalism and ethnographer: Said, Herodotus, and the discourse of alterity. *Criticism, 32*(4), 511-530.

Martinez, E. (1992). Beyond black/white: The racisms of our time. *Social Justice, 20*, 22-34.

Maslow, A. (1968). *Towards a psychology of being.* New York: D. Van Nostrand.

Mass, A. (1992). Interracial Japanese Americans: The best of both worlds or the end of the Japanese American community? In M. P. P. Root (Ed.), *Racially mixed people in America* (pp. 265-279). Newbury Park, CA: Sage.

Matiella, C. A. (1991). *Positively different. Creating a bias-free environment for children.* Santa Cruz, CA: ETR Associates.

Mays, V., & Comas-Dìaz, L. (1988). Feminist therapies with ethnic minority populations: A closer look at blacks and Hispanics. In M. A. Dutton-Douglas & L. E. Walker (Eds.), *Feminist psychotherapies: Integration of therapeutic and feminist systems* (pp. 228-251). Norwood, NJ: Ablex.

McAdoo, H. (1985). Racial attitude and self-concept of young black children over time. In H. McAdoo & J. McAdoo (Eds.), *Black children* (pp. 213-242). Beverly Hills, CA: Sage.

McAuliffe, Jr., D. (1994). *The deaths of Sybil Bolton.* New York: Random House.

McCarthy, C. (1988). Rethinking liberal and radical perspectives on racial inequality in schooling: Making the case for non-synchrony. *Harvard Educational Review, 58*(3), 265-279.

McCarthy, C. (1993). After the canon: Knowledge and ideological representation in the multcultural discourse on curriculum reform. In C. McCarthy & W. Crichlow (Eds.), *Race, identity, and representation in education* (pp. 289-305). New York: Routledge.

McCracken, J. B. (1993). *Valuing diversity.* Washington DC: NAEYC.

McCunn, R. L. (1988). *Chinese American portraits.* San Francisco: Chronicle Books.

McGoldrick, M., Pearce, J., & Giordano, J. (Ed.). (1982). *Ethnicity and family therapy.* New York: Guilford.

McKelvey, R., Mao, A., & Webb, J. (1992). A risk profile predicting psychological distress in Vietnamese Amerasian youth. *Journal of the American Academy of Child Adolescent Psychiatry, 31*, 911-915.

McKelvey, R., Mao, A., & Webb, J. (1993). Premigratory expectations and mental health symptomology in a group of Vietnamese Amerasian youth. *Journal of the Academy of Child and Adolescent Psychiatry, 32*, 414-418.

McKenney, N. R., & Cresce, A. R. (1992, April). *Measurement of ethnicity in the United States: Experiences of the U.S. Census Bureau.* Paper presented at the joint Canada-United States Conference on the Measurement of Ethnicity, Ottawa, Canada.

McKenzie, J. (1993). *Adoption of children with special needs.* In R. E. Berman (Ed.), *The future of children* (pp. 62-76). Los Altos, CA: Center for the Future of Children, the David and Lucile Packard Foundation.

McKillop, D. (1994, November). *Conceptualization of human sexuality: A model for clinical training and practice.* Paper presented at the National Conference of the Society for the Scientific Study of Sex, Miami, FL.

McRoy, R. (1989). An organizational dilemma: The case of transracial adoptions. *The Journal of Applied Behavioral Sciences, 25*(2), 145-160.

McRoy, R. (1990). Cultural and racial identity in black families. In S. Logan (Ed.), *Social work practice with black families* (pp. 97-112). New York: Longman.

McRoy, R. (1994). Attachment and racial identity: Implications for child placement decision making. *Journal of Multicultural Social Work, 3*(3), 59-75.

McRoy, R. (in press). Racial identity issues for black children in foster care. In S. Logan (Ed.), *Black families: Building strengths, self-help, and positive change.* New York: Longman.

McRoy, R., & Freeman, E. (1986). Racial identity issues among mixed-race children. *Social Work in Education, 8*, 164-174.

McRoy, R., & Zurcher, L. (1983). *Transracial and inracial adoptees: The adolescent years.* Springfield, IL: Charles C Thomas.

McRoy, R., Zurcher, L., Lauderdale, M., & Anderson, R. (1984). The identity of transracial adoptees. *Social Casework, 64*(1), 34-39.

Mead, G. H. (1934). *Mind, self, and society.* Chicago: University of Chicago Press.

Melina, L. (1990). Racial identity of children of mixed heritage still controversial. *Adopted Child, 9*(5), 1-4.

Menchú, R. (1984). *I, Rigoberta Manchú: An Indian woman in Gualemala* (pp. 165-170). New York: Verso.

Mennell, S. (1995). The formation of we-images: A process theory. In C. Calhoun (Ed.), *Social theory and the politics of identity* (pp. 175-197). Cambridge, MA: Basil Blackwell.

Miles, R. (1989). *Racism.* London: Routledge.

Miles, R. (1993). *Racism after "race relations."* London: Routledge.

Miller, R. L. (1992). The human ecology of multiracial identity. In M. P. P. Root (Ed.), *Racially mixed people in America* (pp. 24-36). Newbury Park, CA: Sage.

Miller, R., & Miller, B. (1990). Mothering the biracial child: Bridging the gaps between African American and white parenting styles. *Women and Therapy, 10*(1-2), 169-179.

Mills, C. (1992, May/June). Mixed couples: Popular myths about interracial couples. *Interrace*, pp. 20-21.

Mills, C. (1993, November). Worth fighting for? Multiracial. *Interrace*, pp. 21-28.

Mirkin, M. P. (Ed.). (1994). *Women in context: Toward a feminist reconstruction of psychotherapy.* New York: Guilford.

Mitchell, A. (1990). *Cultural identification, racial knowledge, and general psychological well-being among biracial young adults.* Unpublished doctoral dissertation, California School of Professional Psychology, Los Angeles.

Mitchell-Kernan, C., & Tucker, B. (1990). New trends in black American interracial marriage: The social structural context. *Journal of Marriage and the Family, 52,* 209-219.

Mizio, E. (1983). The impact of macro systems on Puerto Rican families. In G. J. Powell (Ed.), *The psychosocial development of minority group children.* New York: Brunner/Mazel.

Monahan, T. (1970). Are interracial marriages stable? *Social Forces, 48*(4), 461-472.

Money, J. (1987). Sin, sickness, or status? Homosexual gender identity and psychoneuroendocrinology. *American Psychologist, 42*(4), 384-399.

Money, J., & Ehrhardt, A. (1972). *Man & woman, boy & girl: The differentiation and dimorphism of gender identity from conception to maturity.* Baltimore: Johns Hopkins University Press.

Monroe, S. (1992, March). Love in black and white: Couples who confront the taboo. *Elle,* pp. 92-96, 100-102.

Moraga, C. (1981). La Guera. In C. Moraga & G. Anzaldúa (Eds.), *This bridge called my back: Writings by radical women of color* (pp. 27-34). Watertown, PA: Persephone Press.

Moraga, C. (1983). *Loving in the war years.* Boston: South End Press.

Moraga, C. (1993). *The last generation.* Boston: South End Press.

Moraga, C., & Anzaldúa, G. (1981). *This bridge called my back: Writings by radical women of color.* Watertown, MA: Persephone Press.

Morgenstern, J. (1971, September 13). The new face of adoption. *Newsweek,* pp. 67-72.

Moritsugu, J. L., Forester, L., & Morishima, J. (1978). *Eurasians: A pilot study.* Paper presented at the Western Psychological Association, San Francisco.

Morrison, T. (1992). *Playing in the dark.* New York: Vintage.

Motoyoshi, M. M. (1990). The experience of mixed-race people: Some thoughts and theories. *Journal of Ethnic Studies, 18*(2), 77-94.

Munro, D. (in press). The continuing evolution of Affirmative Action under Title VII: New directions after the Civil Rights Act of 1991. *Virginia Law Review.*

Murphy-Shigematsu, S. L. (1986). *The voices of Amerasian: Ethnicity, identity, and empowerment in interracial Japanese Americans.* Unpublished doctoral dissertation, Harvard University.

Murphy-Shigematsu, S. L. (1988). Addressing issues of biracial/bicultural Asian Americans. In G. Y. Okihiro (Ed.), *Reflections on shattered windows: Promises and prospects for Asian American studies* (pp. 111-116). Pullman: Washington State University Press.

Myrdal, G. (1962). *An American dilemma: The Negro problem and modern democracy* (20th ed.). New York: Harper & Row. (Original work published 1944)

Nakashima, C. (1988). Research notes on Nikkei hapa identity. In G. Y. Okihiro (Ed.), *Reflection on shattered windows: Promises and prospects for Asian American studies* (pp. 206-213). Pullman: Washington State University Press.

Nakashima, C. (1992). An invisible monster: The creation and denial of mixed-race people in America. In M. P. P. Root, (Ed.), *Racially mixed people in America* (pp. 162-178). Newbury Park, CA: Sage.

Nandy, A. (1983). *The intimate enemy: Loss and recovery of self under colonialism.* New Delhi, India: Oxford University Press.

Nash, G. B. (1982). *Red, black, and white: The people of early America* (2d ed.). Englewood Cliffs, NJ: Prentice Hall.

Nash, G. B., & Weiss, R. (Eds.). (1970). *The great fear: Race in the mind of America.* New York: Holt, Rinehart, & Winston.

National Association of Black Social Workers (NABSW). (1972, April). Position statement on transracial adoptions, presented at the National Association of Black Social Workers Conference, Nashville, TN.

National Association of Black Social Workers (NABSW). (1994, April). Position statement on transracial adoptions, presented at the National Association of Black Social Workers Conference, Nashville, TN.

Njeri, I. (1991, January 13). Taking a step beyond the melting pot. *Los Angeles Times,* pp. E1, E9-10.

Nobles, W. (1980). Extended self: Rethinking the so-called Negro self-concept. In R. H. Jones (Ed.), *Black psychology.* New York: Harper & Row.

No Collective (Eds.). (1992). *Voices of identity, rage, and deliverance: An anthology of writings by people of mixed descent.* Oakland, CA: GRT Book.

No place for mankind. (1989, September 4). *Time,* p. 17.

Nunez, S. (1995). *A feather on the breath of God.* New York: HarperCollins.

O'Hare, W. P., & Felt, J. C. (1991). *Asian Americans: America's fastest-growing minority group.* Washington DC: Population Reference Bureau.

Omi, M., & Winant, H. (1986). *Racial formation in the United States from the 1960s to the 1980s.* New York: Routledge & Kegan Paul.

Omi, M., & Winant, H. (1993). On the theoretical concept of race. In C. McCarthy & W. Crichlow (Eds.), *Race, identity, and representation in education* (pp. 3-10). New York: Routledge.

Ottley, R., & Weatherby, W. J. (Eds.). (1967). *The Negro in New York: An informal social history.* Dobbs Ferry: Oceana.

Pagnozzi, A. (1991, September). Race in America: Mixing it up. *Mirabella,* pp. 130-134.

Parham, T. A., & Helms, J. E. (1985). Relation of racial identity attitudes to self-actualization and affective states of black students. *Journal of Counseling Psychology, 32*(2), 431-440).

Park, R. E. (1928). Human migration and the marginal man. *American Journal of Sociology, 33,* 881-893.

Park, R. E. (1937). Introduction. In E. V. Stonequist, *The marginal man: A study in personality and culture conflict* (p. xvii). New York: Russell & Russell.

Pascoe, P. (1991). Race, gender, and intercultural relations: The case of interracial marriage. *Frontiers—A Journal of Women's Studies, 1,* 5-18.

Pederson, L. (1991). *Dark hearts: The unconscious forces that shape men's lives.* Boston: Shambala.

Pharr, S. (1988). *Homophobia: A weapon of sexism.* Little Rock, AR: Chardon Press.

Phinney, J. (1990). Ethnic identity in adolescents and adults: Review of research. *Psychological Bulletin, 108,* 499-514.

Phinney, J. S., & Rotheram, M. J. (1987). *Children's ethnic socialization.* Newbury Park, CA: Sage.

Pinderhughes, E. (1995). Biracial identity—asset or handicap? In H. W. Harris, H. C. Blue, & E. E. H. Griffith (Eds.), *Racial and ethnic identity* (pp. 73-93). New York: Routledge.

Piper, A. (1992). Passing for white, passing for black. *Transition, 58,* 4-32.

Piskacek, V., & Golub, M. (1973). Children of interracial marriages. In I. R. Stuart & L. E. Abt (Eds.), *Interracial marriage: Expectations and realities* (pp. 53-61). New York: Grossman.

Pitt, L. (1966). *The decline of the Californios.* Berkeley: University of California Press.

Pleasant, W., & Hardy, M. (1990). Interview with Louis Farrakhan. In W. Pleasant (Ed.), *Independent black leadership in America* (pp. 26-51). New York: Castillo International.

Plessy v. Ferguson, 163 U.S. 537 (1896).

Poldnak, A. P. (1989). *Racial and ethnic differences in disease.* New York and London: Oxford University Press.

Porter, J., & Washington, R. (1993). Minority identity and self-esteem. *Annual Review of Sociology, 19,* 139-161.

Posadas, B. M. (1989). Mestiza girlhood: Interracial families in Chicago's Filipino American community since 1925. In Asian Women United of California (Ed.), *Making waves: An anthology of writings by and about Asian American women* (pp. 273-282). Boston: Beacon.

Poston, W. S. C. (1990). The biracial identity development model: A needed addition. *Journal of Counseling and Development, 69,* 152-155.

Poussaint, A. P. (1984). Study of interracial chidlren presents positive picture. *Interracial Books for Children Bulletin, 15*(6), 9-10.

Powell, A. (1988). Raise your child with ethnic pride. *OURS, 21*(6), 26-29.

Powlishta, K. K., Serbin, L. A., Doyle, A., & White, D. R. (1994). *Developmental Psychology, 30*(4), 526.

Prager, J. (1982). American racial ideology as collective representation. *Ethnic and Racial Studies, 5,* 99-119.

Price, G. W. (1967). *Origins of the war with Mexico.* Austin: University of Texas Press.

Proctor, R. (1988). *Racial hygiene.* Cambridge, MA: Harvard University Press.

Puig, A. (1991). A traumatic-stress model for EPAs. *EPA Digest, 12*(22), 53-54.

Rajs, E. C. (1991). Pros, cons of ethnic labels: Standard categories don't fit multi-ethnic population. *UC Focus, 5*(5), 8.

Ramirez, G., & Ramirez, J. L. (1994). *Multicultural children's literature.* Albany, NY: Delmar.

Ramirez, III, M. (1983). *Psychology of the Americas: Mestizo perspectives on personality and mental health.* New York: Pergamon.

Ramos Rosado, M. (1986). La mujer puertoriquena negra, "La otra cara de la historia" [The Black Puerto Rican woman, "The other face of history"]. *Homines, 10*(2), 491-497.

Rawls, J. (1971). *A theory of justice.* Cambridge, MA: Harvard University Press.

Reed, D. (1981). *Education for building a people's movement.* Boston: South End Press.

Regents of the University of California v. Bakke, 438 U.S. 265 (1978).

Report of the National Advisory Commission on Civil Disorders, 1 (1968).

Rich, A. (1986). *Blood, bread, and poetry: Selected prose 1978-1985.* New York: Norton.

Richmond v. Croson, 488 US 469 (1989).

Ridgeway, J. (1990). *Blood in the face.* New York: Thundermouth.

Ringer, B. (1983). *We the people and others: Duality and America's treatment of its racial minorities.* New York: Routledge, Chapman & Hall.

Ringer, B., & Lawless, E. (1989). *Race-ethnicity and society.* London: Routledge, Chapman & Hall.

Rivera, E. (1982). *Family installments: Memories of growing up Hispanic.* New York: William Morrow.

Rodriguez, C. E. (1992). Race, culture, and Latino "otherness" in the 1980 Census. *Social Science Quarterly, 73*(4), 930-937.

Rodriguez, C. E. (1994). Challenging racial hegemony: Puerto Ricans in the United States. In S. Gregory & R. Sanjek (Eds.), *Race* (pp. 131-145). New Brunswick, NJ: Rutgers University Press.

Roman, L. G. (1993). White is a color! White defensiveness, postmodernism, and antiracist pedagogy. In C. McCarthy & W. Crichlow (Eds.), *Race, identity, and representation in education* (pp. 71-188). New York: Routledge.

Root, M. P. P. (1990). Resolving "other" status: Identity development of biracial individuals. In L. Brown & M. P. P. Root (Eds.), *Complexity and diversity in feminist theory and therapy* (pp. 185-205). New York: Haworth.

Root, M. P. P. (1992a). Back to the drawing board: Methodological issues in research on multiracial people. In M. P. P. Root (Ed.), *Racially mixed people in America* (pp. 181-189). Newbury Park, CA: Sage.

Root, M. P. P. (Ed.). (1992b). *Racially mixed people in America*. Newbury Park, CA: Sage.

Root, M. P. P. (1992c). Reconstructing the impact of trauma on personality. In L. S. Brown & M. Ballou (Eds.), *Personality and psychopathology: Feminist reappraisals* (pp. 229-265). New York: Guilford.

Root, M. P. P. (1992d). Within, between, and beyond race. In M. P. P. Root (Ed.), *Racially mixed people in America* (pp. 3-11). Newbury Park, CA: Sage.

Root, M. P. P. (1994a). Mixed-race women. In L. Comas-Díaz & B. Greene (Eds.), *Women of color: Integrating ethnic and gender identities in psychotherapy* (pp. 455-478). New York: Guilford.

Root, M. P. P. (1994b, Summer). Reasons racially mixed persons identify as people of color. In M. Garcia (Ed.), *FOCUS: Newsletter for the Psychological Study of Ethnic Minority Issues in the American Psychological Association*, pp. 1-5.

Root, M. P. P. (1995). The psychological browning of America. In N. Zack (Ed.), *American mixed race: The culture of microdiversity* (pp. 231-236). Lanham, MD: Rowman & Littlefield.

Ropp, S. M., Williams, T. K., & Rooks, C. (1995). *Prism lives/emerging voices of multiracial Asians: A selective, partially annotated bibliography*. Los Angeles: University of California Press.

Roseberry, W. (1992). Multiculturalism and the challenge of anthropology. *Social Research, 59*(4), 841-858.

Rosner, A. (1993). *Choosing sides: How black/white biracial Amherst college students mediate a racial identity*. Senior honor's thesis, Amherst College, Department of Black Studies, Amherst, MA.

Ruddick, S. (1989). *Maternal thinking: Toward a politics of peace*. Boston: Beacon.

Ruiz, A. S. (1990). Ethnic identity: Crisis and resolution. *Journal of Multicultural Counseling and Development, 18*, 29-40.

Russell, K., Wilson, M., & Hall, R. (1992). *The color complex: The politics of skin color among African Americans*. New York: Harcourt, Brace, Jovanovich.

Ryan, A. (1994, November 17). Review of Herrnstein and Murray (1994). *New York Review of Books, 41*(19), 7-11.

Said, E. (1978). *Orientalism*. New York: Vintage.

Said, E. (1990). Reflections on exile. In R. Ferguson, M. Gever, M.-H. Trinh, & C. West (Eds.), *Out there: Marginalization and contemporary cultures* (pp. 357-366). New York: MIT Press.

Saint Francis College v. Al-Khazraji, 481 US 604, (1987).

Samovar, L. A., & Porter, R. E. (Ed.). (1988). *Intercultural communication: A reader* (5th ed.). Belmont, CA: Wadsworth.

Sanjek, R. (1994). Intermarriage and the future of races in the United States. In S. Gregory & R. Sanjek (Eds.), *Race* (pp. 103-130). New Brunswick, NJ: Rutgers University Press.

Sartre, J.-P. (1965). *Anti-semite and Jew.* New York: Schocken.

Sartre, J.-P. (1976). *Critique of dialectical reasoning: Theory of practical ensembles* (A. Sheridan-Smith, Trans.). London: New Left Books.

Scales-Trent, J. (1990). Commonalities: On being black and white, different and same. *Yale Journal of Law and Feminism, 2*(2), 305-327.

Scales-Trent, J. (1995). *Notes of a white black woman.* University Park: Pennsylvania State University Press.

Scheick, W. J. (1979). *The half-blood: A cultural symbol in 19th century American fiction.* Lexington: The University of Kentucky Press.

Searle, G. (1994). Unpublished student paper for English 556, University of Washington, Spring Quarter.

Seda Bonilla, E. (1970). *Requiem por una cultura.* Rio Piedras, Puerto Rico: Editorial Edil.

See, K., & Wilson, W. (1988). Race and ethnicity. In N. Smelser (Ed.), *Handbook of sociology* (pp. 223-242). Newbury Park, CA: Sage.

See, L. (1995). *On gold mountain.* New York: St. Martin's.

Seller, M. (1977). *To seek America: A history of ethnic life in the United States.* Englewood, NJ: Jerome S. Ozer.

Seligman, H. J. (1939). *Race against man.* New York: G. P. Putnam.

Shah, H., & Thornton, M. C. (1994). Racial ideology in U.S. news magazine coverage of black-Latino interaction, 1980-1992. *Critical Studies in Mass Communication, 11,* 141-161.

Sharp, G. (1973). *The politics of nonviolent action.* Boston: Porter Sargent.

Sherriffe, L. (1994, May 27). *Eye on America* (Narr. W. Andrews and C. Chung). New York: CBS Evening News.

Shinagawa, L. H. (1994). *Intermarriage and inequality: A theoretical and empirical analysis of the marriage patterns of Asian Americans.* Unpublished doctoral dissertation, University of California, Berkelely.

Shinagawa, L. H., & Pang, G. Y. (1988). Intraethnic, interethnic, and interracial marriages among Asian Americans in California, 1980. *Berkeley Journal of Sociology, 33,* 95-114.

Shohat, E. (1992). Notes on the "post-colonial." *Social Text, 30/31,* 99-113.

Shrage, L. (1995). Ethnic transgressions: Confessions of an assimilated Jew. In N. Zack (Ed.), *American mixed race: Exploring microdiversity* (pp. 287-296). Lanham, MD: Roman & Littlefield.

Silko, L. M. (1977). *Ceremony.* New York: Penguin.

Silko, L. M. (1991). *Almanac of the dead.* New York: Penguin.

Simon, R. (1984). Adoption of black children by white parents in the USA. In P. Bean (Ed.), *Adoption essays in social policy, law, and sociology* (pp. 229-242). London/New York: Tavistock.

Simon, R. J., & Alstein, H. (1987). *Transracial adoptees and their families.* New York: Praeger.

Simon, R., Alstein, H., & Melli, M. S. (1994). *The case for transracial adoption.* Washington DC: The American University Press.

Singer, J. (1976). *Androgyny: Toward a new theory of sexuality.* New York: Anchor Press/Doubleday.

Sirk, D. (producer), & Stahl, J. (Director). (1934). *Imitation of life.* Universal Pictures.

Sleeter, C. (1993). How white teachers construct race. In C. McCarthy & W. Crichlow (Eds.), *Race, identity, and representation in education* (pp. 157-171). New York: Routledge.

Sleeter, C. E., & Grant, C. A. (1987). An analysis of multicultural education in the United States. *Harvard Educational Review, 57*(4), 421-443.

Smolowe, J. (1993). Intermarried . . . with children. *Time, 142*(21; Fall special issue), pp. 64-65.

Sobel, M. (1987). *The world they made together: Black and white values in eighteenth-century Virginia.* Princeton, NJ: Princeton University Press.

Sommers, V. S. (1964). The impact of dual-cultural membership on identity. *Psychiatry, 27,* 332-344.

Soto, N. E. (1994). Woman of color. In E. Featherston (Ed.), *Skin deep: Women writing on color, culture and identity* (pp. 5-6). Freedom, CA: The Crossing Press.

Spencer, J. M. (1993). Trends of opposition to multiculturalism. *The Black Scholar, 23*(2), 2-5.

Spencer, M. B. (1984). Black children's racial awareness, racial attitudes, and self-concept. *Journal of Child Psychology and Psychiatry, 25,* 433-441.

Spencer, M. B., & Markstrom-Adams, C. (1990). Identity processes among racial and ethnic minority children in America. *Child Development, 61,* 290-310.

Spencer, R. (1994, October/November). Notes from the struggle against racial categorization: Challenge or collaboration? *Interrace,* pp. 18-22.

Sperber, J. (1991, September/October). Not one or the other: Teens want their multiracial identities to be recognized. *LA Youth,* pp. 1-11.

Spickard, P. R. (1983). *Mixed marriage: Two American minority groups and the limits of ethnic identity, 1900-1970.* Unpublished doctoral dissertation, University of California, Berkeley.

Spickard, P. R. (1989). *Mixed blood: Intermarriage and ethnic identity in twentieth-century America.* Madison: University of Wisconsin Press.

Spickard, P. R. (1992). The illogic of American racial categories. In M. P. P. Root (Ed.), *Racially mixed people in American* (pp. 12-23). Newbury Park, CA: Sage.

Stanford group aims to unite students of different cultures. (1994, April 1). *Asian Week,* p. 16.

Steele, S. (1990). *The content of our character: A new vision of race in America.* New York: St. Martin's.

Stehno, S. M. (1990). The elusive continuum of child welfare services: Implications for minority children and youths. *Child Welfare, 69*(6), 551-562.

Stephan, C. W. (1991). Ethnic identity among mixed-heritage people in Hawaii. *Symbolic Interaction, 14,* 261-277.

Stephan, C. W. (1992). Mixed-heritage individuals: Ethnic identity and trait characteristics. In M. P. P. Root (Ed.), *Racially mixed people in America* (pp. 50-63). Newbury Park, CA: Sage.

Stephan, C., & Stephan, W. (1989). After intermarriage: Ethnic identity among mixed-heritage Japanese-Americans and Hispanics. *Journal of Marriage and the Family, 51,* 507-519.

Stolley, K. (1993). Statistics on adoption in the United States. In R. E. Berman (Ed.), *The future of children* (pp. 26-43). Los Altos, CA: Center for the Future of Children, The David and Lucile Packard Foundation.

Stonequist, E. V. (1937). *The marginal man: A study in personality and culture conflict.* New York: Russell & Russell.

Strong, N. (1978). *Patterns of social interaction and psychological accomodations among Japan's Konketsuju population.* Unpublished doctoral dissertation, University of California, Berkeley.

Stuart, I. R., & Abt, L. E. (1973). *Interracial marriage: Expectations and realities.* New York: Grossman.

Sue, D. W., & Sue, D. (1990). *Counseling the culturally different: Theory and practice* (2d ed.). New York: John Wiley.

Sue, S., & Sue, D. W. (1971). Chinese-American personality and mental health. *Amerasia Journal, 1,* 29-36.

Sullivan, A. (1994). On transracial adoption. In *Children's voice* (pp. 4-6). Washington DC: Child Welfare League of America.

Sung, B. L. (1990). *Chinese American intermarriage.* New York: Center for Migration Studies.

Surrey, J. L. (1991). Relationship and empowerment. In J. Jordan, A. Kaplan, J. B. Miller, I. Stiver, & J. Surrey (Eds.), *Women's growth in connection: Writings from the Stone Center* (pp. 162-180). New York: Guilford.

Takagi, D. Y. (1994). Maiden voyage: Excursion into sexuality and identity politics in Asian America. *Amerasia Journal, 20*(1), 1-17.

Takaki, R. (1979). *Iron cage.* New York: Knopf.

Takaki, R. (1989). *Strangers from a different shore.* New York: Penguin.

Takaki, R. (1993). *A different mirror: A history of multicultural America.* Boston: Little, Brown.

Tamagawa, K. (1932). *Holy prayers in a horse's ear.* New York: Ray Long & Richard R. Smith.

Taussig, M. T. (1993). *Mimesis and alterity: A particular history of the senses.* New York: Routledge.

Teicher, J. (1968). Some observations on identity problems in children of Negro-white marriages. *Journal of Nervous and Mental Disease, 146,* 249-256.

Tenzer, L. R. (1990). *A completely new look at interracial sexuality: Public opinion and select commentaries.* Manahawkin, NJ: Scholars' Publishing House.

Thomas, L. (1993). *Vessels of evil.* Philadelphia: Temple University Press.

Thomas, L. (in press). The soul of identity: Jews and blacks. In J. Rubin-Dorsky & S. Fisher-Fishkin (Eds.), *Reconfiguring Jewish indentity.* Madison: University of Wisconsin Press.

Thomas, P. (1967). *Down these mean streets.* New York: New American Library.

Thompson, E. (1967). Japan's rejected. *Ebony, 22,* 42-52.

Thorne, B. (1994). *Gender play: Girls and boys in school.* New Brunswick, NJ: Rutgers University Press.

Thornton, M. C. (1983). *A social history of a multiethnic identity: The case of black Japanese Americans.* Unpublished doctoral dissertation, University of Michigan.

Thornton, M. C. (1992). Is multiracial status unique? The personal and social experience. In M. P. P. Root (Ed.), *Racially mixed people in America* (pp. 321-325). Newbury Park, CA: Sage.

Thornton, M. C. (forthcoming). Dimensions of racial socialization among black parents: Minority, mainstream, and cultural components. In R. Taylor, L. Chatters, & J. Jackson (Eds.), *Family life in black America.* Thousand Oaks, CA: Sage.

Thornton, M. C., & Shah, H. (1995). U.S. news magazine images of black-Asian American relationships, 1980-1992: Enclosed worlds collide. Manuscript submitted for publication.

Thornton, M. C., & Wason, S. (1995). Intermarriage. In D. Levinson, (Ed.), *Encyclopedia of marriage and the family* (396-402). New York: Macmillan.

Tinker, J. (1973). Intermarriage and ethnic boundaries: The Japanese American case. *Journal of Social Issues, 29,* 49-66.

Tizard, B., & Phoenix, A. (1993). *Black, white, or mixed?: Race and racism in the lives of young people of mixed parentage.* New York: Routledge.

Tjerandsen, C. (1980). *Education for citizenship*. Santa Cruz, CA: Emil Schwarzhaupt Foundation.

Toomer, J. (1988). *Cane* (D. T. Turner, Ed.). New York: Norton. (Original work published 1923)

Trinh, T. M-H. (1991). *When the moon waxes red: Representation, gender, and cultural politics*. New York: Routledge.

Troyna, B., & Hatcher, R. (1992). *Racism in children's lives*. New York: Routledge.

Tucker, C. (1994, March 16). A silver lining in saga of a prom (Editorial). *Atlanta Journal/Constitution*.

Tucker, M. (1990). Director's foreword. In R. Ferguson, M. Gever, M.-H. Trinh, & C. West (Eds.), *Marginalization and contemporary cultures* (pp. 7-9). New York: MIT Press.

Twine, F. W. (forthcoming). Brown-skinned white girls: Class, culture and the construction of whiteness in suburban communities. *Gender, Place and Culture: A Journal of Feminist Geography, 3*(2).

Twine, F. W., Warren, J. W., & Ferrandiz, F. (1991). *Just black? Multiracial identity*. New York: Filmakers Library.

Tyack, D. (1974). *The one best system*. Cambridge, MA: Harvard University Press.

U.S. Bureau of the Census. (1964). *Census of population, 1960, Volume 1: Characteristics of the population* (Part I, U.S. Summary, Table 44). Washington, DC: Government Printing Office.

U.S. Bureau of the Census. (1970). *Characteristics of the population* (Vol. 1, Part 1, Sections 1 and 2). Washington, DC: Government Printing Office.

U.S. Bureau of the Census. (1990). *Census of population: General population characteristics—United States* (Vol. 1990 CP-1-1). Washington, DC: Government Printing Office.

U.S. Bureau of the Census. (1992). Marital status and living arrangements: March 1992 (*Current Population Reports*, Population characteristics, Series P20-468, December). Washington DC: Government Printing Office.

U.S. Bureau of the Census. (1993). *We, the American . . . Hispanics*. Washington, DC: Government Printing Office.

U.S. Department of Human Services, Administration for Children, Youth, and Families, Head Start Bureau. (1991). *Multicultural principles* (ACYF-IM-91-03). Washington, DC: Author.

Valverde, K.-L. (1992). From dust to gold: The Vietnamese American experience. In M. P. P. Root (Ed.), *Racially mixed people in America* (pp. 144-161). Newbury Park, CA: Sage.

Vargas, L. A., & Koss-Chioino, J. D. (Ed.). (1992). *Working with culture*. San Francisco: Jossey-Bass.

Vasquez, M. J. T. (1994). Latinas. In L. Comas-Díaz & B. Greene (Eds.), *Women of color: Integrating ethnic and ethnic identities in psychotherapy* (pp. 114-138). New York: Guilford.

Vizenor, G. R. (1981). *Earthdivers: Tribal narratives on mixed descent*. Minneapolis: University of Minnesota Press.

Vizenor, G. R. (1990). *Crossbloods: Bone courts, bingo, and other reports*. Minneapolis: University of Minnesota Press.

Vizenor, G. R. (1991). *Landfill meditation: Crossblood stories*. Hanover, PA: Wesleyan University Press.

Vroegh, K. (1992). *Transracial adoption: How is it 17 years later?* Chicago: Chicago Child Care Society.

Wacker, F. R. (1983). *Ethnicity, pluralism, and race*. Westport, CT: Greenwood.

Wagatsuma, H. (1976). Mixed-blood children in Japan: An exploratory study. *Journal of Asian Affairs, 2,* 9-16.

Walker, A. (1983). *In search of our mothers' gardens.* San Diego, CA: Harcourt Brace Jovanovich.

Walters, L. (1953). *A study of the social and marital adjustment of thirty-five American-Japanese couples.* Unpublished master's thesis, Ohio State University.

Walters, M., Carter, B., Papp, P., & Silverstein, O. (1988). *The invisible web: Gender patterns in family relationships.* New York: Guilford.

Wardle, F. (1987, January). Are you sensitive to interracial children's special identity needs. *Young Children,* pp. 53-59.

Wardle, F. (1988). Who am I? Responding to the child of mixed heritage. *PTA Today, 13*(7), 7-10.

Wardle, F. (1989). Children of mixed heritage: How can professionals respond? *Children Today, 18*(4), 10-13.

Wardle, F. (1991a). Interracial children and their families: How school social workers should respond. *Social Work in Education, 13*(4), 209-272.

Wardle, F. (1991b, Winter). Raising interracial children. *Mothering,* pp. 111-117.

Wardle, F. (1992). *Biracial identity: An ecological and developmental model.* Denver, CO: Center for the Study of Biracial Children.

Wardle, F. (1993a). Biracial profile: John James Audubon is a perfect role model for biracial children. *New People, 3*(5), 9.

Wardle, F. (1993b, March/April). Interracial families and biracial children. *Child Care Information Exchange, 90,* 45-48.

Wardle, F. (1993c). Why young children should learn a foreign language. *American Family, 1*(1), 4-6.

Wardle, F. (1994a). *An anti-bias and ecological model for multicultural education.* Denver, CO: Center for the Study of Biracial Children.

Wardle, F. (1994b, September). *An anti-bias and ecological model for multicultural education.* Paper presented at the fall CAEYC Conference, Denver, CO.

Wardle, F. (1994c, April 10). Biracial burdens: Interracial families struggle against societal myths. *Rocky Mountain News,* p. 83a.

Wardle, F. (1994d). What about the other kids in the neighborhood? *New People, 4*(5), 10-19.

Warmbold. J. (1992). If only she didn't have negro blood in her veins: The concept of Métissage in German colonial literature. *Journal of Black Studies, 23*(2), 200-209.

Warner, D. (Secretary for the European American Studies Group) (1992, August) Letter to the editor. *I-Pride Newsletter, 14*(6), 2.

Waters, M. C. (1990). *Ethnic options: Choosing identities in America.* University of California Press.

Waters, M. C. (1994, April). *The social construction of race and ethnicity: Some examples from demography.* Paper presented at American Diversity: A Demographic Challenge for the Twenty-First Century, Center for Social and Demographic Analysis Conference, SUNY, Albany.

Wattenberg, B. J. (1991). *The first universal nation.* New York: Free Press.

Weaver, K. (1994, March 15). Prinicipal's racial remarks anger students, community. New Orleans, LA, *Times Picayune,* p. A1.

Webb, F. J. (1969). *The Garies and their friends.* New York: Arno Press. (Original work published 1857)

Weinberg, M., Williams, C., & Pryor, D. (1994). *Dual attraction: Understanding bisexuality.* New York: Oxford University Press.

Weis, L. (Ed.). (1988). *Class, race, and gender in American education.* Albany: SUNY Press.

Wellman, D. T. (1993). *Portraits of white racism* (2nd ed.). Cambridge, UK: Cambridge University Press.

Welter, B. (1966). The cult of true womanhood: 1820-1860. *American Quarterly, 18,* 151-174.

West, C. (1993). *Race matters.* Boston: Beacon.

West, C., & Zimmerman, D. (1991). Doing gender. In J. Lorber & S. Farrell (Eds.), *The social construction of gender* (pp. 13-37). Newbury Park, CA: Sage

Wetherell, M., & Potter, J. (1992). *Mapping the language of racism: Discourse and the legitimation of exploitation.* New York: Columbia University Press.

Wheeler, D. L. (1995, February 17). A growing number. *The Chronicle of Higher Education,* pp. A9-10, 15.

Wilkinson, D. (1984). Afro-American women and their families. *Marriage and Family Review, 7,* 125-142.

Wilkinson, D., & King, G. (1987). Conceptual and methodological issues in the use of race as a variable: Policy implications. *Milbank Quarterly, 65,* 56-71.

Williams, G. H. (1995). *Life on the color line: The true story of a white boy who discovered he was black.* New York: Dutton.

Williams, J. (1990, December 20). Amerasian experience: Within, between, & beyond the limits of race, culture, community. *RAFU SHRIMP, 3.*

Williams, P. J. (1991). *The alchemy of race and rights.* Cambridge, MA: Harvard University Press.

Williams, T. K. (1991). *Multiethnic identity construction of Japanese-descent Amerasians.* Unpublished master's thesis, University of California Sociology Department, Los Angeles.

Williams, T. K. (1992). Prism Lives: Identity of binational Amerasians. In M. P. P. Root (Ed.), *Racially mixed people in America* (pp. 280-303). Newbury Park, CA: Sage.

Williams, T. K. (1993, April). *The mulatto metaphor.* Unpublished paper, Pacific Sociological Association Meeting.

Williams, T. K. (1994-1995). *In our very own arena: The social construction and presentation of a gay homeboy identity.* Unpublished fieldnotes.

Williamson, J. (1984). *New people: Miscegenation and mulattoes in the United States.* New York: New York University Press.

Wilson, A. (1984). "Mixed race" children in British society: Some theoretical considerations. *The British Journal of Sociology, 35,* 42-61.

Wilson, B. L. (1985). *Racial identification of black-Asian children: Four to eight years old.* Doctoral dissertation, The Wright Institute of Professional Psychology, Berkeley, CA.

Wilson, T. (1992). Blood quantum: Native American mixed bloods. In M. P. P. Root (Ed.), *Racially mixed people in America* (pp. 108-125). Newbury Park, CA: Sage.

Wilson, W. J. (1980). *The declining significance of race* (2nd ed.). Chicago: University of Chicago Press.

Wilson, W. J. (1987). *The truly disadvantaged: The inner city, the underclass, and public policy.* Chicago: University of Chicago Press.

Winant, H. (1994). *Racial conditions.* Minneapolis: University of Minnesota Press.

Winn, P. (1994). *Americas: The changing face of Latin America and the Caribbean.* New York: Pantheon.

Wong, S. C. (1992). Ethnicizing gender, gendering ethnicity. In S. G. Lim & A. Ling (Eds.), *Reading the literatures of Asian America* (pp. 111-129). Philadelphia: Temple University Press.

Wright, L. (1994, July 25). One drop of blood. *The New Yorker*, pp. 46-49.

Wright, R. D., & Wright, S. N. (1972). A plea for a further refinement of the marginal man theory. *Phylon, 33*, 361-368.

Xicay-Sartos, L. (1993, April). Reconcilable differences: Soy Guatemalteco! Soy Mestizo! *Interrace*, pp. 28-30.

Yee, A., Fairchild, H., Weizman, F., & Wyatt, G. (1993). Addressing psychology's problem with race. *American Psychologist, 48*, 1132-1140.

Yinger, M. J. (1981). Toward a theory of assimilation and dissimilation. *Ethnic and Racial Studies, 4*, 249-263.

York, S. (1991). *Roots and wings*. St. Paul, MN: Redleaf Press.

Zack, N. (1992). An autobiographical view of mixed-race and deracination. *American Philosophical Association Newsletter on Philosophy and the Black Experience, 91*(1), 6-10.

Zack, N. (1993). *Race and mixed race*. Philadelphia: Temple University Press.

Zack, N. (1994a). My racial self over time. In C. Camper (Ed.), *Miscegenation blues: Voices of mixed race women* (pp. 20-27). Toronto: Sister Vision Press.

Zack, N. (1994b, Fall). Race and philosophic meanings. *Newsletter on Philosophy and the Black Experience, 94*(1), 11-18.

Zack, N. (Ed.) (1995a). *American mixed race: The culture of microdiversity*. Lanham, MD: Rowman & Littlefield.

Zack, N. (1995b). Mixed black and white race and public policy. *Hypatia, 10*(1), 119-132.

Zanuck, D. (Producer), & Kazan, E. (Director). (1949). *Pinky*. Los Angeles: 20th Century.

Zenón Cruz, I. (1975). *Narciso descubre su trasero* [Narcissus discovers his buttocks]. Humacao, Puerto Rico: Editorial Furidi.

Zinik, G. (1985). Identity conflict or adaptive flexibility? Bisexuality reconsidered. *Journal of Homosexuality, 11*(1-2), 7-20.

Index

About the Authors

Karen Maeda Allman, MS, RN, is currently working on her doctorate in nursing and has been a Fellow of the National Center for Nursing Research, National Institutes of Health. She also teaches women's studies at the University of Washington. A member of Sigma Theta Tau, the international nursing honorary society, she was distinguished as the Outstanding Graduate Student for 1987 at Arizona State University. Her publications and dissertation focus on the interrelatedness of mental health, racism, and health practices. Her mother is from Japan and her father from the United States; she is of Japanese, English, French Canadian, and Norwegian descent.

Nancy G. Brown, RN, MN, a graduate of Boston University and UCLA, is a Clinical Nurse Specialist in mental health, works as a psychotherapist for Kaiser Permanente in California, is a consultant trainer for the Anti-Defamation League's "A World of Difference" prejudice-reduction program, and is

467

a private practitioner. She co-founded and holds leadership roles in both Multiracial Americans of Southern California (MASC: past president and current board member) and the Association of Multi-Ethnic Americans (AMEA: vice president), a national organization. In these roles, she is a major spokesperson and educator for the media, schools, colleges, and professional conferences. She is of German-Jewish American heritage, and she is married to a man of African American heritage; they have two multiracial daughters.

Lillian Comas-Díaz received her PhD in clinical psychology from the University of Massachusetts. She is Executive Director of the Transcultural Mental Health Insitute and maintains a private practice of clinical psychology in Washington, DC. She is the Editor-in Chief of the journal, *Cultural Diversity and Mental Health.* She is the former director of the American Psychological Association's Office of Ethnic Minority Affairs and the former director of the Hispanic Clinic at Yale University School of Medicine. A fellow of the APA and the American Psychological Society, she is the recipient of the APA Committee on Women in Psychology's Award for Emerging Leader for Women in Psychology. She has published extensively on the topics of ethnocultural mental health, gender and ethnic factors in psychotherapy, treatment of torture victims, international psychology, and Latino mental health. She is the senior editor of two mental health textbooks: *Clinical Guidelines in Cross Cultural Mental Health* and *Women of Color: Integrating Ethnic and Gender Identities into Psychotherapy.* Her book, *Ethnocultural Psychotherapy,* is in preparation.

Kimberly McClain DaCosta received her BA, magna cum laude, from Harvard University. While at Harvard, she co-founded Prism, a discussion group for mixed-race people. She is currently a PhD candidate in the Department of Sociology at the University of California at Berkeley, where she co-founded the Multiracial Alternatives Project and is on the editorial board of the Berkeley *Journal of Sociology*. She is a National Science Foundation Fellow. Her research interests are in race, specifically collective mixed-race identity, and family. She received the Katherine Huggins Prize for her work, "From Black to Indian: The Racial Identity of the Haliwa-Saponi Indians of North Carolina," which focused on collective efforts to change racial classifications. She was born and raised in Massachusetts by her African American father and Irish American mother. She currently lives in Oakland, CA, with her husband, Rich, and her children, Gabrielle and Damian.

G. Reginald Daniel, PhD, received his degree in hispanic languages and literatures and is a Lecturer in Sociology at the University of California, Santa Barbara, and in Latin American Studies and Afro-American Studies at UCLA. His teaching and research focus is on comparative issues of race and identity in the Americas. Since 1989, he has taught several of the first university courses in the United States on multiracial topics. In 1995, he taught the first course devoted specifically to exploring the experience of individuals of African and European descent. He contributed two chapters to the first comprehensive examination of multiracial identity in the United States, *Racially Mixed People in America* (Sage, 1992). He has conducted numerous interviews in the popular press, made television and radio appearances, and participated as a panelist at various conferences dealing with multiracial identity.

He is also a member of the Advisory Boards of the Association of MultiEthnic Americans (AMEA) and Project RACE (Reclassify All Children Equally). His own multiracial identity includes African, Native American, Irish, East Indian, and French backgrounds.

Ramona E. Douglass, BS, is a graduate of Colorado State University and the first woman of color to attend the Colorado School of Mines in 1966. She is currently Senior Sales Manager for a medical manufacturing firm. She is a founding member of the *National Alliance Against Racist and Political Repression* and more recently a founding member of the *Association of Multiethnic Americans,* in which she has held the posts of president and vice president. She has served 7 years on the board of directors for the *Biracial Family Network of Chicago* and is a past president. Her commitment to multicultural/multiracial education has resulted in her co-producing a television documentary, *The Biracial Family Network,* guest lecturing at universities and colleges, and appearing on numerous nationally televised talk shows. In June 1993, her personal testimony was presented at a congressional hearing on the U.S. Bureau of the Census's consideration of a multiracial category. She is of African, Italian, and Native American descent.

Carlos A. Fernández, JD, is an attorney in private practice and a writer. He is the son of a psychiatrist of Mexican birth and mixed Native American and Spanish ancestry. His mother is a psychiatric social worker of diverse European ancestry. Both parents were active in civil rights, especially in support of the farm workers' movement. Members of his extended family include people of diverse ethnic, racial, and religious origins. He was the founding president (1988) of the Association of MultiEthnic Americans (AMEA) serving in that capacity until

1994. He is currently AMEA's Coordinator for Law and Civil Rights and its representative to the 50th Anniversary Commemoration of the United Nations in San Francisco (1995). He has lectured extensively at various universities and colleges on issues of multiethnicity, especially with respect to the recognition of multiracial/multiethnic people. He was a contributing author to *Racially Mixed People in America* (Sage, 1992). He drafted and delivered AMEA's testimony to Congress in 1993.

Lynda D. Field, PhD, received her doctorate and master's degree from the University of Denver. She is a clinical child psychologist on staff in the Children and the Law Program at Massachusetts General Hospital, a clinical instructor at the Harvard Medical School, and staff member at the Boston Juvenile Court Clinic. She has joint clinical and research interests in child mental health and in multicultural approaches to understanding human development. She received a dissertation research award from the American Psychological Association to support her study of self-concept in biracial adolescents. She is of Puerto Rican, Russian, and Jewish ancestry and was raised in Chicago.

Ronald David Glass, MA, is a Lecturer in Social and Cultural Studies in the School of Education at the University of California, Berkeley. He holds BA and MA degrees from Harvard University and has completed advanced degrees at UC Berkeley and Stanford University, where he is finishing his PhD in philosophy of education. From 1990 to 1994, he had a joint appointment in the Philosophy Department and in the School of Education at Stanford University, and he was coordinator of the Program in Cultures, Ideas, and Values. His research focuses on freedom, equity, and justice, as well as the role of formal and nonformal education in giving these values substance within contested contexts. He teaches courses on education and race, class, and gender formation, as well as various other topics in moral and political philosophy and education. He has consulted with a wide variety of organizations, from community-based groups to colleges and universities, on long-range planning and race-related issues. Currently, he is helping to facilitate the formation of a strategic plan for diversity at the 2,500-student Berkeley High School.

Susan R. Graham is Founder and President of PROJECT RACE (Reclassify All Children Equally). In June 1993, she testified before a congressional subcommittee in Washington, DC, about the plight of multiracial children without a classification, which resulted in her invitation to the National Academy of Sciences. She has been featured on the CBS news show *48 Hours* and on *Nick News* on National Public Radio, and she has been quoted in national newspapers and magazines. She is a contributor to *American Mixed Race*. She is active in community and educational organizations and helps others learn the grassroots process to further civil rights, women's, and children's issues. A professional journalist, she writes a popular editorial column for an Atlanta newspaper. She is white, her husband is black, and they have two multiracial children.

Christine C. Iijima Hall, PhD, is Associate Vice Provost for Academic Affairs at Arizona State University West. She received her PhD in social psychology from UCLA in 1980. Her dissertation was one of the pioneer works in the area of ethnic identity of racially mixed people in the United States. She continues to write, to give interviews, and to lecture nationally on issues of ethnic identity, interracial relations, and cultural diversity. She is a licensed psychologist in California and Arizona. She is the youngest child of Roger and Fumiko Hall, an African American retired Army master sergeant and a Japanese war-bride nurse. They have been married for almost 50 years. She has one sister, Juanita, and one brother, Roger. She is the proud aunt of four wonderful nieces and nephews who are the newest generation of multiracial people. Christine, a first-time bride at the age of 39, is married to Matthew Crum.

George Kitahara Kich, PhD, is a psychologist in private practice in Berkeley, California, and Associate Professor in the graduate psychology department (Drama Therapy Program) at the California Institute of Integral Studies in San Francisco, where he is also a consultant on multicultural diversity. He received his PhD in social-clinical psychology from Wright Institute in Berkeley. Research, clinical practice, and public papers and presentations about biracial people, identity, and families have been an important aspect of his life and work since 1975. He was a co-founder of I-Pride, the first multiracial family network in California, and its first president. He was born in Japan and immigrated to the United States when he was 6 years old with his Japanese mother and sister. His father is English-German American from the Bronx. His wife and two daughters are constant sources of energy and love and creativity and growth. Ikebana, moderation, passion, computers, poetry, and research on psychosocial theory and psychotherapy, race and sexuality, occupy him. He continues to have faith in humanity and in the nature of change and substantial transformation in the world.

Rebecca Chiyoko King, MA, received her BA from Carleton College and her MA from the Department of Sociology at the University of California, Berkeley, where she is currently a PhD candidate. She has been a Graduate Opportunity Fellow, a founding member of the Asian Pacific Graduate Alliance, and a co-founder of the Multiracial Alternatives Project while at Berkeley. As a certified secondary social science teacher, she has taught in the public schools both in the United States and in Japan. She is currently the Irvine Scholar in the Department of Sociology at the University of San Francisco. Her research interests are in race, education, and gender; she is currently working on her dissertation, which focuses on the politics of mixed-race identity and its implications for the Japanese American community. She was born in Evanston, Illinois, is of Japanese and European American heritage, and currently lives in San Francisco with her husband.

Ruth G. McRoy, PhD, holds the Ruby Lee Piester Centennial Professorship in Services to Children and Families and is Director of the Center for Social Work Research at the School of Social Work at the University of Texas at Austin. She also holds a joint appointment at the Utah Center for African and African American Studies. She received her BA degree in psychology and sociology and her MSW from the University of Kansas in Lawrence. She received her PhD in social work from the University of Texas at Austin in 1981 and joined the faculty there. Her research interests include open adoptions, emotionally disturbed adopted children and adolescents, transracial adoptions, cross-cultural relationships, racial identity development, black adoptions, kinship placements, and special needs adoptions. She has authored or co-authored numerous articles and book chapters and has presented many invited papers at national and international conferences. She has co-authored four books titled: *Transracial and Inracial Adoptees: The Adolescent Years; Emotional Disturbance in Adopted Adolescents; Openness in Adoption: New Practices, New Issues;* and *Social Work Practice With Black Families.*

Cynthia L. Nakashima is a doctoral student in ethnic studies at the University of California at Berkeley, working on her dissertation tentatively titled, *Mixed-Race Women and Their White Mothers: Race and Gender, Close to Home.* She has taught courses on Asian American history and people of mixed racial heritage at UC Berkeley and has been involved in multiracial organizations in the San Francisco Bay Area, such as Hapa Issues Forum and the Mapping Racial and Ethnic Alternative working group at UC Berkeley. She is the daughter of a Japanese American father and a German/English American mother who have recently celebrated their 30th anniversary, and who are favorite playmates of their granddaughter, Madeline Nakashima-Conway, the 4-year-old daughter of Cynthia and her husband, Shawn Conway.

Deborah A. Ramirez, JD, is a Latino lawyer. She teaches criminal law, ethics, and evidence at Northeastern University School of Law in Boston, Massachusetts, where she is an Associate Professor. She received her BA from Northwestern University and her JD from Harvard Law School. Her research interests focus on race, ethnicity, and the criminal justice system. She is of Spanish and Mexican American descent and embraces both heritages. She currently resides in Boston with her husband, Ralph Gants, and her two children, Rachel and Michael.

Maria P. P. Root, PhD, is an Associate Professor in the Department of American Ethnic Studies at the University of Washington in Seattle. Her publications cover such subjects as disordered eating, trauma, Asian American mental health, and racial identity of multiracial people. Her most recent edited book, *Racially Mixed People in America* (Sage, 1992), received the Myers Center Award for the study of human rights in the United States. She is also a past recipient of the Washington State Psychological Association's Distinguished Psychologist Award, the Filipino American National Historical Society's VIP Award, and leadership awards from the American Psychological Assocation. Born in Manila, the Philippines, she is of Filipino, Spanish, Chinese, Portuguese, German, and Irish heritage.

Brian Chol Soo Standen received his BA in Anthropology, magna cum laude, and in English from the University of Colorado at Boulder. His senior thesis is the first focused study of biracial Korean Americans. He has presented the findings of his research at the 1994 Colorado Asian American Studies Conference and also at the 1995 National Association of Ethnic Studies Conference. During his academic career, he was Northern Colorado representative for the Rocky Mountain Asian American Student Coalition. Currently, he is living in San Diego, California where he is working for a custom software firm as a project manager and spends his free time learning more about his Korean heritage from his mother. In the future, he plans to pursue an Ethnic Studies graduate program and attend law school to establish an Asian American community-based law firm.

Caroline A. Streeter is a doctoral candidate in the ethnic studies program at the University of California at Berkeley. She holds an AB in feminist studies from Stanford University, where she taught a course about mixed-race identity in contemporary literature and media. She leads the Multiracial Alternatives Project study group at UC Berkeley, where she is a teaching assistant and guest lecturer for the course "People of Mixed Racial Descent." She has participated on conference panels about the intersections of marginalized racial and sexual identities. Born in France of a French mother and an African American father, she grew up on U.S. Air Force bases in Europe and the United States, and she also lived in Saudi Arabia. She currently resides in San Francisco, where she is involved in mixed-race, feminist, and queer scholarship and activism. She thanks her family and friends for their indispensable love.

Michael C. Thornton, PhD, is Associate Professor of Afro-American Studies and Acting Interim-Director of Asian American Studies at the University of Wisconsin. He uniquely uses his Afro-Asian American heritage as the foundation to build bridges between the two communities. His research explores bonds between groups of color and how religion, ethnic, and political identity are associated with these relationships. With Hemant Shah, he is writing a book on how mainstream and minority (black, Asian, and Hispanic American) media depicted riots in Los Angeles, Washington, DC, and Miami and the boycott of Korean grocers in New York. He is the product of a black American father and a Japanese mother.

Frances Winddance Twine, PhD, is an Assistant Professor of Women's Studies and an Adjunct Assistant Professor of Anthropology at the University of Washington in Seattle. She received her PhD in anthropology from the University of California at Berkeley in 1994. In 1991, as a graduate student, she co-produced an award-winning film titled, *Just Black? Multiracial Identity.* This film won several awards, including the Special Jury Award at the National Educational Film Festival. *Just Black?* is the first documentary to address the experiences of university students of multiracial heritage. Dr. Twine is a black American and an enrolled member of the Muscogee (Creek) Nation of Oklahoma. She is currently conducting comparative research on the white birth mothers of mixed-race children in England.

Kendra R. Wallace, MA, is currently pursuing a PhD in education at Stanford University where she received a MA in international development education. Her research interests include bi/multiracial identity development, as well as the treatment of race, ethnicity, and culture in education. She has written about culturally sensitive caregiving environments for multicultural children and has worked as an advocate for Project RACE (Reclassify All Children Equally), a nonprofit organization promoting the representational rights of multiracial children. She recently completed a pilot study on student perceptions of ethnicity at a San Francisco bay area high school. She is an adoptee of African-European-American heritage, raised by an interracial couple with two biological, biracial sons. She would like to thank her incredible family for their ongoing love and support.

Francis Wardle, PhD, is Executive Director of the Center for the Study of Biracial Children, a Denver-based organization that works closely with the media, professors, graduate students conducting research, schools, and interracial parents on issues affecting biracial children. He is currently a member of the Board of Editorial Contributors for *The Rocky Mountain News*; a Contributing Editor for the National Association for the Education of Young Children; and a columnist for the national publication, *New People.* His academic interests include self-image, play and designing play environments, and children's information processing. He has published on a vast range of subjects in books, the popular press, and academic journals. He is also a professional photographer whose photographs of children have appeared in a variety of national publications. He has presented at workshops and given invited keynote addresses on biracial children, interracial families, and multicultural education nationally and in Canada. He is white and married to a black woman with Chactaw, Chicasaw, and Asian heritage; they have four biracial children, ages 10 to 18.

Jan R. Weisman, MA, is of black, Jewish, and Native American heritage. She holds a BA in psychology from Roosevelt University, Chicago, and an MA in education from George Washington University, Washington, D.C. She was a Peace Corps volunteer in Thailand from 1982 to 1985, taught the Thai language at the University of California, Berkeley, from 1987 to 1991, and currently teaches the Thai language at the University of Washington. She has sponsored a Thai Amerasian child through the Pearl S. Buck Foundation since 1982. From 1990 to 1993 she served on the board of directors of I-Pride, a San Francisco-based nonprofit organization for interracial individuals and families. She is currently a doctoral student in the University of Washington's Department of Anthropology. In 1994, she developed and team-taught a course on interracial/ interethnic identity at that university. She plans a dissertation on Vietnam War-era Amerasians in Thailand.

Teresa Kay Williams, MA, a Phi Beta Kappa, earned a BA in Japanese studies with an ethnic studies certificate from the University of Hawai'i. She holds an MA in both Asian American studies and sociology from UCLA, where she is currently completing her doctorate in sociology. Her research and teaching interests include examining the construction, presentation, and intersections of race, culture, language, class, gender, and sexual orientation; her academic interests stem from her lived experiences and identity. She has taught ground-breaking ethnic studies and sociology courses at the University of California, Santa Barbara and at UCLA on multiracial and sexual identity. She frequently appears on educational television and radio programs and in documentary films, and gives lectures on international and intercultural issues. Of Japanese and Irish/ Welsh American ancestries, she was born in Sacramento, California, and raised in the Kanto area of Japan, but she considers Southern California—the land of the Chumash and the Mexicano/Chicano people— her adopted home.

Naomi Zack, PhD, received her PhD in philosophy from Columbia University, New York. Her current work proceeds along two main paths—racial theory and history of philosophy. Publications include *Race and Mixed Race* and *American Mixed Race,* an edited anthology that explores microdiversity. Forthcoming projects include *Bachelors of Science: Seventeenth Century Identity, Then and Now,* and *Comparing Sex*

and Race, an anthology that integrates theoretical feminist and racial studies concerns. Since 1993, she has presented her work on race at the American Philosophical Association's regional meetings, and to students and faculty on numerous college campuses. She teaches in the Philosophy Department of the State University of New York at Albany.